Ecologies of Affect

ENVIRONMENTAL
HUMANITIES

Ecologies of Affect

Placing Nostalgia, Desire, and Hope

Tonya K. Davidson, Ondine Park,
and Rob Shields, editors

WLU PRESS

WILFRID LAURIER UNIVERSITY PRESS

This book has been published with the help of a grant from the Canadian Federation for the Humanities and Social Sciences, through the Aid to Scholarly Publications Programme, using funds provided by the Social Sciences and Humanities Research Council of Canada. We acknowledge the financial support of the Government of Canada through the Canada Book Fund for our publishing activities.

Library and Archives Canada Cataloguing in Publication

Ecologies of affect : placing nostalgia, desire, and hope / Tonya K. Davidson, Ondine Park, and Rob Shields, editors.

(Environmental humanities)
Includes bibliographical references and index.
Issued also in electronic format.
ISBN 978-1-55458-258-7

1. Social ecology. 2. Cultural geography. 3. Geographical perception. I. Davidson, Tonya K., 1979– II. Park, Ondine, [date] III. Shields, Rob, 1961– IV. Series: Environmental humanities series

HM861.E36 2011   304.2   C2010-906491-7

Electronic formats.
ISBN 978-1-55458-312-6 (PDF), ISBN 978-1-55458-348-5 (EPUB)

1. Social ecology. 2. Cultural geography. 3. Geographical perception. I. Davidson, Tonya, 1979– II. Park, Ondine, [date] III. Shields, Rob, 1961– IV. Series: Environmental humanities series (Online)

HM861.E36 2011a   304.2   C2010-906492-5

Cover design by Blakeley Words+Pictures. Cover image: *Passing Angel* by Maria-Carolina Cambre and Lorin Yochim. Text design by Catharine Bonas-Taylor.

© 2011 Wilfrid Laurier University Press
Waterloo, Ontario, Canada
www.wlupress.wlu.ca

Contents

List of Figures

Introduction

ONDINE PARK

TONYA K. DAVIDSON

ROB SHIELDS

Places from Which to Think of Place

This book was born in a place with nameless streets. Since 1913, the streets in Edmonton, Alberta, have been numbered, denied the quaint street names of shared city imaginaries like Sesame Street, Broadway, Main Street. The meaningful names of other places evoke a sense of place—place myths—that seems to be absent in a city full of nondescript home addresses like 10731 84 Avenue or 10235 123 Street. The capital of an industrial farming, resource-extracting, boom–bust province, a city of cars that appear to commute endlessly on generic, busy thoroughfares, Edmonton may be an unlikely inspiration for theorizing about affective attachments to place. But Edmonton is born of and shaped by desire. It is an ecology of affect that is placed by and places desire. Stretching out temporally and spatially, it simultaneously desires in pastward-gazing nostalgia and future-looking hope, reaches out toward ever-receding horizons and builds up toward city-ness.

With a footprint larger than New York City, but a population a fraction of its size, Edmonton expands across vast territories. Meanwhile, its core is just beginning to bristle with taller buildings scrambling to meet the desires of a rapidly growing population who seek in Edmonton a place of their own. Much of that population explosion is driven by the oil boom in northern Alberta. But whereas Edmonton is rapidly being reshaped and reimagined by some desires, other desires take a longer time to transform the landscape, and in the meantime can't find a space amidst the expansiveness. When the housing infrastructure couldn't keep up with needs in the last few years, visible tent cities in the heart of the city and invisible working homeless scattered throughout the city ephemerally marked their presence (particularly in summer 2007), adding to the ranks of already existing marginalized populations. Undesired, and the effect of desires unmet, the conditions of the less privileged in this first North American "Human Rights City" (see http://www.pdhre.org) now face the localized fallout of the so-called global economic recession. Perhaps what anchors these fragile, rapid incursions of yearning is a built form that is the nearly ubiquitous domestic architectural style in central Edmonton: 1970s low-rise apartment buildings with unironically kitsch names like "The Branding Place" or "The Shangri-La." These two names speak to ambivalent desires for imagined other times (when ranching was the supposed mainstay) and places (in this case, a mythical utopian place).

A territory shaped by desires and nostalgic in its built environment, Edmonton also brands itself as a place that produces affective, hopeful attachments. Calling itself the "City of Champions," "Festival City," and "Gateway to the North," Edmonton seems to imagine itself as a place whose hope rests on a glorious past, vibrant present, and expansive future. As the triumphs of Edmonton's "Champions" (the Grads, Eskimos, and Oilers) have already faded into sports history, they can now be shared nostalgically by all as the basis for a hope that perhaps similar glory days also still lie ahead.[1] "Festival City" is a branding of hope and a seemingly perpetual deferment of pleasure. In a city with eight-month-long winters and temperatures regularly below −40°C, where plugging in your car to prevent the engine freezing is requisite, celebrating and understanding the city based on a few short months of summer festivals requires a continued hope for the warmer season.[2]

And, as the "Gateway to the North," Edmonton takes very seriously its responsibility to satisfy the consumer desires not only of its own citizens but also of Canada's North, many of whose residents travel to Canada's most northerly large city as their closest urban space to shop. The West Edmonton Mall, still one of the largest and for many years the world's very largest shopping mall, offers a "hyperspace" for actualizing and spatializing desires (see Shields 1989), and competes with the Rocky Mountains as Alberta's top tourist destination. "West Ed" was the first example to showcase the mixture of retail and leisure in a single facility, combining wave pools and aquariums with shoe stores, and juxtaposing skating rinks with the interior facades and merchandise of clothing chain stores and live animal shows. Naively and exuberantly postmodern, the mall has managed to convert the potential of drawing on a huge regional consumer base into actual sales.

West Ed, sitting just beyond the edge of central city dwellers' cognitive maps, vies with Whyte Avenue (the semi-official "other place to shop") and small pockets of fiercely local businesses and artists to make Edmonton's distinct mark on the world (e.g., http://keepedmontonoriginal.com). This competition contradictorily produces and illustrates Edmonton as a space that desires to be recognizably and spectacularly global, and at the same time uniquely and quirkily original. On the one hand is the commercialization and low quality of what is delivered (in the case of much of West Ed's wares), and on the other hand is the perceived (if contradictorily) cosmopolitan elitism of the often high-priced and avant garde local wares. This competition for Edmonton's identity also embodies the inequalities of race, class, and place; the starkness of oppression; and contradictions in the hopes of consumers.

Ecologies of Affect: Placing Nostalgia, Desire, and Hope emerged in this context and out of a nexus of intellectual interests that has been developing at the University of Alberta in Edmonton for several years. This "school" of interdisciplinary thinkers, concerned in particular with issues of space, affect, and virtualities, operates as a rhizomatic network. One node in this network has coalesced around the Space and Culture research group, anchored by Rob Shields. This reading, research, and working group has operated since 2004 with faculty and students in sociology, education, art and design, and others coming together to research, discuss, and puzzle through shared intellectual passions such as theoretical questions of the virtual, space and place, things and the nonhuman, affect and desire, art and representation, the everyday, and much else (http://sites.google.com/site/spaceandculturereadinggroup).

In 2008 the editors, as well as Olga Pak and Mark Jackson, participated in the Association of American Geographers' Conference. There, in Boston, pondering urban geographies over cannoli, we conceived of this book. As an effect of nostalgia, distance allows for an appreciation of home, and we recognized that the University of Alberta's "school of space and culture" was engaging with salient issues of urban geography and sociologies of place in theoretically and empirically complex and rich ways. When we returned to the physical and intellectual context of Edmonton and the University of Alberta, writing and thinking from addresses with too many numbers, we began to bring together work in which we were already engaged regarding ideas of place in relation to affect, experience, representations, and temporality. Some of us were interrogating the effect that temporality and change through time has on understandings of place (Hui, Pak, and Winkler). Many of us were exploring how affect and experience overlay meaning onto spaces, reinterpreting those spaces (Buffam, Cambre, Dorow and Dogu, and Tiessen). Others of us were puzzling through how places are re-presented through objects, stories, and cultural forms (Davidson, Hroch, Park, and Vallee). And some of us were considering how spaces are actualized to give place to desires, ideals, and promises (Jackson and della Dora and Shields).

Defining Affect and Ecology

The sense of the term *affect* has changed over the last couple of decades. It used to be a term that indicated a supplement, the emotive counterpart or element of a concept. Affect was curious extra-academic terrain. The major contemporary theoretical impetus to study affect has come from the work of Gilles Deleuze, whose 1978 lectures on Spinoza revive the concept of *affectus*—Latin for passion, affection, disposition, state, endowed with, or possessed of. (It is derived from *afficere*—to affect, make an impression, or move.) As Deleuze explains, *affectus* is "a melodic line of continuous variation," is "in me" as a change in my *vis existendi*, my "force of existing," or my *potentia agendi*, the lived power or potential to act (Deleuze 1978, n.p.).[3] Deleuze translates *affectus* by the French *l'affect* (usually "affect" in English) rather than "feeling," and differentiates it from *affectio*, or affection—"an effect, or the action that one body produces on another" (Deleuze 1978), such as, but not limited to, an emotion or perception. Even though the Latin *affectio* itself means mood or feeling, Deleuze's decision to distinguish it from *affectus* (from which it is derived) marks his paradigmatic shift to highlight sentiment and disposition over material substance.

Baruch Spinoza himself, however, opposed Descartes' mind–body dualism. This led him to establish "affect" as the ideal-type of *relation*—a preconscious, proto-social moment in which the multitude of potential, but still virtual, interactions crystallize into the actuality of a specific interaction or response. Thus, affective passage is an increase or decrease of capacity, *puissance*, or lived power, rather than an affection per se. From a base of joy, sorrow, and desire, Spinoza builds a discussion of the full range of emotions, tracing experiences such as fear back to the affective dynamics of increasing and decreasing capacity to act.

> *Fear* is a sorrow not constant, arising from the idea of something future or past, about the issue of which we sometimes doubt…. There is no hope without fear nor fear without hope…. [T]he person who fears, that is to say, who doubts whether what he [sic] hates will not come to pass, imagines

something which excludes the existence of what he hates, and therefore (Prop. 20 Part 3) is rejoiced, and consequently so far hopes that it will not happen. (Spinoza 1930, 270: Def. 13 of the Affects)

As Spinoza puts it, this alternating capacity for action is experienced as joy (*laetitia*), "passive joy," or "passion by which the mind passes to a greater perfection" (Spinoza 1930, 218: Prop. 11, Schol.) or sadness (*tristitia*), although some prefer to see these translated as pleasure and unpleasure,

> the mind can suffer great changes, and can pass now to a greater and now to a lesser perfection; these passions explaining to us the affects of joy and sorrow. *By joy* ... I shall understand the passion by which the mind passes to a greater perfection.... The affect of joy, related at the same time both to the mind and the body, I call *pleasurable excitement* (*titillatio*) or *cheerfulness;* that of sorrow I call *pain* or *melancholy.* (Spinoza 1930, 218: Prop. 11, Schol.)

Only in theory of the turn of the twenty-first century has affect returned to the sense Spinoza (1930) gave it in Part 3 of his magnum opus, *Ethics.*[4]

> Emotion and imagining work together; our imaginings are intensified by our loves and hates, and implicated in our fears and hopes. It is in Spinoza's treatment of the operations of hope and fear that we see most clearly the integration of his political philosophy with his metaphysics of human bodies.... In the *Ethics* and the *Tractatus Theologico-Politicus*, he systematically studies the social dimensions of fear and hope. The fluctuations of these two passions form the backdrop to his consideration of political institutions. Vacillation of mind stands to affect, he says, as doubt is related to the imagination. (Gatens and Lloyd 1999, 28)

The contributors to this volume maintain Spinoza's more materialist approach, tying affect to bodies and ecologies rather than Minds, sentiments, or emotions. The concept of affect fuses the body with the imagination into an ethical synthesis that bears directly on the micropowers inherent in everyday interactions. How these are negotiated builds not only an individual temperament but also a persona and habitus, which are as much individual as they are a social style and regime of living. Affect is furthermore a flux that is always in context—immanent—and thus draws on a situational ethics and therefore on the social and spatial milieu. Infused with power, grounded in place and located bodies, affect is viscerally political.[5]

Writers such as McCormack (2003) turn to this philosophical under-standing of affect as a form of allure[6] or attention, which provides the emotional "glue" that drive bodies to assemble into collectives and by which objects are understood to participate in micro-geographies possessed of a spe-cific situational ethos—or what we might call an ecology. Affect is also fused, then, with an *ecology*.

We understand ecology in a critical sense as both natural and human, as a material system in which diverse forces and processes intersect and give rise to new forms. This interactive quality is stressed in the literature (e.g., Gorz 2010) but cannot be reified as a fixed system. Instead, it is always in flux, even while grounded and even as it is a system that is decidedly con-crete and determined. As we discuss in our Conclusion, rather than being sim-plistic determined outcomes, ecologies are always in a state of emergence, hovering on the verge of unpredictability.

The aim of this book is to inspire readers to consider space and place beyond their material properties and attend to the imaginary places, ideals, and real but intangible objects that underpin and produce material places and social spaces. It is in this sense that we are speaking of ecologies. Thus, we approach relations rather than static things or determining structures. While there may be things for the purposes of certain analyses that are addressed as "structures" and as "environments," they are also often treated as limited, autonomous systems. Ecologies sum up the multiple ways of affecting and being affected, of multi-causal processes and contingent out-comes. But they are also nontotal and open systems, criss-crossed by flows. Material and virtual geographies are teased out in this collection of rich ethnographic, phenomenological, and critical analyses that explore the mul-tiple, complicated, and overlapping affective placing of nostalgia, desire, and hope.

Place, Affect, and the Virtual

Places, as well as being functional locations of events and everyday life, pro-duce affective attachments—to people, events, things, times, and other places, within and across different ecologies. In this compilation, chapters explore the sources of attachments to place as operating through a series of affective virtualities: nostalgia, desire, and hope. Central to the cases in this book is an interrogation of places that are or become contested in light of affective relationships. A general consensus across the chapters is that place emerges out of dynamic relationships between humans, things, and environ-ments. This is articulated in Hui's chapter as she works out and develops

Kevin Hetherington's notion of placing. Rather than seeing place as created through a mental process of attributing meaning, Hetherington (1997) foregrounds the interaction of humans with material objects, suggesting that place and affect are therefore results of a process of interacting with the material world. The continual engagement of people with things and in environments creates places and affects that are themselves always shifting, morphing, and flickering. These articles are bound by a commitment to expanding theoretical understandings of the relationships between place and imagined temporalities and desire. The book is informed by the critical insights that social theorists, sociologists, and scholars working across disciplines can make.

The crucial intervention this edited compilation makes is an active, consistent engagement with the virtualities that produce and refract our idealized attachments to place. We understand nostalgia, desire, and hope as *virtual*: that is, even though they are not material, they are nevertheless real and thus must be accounted for. In this book, we take up affect, emotion, and emplacement and consider them in relation to each other and how they work to produce and are themselves produced by certain temporal and spatial dimensions. Recognizing that these affective attachments to place operate across multiple times highlights the *virtuality* of these attachments. Chapters explore this virtuality of affects and of the capacities and affordances of objects and environments. In general, the virtual has been neglected in environmental and urban studies. However, to speak of such things as cities or ecologies is to identify nonmaterial entities that are precisely denoted by the virtual. This builds on the insights of Marcel Proust, C. S. Pierce, and others, that it is necessary to recognize *intangible objects*. Such objects include brands, groups such as communities and classes, sets, and the social—any intangible "thing" that is not a mere fiction but is known only through its effects, "as if" it was a thing. The virtual is thus intangible but not an abstraction or fiction; the virtual is also real but distinct from the material, "ideal but not abstract, real but not actual." As Proust comments on memory,

> let a sound, a scent already heard and breathed in the past be heard and breathed anew, simultaneously in the present and in the past, real without being actual, ideal without being abstract, then instantly the permanent and characteristic essence hidden in things is freed and our true being which has for long seemed dead but was not so in other ways awakes and revives. (Proust 1931, n.p.)

The chapters thus consider the power of the virtual as something conveyed by materialities but greater than these objects at any given moment, where there is more than meets the eye. This includes the potential of objects and bodies, their capacity to support action or to act, to affect or to be affected. Even when latent, this makes it possible for us to place our hope in a better future. Recognizing the virtual enables us to designate elements that allow a place to maintain its ethos or for a picture to maintain its power even as both decay over time. The chapters also consider the shortcomings of the virtual, where overreliance on virtually real objects, like an image in a mirror, leads to a situation where material necessities are not provided. There may also be a faith in the virtual that leads people to trust blindly or to a material situation being discounted—or overestimated, for example, in situations where fear or distrust leads to a perception of danger.

In planning the book, we began by considering three affectual modalities that seemed to operate with different temporal orientations; considering nostalgia as an affect oriented toward the past, desire situated in the present, and hope as an affect directed toward the future. As the contributors came to realize, these affects and temporal orientations are not linear or limited. Nostalgia, desire, and hope often overlap in a particular place with many different temporal orientations creating multiple, coinciding ecologies in one place. Memories and hopes are often simultaneous. In other words, it is not only possible but more quotidian that one's experience of place can be informed by all three of these registers at the same time. While this simultaneity of affect is the consensus of the contributors, this book is nevertheless organized in three sections; the chapters are placed in the section of the predominant affectual mode their research presents. (For a further discussion, see Conclusion.)

Nostalgia

Nostalgia has emerged in a variety of forms in the contemporary context. As a longing for place, both material and virtual, and implicated in complex relationships between simultaneous temporal and affective dispositions, nostalgia is a condition of great concern to urban geographers and sociologists of place. In this section, the authors tackle four particular personal and collective, historic and contemporary aspects of nostalgia. These chapters demonstrate the capacity of nostalgia to offer an alternative, affective reading of history and a consequently constraining or liberating vision of the future. In this way, this section sets the stage for reconsidering the flickering, overlapping relationships among affects, temporalities, materialities, and virtualities. Anne Winkler opens the section by taking readers to the heart of the former East Germany (German Democratic Republic, or GDR). There, on a nostalgic return visit, she buys a kitschy coffee mug that revels in *Ostalgie*, a form of nostalgia for the former East Germany (German Democratic Republic, or GDR). Winkler uses this mug as a starting point to consider what remains after historical rupture. Winkler asks after the politics of *Ostalgic* representations: How are practices of *Ostalgie* implicated in the context of complicated historicizations of the former GDR? She finds a subversive potential of hope operating through *Ostalgie*, which offers a counter-hegemonic narrative of East German history, in an aesthetic of kitsch that creates an alternative vision of the future. Tonya Davidson's chapter, which also explores the relationship between personal and shared nostalgia, begins an ongoing engagement throughout this book with the theme of virtual places as she offers a nostalgic autoethnographic study of her grandparents' abandoned Croatian village of Kapetanovo. She argues that this village is known to her and others as a "virtual homeland"—a lost place that is felt deeply although not experienced first-hand but instead through a series of memory technologies that have worked to produce "postmemories" of this place. Highlighting technologies of storytelling, "object survivors," and memory texts, her chapter offers up an assortment of virtual engagements with Kapetanovo. Through this deeply intimate collection of stories, things, and texts, Davidson explores the many ways it is possible to feel connected and nostalgic for a place that predates her own birth but to which she nevertheless feels connected and, in a way, remembers. Allison Hui offers a longitudinal understanding of nostalgia and place by asking what happens over time in the constant production and reproduction of places. How is nostalgia activated in this process? In her analysis of travel memoirs, Hui expands on Hetherington's conceptualizations of "placings" to include time and mobility, exploring how places are produced virtually from, and in other times and places as articulations of, nostalgia. To this end, Hui analyzes a series of memoir narratives of second home visitors and returning immigrants. She suggests that in situations where return home is possible, placing involves three phases. In the first phase, material placing results in the virtual affect of home. In the second phase, the place is remembered and nostalgically and virtually placed through memories and memory technologies. Finally, Hui suggests that at the moment of the return visit re-placing occurs: the materiality of the place is engaged and placed in relation to the virtual, remembered place. In revealing the workings and significance of virtual places, Hui offers a new paradigm to understand the material and immaterial processes of placing. Concluding the section, Mickey Vallee offers a history of nostalgia from its emergence as a clinically identifiable psychological disorder of homesickness induced in particular by music to the use of nostalgia as a commodifiable mood by the popular music industry. Vallee shows the mutually constitutive relationship between nostalgia and music, focusing on nostalgia and popular nineteenth-century music to explore the assumed relationship between nostalgia and hope, in which hope is widely understood to be an antidote to pathological nostalgia. Vallee suggests that the music industry has capitalized on the affective potency of nostalgia when performed in the domestic sphere by creating an affective longing for home even when at home. Engaging with some exemplars of nostalgic music production, such as the ballad "After the Ball," Vallee offers a critique of nostalgic music and links vignettes of music history to present nostalgia as an affect with a discursive history.

Desire

In their own ways, all the chapters in this collection deal with desire, so it is a theme that runs through the entire book. But in these chapters that are specifically oriented to desire, there is a heightened sense that desire reveals the impossibilities of the present and of presence. In many ways, we see that desire is less directed than nostalgia or hope: while nostalgia tends toward a pastward, reminiscent desiring, and hope often evokes a future-oriented, aspirational desiring, desire stretches out open-ended in many directions. The potency and possibility of the present and of desire are rendered as deep uncertainty and ambivalence. Tiessen argues that recognizing the capacities and possibilities that places and our relations to and with them afford allows one to enact opportunities. And this is certainly the case in Pak's shape-shifting St. Petersburg, Shields's reinterpreted Las Vegas, and Park's liminal suburbs. However, when considered from the perspective of desire, one also sees, in Pak's, Shields's, and Park's chapters, that St. Petersburg's identity, Las Vegas's place in the world, and the idea of the suburb are fragile, fleeting, and incidental. Full of potency and uneasiness, the openness and flexibility of these places of desire and of the desire for these places are also guarded against, foreclosed, or subverted as opposite expressions of desire.

 This section begins with Rob Shields introducing the seventeenth-century philosopher Baruch Spinoza to a twenty-first-century Las Vegas. Shields describes contemporary Las Vegas as a desert city that is conditioned primarily by the orientation others have toward it as a place of escape. It is a locale marked by overstimulation and the affective registers of desire, fear, and enthrallment. Following Spinoza and Deleuze, Shields develops the notion of affect as dynamism within the body and between bodies and the external environment. Within this framework, Shields engages with particular affective qualities of the Las Vegas Strip such as the teams of hawkers, relations among differentially raced and classed bodies, and the liminal space of the Strip itself. Shields responds directly to the upcoming chapter by Tiessen in suggesting that, while affordances are the present capacities of environments and things, affects are the capacities of dynamic bodies. The affect of escape suggested by the Las Vegas Strip is a flickering syncresis of bodies, time, and space. This affect takes on a political register as experiences of Las Vegas as an escape destination are situated in the naturalized background of service workers, and in the mechanized buzz of slot machines that generate a muted repressed affect.

Matthew Tiessen's chapter follows with a meditation on the relationship between places, things, and human desiring in his Deleuzian reading of place and desire. Tiessen suggests that humans are always mediated by the agency of nonhuman things. He explores human desiring in relation to place as an exemplar of mediations between human and nonhuman entities. Central to the "intra-action" between human and nonhuman agents are the generous offerings of "desire lines," which seduce human actors to play and engage. The following two chapters explore this intra-action between human and nonhuman agents and also with the imaginary, as the site in which desire begins to be actualized. In her chapter on the changing cityscape of post-Soviet cities, Olga Pak investigates how places are actualizations of diverse, often competing sets of desires. Understanding the virtual dimension of the city—the urban—as that generative dimension where affects such as nostalgia, desire, and hope percolate, Pak explores citizens' emotional relationships with their city and the symbolic role of the urban imaginary accompanying the post-Soviet urban transformation of cityscapes by analyzing *responses* to these transformations and the desires that these responses reflect. In her chapter on suburbia and its representation in children's books, Ondine Park suggests that suburbia is imagined as a place promising that desires for a good, happy, well-placed life can be realized. Park suggests that these picture books (like Winkler's kitschy *Ostalgie* and Hroch's "minor art" form of puppetry) open up the *possibility* for a potentially radical reimagining of suburbia as the spatialization of liberatory desire. But the hegemonic ideal that asserts the desirability of a private, interiorized home in the suburb as a locale for self-actualization, a heteronormative family, and a pleasant relation with nature remains fundamentally undisturbed. In reproducing routinized desire through ideologically constrained hopeful and nostalgic evocations of the good home and good family, these books reassert the standard imaginary of suburbia as the spatialization of hegemonic desire.

Hope

In the final section, dreams, the whimsical, longing, failure, inclusions, and exclusions all take their turn at placing hope. Perhaps because a hopeful place or (hope for a place) inspires utopian territorialization, the chapters in this section engage primarily with practices of taking over, reclaiming, or rewriting actual spaces into hopeful places. Such a takeover offers the possibility of remapping, re-visioning, and reworlding toward an other time or an other place. Not surprisingly then, they also all deal with colonialism in some capacity. While Buffam and Jackson and della Dora explore ways in which colonial imaginings continue to propel articulations of hope in places, Cambre and Hroch explore how hopeful places are produced through the use of images of Che Guevara and giant puppets in practices that remap. In between these notions of hope being utilized to liberate or dominate, Dorow and Dogu find that hope is differentially spatialized among communities.

Through ethnographic fieldwork, Bonar Buffam explores how an Edmonton youth centre deems itself a place of hope. Through practices of defining appropriately hopeful futurities for children and excising elements understood as threatening to idyllic "virtualities of childhood," this place of hope exists as a fortress against simultaneously racialized and criminalized aspects of the city. Located in the "inner city," a place imagined to be divested of hope, the centre actively produces itself as a bastion of particular types of childhood, youth, and hope, uncritically and ideologically imbued with middle-class understandings of childhood and public spaces, at the expense of the marginalized youth who actually occupy the space of the inner-city drop-in centre that he studies.

Other articulations of hope are more optimistic, however. Maria-Carolina Cambre shows the many uses of the image of Che Guevara to express a hope to move out of oppression and to actualize liberation. Her chapter offers a phenomenological analysis of the ubiquitously circulating image of Che, which has appeared at student protests in India, on the wall dividing Palestine from Israel, at protests in London, and as graffiti in New York. Cambre offers an exploration of how things and places ontologically flicker in almost magical ways, showing that Che's image circulates as if alchemically, intimating other, outside forms of allegiances that move beyond localized oppressions. While Che's image circulates in many spaces, the image itself produces a space. Here, Cambre engages Deleuze and Guattari's notion of territory to further unpack the workings of an iconic image of resistance in creating places of hope. Petra Hroch explores the creation of ephemeral and unexpected places of hope in her chapter on the French puppet troupe Royal de Luxe. She points to the political potential illuminated by the gigantic puppets: by shaking up an everyday consciousness that is perhaps more dreamlike in its self-exemption from action than the moments of fantasy created by the performance of the giant puppets, the public spirit of the streets is revitalized and an unexpected space of hope is thereby created. Hroch details how the effects of scale are qualitative and affective rather than merely quantitative: the puppets are effective and productive precisely because of their immense scale and slow, yet highly visible mobility.

Shifting to everyday engagements with urban spaces, Sara Dorow and Goze Dogu offer an ethnographic account of hope and the space of Fort McMurray, Alberta—an exemplar of neo-liberal globalization. Expanding on insights from Hage (2003), they find hope unevenly distributed both socially and spatially: participants mapped hope differently onto Fort McMurray based on their differential attachments to that place. In the same space, some hopes liberate, while others are merely escapist. It is, they suggest, simultaneously a node within a spatialization of hope and within itself a place of multiplicities. Congruent with the many chapters on nostalgia, the chapters on hope suggest that hope as an affect operates as a temporal unsettling of place and a multiplicity of co-present places. Perhaps unexpectedly, some articulations of hope draw on nostalgias—erasing and reimagining the past as both more desirable and more capable of sustaining a hopeful vision of the future. While the authors in the nostalgia section engage with virtual places of the past, Mark Jackson and Veronica della Dora engage with the virtual, not-yet-realized places of artificial islands. They suggest the desire and contemporary projects to terraform islands are inspired by nostalgia for when there were still unknown places, and especially unmapped islands. Such places, looking into the unknown, speculative ocean, had offered ideal spaces of hope in travel and adventure narratives. Jackson and della Dora argue that the artificial islands now being produced in the Persian Gulf, however, offer a spectacular *hopeless* hope.

Finally, our conclusion reflects a workshop in which the authors and editors gathered back together in Edmonton to share our ideas on and approaches to affect, places and placing, temporalities and virtualities, nostalgia, desire, and hope. We explored our common and diverging understandings of these key concepts, and considered future directions for these intellectual concerns. Most importantly, we note, all the authors of this volume explore the flickering syncresis between material and virtual places, between affect and ecologies.

Notes

We acknowledge the generous support of the anonymous referees and the Aid to Scholarly Publication Program as well as our editors at Wilfrid Laurier University Press. We are also grateful for the intellectual milieu created by so many of our colleagues and peers at the University of Alberta.

1   The Edmonton Commercial Graduates won 502 out of the 522 games they played, utterly dominating women's basketball for a quarter of a century (1915 to 1940). The Eskimos, Edmonton's professional football team, won five consecutive Grey Cups (1978–1982). And the Oilers, the city's professional hockey team, won five Stanley Cups (1984 and 1990).

2   Although this is changing more recently with Edmonton incorporating a new winter festival and reenvisioning itself as a year-round festival city.

3   See also Spinoza 1930, 270: Def. 3, as well as the influential scholarship of Macherey 1995.

4   The full title is *Ethica ordine geometrico demonstrata et In quinque Partes distincta, in quibus agitur.*

5   Affect is thus "critical" in the political sense of being about force and lived power or the capacity to act.

6   For more on "allure" see Harman 2007.

References

Gatens, M., and G. Lloyd. 1999. *Collective imaginings: Spinoza, past and present.* London; New York: Routledge.

Gorz, A. 2010. *Ecologica*, trans. C. Turner. London; New York: Seagull Books.

Hage, G. 2003. *Against paranoid nationalism: Searching for hope in a shrinking society.* Annandale: Pluto Press.

Harman, G. 2007. On vicarious causation. In *Collapse: Speculative Realism 2*, 187–221. London: Urbanomic.

Hetherington, K. 1997. In place of geometry: The materiality of place. In *Ideas of difference*, ed. K. Hetherington and R. Munro, 183–99. Oxford: Blackwell.

Macherey, P. 1995. *Introduction à l'Ethique de Spinoza–La troisième partie–La vie affective.* Paris: Presses universitaires de France.

McCormack, D. P. 2003. An event of geographical ethics in spaces of affect. *Transactions of the Institute of British Geographers* 28 (4): 488–507.

Proust, M. 1931. *Time regained. Remembrance of things past*, trans. S. Hudson. London: Chatto and Windus. http://ebooks.adelaide.edu.au/p/proust/marcel/p96t/chapter3.html (accessed July 10, 2010).

Shields, R. 1989. Social spatialization and the built environment: The West Edmonton Mall. *Environment and Planning D: Society and Space* 7 (2), 147–64.

Spinoza, B. d. 1930. *Ethic*. Third part: On the origin and nature of the affects, trans. W. H. White. In *Spinoza: Selections*, ed. J. Wild, 204–81. New York; Chicago; Boston: Charles Scribner's Sons.

Section I: Nostalgia

1

"Not everything was good, but many things were better"
Nostalgia for East Germany and Its Politics

ANNE WINKLER

Prologue

During a recent trip to Berlin, I wandered through the shops of Alexander-platz in search of objects invoking the East German past. This square, once the symbolic centre of the German Democratic Republic, is tied inextrica-bly to one of the most vivid memories of my East German childhood. It was early 1990, and I was about to begin a new life with my family in Canada. My grade eight class was in Berlin on *Jugendweihefahrt*, a trip we took as part of a secular rite of passage celebrating our transition into adulthood. Before returning to our hometown, we visited Alexanderplatz with its soar-ing Fernsehturm (Television Tower) and futuristic Weltuhr (World Clock), and the nearby Rote Rathaus (Red City Hall). My classmates and I knew with certainty that this place embodied our nation's technological superior-ity, worldliness, and commitment to socialism, a socialism that, ironically, was crumbling into non-existence at that very moment. I remember dis-tinctly our excitement when we spotted a vendor who was selling Coca-Cola at the base of the television tower. Many of my classmates spent a signifi-cant portion of their allowance on their very first can of Coca-Cola, a drink most of them knew only from western television and magazine ads. Eight-een years later, again at the base of the television tower, I entered a sou-venir shop looking for items that would help me think about what ideas about the East circulate in today's Germany. What I found was a coffee mug, a mug so kitschy that I was a little embarrassed to buy it (see Figure 1.1). Large red letters on the rim of the mug read "Ostalgie," "In memory of East

Germany," and "Not everything was good, but many things were better." Eleven cartoon images "memorialize" lost facets of East German life. This chapter explores why and how this mug matters.

Introduction

In the aftermath of the collapse of socialism in Europe, nostalgic framings of the recent past emerged unexpectedly. In Russia, Poland, the nations of the former Yugoslavia, and other countries, cultural practices appeared that dwelled on ostensibly positive aspects of everyday life under socialism. In this chapter, I examine this phenomenon's German variant, *Ostalgie* (nostalgia for the East). Broadly, *Ostalgie* is the preoccupation with unique facets of the former German Democratic Republic (GDR). It consists of such diverse articulations as the popularity of consumer goods that mimic those that were available in the GDR, television variety programs exploring the nation's oddities, and the "museumification" of East German everyday life. Cultural analyses[1] place the origin of *Ostalgie* in a collective sense of loss and dislocation that resulted from the unequal merging of two cultures (e.g., Bach 2002; Berdahl 2005; Betts 2000; Blum 2000; Boyer 2006; Cooke 2004a; Cooke 2004b). These works explore the ways in which *Ostalgie* entails counter-hegemonic practices that give voice to aspects of the East German past that dominant discourses fail or refuse to address.

In addition to outlining the forms that *Ostalgie* takes, this chapter has two further goals. I highlight the politics of this contemporary form of nostalgia, both in its practice and scholarly analysis. Furthermore, I am concerned with the future-oriented claims *Ostalgie* and other historicizing discourses make. I suggest that a study of *Ostalgie* that takes into consideration its relation to other narratives constructing what kind of a place East Germany was offers possibilities for nuanced understandings of the politics of nostalgia.

This chapter has three parts. I begin with descriptions of *ostalgic* practices and products. In addition, I conduct a cursory reading of a self-designated nostalgic object; I consider an *Ostalgie* coffee mug's form and content and relate its messages to cultural and socio-economic changes that the unification of Germany brought with it. The mug serves as a departure point for the analysis that follows, while also grounding it. Throughout the text, I return to this object to illustrate my developing argument. I do so sparingly and hesitantly, however, because I do not wish to propose that the mug can stand in for *Ostalgie* in all its variation. I would merely like to suggest that this example of *ostalgic* material culture hints at the contradictions, complexities, and political character of the practice.

Figure 1.1 The *Ostalgie* coffee mug. (Photo credit: A. Winkler)

In the second part of this chapter, I turn from describing to theorizing *Ostalgie* in an effort to make explicit the practice's politics. I begin with the possibilities and difficulties that arise when conceptualizing *Ostalgie* as nostalgia. How socio-economic relations of power shape *Ostalgie* becomes increasingly clear in reflections on why it articulates itself primarily through consumer goods. In turn, the purchasing of things and its interpretation as

authentic and subversive practice pose questions about the political limitations of consumption as resistance.

The third part of the chapter concludes that today, twenty years after
the unification of Germany, understandings of *Ostalgie* must situate themselves within the context of other narratives about the East German past, especially as they relate to mythologizing the contemporary German nation.

Articulations

An adequate and satisfying definition of *Ostalgie* is difficult to formulate
because it entails numerous practices and products that have changed over
time. In addition, although the academic literature offers extensive descriptions, it does not provide clear boundaries of the phenomenon. Thus, I begin
with examples of *Ostalgie* and subsequently focus on one specific material
expression.

The rise of *Ostalgie* included the dramatic increase in the availability of consumer products packaged to look like those that were available
in the GDR (see Figure 1.2). Ironically, many former East Germans preferred the one type of laundry detergent or lemonade that mimicked the
product once produced by the centrally planned socialist economy to the
many western product alternatives available on store shelves. In related

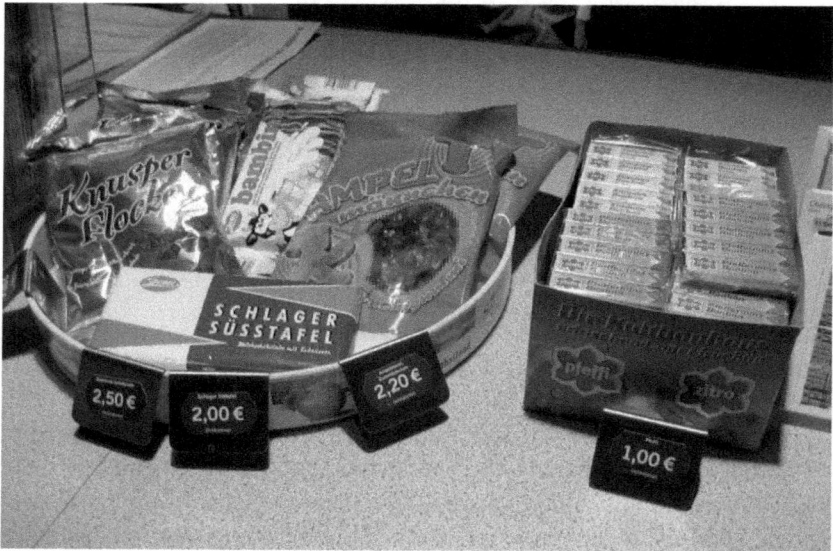

Figure 1.2 Replicas of East German candy. DDR Museum, Berlin (March 2008).
(Photo credit: A. Winkler)

occurrences, the German entertainment industry began making films and television programs that focused on the peculiarities of East Germany and its citizens. One example is the internationally acclaimed film *Good Bye, Lenin!* (Becker 2002), in which a son recreates the former East Germany for his mother who had been in a coma during the collapse of the GDR (see Finger 2005). Every major television network produced an *Ostalgie* show, usually hosted or co-hosted by an East German, demonstrating the various ways in which the GDR was a different, laughable, and backward place.

   Ostalgie also has an experiential component. For example, many of the GDR or *Ostalgie* museums invite guests to relive the East by walking into a typical kitchen, living room, or bathroom (see Scribner 2000) (see Figure 1.3). Visitors can open drawers to touch everyday consumer goods and sit on sofas, imagining themselves as East Germans. The Berlin Ostel hotel offers GDR theme rooms, a store carrying *Ostprodukte* (products of the East), and an in-house gallery exhibiting East German art (see Rethmann 2009). Meals that have disappeared from other restaurants can be ordered at the Berlin Mauerblümchen (Wallflower) pub. For those visitors of the capital city who are interested in its recent history, the Berlin Tourism website (2008) suggests they take *Ostalgie* tours, claiming that this activity will "show both sides," "the difficult historical discussion and the (n)ostalgic mood." Even the hobby of belonging to Trabant car clubs cannot escape the *Ostalgie* label. Rituals such as *Jugenweihe*, the rite of passage marking transition from childhood to adulthood, are also entangled with the notion of romanticizing the East.

   Ostalgie products that I have received or purchased include chocolates wrapped in East German–like currency, a Trabant toy car, jars of pickles made in the Spreewald, and the children's musical instrument Triola. While some of the examples of *Ostalgie* I have listed here and ones I have described above may seem banal to the uninitiated and meaningless outside the context of direct experience, combined they raise the question of why the same term labels so easily such a variety of objects and practices. I would like to suggest that the fact that *Ostalgie* expresses itself with great diversity, or conversely, that the phrase is so broadly applicable, begins to hint at the phenomenon's politics. This observation raises questions about the significance of naming cultural practices nostalgia, a type of affect that from a quotidian perspective refers to a romanticizing and consequently historically falsifying backward gaze in time. In an effort to respond to these questions and thereby render the underlying politics of nostalgia more apparent, I offer the following reading of the *ostalgic* mug. In the absence of definitions,

Figure 1.3 The East German bathroom. DDR Museum, Berlin (March 2008). (Photo credit: A. Winkler)

this cursory reading also offers a deeper consideration of what *Ostalgie* entails in terms of cultural practice.

Three quasi-headlines title the mug: "Ostalgie," "Not everything was good, but many things were better," and "In memory of the GDR." Equally as prominent as these texts are a portrait of Karl Marx and the GDR flag's emblem composed of a hammer, a sickle, and a wreath of wheat. Combined, these words and images guide the reading of the remainder of the surface; the mug addresses itself to its reader as an obituary to an Arcadia, albeit a slightly imperfect one, a time and place when life was easier and more fulfilling than it is now.

On the outside the mug features ten caricatures illustrating written statements that represent ostensibly no longer existing facets of GDR life. The majority of the messages indicate economic security and well-being. "Affordable rents" and "Coffee or beer for 50 Pfennig once again" point directly to a low cost of living. Along with the statement "Work and post-secondary education for everyone," the mug also proclaims that in East Germany employment and employment training were universally accessible. "Pensions were secure" speaks to state support for the elderly and alludes more broadly to a generous welfare system. Even the words "The children were looked after" and the accompanying image of a woman caring for four children conjure the organization of the socialist economy. This message points to the role of the state as caregiver, and with it, indirectly to women's high participation in the workforce. Together, the five scenes paint daily life in the GDR as not only affordable but also worry free, in large part owing to a benevolent state.

In addition to economic well-being, several statements allude to a sense of community, belonging, and connectedness once experienced and now lost. "We still had neighbors and colleagues" and "More time for love" evoke harmonious interpersonal relationships that by implication the individualism of capitalism now undermines. The image of an East German athlete standing at the top of a podium and the phrase "Those were the days" also hints at togetherness, albeit at the level of the nation. The scene suggests that winning international sporting events was closely entwined with national identity and pride (see Fisher 2002; Magdalinski 1999).

"We looked forward to our dearest, our car, for a long time" is the most sarcastic and critical statement. In the GDR, the average wait time for a new car was fifteen years, which from the standpoint of East Germans was a great annoyance and from the perspective of a capitalist economy was a clear indication of the flaws of a centrally planned economy. This assertion recognizes scarcity in the realm of consumer goods while also suggesting a dramatically different relationship between people and products compared to contemporary western consumer culture. At the same time, similar to the other phrases of the mug, being unable to purchase certain types of products when wanted and needed emphasizes the difference between the East and the West.

For those outside of Germany, perhaps the most peculiar statement on the mug reads "Nude beaches—No problem." The idea that East Germans had unique attitudes toward nudity has emerged as a dominant identifier of difference between East and West. In fact, nude bathing *was* more popular in the GDR at the time of unification. However, why this practice has become so central in the insistence of dissimilarity is not entirely clear. One conceivable explanation is that nude bathing entailed a form of resistance to state control. However, McLellan's (2007) history of nudism and nude bathing in East Germany brings forth no evidence that would warrant such a conclusion. In her work on media representation, Hörschelmann (2001) interprets this cliché as shorthand for East Germans as exotic, wild, less civilized, more natural, and more naive compared to their western counterparts. From this perspective, the aim of the mug's statement is primarily to exoticize the Other and devalue easterners. Yet, because the mug implies a reader "in the know," one who understands its messages because he or she experienced personally life in the GDR, the reference to nude bathing might function primarily as an identifier of difference.

In its totality, the most striking aspect of this *Ostalgie* object is the contrast between style and subject matter. In form, the mug stands as an ephemeral, laughable, kitschy,[2] and therefore dismissible object that in its self-representation as obituary lays no claim on the future. When bracketing the banality, the mug's content simultaneously offers a multi-faceted, ironic, and comprehensive system critique. Five of the ten statements refer explicitly to perceived socio-economic deteriorations that appeared with transformations in economic organization. On an emotive level, the loss of a sense of identity and belonging dominate. The mug's mode of address reinforces this affective dimension, for it declares the messages as experientially based truths as opposed to those founded on seemingly objective "facts."

A consideration of the veracity of the object's claims highlights two fundamentally different understandings of the politics of nostalgia in the eastern German context. The cultural studies–oriented literature published predominantly in English and outside of Germany tends to treat *Ostalgic* expressions primarily as subversively playful, emphasizing the active and critical capacity of those who engage in its practice (e.g., Boyer 2006; Cooke 2005; Jozwiak and Mermann 2006). Within this framework, the mug does not represent understandings accurately or falsely, but rather displays authentic sentiments, even if profit interests have co-opted them. In contrast to this agency-centred analysis, much of German literature, academic and popular alike,[3] approaches *Ostalgie* as promoting an incorrect understanding of the past that interferes with the "accurate" historicization of East Germany. For example, Neller (2006) painstakingly gathers evidence that she argues demonstrates clearly that many of the purportedly positive aspects of GDR society, several of which the mug references, have their origin more in a manipulative East German regime than in what truly occurred. Concerned primarily with *Ostalgie*'s false assertions about the past, Neller concludes that politically, GDR-nostalgia[4] undermines democratic thought and the inner unity of Germany, because it romanticizes totalitarianism.

The descriptions of the diversity in the expression of *Ostalgie* and the reading of one example I have undertaken above begin to bring into focus the politics that are at stake in both *ostalgic* practices and their analysis. I now turn to three theoretical approaches that underscore the phenomenon's political dimensions.

Ostalgie as Nostalgia

All analyses of *Ostalgie*, even those that claim that the phenomenon may not exist (e.g., Boyer 2006), take as a given the neologism's root in the word *nostalgia*. Nostalgia itself is part of how scholarly discussions define *Ostalgie*. For example, Betts (2000) describes it as a "(n)ostalgia among ex-GDR citizens for the relics of their lost socialist world, be they everyday utensils, home furnishings, or pop culture memorabilia" (734). The starting point for deliberations on *Ostalgie* as a cultural practice is frequently a consideration of the term's etymological root in longing for the past (*nostos*: homecoming; *algia*: pain or longing). For example, Boyer (2006) and Neller (2006) return to the origin of the word in Johannes Hofer's 1688 dissertation that medicalizes the vernacular term *homesickness* (*Heimweh*). For Neller this starting point leads to framing *Ostalgie* as embedded in psychological and medical discourses; consequently, *Ostalgie* is understood as a practice that is fundamentally regressive (41). Referencing a more recent text, Berdahl draws on Stewart to emphasize and support her assertions about *Ostalgie*'s character as nostalgia: "Hostile to history and its invisible origins, and yet longing for an impossible pure context of lived experience at a place of origin, nostalgia wears a distinctly utopian face, a face that turns toward future-past, a past which has only ideological reality" (Stewart 1993, 23, cited in Berdahl 1999, 201). In other words, identifying *Ostalgie* as nostalgia entangles the practice inescapably with the overarching failure to consider how the past truly unfolded.

Nostalgia's incongruence with history is part of a larger discourse on postmodernity. For example, Fredric Jameson (1991) and Linda Hutcheon (2000) equally condemn nostalgia's failures. For Jameson, nostalgia entails "an elaborate symptom of the waning of our historicity, of our lived possibility of experiencing history in some active way" (21). Hutcheon also deems nostalgia a poor indicator of what has been:

> Nostalgia, in fact, may depend precisely on the irrecoverable nature of the past for its emotional impact and appeal. It is the very pastness of the past, its inaccessibility, that likely accounts for a large part of nostalgia's power.... This is rarely the past as actually experienced, of course; it is the past as imagined, as idealized through memory and desire. (195)

In contrast to Jameson, Hutcheon, and Neller, cultural analyses of *Ostalgie* struggle with this negative connotation of the term, for the approach principally celebrates the practice as productive and counter-hegemonic. Consequently, several authors have developed typologies of nostalgia in an attempt to account for the tensions in how it articulates itself, especially its politically contradictory manifestations. For example, Bach (2002) juxtaposes modern and postmodern nostalgia; Berdahl (1999) differentiates *Ostalgie* in terms of "mere" nostalgia and socially sanctioned commemorative practices, and Boym (2001), examining contemporary nostalgia beyond its German variant, contrasts restorative and reflective nostalgia. While these differentiations identify successfully opposing tendencies of nostalgia by acknowledging its both productive and regressive character, these separations may also obscure just how much these aspects function interdependently.

For Bach (2002), *Ostalgie* consists simultaneously of two forms of nostalgia: a modern and postmodern one. The former is a version grounded in easterners' experience, while the latter is the domain of westerners. In its modernist articulation, the "consumption of *Ostprodukte* [products related to the East] appears as a form of production itself—a re-appropriation of symbols that establishes 'ownership' of symbolic capital" (547). Moreover, this type of *Ostalgie* entails a "longing for the fantasies and desires that were once possible ... longing for a *mode* of longing that is no longer possible" (ibid.).

With postmodern nostalgia, Bach attempts to account for the fact that western Germans and young eastern Germans, both of whom have no direct experience of living in the GDR, purchase *Ostprodukte*. Here, "*Ostprodukte* constitute floating signifiers of 'neokitsch' that undermine consumption as an oppositional practice by at once turning the consumer into the market and the goods into markers of personal ironic expression" (Bach 2002, 547). Postmodern nostalgia, or nostalgia of style, involves no sense of loss, makes no reference to embodied memory, and consequently does not entail an appeal to recreate the past. Rather, individuals use material signifiers of *Ostalgie* arbitrarily as expressions of hipness.

Bach's typology of nostalgia dichotomizes the features of *Ostalgie* to the point where it erases the phenomenon's puzzling complexity, especially its contradictory nature. In the context of consumer products, the dualism implies ignorant easterners who fail to recognize that they are not purchasing the same products that they reincarnate and that with unification the relations of productions have changed entirely. I would suggest that what Bach labels modernist nostalgia is potentially just as playful as postmodern nostalgia. In both instances, *Ostprodukte* can function as floating or even empty signifiers. Moreover, Bach's dichotomy of modern and postmodern nostalgia leads him to an ahistorical conclusion. He writes, "As direct memories of the GDR fade" all that remains is "highly aestheticised and decontextualized sense of camp" (554). In other words, no meaningful trace of the past will exist once those who experienced life in the GDR are no longer alive. I would suggest that Bach's conclusion is implausible in part because *Ostalgie* does not operate as unidimensionally as Bach proposes. However, it does hint at a politics of historicization to which I will speak in the last part of this chapter.

Attempting to account for *Ostalgie* as practices and products that both contest and affirm the new order, Berdahl (1999) distinguishes between "mere" nostalgia and socially sanctioned commemorative practices (193). Here, "mere" nostalgia is "embarrassing, irritating, puzzling, or laughable to many western and eastern Germans alike.... [They are practices] readily dismissed in popular, political and academic discourse ... as the questionable products of 'GDR romantics,' former Communist Party loyalists ... and clever entrepreneurs" (ibid.). What transformed into "mere" nostalgia first appeared as a challenge to discourses and socioeconomic changes that undermined the foundations of easterners' identity. In the examples Berdahl provides, this type of authentic practice emerged from the people, outside of the commercial arena. These articulations subsequently transformed into *Ostalgie*, which she characterizes as an increasingly profitable industry that entails the revival, reproduction, and commercialization of GDR products as well as the "museumification" of GDR everyday life (Berdahl 1999, 193).

Juxtaposed to this mere nostalgia are the more historical and authentic practices of collecting, displaying, and cataloguing of GDR everyday life in public and private commemorative contexts. Berdahl (1999) highlights the emergence of immensely popular informal museums, galleries, and displays in community centres, which, she argues, "strive to preserve, instruct, and dignify" (201). The purpose of these collections is to "counter the dominant images of the GDR as an economy of scarcity" and to "categorically contrast ... 'historical' objects from widespread nostalgia for an 'allegedly better past'" (ibid.).

Similar to Bach, Berdahl aims to distinguish the publically and aca-
demically ridiculed aspects of *Ostalgie* from the role the phenomenon plays
in remembering the past in uncommercialized terms that recognize lived
experience. Yet Berdahl's conclusion that *Ostalgie* functions both hegemon-
ically and counter-hegemonically renders her differentiation meaningless.
Socially sanctioned commemorative practices can always also have elements
of "mereness" and vice versa. The *Ostalgie* card game to which she refers is
on its own "mere" nostalgia, but it also elicits personal, "authentic" reflections on the past in the players. On the contrary, what began as grassroots
collecting of everyday objects has in some communities turned into profit-
oriented *Ostalgie* museums that distribute products mimicking East German
wares.

In contrast to the frameworks Bach and Berdahl propose, Svetlana
Boym's (2001) typology begins to allow nostalgia to be highly complicated
and contradictory. She distinguishes between restorative and reflective nostalgia by differentiating their relation to time. The former invokes the present and future, while the latter lingers in the past.

> Restorative nostalgia puts emphasis on *nostos* and proposes to rebuild the
> lost home and patch up the memory gaps. Reflective nostalgia dwells in
> *algia*, in longing and loss, the imperfect process of remembrance.... Restora-
> tive nostalgia manifests itself in total reconstruction of monuments of the
> past, while reflective nostalgia lingers on ruins, the patina of time and his-
> tory, in the dreams of another place and another time. (Boym 2001, 41)

As opposed to Bach's and Berdahl's classifications, Boym accounts for
the tensions and complexities of nostalgia without disavowing its etymological roots and use in everyday speech. In the context of Germany, restorative nostalgia can be understood as a hegemonic reading of *Ostalgie*,
comprising those perspectives that reject it for its banality or apparent
unwillingness to face historical facts, while reflective nostalgia pertains to
any practice that takes on the past in any manner but its condemnation.
This form does not exclude the purchasing of commercialized *Ostalgie* products, enjoying a pint of beer in the Mauerblümchen restaurant, or in Boym's
case, spending time at Ljubljana's Nostalija Snack Bar. Most significantly,
Boym recognizes that reflective nostalgia can articulate itself as playful and
deeply meaningful simultaneously, for it "can be ironic and humorous. It
reveals that longing and critical thinking are not opposed to one another, as
affective memories do not absolve one from compassion, judgment or critical reflection" (59). Yet despite capturing the complexity of nostalgia, Boym's

typology cannot fully account for *Ostalgie* because *Ostalgie* and nostalgia are not synonymous, even though she and most others do treat them as interchangeable. Linking a broad range of cultural practices and products to the notion of nostalgia has implications for how we can come to know them. Thus, I would like to suggest that the politics of the deployment of the term require further investigation.

Notwithstanding my critique, it is possible to ask how Bach's, Berdahl's, and Boym's typologies illuminate an interpretation of the *Ostalgie* mug. From Bach's perspective, the mug embodies modernist nostalgia because it addresses the person "in the know" and to be understood it requires direct experience with life in the GDR. The dimension that is lost in this classification, however, is the silliness of the mug that Bach reserved for the uninitiated who are permitted to play with meaning infinitely. Thus, the example of the mug makes apparent that the separation of modern and postmodern nostalgia might shed little light on what *Ostalgie* is, for it clearly entails both characteristics. The mug's appearance points to Berdahl's definition of "mere" nostalgia, for its commercial, kitschy aesthetics indicate triteness and banality. Yet, as mentioned several times, the mug also displays politically sensitive subjects. Consequently, do an understanding of these topics as meaningful, a purchase based on this comprehension, and agreement with the messages classify as "socially sanctioned commemorative practice"? Although perhaps not quite so deep or profound, the mug surely entails something more than "mereness." Again, as in Bach's typology, Berdahl's differentiation dichotomizes a phenomenon that its contradictory articulation does not support. *Ostalgie* as embodied in the mug is also not "restorative" in the manner in which Boym describes it, for the object reads like an obituary or a postmodern tombstone; the past is irrevocably dead and has no hope of resurrection. In contrast, reflective nostalgia provides a framework that can decipher and describe the contradictions for which the other categories cannot account. The mug's banality, irony, and lamentation and even its critique of capitalism can operate in synergy.

On the one hand, Boym's "reflective nostalgia" proves to be useful for the analysis of *Ostalgie* and suggests that other works that consider in depth this type of affect could illuminate understanding of the phenomenon further (see Davis 1979; Wilson 2005). On the other hand, too much emphasis on nostalgia in the study of *Ostalgie* is troubling. It presupposes that everything labelled such is inextricably tied to the complex notion of nostalgia, the consequence of which is a tendency to reify the phenomenon and with it neglect an investigation of what exists a priori. Scholars interested in cultural responses to German unification may benefit from remembering that an artist coined the term *Ostalgie*⁵ (Cooke 2005; Neller 2006). While the phrase undoubtedly refers to something operating in the world, reflections on this origin open up possibilities for alternative conceptualizations of the cultural practices that emerged with German unification. It does not suffice to describe how the kitschy mug operates as nostalgia. Rather, the question why it labels itself *Ostalgie* demands asking. Thus, I would suggest that what must be analyzed in more detail are the contexts in which nostalgia is invoked and deployed, by whom, and with what degree of power. Ideas on how and why *Ostalgie* emerged begin to respond to these questions.

Origins

The most astonishing aspect of the unification of the Germanys is how rapidly it occurred. The consensus in the literature is that this abrupt and complete change is the origin of *Ostalgie*. For example, Betts (2000) writes, "No doubt this East German nostalgia is directly linked to the fact that the GDR has literally vanished from the political map" (734). More specifically, integration of West and East took the form of an unequal partnership with the consequence that "cultural ideals once underpinning the GDR's cosmology had all been rudely relegated to the dustbin of history" (743). Broken promises and the realities of living in late-capitalist society, such as individualism, unemployment, uneven wages, and deep cuts to state subsidies, also rapidly confronted many eastern Germans. Consequently, Berdahl (2005) argues that practices of *Ostalgie* have to be understood "in the context of feelings of profound displacement and disillusionment following reunification, reflected in the popular saying that we have 'emigrated without leaving home'" (165).

   While this idea that historical rupture is the foundation of *Ostalgie* is relatively self-evident, why it articulates itself the way it does is a more difficult question to answer. After unification, *Ostprodukte* emerged rapidly as visual shorthand for German–German dissimilarity and as most common articulations of *Ostalgie*. The unchanging design of East German consumer goods over the course of decades, or their "aesthetics of sameness" (Betts 2000, 754), makes them "particularly effective *lieux de memoire*" (Berdahl 2005, 163). The dominance of products in the practice of *Ostalgie* raises the question of why engagement with the eastern German past/present/future occurs so prominently in this particularly realm. Betts posits that consumption is the only safe domain in which to express positive sentiments because negative discourses about the former East Germany implicating both the public and private spheres leave no opening for alternative and more conventional sites. For him, "the long-running *Trauerspiel* of serialized Stasi disclosure about state corruption, widespread denunciation, and personal betrayal effectively blocked any real positive identification with the GDR past" (743). Blum (2000) extends this idea: "[D]iscourse on consumer products is not fraught with nearly as many anxieties as, for instance, the discussion of political or cultural issues. The undeniable moral bankruptcy of the political nomenclature of the GDR, reiterated countless times, forecloses even the possibility of a productive, unemotional engagement with the past" (232). Although both Blum and Betts make a significant contribution by pointing to the existence of barriers to more traditional avenues for negotiating history, a necessary next step must be to examine what forms these barriers take, whose interests their erecting serves, and how they are experienced in the everyday.

Boyer offers some insight in this regard. In his study of eastern media organizations (2006), he found that eastern Germans were excluded from speaking to Germany as a nation and were rather called upon only as experts of regional matters. When eastern Germans "dared to transgress a past-oriented regional identity ... they were disciplined as 'nostalgics' for the GDR" (373). Boyer also claims that eastern journalists whom he interviewed expressed an inability to speak critically about a unified Germany because their western colleagues interpreted their views as "a lack of commitment to democracy and as a yearning for a return to the GDR" (ibid.). In other words, some of those who could produce knowledge to counter dominant discourses find themselves unable to do so.

In addition to journalists, the role not afforded to the intelligentsia suggests why material culture is so significant in producing narratives about what kind of place East Germany was. Betts (2000) observes that "intellectuals played no leading role in the reconstruction fever of 1989 [or] in shaping the demands and sentiments of the people after the Fall" (744). He explains the causes for their absence as a function of their role within the socialist regime:

> Not only do intellectuals have little to offer for the present or future; they have also lost ... their former credibility as spokespeople of their liquidated past. The scandalous revelations about the Stasi complicity of prominent GDR intellectuals ... only deepened this widespread sense of betrayal and disillusionment.... This was all the more disheartening insofar as intellectuals were long regarded both inside and outside East Germany as the very embodiment of what little pluralism and counter culture existed before 1989. (746)

Here, the irrelevance of intellectuals, combined with limits placed on eastern German journalists, points to how groups traditionally charged with constructing discursive frameworks for understanding social change did not play this role as commentators and interpreters of the collapse of socialism and the unification of Germany. Moreover, the broader context of abrupt system transformation and the peculiarity of East German consumer goods begin to hint at the complex context in which *Ostalgie* emerged, why objects such as the *Ostalgie* coffee mug circulate, and what its political significance may be. To shed more light on *Ostalgie*'s politics in the sense of what is at stake and what struggles are at play, I will now examine the phenomenon from the perspectives of agency and authentic cultural practice.

From the People and for the People

Much of the literature describes *Ostalgie* implicitly or explicitly as authentic resistance to dominant discourses, particularly in its less commercialized articulations. An example of this understanding is Berdahl's (2005) juxtaposition of two museums that focus on the GDR: the Leipzig Forum of Contemporary History (ZGF) and the Museum for East German Everyday Life Culture in Eisenhüttenstadt. The explicit focus of the ZGF is on "the history of resistance and opposition during the dictatorship of the Soviet occupation zone and the GDR.... Images of suffering, repression, and state violence are foregrounded alongside a narrative of resistance and opposition" (Berdahl 2005, 159). In contrast, the project of the Museum for East German Everyday Life Culture entails the "museumification of the world of GDR objects as an active and mutual communication that allows for reflective thought in a period of individual and often painful reorientation" (Ludwig 1996; Ludwig and Kuhn 1997, cited in Berdahl 2005, 162).

Berdahl asserts that the ZGF houses and propagates inauthentic, hegemonic history while the Museum for East German Everyday Life Culture makes accessible a more authentic version of the past, one based on life experience. At the same time, Berdahl situates the Museum for East German Everyday Life Culture within the context of *Ostalgie*, which she defines as the production of counter-memories and identities. I would suggest that the combining of *Ostalgie* with "more authentic" history becomes problematic when considering that the museum presents itself as functioning outside of the political. Berdahl (2005) writes, "My hosts repeatedly stressed that they did not want to glorify the GDR, that this was intended as a completely 'apolitical exhibit.' As evidence of this, they cited their 'strategic decision' not to include political memorabilia like pins, medals, uniforms, or FDJ scarves [*sic*—Free German Youth members wore blue shirts]" (164). This refusal to recognize the overtly political indicates a denial of something that is unavoidably part of the museum's endeavour. Although Berdahl suggests that comments left in the museum's guest book indicate the political nature of the exhibit, she does not consider further the impact of the official apolitical status. Her descriptions lead to a conceptualization of the ZGF's project as political, inauthentic, and hegemonic and the Museum for East German Everyday Life Culture as authentic, subversive, yet apolitical. As indicated above, the latter's subversive and apolitical character is incongruous, which poses an analytical and political problem. This contradiction puts into question the Museum for East German Everyday Life Culture's status as a site that articulates counter-narratives. More importantly, the example highlights a much greater problem for attempts to engage with the GDR past and the eastern German present and future. *Ostalgie* is permissible as long as it is not political. Here, the political and a glorification, or at least uncritical appraisal, of the GDR are equivalent. The assertion of *Ostalgie* as authentic resistance also emerges in deliberations on the popularity of *Ostprodukte*. This type of discussion often links resistance and identity by way of stating that eastern Germany's second-class status is preventing an affirmation of eastern German identity in a more political forum. For example, Bach (2002) writes, "Articulating an East German identity ... is a precarious task, since the East firmly occupies the discursive space of inferiority and practically speaking, western Germans dominate the economic, cultural, and political landscape of the East" (548–49). He concludes that purchasing consumer goods that mimic East German products is one of the only options for resisting this dominance. Advertisers take advantage of this assertion of eastern identity by marketing *Ostprodukte* as symbolizing the real and the natural. Many ads play on easterners' wish for their products, and by extension themselves, to be perceived as "normal" and "down-to-earth" (Hogwood 2002, 50).

Yet the triad of consumption, resistance, and authenticity is unavoidably also a contradictory and uneasy one. Berdahl (1999) calls upon Michel de Certeau (1984) to support her beginning suspicion that what appears to be an act of resistance is in fact a form of complicity. Here, she paraphrases de Certeau, thereby highlighting the entanglement of the hegemonic and the subversive. She writes, "[C]onsumers of *Ostalgie* may escape the dominant order without leaving it" (206).

A concrete example of *Ostalgie* allows specific elaboration on the practice as authentic and subversive. One of the most successful efforts to save GDR iconography from oblivion is the *Ampelmann* (traffic light man), a

Figure 1.4 *Ampelmann* store and *Fernsehturm*, Berlin. (Photo credit: A. Winkler)

pedestrian traffic light in the shape of a chubby, masculine figure wearing a hat. Attempts to replace it with traffic lights according to European standards in the early 1990s quickly met with outrage in eastern Germany. Opposition to removal led not only to the *Ampelmann*'s survival but also to a highly lucrative business. Today, souvenir shops and specialty *Ampelmann* stores (see Figure 1.4) carry countless products featuring the character, including purses, towels, pencils, erasers, T-shirts, and drinking glasses. Its commercial success and ubiquity have imbued it with such symbolic power that it stands in loosely for the entire contemporary East. For example, a cover of the popular German weekly *Der Spiegel* features a green *Ampelmann* half submerged in water and the headline "Jammertal Ost" ("The East: Landscape of Misery"). Yet, here also emerges one of the central problems of *Ostalgie*, particularly in reference to authenticity and resistance. Although the mere survival, and more significantly the commercial success of the *Ampelmann*, may point to triumphant resistance to attempts to assimilate the East, not all might be as it seems. Today, the figure is stripped of any specific reference to the former East; it is an empty signifier that alludes merely to some kind of difference. What this difference entails is unclear, as is how purchasing it might oppose dominant understandings of the GDR past.

Returning to the *Ostalgie* coffee mug, questions about how it might embody authenticity and resistance can also be posed. Its kitschy aesthetic and the location of its purchase, that is, the souvenir shop, would suggest it entails neither. However, unlike the *Ampelmann*, the mug displays politically controversial and potentially potent ideas. Does this mean that buying the mug is an authentic act and a form of resistance? Perhaps this question is not particularly relevant because attempts to answer it yield only the conclusion that *Ostalgie* can be simultaneously hegemonic and counter-hegemonic and that it is sometimes an authentic form of resistance and other times is not. In addition to the theoretical framing of *Ostalgie* as nostalgia, questions about authenticity and resistance, although providing fascinating descriptions, frequently leave unexamined the wider politics of the phenomenon. Here, I wonder in particular about the ongoing implications of the practice, especially in reference to other, more powerful historicizing discourses.

What Remains: Historicization and *Ostalgie*

With its emphasis on agency, cultural studies–oriented literature places nostalgia in the contexts of contemporary socio-economic conditions. Here, *Ostalgie* emerges politically as a "critical tool to promote and enable an active engagement with the present" (Enns 2007, 478), and as resistance to colonization by western Germany and globalization more broadly (Jozwiak and Mermann 2006). In contrast to this focus on the present, perspectives such as Neller's (2006) emphasize the relevance of the past by describing nostalgia as dehistoricizing and depoliticizing. Nostalgia impedes an objective and truthful appraisal of the past and jeopardizes the unified and democratic Germany.

Yet, the collapse of the European socialist nations highlights the impossibility of objectively true understandings of the past, for it has rendered the social construction of historical discourses blatant and visible, particularly as they articulate themselves in public spaces. The swift renaming of cities and streets and the removal of monuments that occurred nearly overnight seemed inevitable and almost natural. Although the majority of overt public markers of the socialist past disappeared rapidly and without much fanfare, fierce public struggles over what traces would continue to project themselves into the future also erupted. For example, for over a decade citizen groups actively attempted to rescue the Palast der Republik (Republic's Palace) in Berlin, former seat of the East German parliament and venue for major cultural events, by attempting to reframe its political symbolism. This project included expensive asbestos removal, renaming the building Volkspalast (People's Palace), and staging successful art exhibits and theatre performances. Restoration funds and energy were invested to no avail. In 2006 the federal government prohibited any further delay of demolition and with this decision made room for the long-planned rebuilding of the Berliner Stadtschloss (Berlin City Palace), principal residence of Prussian regents since the eighteenth century. The palace had been damaged during the final days of the Second World War and the new East German government subsequently tore it down, for it deemed reconstruction politically undesirable. According to the project's proponents, the building anew of the Stadtschloss entails a symbolic spatial and historical restoring of order (see Boym 2001, 180–90; Till 2005).

While this example illustrates public resistance to top-down reshaping of the material historical landscape, it also provides evidence of a government-sanctioned process that overtly moulds understanding of the East German past. In this case, the destruction of a structurally sound building and its replacement with a costly copy of a Prussian palace points toward ideologically motivated construction of what kind of a place East Germany was and what the new Germany imagines itself to be. The demise of the Palast der Republik signals clearly that symbols of the East have no place in a unified Germany. It is in this context of the mythologizing of the new Germany that *Ostalgie* as a memory-based cultural practice appeared and continues to operate today.

Conclusion

What is the significance of the *Ostalgie* coffee mug, belonging to a Trabant car club, celebrating *Jugendweihe*, purchasing replicas of East German consumer goods, and visiting GDR museums, objects and practices so easily characterized as *Ostalgie*? While the authenticity and subversive character of *Ostalgie* is not as evident as some commentators claim and hope, the phenomenon projects forward aspects of the East German past that other discourses reject or omit. At the same time, the association of these object and practices with the notions of nostalgia and kitsch renders them dismissible and usually insignificant in comparison to more traditional and government-sanctioned commemorative practices and framings of the GDR as a dictatorship and *Unrechtsstaat* (illegitimate state). Analytical frameworks that replace or work alongside the concept of nostalgia are one possibility for bringing together these contradictory aspects of this cultural response to post-socialism.

Another strategy is to "keep up" with *Ostalgie*. Although the literature traces extensively the emergence of this phenomenon, in recent years few contributions examine how it has changed over time, how it articulates itself today, and how it relates to other discourses staking an interpretive claim on the past. I would like to suggest that an approach that considers these not only can bring to the fore competing interests in the interpretation of the GDR but can also illuminate the struggle over mythologizing the unified Germany. Broader contextualization of *Ostalgie* makes visible hegemonic discourses attempting to create new narratives about a unified Germany in which the GDR can play only a very narrow role. These types of stories intersect and collide with more marginal meaning-making efforts of individuals and small interest groups who operate primarily from a localized standpoint. In addition, placing *Ostalgie* into the context of specific sites and material expressions will further contribute to a more nuanced understanding of contemporary cultural responses to post-socialism. For example, in my work, I am now beginning to embark on an analysis of museum representations of Germany's recent history, such as in the popular GDR museums that can be found in many communities of the former East and that the literature describes frequently as nostalgic expression. The historicizing work of the German federal government through such organizations as the Bundesstiftung für Aufarbeitung der SED Diktatur (Federal Foundation for the Reconciliation of the SED Dictatorship) can further shed light on the tensions and interactions between competing understandings of the past, particularly in relation to the present and the future, and the role that nostalgia can and cannot play within these processes.

Notes

1 German analyses of this subject tend to present a much more negative per-spective. I will address this difference below.

2 Popular and academic discourses assume that *Ostalgie* expresses itself pre-dominantly through the aesthetic of kitsch. For example, Boyer refers almost in passing to the "lightness and kitschiness of *Ostalgie*" (Boyer 2006, 380). Even texts that would not ordinarily be described as kitsch, such as the litera-ture of the acclaimed East German writer Christa Wolf, has been dismissed as kitsch when its critics deemed it not sufficiently critical of the GDR (Cole 1999, 406). In recent years, particularly in responses to the fall of communism, schol-arly discourses have grappled with the tensions between celebrating the creativ-ity of kitsch and its aesthetics' more retrogressive characteristics.

3 Cooke (2005) responds to the German concern that *Ostalgie* threatens Ger-man unity. He concludes that "although the way the GDR is used is still wor-thy of exploration, the vast majority of this use is generally far more mundane than much of its reporting" (203).

4 Although Neller differentiates GDR-nostalgia and *Ostalgie*, her definition of the former as the "positive Orientierugen gegenüber der ehemaligen DDR" (positive orientation toward the former GDR) does not contradict other descrip-tions or conceptualizations of *Ostalgie* (Neller 2006, 37).

5 According to Cook (2005, 8), the Dresden cabaret artist Uwe Steimle coined the term. Neller (2006, 42) credits the lyricist Günter Kunert.

References

Atkinson, D. 2007. Kitsch geographies and the everyday spaces of social mem-ory. *Environment and Planning A* 39 (2): 521–40.

Bach, J. 2002. "The taste remains": Consumption, (n)ostalgia, and the produc-tion of East Germany. *Public Culture* 14 (3): 545–56.

Becker, W., dir. 2002. *Good Bye, Lenin!* DVD. Berlin: X Verleih AG.

Berdahl, D. 1999. "(N)ostalgie" for the present: Memory, longing, and East Ger-man things. *Ethnos* 64 (2): 192–211.

———. 2005. Expressions of experience and experiences of expression: Museum re-presentation of GDR history. *Anthropology and Humanism* 30 (2): 156–70.

Berlin Tourism. 2008. "East Berlin nostalgia tours." http://www.visitberlin.de/english/sightseeing/e_si_berlinprogramme_ostalgie.php (accessed Novem-ber 2, 2008).

Betts, P. 2000. The twilight of the idols: East German memory and material cul-ture. *The Journal of Modern History* 72 (3): 731–65.

Blum, M. 2000. Remaking the East German past: *Ostalgie*, identity, and mate-rial culture. *Journal of Popular Culture* 34 (3): 229.

Boyer, D. 2006. *Ostalgie* and the politics of the future in eastern Germany. *Pub-lic Culture* 18 (2): 361–81.

Boym, S. 2001. *The future of nostalgia.* New York: Basic Books.

Cole, J. 1999. The difficulty of saying "I." *Journal of European Studies* 29 (4): 405–16.

Cooke, P. 2004a. *Ostalgie*'s not what it used to be. *German Politics and Society* 22 (4): 134–50.

———. 2004b. Surfing for eastern difference: *Ostalgie*, identity, and cyberspace. *Seminar—A Journal of Germanic Studies* 40 (3): 207–20.

———. P. 2005. *Representing East Germany since unification: From colonization to nostalgia.* Oxford: Berg.

Davis, F. 1979. *Yearning for yesterday: A sociology of nostalgia.* New York: Free Press.

de Certeau, M. 1984. *The practice of everyday life*, trans. S. Rendall. Berkeley: University of California Press.

Enns, A. 2007. The politics of *Ostalgie:* Post-socialist nostalgia in recent German film. *Screen* 48 (7): 475–91.

Finger, A. K. 2005. Hello Willy, Good-Bye Lenin! Transitions of an East German family. *South Central Review* 22 (2): 39–58.

Fisher, P. 2002. Creating a Marxist-Leninist cultural identity: Women's memories of the German Democratic Republic's Friedensfahrt. *Culture, Sport, Society* 5 (1): 39.

Haußmann, L., dir. 1999. *Sonnenallee.* DVD. Berlin: Bojebuck Delphi Filmverleih GmbH & Co.

Hogwood, P. 2002. "Red is for love ...": Citizens as consumers in East Germany. In *East German distinctiveness in a unified Germany*, ed. J. Grix and P. Cooke, 41–54. Birmingham, UK: University of Birmingham Press.

Hörschelmann, K. 2001. Audience interpretations of (former) East Germany's representation in the German media. *European Urban and Regional Studies* 8 (3): 189–202.

Hutcheon, L. 2000. Irony, nostalgia, and the postmodern. In *Methods for the study of literature as cultural memory*, ed. R. Vervliet and N. Estor, 189–207. Amsterdam: Rodopi.

Jameson, F. 1991. *Postmodernism, or, the cultural logic of late capitalism.* Durham, NC: Duke University Press.

Jozwiak, J. F., and E. Mermann. 2006. "The wall in our minds?": Colonization, integration, and nostalgia. *Journal of Popular Culture* 39 (5): 780–95.

Lee, M. J. 1993. *Consumer culture reborn: The cultural politics of consumption.* London: Routledge.

Ludwig, A. 1996. *Alltagskultur der DDR: Begleitbuch zur Austellung "Tempolinsen und P2."* Berlin-Brandenburg: be.bra-Verlag.

Ludwig, A., and G. Kuhn. 1997. *Alltag und soziales Gedächtnis: Die DDR-Objektkultur und ihre Musealisierung.* Hamburg: Ergebnisse Verlag.

Magdalinski, T. 1999. Sports history and East German national identity. *Peace Review* 11 (4): 539.

McLellan, J. 2007. State socialist bodies: East German nudism from ban to boom. *Journal of Modern History* 79 (1): 48–79.

Neller, K. 2006. *DDR-Nostalgie: Dimensionen der Orientierungen der Ost-deutschen gegenüber der ehemaligen DDR, ihre Ursachen und politschen Konnotationen*. Wiesbaden: VS Verlag für Sozialwissenschaften.

Rethmann, P. 2009. Post-communist ironies in an East German hotel. *Anthropology Today* 25 (1): 21–23.

Scribner, C. 2000. Tender rejection: The German democratic republic goes to the museum. *European Journal of English Studies* 4 (2): 171–87.

Stewart, S. 1993. *One longing: Narratives of the miniature, the gigantic, the souvenir, the collection*. Durham, NC: Duke University Press.

Till, K. E. 2005. *The New Berlin: Memory, politics, place*. Minneapolis: University of Minnesota Press.

Wilson, J. 2005. *Nostalgia: Sanctuary of meaning*. Cranbury: Associated University Press.

2

Nostalgia and Postmemories of a Lost Place
Actualizing "My Virtual Homeland"

TONYA K. DAVIDSON

> *My mother has not been to Kapetanovo, the small Croatian village of her parents. She was born in London, Ontario, in 1951, two years after my grandparents settled in Canada. When she was born, her parents were farmhands, learning English, sending their seven-year-old daughter, Inge, to school. Imagining this period, I see my infant mom, with her round face, in a porcelain doll dress, plopped on the porch of a white farmhouse. It is an image directly imported from family albums. Although she doesn't know it in her infancy, she will be shaped by a place very distant from this southwestern Ontario homestead. Now, I ask my mom if she feels connected to the distant place that has had a shadow presence in her life. My mom answers, "The feeling I have with my Kapetanovo connection, it's not just through words and pictures. There is something intangible there, more of a spiritual connection that carries on."*

This project asks how it becomes possible to feel and remember an unvisited, unknown place as lost. What are the mechanisms of memory and representation that lead descendants of exiles to continue to feel a sense of loss of place? Considering Proust's conceptualization of the virtual as "real without being actual, ideal without being abstract" (Shields 2003, 25), my grandparents' Croatian village, Kapetanovo, has become a *virtual homeland* for many people, constituted through texts and memories. What is a homeland without access to the materiality of the land? While the idea of "home" is itself a process of constant re-creation (Gonzales 2005; Wilson 2005), in cases of exile or forced relocation, both home and land become virtualized. A virtual homeland is accessible through actualizations, through the residue that gathers, collects, and reconstitutes places: blueprints of proposed monuments, maps of the town sketched by a daughter, amateur vacation videos made by some who have returned.

In 1944 my grandparents Margaret and Stefan Torau, their families, and the majority of the German population of their small town in Eastern Croatia (then Yugoslavia) were forced to flee from Josef Tito's partisans. Kapetanovo was their hometown. In their sixty years in Canada, surrounded by other "Kapetanovers," this village became constituted as a virtual homeland for their children and grandchildren. In this chapter, I explore the residual, virtual Kapetanovo and argue that new articulations of a virtual place known only through traces offer up new possibilities for understanding. The traces of a virtual homeland, the accessible actualizations of this place, are found in storytelling, things, and memory texts. Actualizing a virtual homeland emphasizes the gaps, the trace-like nature of memory practices, and the affect imbued and performed in memory practices across generations.

The unarticulated connection to a place that played out as a phantom background to my mother's childhood defines a relationship to a virtual place. A virtual place is one that's defined not by its materiality, but rather through its loss of materiality.[1] This connection, I would argue, is propelled by what Svetlana Boym (2001) describes as "reflective nostalgia." For Boym there are two types of nostalgia: restorative and reflective. "Restorative nostalgia manifests itself in total reconstructions of monuments of the past, while reflective nostalgia lingers on ruins, the patina of time and history, in the dreams of another place and another time" (41). While restorative nostalgia is engaged in homecomings, returning places to their "original" states, reflective nostalgia "cherishes shattered fragments of memory and temporalizes space" (49). My virtual homeland, as actualized through stories, photography, and memory texts, operates as a form of the latter.

A Note on Postmemory and Autoethnography

The distances between generations, homes, places, and times cannot be measured in latitudes and longitudes. Writing about the children of exiled parents, Marianne Hirsch (1996) states, "The distance separating them from the locus of origin is the radical break of unknowable and incomprehensible persecution; for those born after, it is a break impossible to bridge. Still, the power of mourning and memory, and the depth of the rift dividing their parents' lives, impart them something that is akin to memory" (662) What is "akin to memory" is a sense of feeling and knowing a place that is considerably "unknowable." This is what Hirsch defines as "postmemory," a phenomenon particular to descendants of the exiled. She writes, "Postmemory characterizes the experience of those who grow up dominated by narratives that preceded their birth, whose own belated stories can be neither fully understood or re-created" (659). Postmemories are the feelings of "home" as a place that "would remain, out of reach" (661). Postmemories emerge and are constructed as new articulations, as the bearers of postmemories attempt "to re-build, to re-incarnate, to replace and to repair" (661). In this way, the production of postmemory has elements of reclamation and dialogism.[2] Hirsch explores postmemory through memory texts created by "agents" of postmemory using aesthetic creations such as memory books and workings with family photography as examples.

An emphasis on new creations of memory is echoed in Alison Landsberg's (1997) writings on Art Spiegelman's graphic novel *Maus*. In this graphic novel, Spiegelman uses cartoon mice and cats to depict his father's stories of Auschwitz. Landsberg writes about a story in *Maus* in which the father, Vladek, finds some wire and picks it up, explaining the usefulness of the wire, and how "inside it's little wires. It's good for tying things" (67). Landsberg writes, "The recirculation of the wire becomes a metaphor for the recirculation of the Holocaust through a different medium (the comic book) suggesting that when one puts the story into a different medium, new insights, new possibilities, emerge" (67). Learning from works such as *Maus* and their interpretations, my project explores some of the ways in which a "lost place" becomes circulated in new ways by subsequent generations through mechanisms of postmemory.

Using my grandparents' village as the place of study, this project has emerged as a form of narrative ethnography. I have been inspired by the techniques of autoethnography, a methodology that uses stories as means of analysis, rather than as content for analysis (Denzin 2003, 2006; Ellis 2004; Ellis and Bochner 2006; Pelias 2005; Richardson 2000; Spry 2001). This methodology emphasizes writing narratives and working stories in a way "that shows rather than tells" (Ellis and Bochner 2006, 445). My intimate relationship with the subject of analysis and my desire to explore how postmemories emerge and produce place call out for this type of analysis. Through a modified form of narrative ethnography, I hope to *show* how places come to haunt through storytelling and things. There is a further level of haunting

Figure 2.1 Kapetanovo, 1930s. (Photo courtesy of Katherine Davidson)

in this text: absent are the voices of other family members such as my oma Margaret Torau, who died in 1996, and others who remain distanced by physical and emotional geographies.

Working Stories

My opa talks and talks. Sometimes if I stop paying attention I look up and notice he is now standing in front of me, having moved from his regular chair. His own words move him to move. Often he interrupts himself, dismissing his stories, looking at me with a bit of disgust. "You don't understand. How could you possibly understand? I don't know why I keep saying." The fact that I have trekked to his small abandoned town in eastern Croatia, or am embarking on this project of his life, is little proof of my interest and willingness to understand. Other times he interrupts himself and looks up at me, bemused. "But why do you want to know?" He almost smiles. "You could never know. He confirms what Schreiber Weitz says, in relation to Holocaust survivors, that "to speak is impossible, and not to speak is impossible" (in Caruth 1995, 154). But I try. I ask him about how many pigs they took, how they fed their horses, what they left behind. My opa refuses to acknowledge that they have become my stories too. I have favourites that I similarly retell: the one about the bicycle man, the one about the disabled soldier who gave up forever his chance for true love. To him I am a Canadian child, raised on Fun Dips

*and Saturday morning cartoons. My opa simultaneously holds on
to and transmits his past.*

Storytelling is one of the mechanisms of postmemory generation, as stories
work to produce what Allison Landsberg (1997) calls a "transferential space."
These are spaces in which "people are invited to enter into experiential relationships with events through which they themselves did not live" (66). Stories produce the metaphoric bridges across times and place, allowing a
virtual place to be felt and remembered. In relation to loss and place, how
does storytelling work? What did his stories do? What have they done? And
how can or should the listener or ethnographer work these stories?

This project is also about the loss of stories, another layer of complication that has been the unintended effect of my grandfather's passing in the
spring of 2007. When I began working on this project I tried to remember
the stories and I couldn't. I had actively listened for my whole life, many
Sundays in a row—to stories, whole Christmas, Easter, Mother's Day, and
Father's Day holidays devoted to stories. Movies were shut off after acknowledging that there was no way the movie could coincide with an evening performance of Opa stories. So instead, we all listened. They weren't
conversations, they were performances. But what, after all of this listening,
can I say? Can I perform? I am struck by this loss, by my inability to have
captured the nuanced textures of these performances, to have only a sense.
I am frustrated also by the moments I wanted to watch the movie, to escape
to town to pick up the pizza in lieu of more performances.

To negotiate with the loss of stories I am invoking Walter Benjamin's
conception of the storyteller as a way of understanding what one can learn
from stories. Storytelling produces a space that works in many ways. For
the generation exiled, storytelling can become a way of conceptualizing loss.
For the listeners, storytelling allows for the generation and maintenance of
a virtual place; in particular, listening through the juxtaposition of stories
to emergent details can allow stories to offer remembrance in ways previously unnoticed.

The Storyteller

For Walter Benjamin (1969), storytelling is a form of counsel that works
through producing experiences rather than parlaying information. Benjamin states that "the storyteller takes what he tells from experience—his
own or that reported to others. And he in turn makes it the experience of those
who are listening to his tale" (87). In this way, rather than presenting

history, storytelling generates memories of the experiences of listening to stories. For Benjamin, stories are told without judgment or analysis. They are offered generously and openly. He explains:

> Actually, it is half the art of storytelling to keep a story free from explanations as one reproduces it.... The most extraordinary things, marvelous things, are related with the greatest accuracy, but the psychological connection of the events is not forced on the reader. It is left up to him to interpret things the way he understands them. (89)

Listening to stories, likewise, takes a unique form. Because storytelling works through multiple retellings (Benjamin 1969, 93), the best listener engagement requires a state of relaxation, even boredom (91). For Benjamin, "The more self-forgetful the listener is, the more deeply is what he listens to impressed upon his memory" (91). I consider my opa a Benjaminian storyteller who produced countless experiences of Kapetanovo for my sister and me. His stories, rather than transferring information, worked to produce experiences, affect, and relationships. What can I say, then, after all of this both engaged and uninterested listening? Beyond my relationship with my opa, his endless stories have produced a memory of his village as a lost place.

There are some stories whose performances I can recall. I have written these stories as short vignettes, which I will offer together. In suggesting an opportunity to "remember otherwise," Roger Simon (2005) suggests that certain details emerge through the juxtaposition of stories. These details signal a doing and work as the "persistent moment of saying" (113) and "an interruption of 'more of the same'" (114). What can emerge through juxtaposing stories, reconsidering testimonies in this way, are surprises. To reconcile my loss of stories, I have returned, to hear differently, what these insistent anecdotes are saying, what learning I am being offered. Here, I have three vignettes, which, juxtaposed, offer up a new understanding of loss of stories and stories of loss.

> *He is telling me this story at his kitchen table, wearing his slippers; we've just had lunch, my mom is cleaning, and I am "listening." He was probably telling a story about Heinz (where he worked for thirty years) or something I found less interesting. I usually ended up interjecting, "Tell me about the trek." This was a shorthand way for me to get him on to my favourite subject—their horse-drawn wagon trip fleeing from Croatia to Austria in 1944. I am fifteen and record the story in a pink notebook I carry around for such purposes. In my notebook, I have written: First they left in May for another province in Yugoslavia*

Ssram, where they stayed until October. In October, they had to leave Ssram in the middle of the night. Oma and her sister slaughtered a pig and packed it in lard; Opa went to the mill to make some flour, but the mill man had already left. On the trek, a series of wagons (their entire village sticking together), they see a bunch of things thrown into the ditch—they are too heavy to burden their horses with on the soft ground: knitting, bicycles, and bundles of knit slippers. The horses, even Opa's strong horses, Wilma and Zorca, are exhausted; they have to run through towns in the middle of the night with heavy loads, and there is not enough hay. In Hungary, Opa trades a good pair of never-worn Italian shoes for fifty kilos of oats for his horses.

My opa is in the hospital, his lungs are failing. His roommate has been sleeping all day. "Look at him," he says, "sleeping away his memories. My opa doesn't sleep away his memories, but he is too weak to talk at his normal velocity. This day, he sits up for lunch and motions toward his shoes—brown leather slippers I have seen a million times. "These," pointing, "my brother made; he was a shoemaker. He was a shoemaker because he had polio. Couldn't work, or do the army." He continues to talk about his brother while picking at the hospital tray of food. The gist of this story is his typical conclusion that his younger brother was generally "up to no good." "There is another pair of shoes at the house that he made. They are pointy and too tight."

It is Christmas Day, a moment of lull and feast-fuelled exhaustion in between meals at my parents' place. My sister and I are on the couch comparing our crocheting. Opa is in his chair, the stiff high-backed chair that no one minds giving up to him. He makes this sound with his mouth—put-put, that my mom says he picked up after he quit smoking. He is put-putting in his chair, thinking. Spontaneously he starts a story in German to my mom. He has stood up and started pantomiming, so I insist on a language switch. He is talking about the trek and his wedding shoes. The shoes, along with both of their wedding outfits, made it from Kapetanovo, through Hungary and Austria to Rodney, Ontario. The shoes were black leather, Italian. He explains, in some detail I can't recall, why they were so good—something about the stitching, the sole? When they arrived in Canada, they were his only shoes, and his first job was as a farmhand working in the fields. Within a week, they were ruined. He ends the story deflated, sits down, and resumes put-putting.

What was offered in these anecdotes, some known and repeated more than others? How can I learn from, rather than learn about,[3] my grandfather, Kapetanovo, loss? In the three stories, shoes work as the vehicle or the exemplar of loss. As a result of exile, my grandfather is forced into a position of selling his shoes to feed his horses or destroying his shoes in the physical process of working for a new life. Talking about his long-lost brother, who never came to Canada, whose image is stuck at young adulthood in the stories, my opa uses the shoes as a material testament to loss, a memory object. Through their materiality, the shoes also offer up a sentiment about work. They are worked through, worked on, made to work as capital. As my grandfather slumps into his chair defeated, I get a sense through this and other stories of the trying, exhausting labour of exile, labouring for a new life. I also gain from the shoes a well-learned understanding of my opa's endearing and enduring vanity. His loss and destruction of shoes is further marked by his sense of pride in self-presentation. This marks Walter Benjamin's (1969) claim that "traces of the storyteller cling to the story the way the handprints of the potter cling to the clay vessel" (92). These stories, offered up in their remembered partiality, suggest the ways in which storytelling, as an imparting of sentiment, rather than information, works to offer counsel.

Storytelling is both an intra-generational bridge, a means of forging understandings of other times and places, and a solitary ontological endeavour, to which there are witnesses (Felman 1992; Laub 1995). It is impossible for my grandfather to keep his memories to himself, to refuse us ownership of his past. It is impossible because I claim ownership, and because he has to share. We are both selfish and creative in our understandings of this past. Rachel Baum (2000) writes that "while memory is given shape through stories, it is never fully contained within them" (92). Stories likewise can only be traces; in the process of actualization, there is always still some loss. Kapetanovo is flattened from a three-dimensional world, feeling breezes and memories of the pitch black night sky, to a two-dimensional series of narratives with residual affect. Jackson (2002) explains that while storytelling is instrumental in creating social cohesion, there can never be a full, complete exchange: "every person's story remains, therefore, irreducibly his or her own, imperfectly incorporated into the collective realm" (64). At the same time, storytelling is one way to reconstitute some of the texture of places and times lost. What is felt in subsequent generations, while largely conveyed through a ritualized space of storytelling, has a subtle beyond. At moments of loss, we have access only to the traces.

In working stories of Kapetanovo, I realize that while I feel that I have many stories, in reality I can account for only a few. In his years of storytelling as a grandfather, the last thirty years of his life, my opa produced new experiences and new, real relationships with his past, in particular, his home—Kapetanovo. What I know is less than what I feel, a testament to successful storytelling.

Memory Objects and Texts

Stories and objects have a reciprocal relationship. Objects inspire stories; stories are contained in objects invested with meaning. Stories also work up and conjure lost objects. In Rob Shields's (2003) tetrology of the virtual, objects exist in the realm of the actually real: the concrete (29). In fact, "the virtual is fully real but can be actualized as the concrete" (30). Things are the concrete result of and means toward actualizing real moments, memories, desires. While Landsberg uses prosthetic memory to describe how forms of mass media produce memory technologies, in this section I explore how objects such as photography or baby clothes, more intimate family heirlooms, similarly act as 'transferential sites" for postmemories. Elizabeth Spelman (2008) argues that objects provide a "scaffold for memory, in the sense that they provide a kind of platform through which memories are reached for, a guiding structure through which the past is recalled" (11). In intergenerational memory, objects provide tangible forms that can outlive places and people. In this study, objects emerge at multiple junctures. There are "object survivors" (Liss 2000): things from Kapetanovo. There are also *memory texts*: memory performances actualized, made concrete. Memory texts are produced to perform postmemory by both first and subsequent generations.

Object Survivors

Objects are central to postmemory. The United States Holocaust Memorial Museum refers to objects recovered or safeguarded from incidents of trauma as "object survivors" (Liss 2000, 124). For Liss, "The artifact intrudes in the realm of the present through its hyperreality and, paradoxically, through the utter concreteness it signals. It brings one closer to the historical real, supposedly closer to the tangibility of the events and to the experiences of those who did and did not survive" (121). "Object survivors" in their material tangibility stand in for both the unrepresentability of the trauma and the human loss. Object survivors exist in part because of deliberate decisions, acts of constructing memory that result from attachments to things. In the context of exile, how to remember home is forged in the brief moments of packing during exile. This packing is infused with both nostalgia for a life that is at that moment being lost and an impetus to plan for the future (Parkin 1999). In the process of choosing what to discard and what to hold close, objects are transformed into "object survivors" and take on a dynamic that exceeds their original use value. Wedding shoes, taken for their utility and quality, become poignant signifiers of further loss through their association with happier times and their ultimate destruction.

In their ability to structure memory, feelings of belonging, and understandings of loss, objects offer up affordances for remembering.[4] Andrea Liss writes about a Polish train car used to deport Jews that is now an exhibit at the United States Holocaust Memorial Museum. She (2000) explains that "the artifact functions as a marker of the trauma through its status as representation—that is, as lack and loss yet also as evidence of the real—which signals its potent and ambivalent inaccessibility" (125). Object survivors, in their tactility, allow some physical, literal connection while reconfirming distance. Holding and being close to an object brings a sense of closeness with the experience imbued in the object. Yet the object's foreignness reasserts the distance of the experiences. This distance is structured and emphasized with the sacred distance that we award to museum artifacts. In relation to family heirlooms, object survivors offer an emphasized sense of intimacy as objects that can be held and incorporated into domestic spheres. Some objects from Kapetanovo, like a pair of good shoes or baby clothes, create a framework around which remembering (and necessarily forgetting) becomes possible.

My grandparents lost three children in infancy in Kapetanovo and in their few years in Austria before coming to Canada. My mother (Kathe Davidson) describes her childhood: "I usually asked questions, I remember asking questions a lot about my brothers and sister that died. I asked a lot about them and I always wanted to see baby clothes that my mother had for them. And she'd bring out a box of these little baby clothes that she had for them, and I loved looking at them." Her siblings' clothes, as object survivors, provide my mother some intimacy with her siblings who were absent in her childhood. In Art Spiegelman's autobiographical graphic novel *Maus II: And Here My Troubles Began*, Art comments to his wife on being haunted by his ghost brother, Richieu, who was killed during the Nazi genocide. During Art's childhood, Richieu's photo was hung prominently in his parents' bedroom. For Art, Richieu's photo performed unintelligible memories. Art's (1986) character states, "They didn't talk about Richieu, but that photo was a kind of reproach, he'd have become a doctor, and married a wealthy Jewish girl" (15). For Spiegelman, his brother's photo performs the haunting presence of his ghost brother and has the effect of producing survivor guilt. My mother's deceased siblings' baby clothes similarly have

Figure 2.2 Baby clothes from Kapetanovo. (Photo courtesy of Katherine Davidson)

affective consequences, highlighting to child Kathe her distance from her parents' exile, while she attempts through these objects to forge closeness. In another instance my mother articulates a distinct relationship to her parents based on her Canadian birth—a type of survivor guilt similar to Art's. Talking about her Yugoslavian-born sister, Inge, my mother states:

> She was born while they were refugees. She was born in Surcin, in the middle of it. Did they even recognize that she was there? They lost Stephan, they lost Kathy, and meanwhile Inge is there, what are they doing with her? I think, my feeling is, that she is one of them. Inge told me, my mother said that to her, that she was one of them, but in a negative way, it had a negative connotation, but that I wasn't.

Reaching out to the baby clothes, she attempts to reconcile her Canadian birth. The unbridgeable distance between my mother and her deceased siblings is mediated through these object survivors.

If places are arrangements of things (Hetherington 1997; Hui in this volume; Tuan 1977), simultaneous to the destruction of homes and places is the destruction of objects and collections of material meaning-infused goods. Being unable to hold objects pushes some things into the realm of constant re-creation that is storytelling. The surviving things take on new responsibilities, having to stand in for the many other objects lost and stolen and the vibrant places that have been destroyed. The portability of object survivors ensures their suitability to the nature of postmemory, as memories that can be transported from person to person, among times and places.

In relation my grandfather's story of his ruined wedding shoes, the destruction of shoes kept safe for their connection to a past time and place and the envisioning of a Canadian future signals the salience of objects in relation to home. The transportation of old, special shoes to a new place is not seamless. Objects can bridge one's relationship to places. The loss and destruction of these place-tying things serves to reinforce the destruction of a material home, necessitating its creation through virtual actualizations.

Memory Texts

My great-oma, Katharina Torau née Bauer, was an avid memory keeper. In her eighties she continued to walk, wearing an old kerchief, to the Leamington Public Library, coming home with a bag full of books. She died when I was five. I remember only that she had impossibly old hands, and if she hadn't been my great-oma, whose face opened up into a smile because I was her kleine, she might have made me nervous. As a committed letter writer, she was always interested in inscribing memory in a variety of ways.

Distinct from object survivors, memory texts represent the deliberate inscribing of memory. Since I began this project, texts demanding attention have materialized within my reach. While object survivors can be the result of deliberate choices of preservation, memory texts are reflexive inscriptions of memory-as-texts. Examples of memory texts abound in art and literature.[5] Memory texts are a concrete, portable form of memory and postmemory making, inscribed at both primary and post levels of remembering. Memory texts also represent the dialogue between bearers of memory and postmemory. Andrea Liss (2000) describes Tatana Kellner's artist book *71125: Fifty Years of Silence, Eva Kellner's Story* (1992), which exemplifies this type of memory inscription. This artist book is the result of the artist's relationship with her mother, Eva. The book consists of Eva's autobiographical text about her experiences throughout the Holocaust, written in Czech. Alongside the Czech text is Tatana's English translation. The texts together create an overlay that is interrupted by a pink cast of Eva's arm with its tattooed Auschwitz number (Liss 2000, 127). Liss (2000) describes the project: "The very enormity and detail of her stories confront readers with the utter incomprehensibility and horror that Eva lived through. In its paradoxical silence, absence and fullness, her hand stands in as the uncanny trace of impossible evidence" (128).

The Kellners' project exemplifies the possibilities of memory and postmemory texts in making material the intangibilities of memory. In words and in form cast from the actual remembering body, the Kellner book is an actualization of two sets of memories. In this section, I work through texts that represent the beginning of an actualized/textualized virtual Kapetanovo at two moments of remembering: original memories and memories of second and third generation Kapetanovers.

Text One In her Bible, on the inside covers and on two pages of paper affixed with masking tape, my great-oma Katharina Bauer has inscribed her story. She records the dates of birth and death of her children, her parents' and grandparents' names, and biographical details. She writes, "In the WW 2 we were driven out of our homes by the Partisans in the year 1944, to Ober Austria. In the year 1949 we left for Canada, Leamington, Ontario." My great-oma concludes her short autobiography, "This I have written in order that the children will know how we came here ... written by mother Katharina Torau in the year 1980 Leamington." She wrote her autobiography when she was eighty-seven years old.

Text Two There is a photograph of four young boys in front of the Gasthaus (tavern) of Kapetanovo. The images of the boys are all fuzzy; one sits in a tree. From his posture, I can tell that one of the boys is my opa. Turning this photo over, I find a verse, written by Katharina Ellenberger, a Kapetanover of my great-oma's generation. Katharina Ellenberger has written:

> Zur Erinnerung an euer Elternhaus
> aus dem Heimatland
> Wo eure Wiege stand
> und heute ist es für uns
> ein fremdes Land.
>
> Seit dem Jahre 1944-5-10
> verlieren wir unsere Heimat.[6]
>
> *For remembrance of your parental home*
> *In the homeland*
> *Where your cradle stood*
> *And today for us is*
> *A strange unfamiliar land.*

In the year 1944-5-10
We lost our home.
(translation Kathe Davidson, 2006)

Katharina Ellenberger and Katharina Torau have created memory texts that reach out to engage with subsequent generations. In the verse, the intimacy of a home lost is emphasized. The link in this verse between home, intimacy, and identity is made clear. For Katharina Ellenberger, the home lost was the place that witnessed her children's infancy. Without these connections, the place was emptied and made foreign.

These texts reach out to a particular though not always well-defined audience. In both texts there is a mode of address: read this, turn over this photo. In my grandparents' Swabish dialect of German they often exclaimed *Kuk ein mal!* (which sounded to my ears like *gookamollie!*). It meant "Look here!" These texts exclaim, from a beyond—*Kuk ein mal!* This address echoes Roland Barthes' (1981) idea of the photograph, which he writes "is never anything but an antiphon of 'Look', 'See' and 'here it is'; it points a finger at certain vis-à-vis, and cannot escape this pure deictic language" (5). Memory texts, like storytelling, demand an audience. These objects induce the readers to perform, in new articulations, the memory of their exile. These inscriptions offer a form of objectified narrative, a means of transforming an uneasy life into a more coherent narrative. "In order that the children will know," says Katharina Torau, "we lost our home" (Katharina Ellenberger).

Figure 2.3 Boys at Gasthaus, Kapetanovo. (Photo courtesy of Katherine Davidson)

Text Three: Postmortem Maps I have a map that my mom created on a weekend visit to her father, my opa, in January 1997. This map represents a particular type of post-mortem map making. It is a map of Kapetanovo in the 1940s. On this map there is one street with sixty homes. I imagine that my mom and opa are sitting at my opa's kitchen table. My mom is writing down the names as my opa talks. But no, my opa objects, that was the Gus Pimiskern home; the Pichlers lived there (he points), closer to the Bauers. There are scratches on the map and revisions, and in the end, he is satisfied. His Kapetanovo has been recovered, actualized on this Sunday afternoon. In fact, two sets of desires are present in this map, my grandfather's and my mother's, representing both the need to tell and the need to know.

Mapping ghost towns is another form of creating memory texts. Understanding radical etymologically as "of or having roots," maps of exiled homes are a form of radical cartography. For communities in a diaspora, maps legitimize both the roots and routes that define them.[7] Maps can also be products of desire. Lozanovska (2002) writes: "Thinking about maps as tools of travel, maps and mapping are trajectories of desire. To place a dot is also to trace a line between one site and another, and this line is a trace of desire. Desire is articulated through visibility. The trace of the dot and the line bring into visibility what was invisible" (144). The maps that emerge as postmemory texts make visible what is erased through global patterns of movement, war, and erasure.[8]

One summer my mom and I were visiting my opa. We had just harvested some tomatoes from his garden and were taking a break in the sun. On this visit, in our lawn chairs, my mother created another map for me, a map of Leamington in the 1950s. On this map she indicated her childhood home and the homes of many Kapetanovers in her neighbourhood. She narrates as she draws. The maps represent the relocation of a community, maps of movement. Sketching and describing, her mapping becomes a performance. The woman in this house, a friend of her grandmother's, served her bread with salted butter, a special treat. And here was her cousin's house, and here was where the old Pimiskerns lived; it goes on. My map-making mother is compelled by a desire to sketch and evoke her childhood community. Her desire is to remember for herself and to remember for me. Both maps indicate the family names of the homeowners: Pimiskerns, Felders, Toraus. The two maps, 1940s Kapetanovo, 1950s Leamington, both created by my mother, when overlaid, construct a map of movement and identity. The actualization of this virtual homeland operates at the level of inscription, as my mother sketches, and in viewing the map.

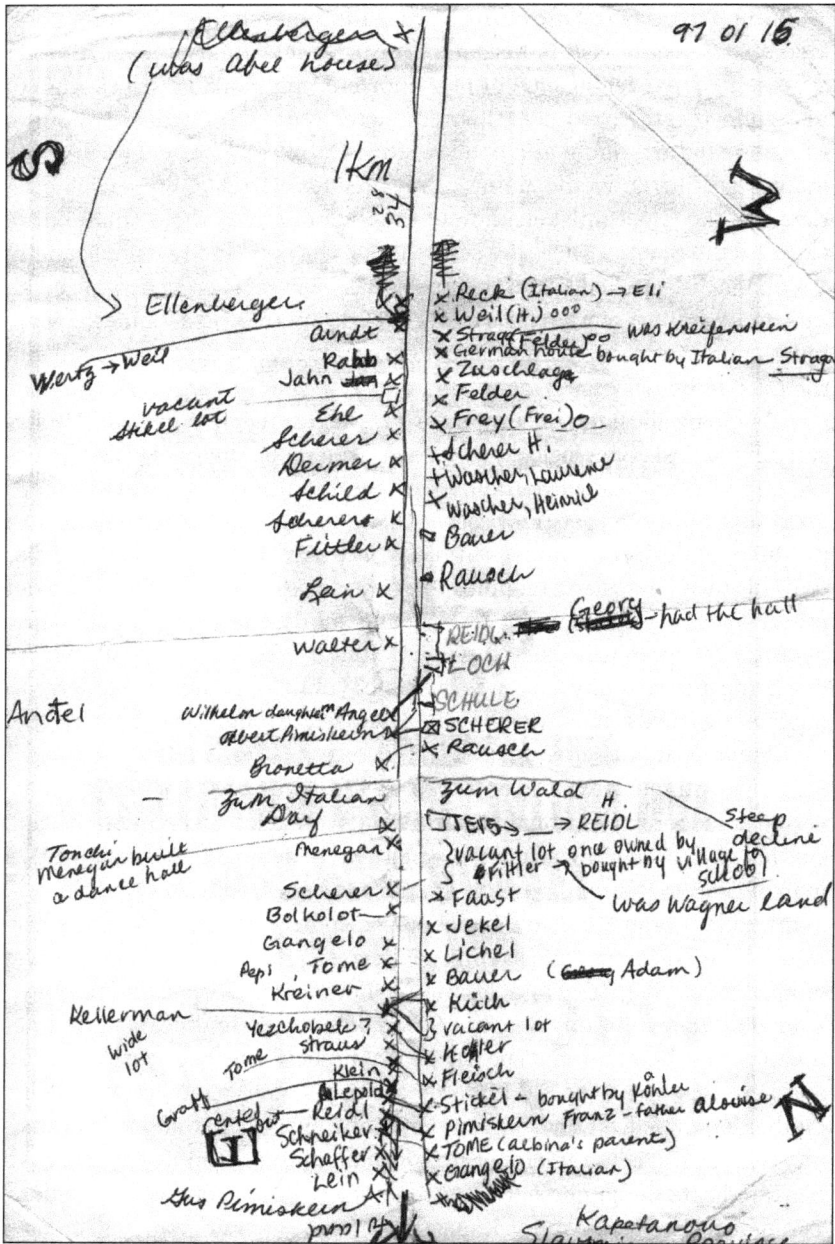

Figure 2.4 Map of Kapetanovo, 1997. (Map and photo credit: Katherine Davidson)

Implicit in these overlaid maps are the differences, the spaces between places that are the salient meaning and memory-making gaps—the subtle beyond of what is lost in postmemories. Mapping ghost towns is a post-mortem engagement. In between the lines, maps create spaces for perform-ance. Mapping a ghost Kapetanovo of the 1940s makes evident the relations among place, identity, and history. Mapping is an articulation of two types of traces. Maps trace the outlines of much fuller places. They also trace shadows, making visible the places erased by history and dominant forms of cartography.

Text Four: Pink Notebook I have a pink notebook from when I was fifteen. Under "subject" on the cover I have written "Oma and Opa's story." This is the most unsophisticated of my memory texts. It is a constellation of "facts," things I thought or was persuaded were important for me to know. There is a half-done map of Kapetanovo: "Pacrac 14 km ... 13 families with sons in the army, 60 houses, 300 people." On one page I had scrawled a family tree, on the other a timeline from Kapetanovo to Canada. And then I find a recipe (with diagrams) of how to make "Oma's fried chicken." There are biographies of my oma's friends who must have been visiting when I was there with my pink notebook. And then there is a page of basic German verb conjugations. On one page there is both "how to make cottage cheese" and a description of army madness. From my notebook I learn an organic methodology of postmemory making. How is it to know another time, another place? I have it all here: maps, language, recipes, diagrams, stories, dates, and genealogies. What I wanted to know is reflected in the stories, as is what was important for me to know. What are consistent throughout are stories about dances. My opa wanted me to know things like this: "when he was 17 he played violin. He'd play at an Italian dance. Two Italian girls had crushes on him. One was beautiful but a bit crazy, the other one was not as beauti-ful but quieter."

There are many accounts of my opa's charm, aptitude, and intelligence. These stories confirm Hannah Arendt's (1958) statement, "Who somebody is or was we can know only by knowing the story of which he is himself the hero—his biography, in other words" (186). Incidentally, there are no sto-ries about my grandparents' thirty years working for Heinz in my notebook, and few about Canada at all. He told me lots of Heinz stories, but I never wrote them down. In the notebook are some unwilling stories, stories I didn't ask for, that didn't even want to be told. So, let's turn the page and talk more about how he was such a great, smart violinist, charming the Italian girls from the neighbouring village. My notebook speaks to multi-ple organic methods of actualizing postmemories. Compelled by the stories,

I sat and drew, doodled, asked questions, and made lists. I attempted to capture the multiple performances that were in the process of producing my own shadow geography of belonging.

Conclusion

Both Landsberg (1997) and Hirsch (1996) argue that the end result of prosthetic memory and postmemory is to create spaces that further possibilities for empathetic understanding and possible reclamation. While Landsberg and Hirsch focus on the effects of memories of trauma on others, in this project I explore a particular aspect of postmemory, the postmemories of a particular place, how a materiality or physical geography that is lost is circulated and constituted through technologies of memory. In order to extend Hirsch's understanding of postmemory to an understanding of postmemories of places, I have invoked an understanding of these places through the concept of the virtual. Virtual places as real and ideal are constituted through technologies of memory, storytelling, objects, and texts. Objects and texts act as mediums for storytelling and intergenerational dialogue and for conjuring a place lost. In this way, objects and texts are both actualizations and mediations. They exist as the end result, active creations of workings of memory and translation, as well as the in-betweens, mediations between generations, the workings through memory. None of the things or texts are silent. While the dictating and drawing of maps is remembered as a memory performance, the texts that compel looking—the photograph with verse and the Bible inscription—likewise become enacted through practices of looking.

At the end of this project I am left with two questions: Why and how do I know Kapetanovo? My other grandparents could point out to me, on a drive, "there—that house is where I grew up." That house still stands. For my opa, when pointing to his ancestral home was impossible, it became necessary to actively evoke the place. What does it mean that I do not know Kapetanovo in one way ("you cannot possibly understand") but do, in another way, know Kapetanovo quite intimately? This is, in fact, the nature of virtual places: always partial, in-between, simultaneously there and never there. When a place is lost, it is never truly lost; there are remainders: the traces. The traces of places lost are the place's virtuality, a real and ideal place.

Actualizing my virtual homeland, through conversations with my mother, my grandfather, and other relatives, I realize that my understandings and attachments are partial and can only outline a translation of a lost place. Traces can illuminate—outlining absences, shapes. Traces also make visible all that cannot be known. The traces are both the remainders and the mediums through which this place can be known. As my mother creates a map of her parents' village, she draws, knowing that it is insufficient, but feeling that it is necessary.

Notes

I would like to thank Rob Shields, Sharon Rosenberg, Julie Rak, Bonar Buffam, and Ondine Park for reading various versions of this paper. I would also like to thank my mother, Kathe Davidson, for her generous participation in this project. This chapter is dedicated to my grandparents Margaret Torau (1920–1996) and Stefan Torau (1918–2007).

1   In contrast, Hui (in this volume) follows Kevin Hetherington to suggest that all place is virtual.

2   Postmemory is similar to Alison Landsberg's (1997, 2004) concept of "prosthetic memory." Landsberg (1997) has defined feeling memories of absent experiences as "prosthetic memories." She writes, "[P]rosthetic memories are memories that circulate publicly, are not organically based, but are nevertheless experienced with one's personal archive of experience, informing not only one's subjectivity, but one's relationship to the present and future tenses" (66). Prosthetic memory differs from postmemory in that postmemory stresses intergenerational memory, while prosthetic memory focuses on the circulation of memories not experienced first-hand but experienced through media and various memory technologies.

3   The distinction between learning about and learning from is one made by Roger Simon (2005): "to learn from attempts to face the traces of lives lived in times and places other than one's own" (105). Learning from is a transitive form of remembrance, a type of remembrance that takes hold and offers a "critical recognition or discovery that unsettles the very terms on which our understandings of ourselves and our world is based" (106).

4   See Tiessen in this volume.

5   For Holocaust fiction see Kirmayer 1996; Baum 2000; Langer 1995; King 1996. For film see Lanzmann 1995; Laub 1995; Landsberg 2004; Felman 1992.

6   The verse has been edited for spelling.

7   James Clifford (1994) defines diasporas: "It involves dwelling, maintaining communities, having collective homes away from home.... Diaspora discourse articulates, or bends together, both roots and routes to construct what Gilroy describes as alternate public spheres (1987), forms of community consciousness and solidarity that maintain identifications outside the national time/space in order to live inside, with a difference" (308).

8   My mother's maps echo the back of Art Speigelman's *Maus* comic series. On the back of volume 1, a map of Eastern Europe (Poland, Slovakia, Hungary) is inlaid with a map of Rego Park, New York. On the back of volume 2, inlaid in a map of Auschwitz is a map of the Catskill Mountains, New York.

References

Arendt, H. 1958. *The human condition*. Chicago: University of Chicago Press.

Barthes, R. 1981. *Camera lucida*. New York: Hill and Wang.

Baum, R. 2000. Never to forget: Pedagogical memory and second-generation witness. In *Between hope and despair: Pedagogy and the remembrance of historical trauma*, ed. S. Rosenberg, R. Simon, and C. Eppert, 91–115. Lanham: Rowman and Littlefield.

Benjamin, W. 1969. The storyteller. In *Illuminations*, 83–109. New York: Schocken Books.

Boym, S. 2001. *The future of nostalgia*. New York: Basic Books.

Caruth, C. 1995. *Trauma: Explorations in memory*. Baltimore: Johns Hopkins University Press.

Clifford, J. 1994. Diasporas. *Cultural Anthropology* 9 (3): 302–38.

Denzin, N. 2003. *Performance ethnography: Critical pedagogy and the politics of culture*. London: Sage.

———. 2006. Analytic autoethnography, or déjà vu all over again. *Journal of Contemporary Ethnography* 35 (4): 419–28.

Ellis, C. 2004. *The ethnographic I: A methodological novel about autoethnography*. New York: Altamira Press.

Ellis, C., and A. Bochner. 2006. Analyzing analytic autoethnography. *Journal of Contemporary Ethnography* 35 (4): 429–49.

Felman, S. 1992. The return of the voice: Claude Lanzmann's *Shoah*. In *Testimony: Crises of witnessing in literature, psychoanalysis, and history*, ed. S. Felman and D. Laub, 57–76. New York: Routledge.

Gonzales, B. M. 2005. Topophilia and topophobia: The home as an evocative place of contradictory emotions. *Space and Culture* 8 (2): 193–213.

Gross, D. 2000. *Lost time: On remembering and forgetting in late modern culture*. Amherst: University of Massachusetts Press.

Hetherington, K. 1997. In place of geometry: the materiality of place. In *Ideas of difference*, ed. K. Hetherington and R. Munro, 183–99. Oxford: Blackwell.

Hirsch, M. 1996. Past lives: Postmemories in exile. *Poetics Today* 17 (4): 659–86.

King, N. 1996. Autobiography as cultural memory: Three case studies. *New Formations* (Winter): 50–62.

Kirmayer, L. 1996. Landscapes of memory: Trauma, narrative and dissociation. In *Tense past: Cultural essays on memory and trauma*, ed. P. Antze and M. Lambek, 173–98. New York: Routledge.

Jackson, M. 2002. *Politics of storytelling, violence, transgression and subjection*. Copenhagen: Museum of Tusculanum Press.

Landsberg, A. 1997. America, the holocaust, and the mass culture of memory: Toward a racial politics of empathy. *New German Critique* 71: 63–86.

———. 2004. *Prosthetic memory: The transformation of American memory in the age of mass culture*. New York: Columbia University Press.

Langer, L. 1995. *Admitting the Holocaust*. Oxford: Oxford University Press.

Lanzmann, C. 1995. The obscenity of understanding. In *Trauma: Explorations in memory*, ed. C. Caruth, 200–20. Baltimore: Johns Hopkins University Press.

Laub, D. 1995. Truth and testimony: The process and the struggle. In *Trauma: Explorations in memory*, ed. C. Caruth, 61–75. Baltimore: Johns Hopkins University Press.

Liss, A. 2000. Artifactual testimonies and the stagings of Holocaust memory. In *Between hope and despair: Pedagogy and the remembrance of historical trauma*, ed. S. Rosenberg, R. I. Simon, and C. Eppert, 117–33. Lanham: Rowman and Littlefield.

Lozanovska, M. 2002. Architectural frontier / Spatial story. *Space and Culture* 5 (2): 140–51.

Parkin, D. 1999. Mementoes as transitional objects in human displacement. *Journal of Material Culture* 4 (3): 303–20.

Pelias, R. J. 2005. Performative writing as scholarship: An apology, an argument, an anecdote. *Cultural Studies—Critical Methodologies* 5 (4): 415–24.

Richardson, L. 2000. Writing: A method of inquiry. In *Handbook of qualitative research*, ed. N. Denzin and Y. S. Lincoln, 516–29. Thousand Oaks, CA: Sage.

Shields, R. 2003. *The virtual*. New York: Routledge.

Simon, R. 2005. *The touch of the past*. New York: Palgrave Macmillan.

Spelman, E. 2008. Repair and the scaffold of memory. In *What is a city? Rethinking the urban after Hurricane Katrina*, ed. P. Steinberg and R. Shields, 140–53. Athens: University of Georgia Press.

Spiegelman, A. 1973. *Maus I: My father bleeds history*. New York: Pantheon Books.

———. 1986. *Maus II: And here my troubles began*. New York: Pantheon Books.

Spry, T. 2001. Performing autoethnography: An embodied methodological praxis. *Qualitative Inquiry* 7 (6): 706–32.

Tuan, Y.-F. 1977. *Space and place: The perspective of experience*. Minneapolis: University of Minnesota Press.

Wilson, J. 2005. *Nostalgia: Sanctuary of meaning*. Lewisburg: Bucknell University Press.

3

Placing Nostalgia
The Process of Returning
and Remaking Home

ALLISON HUI

When you embark on a journey, you have already arrived. The world you are going to is already in your head. You have already walked in it, eaten in it; you have already made friends; a lover is already waiting. (Brand 2001, 115)

Nostalgia is often understood as an inability to go back, a sickness from being unable to return. Though temporally this may be the case, as the past cannot be revisited, affects such as nostalgia are linked to material spaces, and can have enduring relationships with space. Like Stewart (1988), I see nostalgia as "a cultural practice, not a given content; its forms, meanings, and effects shift with the context—it depends on where the speaker stands in the landscape of the present" (227). Space then is referred to by nostalgia (one is sick from being unable to return *somewhere*) and affects people's practices of nostalgia. Similarly, nostalgia is temporal both because it gestures to the past and because it changes as people engage with it over time. This suggests that the space and time from which people evoke nostalgia are as important as the space and time nostalgia evokes. The contexts of practising nostalgia, however, change. People can move and travel a significant amount, and this alters their relationships with, and enactments of, nostalgia. This chapter thus seeks to set nostalgia in motion, examining changing and mobile engagements with nostalgia in the context of visits to previous or second homes.

A focus on homes is an apropos starting point for discussions of nostalgia. The term *nostalgia* itself comes from the Greek root *nostos,* "return home," and speaks not only to an excessive and sentimental desire for the past but also "the state of being homesick" (Nostalgia). Furthermore, the experience of leaving home is one shared by many. For some, leaving home is a seasonal experience, with second homes or vacation homes serving as seasonal residences that are perpetually left and revisited. For others, leaving home is marked by permanence, as when people emigrate and reside in new countries for indeterminate or fixed periods of time. The affects resulting from these departures can vary significantly, as is evident when comparing voluntary and forced departures. Focusing specifically on nostalgia, then, this chapter uses return-home mobilities[1] to consider the different relationships nostalgia can have with space and place.

Despite a continuing interest in issues related to home, little has been written about the process of returning home. The return-home mobilities of those with second homes or previous homes have remained largely outside the sphere of tourism studies (Bell and Ward 2000) and have received limited attention as means of maintaining transnational communities (Duval 2004, 2005; Long 2004), preparing for retirement (Casado-Diaz 2004; Williams and Hall 2000), or encouraging return migrations (Ghosh 2000; Potter, Conway, and Phillips 2005). Conceptually, the physical mobilities of people to previously visited spaces are challenging because they are marked solely by neither the exceptionality or "other" that is often seen to ground tourism nor the familiarity of spaces of permanent residence. They lie between the familiar and unfamiliar, and, as this chapter will show, it is in the negotiation of these two facets that mobilities of return demonstrate a unique relationship with place and affect.

Narratives from the travel memoirs of people who have returned to previous or second homes will be used to illustrate one process through which nostalgia might be created and recreated. The larger project from which this chapter draws involved the analysis of five memoirs written since the late twentieth century (Blaise and Mukherjee 1977; Chiang 1977; Gable and Gable 2005; MacGregor 2002; Phillips 1990) and additional supportive texts (Bainbridge 2002; Gordon 1989, 2006; Liu 2005; MacGregor 2005). These memoirs were sampled theoretically for their extended and diverse discussions of returns to previous or second homes. Though literary journeys are themselves constructed, and the privileged position of these authors is unrepresentative of many return experiences, this did not hinder the project's discussion of the theoretical relationships between spaces, places, and practices. In this way, the memoirs were valuable in providing framings of spaces and places, which were then used as foils for alternative framings of these concepts.

This chapter, and the project it emerges from, is concerned then with relationships between space, place, the material, and the virtual as they interweave and overlap in practice. Using the concepts of material spaces, virtual places, and affects, I argue that nostalgia emerges from and is shaped by particular relationships between space and place. The next section uses an art installation entitled *Linked* to introduce these themes, which I subsequently develop.

Linked: Visiting Homes That Are Not There

Most of those who have visited the installation space since 1999 first encounter what appears to be unremarkable: it is a road like many others, which links the East End of London with the M11 that heads north to Cambridge. At one time, however, there was no road, and in its place were the homes of four hundred families. Since July 2003, visitors to this stretch of road have been able to sense some of what is absent, thanks to Graeme Miller's sound installation *Linked*.

Linked is "a landmark in sound—an invisible artwork—a walk" (*Linked*). Participants borrow a transmitter and a map from one of several pick-up locations and then walk some or all of the three-mile route, along which "20 transmitters continually broadcast hidden voices, recorded testimonies and rekindled memories of those who once lived and worked where the motorway now runs" (*Linked*). Thanks to *Linked*, a world of sound and memory speaking from the past is superimposed upon the material world. *Linked* documents what is not there anymore and voices the nostalgic absence of homes that cannot be revisited or reclaimed. The homes that people speak of are lost places, marked now only by the constant sound waves that whisper of the past even, as Miller (2008) acknowledges, when no one is listening.

Linked is situated in a material space but invites people to visit in order to see what is not there. Participants travel not to the physical homes of the past but to places of memory—the memory of those who once lived where they can live no more (see Davidson in this volume). The place participants experience through their walking and looking is very different from the place described by voices in the transmitters. The places evoked by audio presences make the material absences of the space jarring. As this chapter will show, it is this gap between the immaterial and the material that can breed and feed nostalgia.

As *Linked* illustrates, homesickness and nostalgia can be experienced in many different ways. For the four hundred families who were displaced, visiting *Linked* is a moment of return that is compared to and weighed up against previous experiences in their homes. For other visitors, the original homes are unfamiliar, a mystery, and accessible only through descriptions and recollections. This chapter concentrates upon people who have first-hand experiences of the places being pined for, but it is important to note that complex manifestations of nostalgia are produced. Though only some participants in *Linked* have first-hand experience of the destroyed home, both groups can share in feelings of loss and sickness for these homes and the past in which they existed. Creating these different feelings of loss is, I argue, the result of distinct processes of interacting with space and place, two concepts that are outlined in the next section.

From Materiality to Immateriality: Space, Place, and Affect

When considering *Linked*, it is quite obvious that a significant difference exists between the materially present M11 link road and the immaterial place that is described on the audio feed. This distinction between material space and immaterial place, however, could have been identified even before the homes were destroyed. In order to speak more precisely about how materialities and immaterialities relate, this section defines place, space, and affect, as well as how people's practices and interactions link them.

Following Hetherington (1997), I identify place as an immaterial entity arising from the placing, ordering, and representing of material objects (192). That is, place results from the process of interacting in material surroundings. Places themselves, however, are virtual in Shields's sense of being "real idealizations" that are immaterial but not abstract (2003, 28–29).[2] The homes described in *Linked*, for example, are virtual because they do not have a material existence but are nonetheless specific, and therefore unlike abstract generalizations of home. While virtualities are not material, they can be actualized into concrete forms through activities such as drawing pictures (see Dorow and Dogu in this volume). This framing of place is contrasted by an understanding of space as material forms and geographic locations in and with which people undertake the process of placing.

To understand this distinction between space and place, consider the space of a house—a physical built structure that might be appropriately labelled with a street address, denoting its mapped location. Space and place are distinct, and thus the space of the house does not become a place of "home" until people have gone through the process of placing and ordering furniture and other objects. Moving and arranging desks and examining tables within the house could result in a place of "office" or "clinic," whereas placing instead couches, beds, pictures, and personal mementoes could result in a place of "home." Though constituted through interactions with material objects, this place of home is immaterial and can travel with people to different spaces in the mental images and memories that result from placing objects in the house. In addition to being independently mobile of the house, the spatialized limits of a place of home need not correspond to the spatial limits of a house (Gough 2007). That is, the place of home could include the street or neighbourhood in which the house is situated, and sometimes the place of home can encompass an entire country. Though certainly differing scales of home come with unique issues in terms of what type of material interactions can create them, the importance of interactions with materialities remains.

Since this understanding of place is based upon people doing things, practices can be seen to tie space and place together. Practices are embodied activities performed by people, and these occur in and transform spaces. Practices, however, also create places—it is by doing things with things that people make the relationships that compose place. People's practices of creating place are interactive—with both living and nonliving materialities—and continuous. Though often practices in one space create a place associated with that space, this is not always the case. People can inhabit one location, such as a dentist's office, and interact with the memories of an unrelated place, like a beach, just as surely as they can actively order and create the place of the office.

Spaces and places thus have a flexible relationship that is dependent upon the practices of people. While there may be a strong probability that some spaces will be transformed by people into certain types of places, this relationship is not deterministic. As noted above, houses are most often arranged into homes, but they are also sometimes offices. There is no linear relationship between houses and homes, so one house can be more than one home. Space and place are thus independent entities yet are in constant relationship thanks to the practices of people.

It is important to note that this distinction between space and place differs from those used by other authors. Tuan has also articulated differences between space and place, but for him space is more abstract than place, and is distinguished by having no significance in itself. Whereas place is made concrete for Tuan (1977) through meanings attached to it, space concerns more abstract potentials for movement, as experienced through distances, areas, and relative locations. Other authors are often less clear about the distinction they make between space and place, although many such as McDowell (1999) and Davis (2005) make implicit distinctions between space, which is geographic and can be mapped, and place, which involves something more, such as interactions of power or socio-cultural ideas that change over time.

Having established a distinction between space and place, it is now possible to consider where affect fits in. Within Hetherington's understanding of place, an emphasis upon material interactions is important precisely because of what it contributes to understanding affects, or emotions and meanings. Though human geographers have tended to see place as subjective assessments of space and the attachment that arises from giving space meaning (Williams and Patterson 1996 in Kaltenborn 1997, 176), Hetherington (1997) notes that this definition fails to incorporate an understanding of the material objects involved (187). By considering place instead as something constituted in the placing, ordering, and representing of material objects, Hetherington emphasizes the interactive and embodied process of creating. He argues that

> Rather than taking a place as a site that stands for something, that has intrinsic or mythic meaning because of its supposed fixity in space, we should think of places as relation, as existing in similitude: places as *being in the process of being placed in relation to* rather than being there. (1997, 187–88)[3]

As a result, affects and subjective assessments are seen to come from, and feed back into, the process of placing and ordering. Assessments of safety that might be attached to the place of home, for example, emerge not through an abstract process of attributing meaning, but through the materially based process wherein people interact in their homes. It is through locking doors and returning to find the house still secured that the place of home becomes enacted as safe. Affect then is a product of this process. Within this conceptualization, places do not produce affective attachment—rather, people do, through their practices. The cultural practice of nostalgia that Stewart refers to is thus intertwined with the process of placing.

Though Hetherington's formulation of place provides an interesting starting point, thinking about return-home mobilities reveals areas in which the relationships between spaces, places, and affect need more development. There is a difference, for example, in the temporality of affects. The difference between placing "home" as temporally present and placing "nostalgia" as pointing to the past needs to be addressed. If places are "in the process of being placed in relation to" (Hetherington 1997, 188), then understanding the temporality of affects requires a consideration of this process over time. Additionally, Hetherington does not examine what happens to places when people leave the spaces in which they were created. People may, for instance, move houses but retain a sense of them as virtual homes. The process of creating and interacting with place and nostalgia is mobile, and the following sections articulate three separate types of placing to account for the movement of people and the temporality of affects.

Material Placing and Virtual Placing

Turning to the case of return-home mobilities, I argue that people's mobilities necessitate more nuanced understandings of practices of placing and nostalgia. While the three types of placing I outline below build upon the process detailed in the previous section, they also complicate understandings of how placing and nostalgia articulate over time and space. In return-home mobilities, there are particular patterns of interaction with space and place. People start out in a house, where they arrange a virtual place of home. They then leave the space of the house but continue to have access to the place of home. Later they can return to the house, and upon doing so they may find that its materiality and the place that can be enacted in it are quite different. These different interactions correspond to three types of placing: material placing, virtual placing, and re-placing. By identifying the shifts between these types of placing, I show how nostalgia emerges and is negotiated through specific types of placing, namely virtual placing and re-placing. This section starts then by addressing the first phase in return-home mobilities: material placing.

Before places can move, they must be created, and this initial phase, outlined in the previous section, can be understood as material placing. People undertake a period of placing while they are physically present at one location, interacting with the co-present materialities of that space. As Hetherington suggests, through this process they create the virtual place of home and the various affects that accompany it. During material placing, then, people interact in a house and create a place of home and affects attached to it.

Following this phase, which could last a month or many years, people leave their house, and this travel marks the beginning of a period of virtual placing. Having left the space of the house, it is no longer possible to undertake a material process of placing home. People continue, however, to interact with their former home and to compare it to other spaces and places. Placing therefore continues, but rather than arranging materialities, people arrange their immaterial home in relation to other materialities or places. This acknowledgment of virtual placing suggests that places remain present and continue to change after leaving the space they are attached to. A former home can, for instance, be deemed more treasured, more convenient, or more confined once it is compared to subsequent homes. This phase thus both builds upon and departs from Hetherington's work to suggest that once a place is created, people can still order and compare it with other places and spaces, even though they may not be physically co-present with its materiality.

It is in this phase of virtual placing that the present affects of placing can become transformed into the longing past of nostalgia. People are no longer interacting with materials to create relationships to place, and they may find that the affects connected to home recede into the past. These affects can still be accessed but retain no immediacy, as they cannot be directly evoked through the process of material placing. The present experience of material placing, which continues in other spaces, becomes contrasted with the past experience of material practices linked to a former house. In this way, connections between nostalgia and the past are the result of not just temporal separation, but also physical separation, which halts the process of materially arranging relationships to space.

Recognition of this phase of virtual placing creates room not only for considering what happens when people leave familiar spaces, but also for considering how virtual or imaginative travel (Urry 2000, 66) might contribute to the practice of creating place. In preparation for tourism, for example, people can spend a significant period of time interacting with guidebooks, websites, and other resources that allow them to imagine and construct relationships with the space they are planning to visit. Though these interactions do not involve practices in the space of their destination, they do involve material interactions with books and images that can begin to create a virtual place of their destination even before they depart.

Many visitors to *Linked* have this kind of indirect link to the material houses of former residents. Though they were never in or around these houses, hearing about them can be part of a process of virtual placing. By comparing the virtual place of residents' former homes with the materiality of the link road, visitors can recognize a nostalgia that exists for residents. Indeed, those interacting with *Linked* can experience their own nostalgia by creating relationships between the loss of these particular homes and similar losses of homes and landscapes to roads and motorways elsewhere.

As noted earlier, this type of nostalgia is different from that of residents who were familiar with the space before *Linked*. Different types of nostalgia can emerge, then, through different processes of placing. Though material placing is the first phase featured in this discussion of returning home, it need not always come first, and this emphasis is solely the result of choosing to follow people who return home after periods of absence.

Re-placing and the Virtual Gaze

Having first materially placed and then virtually placed a second or former home, people can be left with a significant desire to physically return home. Such a return to the space of the virtual home marks the beginning of the third phase—one of re-placing. Having returned to where the place was first created, people can begin the process of placing again, establishing relationships with material objects and surroundings. Unlike the first visit, however, the return involves interactions with not only the materialities of the location, but also with the virtualities of the place that was previously created there.

Though placing is primarily about interactions with materialities for Hetherington, it cannot be limited in this way when people are already familiar with a space. I suggest instead that return trips involve re-placing, which also interacts with pre-existing virtualities of place and affect. In this way, the practice of placing at a former home is not just about relating materialities to each other, but also about relating them to the affects, memories, and places carried from previous experiences there.

This relationship between experiences of return and previous interactions is discussed at length in Chiang's memoir (1977). Chiang is an author and artist who was born and lived in China for many years before political issues led him to flee the country in 1933. His absence was originally intended to be short, but a series of events, including the Sino-Japanese War, the Second World War, and the spread of McCarthyism, prevented his return. As a result, he spent many years in the United Kingdom and the United States, where he eventually became a citizen. *China Revisited, After Forty-Two Years* (1977) includes a brief discussion of Chiang's departure from China and his time away, and then gives a detailed log of his travel and experiences upon return. In this memoir, Chiang recognizes the inevitability of comparing the places he knew in the past and the spaces he encounters during his trip: "My thirty years of life in China before 1933 as well as my personal experiences as the head civil servant of three big counties put me into a rather different category as a visitor to the present-day China. I would undoubtedly compare what I could see now in China with what I knew of her before 1933" (54). Unlike other visitors, Chiang observes changes within spaces, comparing the current state of China with the virtual place he carries with him. Confronted by new built spaces and new experiences, as well as new understandings gained from the spaces and mobilities he has experienced since his departure, Chiang must rearrange and reorder the place of China that he has carried with him during his absence. Chiang's practices during his return thus help to enunciate a revised understanding of the place of China by adding layers of meaning and memories from his new experiences there.

This process of re-placing is made possible by a period of absence from a space, and is therefore distinct from the placing that can occur in one space over time. When people maintain consistent contact with a material space, interactions with place can be continuous, and incremental changes to the virtuality of place can be regularly incorporated. After departing for a significant length of time, however, these kinds of interactions are put on hold. As a result, upon their return to a former house, people are faced with the task of creating relationships among the material space, its contents, and the memories and affects that were created during previous interactions there.

The comparisons and negotiations of change that are involved in re-placing hold similarities to Perniola's conception of transit. Rather than discussing movement or travel, Perniola focuses on transit, a concept that attempts to avoid binaries, dualisms, and teleological thinking by invoking movement that goes from the same to the same (Verdicchio in Perniola 2001, 18). Perniola (2001) does not take this sameness to imply equality, and suggests that transit involves the introduction of difference, which is seen to be not an inherent characteristic of things, but a property of transit itself (47–48). Transit introduces differences between similar spaces. For memoir authors, leaving previous houses introduces difference that they incorporate into their experiences of home upon return. These patterns of mobility are transitions from the same to the same, in that certain spaces are still/always known as home places, and yet they are unequal because the transit itself affects whether they are former or current homes. So whereas Perniola frames this in terms of difference that emerges in transit and must be reincorporated, I focus upon different types of placing that become the markers of difference and the focus of reincorporation. Travel disrupts material co-presence and thereby introduces a difference between material placing and virtual placing. When material placing is again possible upon return, the virtual place must be incorporated into re-placings.

People "re-place" places, then, by rearranging and reordering material objects to represent a space and experiences in it anew. This process may be uncomfortable, as the material form of a space can contradict memories of it. Especially if someone returns hoping to find that little has changed, the process of re-placing and rearranging knowledge about a space can be quite stressful.

Though re-placing is not only about material interactions, it does mark the importance of material co-presence. People often continue to interact with the place of previous or second homes through photographs, television, newspaper stories, and conversations with those left behind, but these practices all remain mediated means of virtual placing. As such, they lack sensuous elements that would be attainable through first-hand experience. The opportunity to interact in a personal, embodied way with the space and materiality of a second home or previous home can therefore be very appealing. Duval (2005) notes that despite improvements in communications technology, physical return is still seen as the best way of keeping track of the changes in one's homeland (255). Similarly, returnees to Vietnam have spoken of the desire to reconnect with space and relocate places on their return:

> Memories of former houses, streets, fields, and trees became specific experiences with normal dimensions again. Certain smells were associated with a specific fruit. Space being relocated in place was not just a set of distant images, stories, or disembodied voices but encompassed specific sensory experiences, histories and relationships. (Long 2004, 88)

Returning thus allows migrants to reconnect with the particularities of important spaces and places, and this reconnection can involve anticipating and comparing the memories and experiences of many senses.

Chiang (1977) notes a similar desire to personally engage with changes within his homeland. In the prologue to his memoir, he speaks of how engaging with change is a central focus of his return:

> I was so anxious and curious to learn about these great changes that I read whatever accounts I could get hold of in the daily papers and also in books written by people who had recently made visits to China. But a Chinese popular saying, "Seeing once is better than hearing about it a hundred times," kept telling me that I must go to see the changes myself. (13–14)

Returning, then, is an important opportunity for sensuous material engagement with spaces, and second-hand accounts from friends or the media cannot substitute for this material engagement. At the same time, however, being able to "see the changes," as Chiang phrases it, depends on attention being directed not only to the present materialities, but also to the seemingly absent virtualities—to the places that are not materially there. It is in the comparison between these material and virtual gazes that change exists.

In summary, re-placing involves both the immaterial and the material, and is predicated upon a prior period of placing and subsequent travel. Travel away from a space prevents material interactions with place, and so another episode of travel is necessary to return and reconvene with the materiality of space. Such travel can be highly valued because it makes memories "specific experiences ... again" (Long 2004, 88). With material co-presence, however, comes a need to address changes, and re-placing involves integrating remembered places and revisited spaces into new understandings of place. In the next section, these dynamics of re-placing are examined in more detail, drawing upon Chiang's stories of returning to China.

Re-placing China

These interactions between remembered places and revisited spaces are evident in Chiang's narrative of return. During his return to China, Chiang is always accompanied by guides from the Chinese Travel Service, who facilitate all his trips to tourist attractions, as well as locating and arranging meetings with former friends he wishes to see. With the help of the CTS guides, Chiang actively searches out familiar spaces along his journey, so that he can return to re-experience places that are entrenched in his memory.

One location Chiang revisits is Lu Mountain, a well-loved and oft-frequented retreat from his past (1977, 133). An entire chapter is devoted to Chiang's return to this space after a long separation: "Though I have been to Lu Mountain again and again and stayed on it over six months since [the age of eleven], it had been more than forty-two years since I saw it last" (134). While spending two days visiting both beautiful locations that he frequented in the past and those he knew only through paintings, Chiang recalls and interacts with his memories of the place. At Han-p'o-kou he stands,

> facing the gap between two mountain slopes with the wide expanse of Lake P'o-yang in the far distance. This was where I had watched the sunrise with my father more than sixty years ago. My father's love for me and his training to make me a painter filled my heart with poignant feeling. I grieved that he was no longer here to join his long-wandering son who had come back to see his beloved mountain. (135)

In this situation, the experience of re-placing becomes invested with nostalgia and grief because, though the materiality of the mountain remains, his father is no longer present. The virtual place of Han-p'o-kou is composed of relationships among a mountain, a sunrise, a father, and a son. The re-placing, however, involves the material presence of only three of these four elements, and thus Chiang negotiates grief at the absence of his father.

On other parts of the mountain, Chiang encounters the absence of not only former companions, but also former materialities. He visits the site of a famous waterfall that was represented in paintings, and finds "only a tiny trickle of water coming down through the thickets" (138). Though the water no longer resembled its famous representation, Chiang notes, "A stone bridge was still there as I remembered it" (138). Visiting Lu Mountain thus becomes an exercise in which Chiang interacts with places made in the past and creates new understandings of place that incorporate altered materialities and experiences.

When in his home city of Kiukang, Chiang similarly tries to revisit places linked to important memories, but finds in several cases that the passage of time has made this impossible. Speaking about the city, Chiang (1977) states:

> Every inch reminded me of something, yet everything looked so different from what I had known before. I insisted on being taken to where my old home had been, but there was no trace of it, or of my old official residence, for both had been destroyed by the Japanese invaders in 1938. I gazed at the stones on the road and the walls of the new houses, and could find no thought or words to describe my feelings. Everything told me that my past had gone forever. (130)

The lack of material similarities between the space he encounters and the place of his memory mark for Chiang a significant break, which he re-places as the gap between the irretrievable past and the present.

The role of the present materiality of spaces is central to Chiang's varied experiences of return. The material things Chiang encounters affect his assessments of the change between virtual places and material spaces, as well as the emotions that arise in this process of re-placing. Sometimes, as with the stone bridge on Lu Mountain, remaining material elements help to signal that the space he is presently occupying is indeed the same space where his virtual place was created. With his former house, however, Chiang returns to find no trace of its materiality. In this instance the connection between the place and space, between his past and the present, remains virtual.

This marks another connection between placing and re-placing. If it is the interactions with materiality that identify placing, then the return or repetition involved in *re*-placing can take place only if there is some consistent materiality with which to engage. It is this consistent materiality that creates a link between the placing of the present and of the past. The materiality acts as an anchor for the virtual places, and connects the places created in different temporal periods. When no materiality can be found in common, as with Chiang's failed attempt to detect anything recognizable in the location of his former home, the link between the place created through present interactions and the place of memories is never actualized. Thus the place of his former home and the present location of his former house remain unconnected, marking the gap between the past and present.

Entering a "Home That Is No Longer Standing"

Though the absence of Chiang's former home convinces him that his past is lost, in other cases the disjuncture between past and present can be less apparent. Sometimes, the materiality of a space remains similar enough that re-placing can easily forge links between the present space and the virtual places created in the past. When this occurs, the sickness of separation can be tempered by a sense of reunion and joy.

This is apparent in MacGregor's (2005) story of returning to the site of his grandparents' former home in Algonquin Park in central Canada. A Canadian journalist, MacGregor shares stories of his interactions with summer homes in both *Escape: In Search of the Natural Soul of Canada* (2002) and *The Weekender: A Cottage Journal* (2005). After the death of his father and sister, MacGregor returns with his mother and cousin in order to reflect upon the loss of family members and their past summers spent together:

> *We cannot enter a log home that is no longer standing, but we enter, easily and happily*, the sounds that stand guard for us, waiting: the wind and the water, the sound of this lake on this point—a voice that belongs nowhere else....
>
> My mother sits on a large stone and watches Don and I dive from the high rocks much as we dove in the '50s and '60s, *the splash the same, the whoop the same, the footholds getting back out the same*, only slippery from disuse.
>
> I wander off and find, back of where the outhouse once stood, a rusted old straight pipe that once carried the exhaust from our coal-oil-driven washing machine out the porch door. I cart it back and we stand and marvel at

it, *each hearing again* the heavy burp of the machine in full throttle, the memory bittersweet in that it speaks to us of summers lost, but reminds, as well, of the rule that forbade swimming when the washing machine was on because no one, we were told, would ever hear our cries for help if we got in trouble. (MacGregor 2005, 120–21, emphasis added)

Being in the space again, these visitors actively experience it both as it is and as it was—engaging with the space in such a way that they can re-place the boundaries of the log home, the experience and role of water and swimming, and even the connection of objects to sounds and rules that defined the place of this home. MacGregor re-places the sounds and sensations as being the same, things heard again, and relates them not only to each other, but also to his memories and the place he knew as a child. The visitors create relationships to the place and interactions of the past that are both bittersweet and a source of happiness. The affective ties MacGregor has maintained with this cottage place during his absence are reorganized in light of the loss of family members and his return to the space, which confirms that though time has moved on, in some ways the space remains unchanged.

Attempts to revisit familiar spaces in order to get in touch with places from the past can thus invoke a multitude of emotions and outcomes as the similarities or discrepancies between intangible places and the reality of present spaces become apparent. These experiences are practices that rearrange and reorder previous understandings of space, creating new layers of memories and a sense of how the places of past experience are set apart from, but also related to, places of current interactions.

Nostalgia, *Saudade*, and Hope

Within the process of placing, travel, and re-placing that this chapter has discussed, nostalgia can be identified with the longing for material placing. It is not that virtual interactions with the place of home are lacking, for the virtual place is mobile and can travel anywhere in the form of personal memories. The withdrawal and sickness occurs because people are separated spatially from the materiality used in practices of placing, and thus must end their temporal period of material placing. Through physical travel and the passage of time, both the process of placing and the virtual place of home itself become imbued with a sense of loss and homesickness.

While some definitions of nostalgia take the lost time or state to be irrecoverable, a consideration of cases of return-home mobilities, when people do in fact return to where they created virtual places, reveals that in a limited sense one can return home again. As Brand (2001) suggests, some people set out on journeys having "already arrived" (115), for they know the worlds to which they are headed, and these virtual places precede and accompany them. Those who return to the birthplace of the virtual places they carry with them may find opportunities for re-placing, for relating and forging new relationships not only with the materiality, but also with the nostalgic absence of virtual places. Through re-placing people negotiate the gaps between familiar places and somewhat unfamiliar spaces, in the process layering new affects on top of old ones. Returning to such spaces can lead to joy at the discovery that little has changed, or disappointment and a sense that the place of home is irrecoverable.

Given this possibility of return, the type of nostalgia present in return-home mobilities is more akin to the untranslatable Portuguese term *saudade*. Where nostalgia involves longing, *saudade* also incorporates a hope that the object of longing might return (Feldmann 2007). *Saudade* thus infects nostalgia with the cure that Vallee (in this volume) discusses, treating the sickness of nostalgia with the hope that one will be able to return home.

Those who leave willingly from vacation homes or previous homes are often able to keep nostalgia and hope closely linked, since the possibility of a later return remains. MacGregor (2002), for example, has become familiar with a yearly ritual wherein the longing for his second home is always rewarded by eventual return. For Chiang, what was hoped to be a short absence became extended by circumstances beyond his control. His nostalgia and hope of returning likely changed many times as the possibility of return became more or less plausible. Eventually, Chiang (1977) is able to "fulfil [his] great longing to see [his] home cities" (119), but he finds some spaces forever changed.

While these memoir writers are able to link nostalgia and hope, for others, the circumstances of departure can make *saudade* or hope difficult to sustain. The families whose houses were destroyed in the building of the M11 link road have no hope that the materiality of their houses will ever return. Yet even if they cannot return home, they can still return, along with many others, to the space where their houses were. Like Chiang, visitors to *Linked* are unable to find the materiality of the neighbourhoods that were destroyed, but they visit nonetheless, in order to interact with maps and transmitters and to gaze upon the virtual places they can't see. This ability to return to spaces does not make up for the inability to return to lost places; however, it is still important because it points to a politics of not only departure, but also return.

In this way, the circumstances of leaving home are undoubtedly important for subsequent interactions with the place and affects of home. Stories of return-home mobilities have demonstrated that virtual places of home can remain present and active in people's interactions. Just as homes can travel with people, so too do they change with people, becoming places of nostalgia and adapting to changing possibilities of hope for a return. Whether or not materiality remains during people's absence, however, has a significant effect by shaping the possibilities for hope, and for interactions upon their return.

The dynamics of affects such as nostalgia, then, are significantly shaped by the possibility of hope and a return home. Nostalgia can be fostered both because home spaces no longer exist—as with *Linked*, Kapetanovo (Davidson in this volume), and the German Democratic Republic (Winkler in this volume)—and because they are presently inaccessible, perhaps owing to the global political situations that long prevented Chiang's return. Depending on its relationship to hope and return, nostalgia can be practised in different ways.

Separating out phases of material placing, virtual placing, and re-placing offers an opportunity to consider interactions between places and affects over time, and within personal histories of physical travel. Basing this exploration on Hetherington's formulation of place both emphasizes and reinforces the link between people's material and immaterial interactions, and offers the challenge of thinking about place and affects as not static states or entities but rather mobile processes that are practised over and over again. People can return home through imaginative mobilities to their places of memory, and these imaginative mobilities are unhindered by financial resources or temporal constraints. Nonetheless, the hope or enactment of return travel can remain important, as sensuous material interactions create different relationships to place and different affects than virtual ones. If, or when, people do undertake a physical return to engage with the nostalgic absence of home, their process of placing and re-placing, enacting and re-enacting nostalgia, continues.

Notes

The research upon which this chapter draws was gratefully supported by a Canadian Graduate Scholarship from the Social Sciences and Humanities Research Council of Canada. Many thanks to the editors, to the other contributors to this collection, and to Dana Bentia, Sergio Fava, Tom Roberts, and James Tomasson for their helpful comments on earlier versions of this chapter.

1 The term "mobilities" highlights that people can return home both through physical travel and by other means, including imaginative and communicative mobilities (Urry 2007).
2 This usage differs from Deleuze's understanding of the virtual, which includes a sense of unrealized potentialities (Deleuze and Parnet 2006, 112–15).
3 Here Hetherington articulates an understanding of how places are defined relationally, which he has used in other work to consider heterotopias and the relationship between marginal sites, marginal groups, and identity (1993, 1998).

References

Bainbridge, J. 2002. *Above the sea: Expat in China*. New York: Writers Club Press.

Bell, M., and G. Ward. 2000. Comparing temporary mobility with permanent migration. *Tourism Geographies* 2 (1): 87–107.

Blaise, C., and B. Mukherjee. 1977. *Days and nights in Calcutta*. New York: Doubleday.

Brand, D. 2001. *A map to the door of no return: Notes to belonging*. Toronto: Doubleday.

Casado-Diaz, M. A. 2004. Second homes in Spain. In *Tourism, mobility, and second homes: Between elite landscape and common ground*, ed. C. M. Hall and D. K. Müller, 215–32. Clevedon, UK: Channel View.

Chiang, Y. 1977. *China revisited, after forty-two years*. New York: W. W. Norton & Co.

Davis, J. S. 2005. Representing place: "Deserted isles" and the reproduction of Bikini Atoll. *Annals of the Association of American Geographers* 95 (3): 607–25.

Deleuze, G., and C. Parnet. 2006. *Dialogues II*, trans. H. Tomlinson, B. Habberjam, and E. R. Albert. London: Continuum.

Duval, D. T. 2004. Conceptualizing return visits: A transnational perspective. In *Tourism, diasporas and space*, ed. T. Coles and D. Timothy, 50–61. London: Routledge.

———. 2005. Expressions of migrant mobilities among Caribbean migrants in Toronto, Canada. In *The experience of return migration: Caribbean perspectives*, ed. R. B. Potter, D. Conway, and J. Phillips, 245–61. Aldershot, UK: Ashgate.

Feldmann, L. 2007. Aesthetics of saudade. http://www.proz.com/translation
-articles/articles/1399/1/Aesthetics-of-Saudade (accessed February 25,
2010).

Gable, S., and C. I. Gable. 2005. *Palladian days: Finding a new life in a Venetian country house*. New York: Alfred A. Knopf.

Ghosh, B., ed. 2000. *Return migration: Journey of hope or despair?* Geneva:
International Organization for Migration and the United Nations.

Gordon, C. 1989. *At the cottage*. Toronto: McClelland and Stewart.

———. 2006. *Still at the cottage*. Toronto: McClelland and Stewart.

Gough, K. 2007. Thinking geographically about house and home panel. Paper
presented at the Association of American Geographers Annual Meeting,
April 21, in San Francisco, California.

Hetherington, K. 1993. The geography of the other: Lifestyle, performance, and
identity. Doctoral dissertation, Lancaster University.

———. 1997. In place of geometry: The materiality of place. In *Ideas of difference*, ed. K. Hetherington and R. Munro, 183–99. Oxford: Blackwell.

———. 1998. *Expressions of identity: Space, performance, politics*. London:
Sage.

Kaltenborn, B. P. 1997. Nature of place attachment: A study among recreation
homeowners in southern Norway. *Leisure Sciences* 19: 175–89.

Linked. http://www.linkedm11.net/ (accessed February 25, 2010).

Liu, H. 2005. *The transnational history of a Chinese family: Immigrant letters,
family business, and reverse migration*. New Brunswick, NJ: Rutgers University Press.

Long, L. D. 2004. Viet kieu on a fast track back? In *Coming home? Refugees,
migrants, and those who stayed behind*, ed. L. D. Long and E. Oxfeld,
65–89. Philadelphia: University of Pennsylvania Press.

MacGregor, R. 2002. *Escape: In search of the natural soul of Canada*. Toronto:
McClelland and Stewart.

———. 2005. *The weekender: A cottage journal*. Toronto: Penguin.

McDowell, L. 1999. *Gender, identity and place: Understanding feminist geographies*. Cambridge: Polity.

Miller, G. 2008. Keynote address. Paper presented at the Graeme Miller symposium: Landscapes of memory, May 30, at Lancaster University, UK.

Nostalgia. 2010. *Merriam-Webster online dictionary*. http://www.merriam
-webster.com/dictionary/nostalgia (accessed February 25, 2010).

Perniola, M. 2001. *Ritual thinking: Sexuality, death, world*, trans. M. Verdicchio. Amherst, NY: Humanity Books.

Phillips, M. 1990. *I saw three Chinas*. Victoria, BC: Orca.

Potter, R. B., D. Conway, and J. Phillips, ed. 2005. *The experience of return
migration: Caribbean perspectives*. Aldershot, UK: Ashgate.

Shields, R. 2003. *The virtual*. New York: Routledge.

Stewart, K. 1988. Nostalgia—a polemic. *Cultural Anthropology* 3 (3): 227–41.

Tuan, Y.-F. 1977. *Space and place: The perspective of experience*. Minneapolis: University of Minnesota Press.

Urry, J. 2000. *Sociology beyond societies: Mobilities for the twenty-first century*. London: Routledge.

———. 2007. *Mobilities*. Cambridge: Polity Press.

Williams, A. M., and C. M. Hall. 2000. Tourism and migration: New relationships between production and consumption. *Tourism Geographies* 2 (1): 5–27.

Williams, D. R., and M. E. Patterson. 1996. Environmental meaning and ecosystem management: Perspectives from environmental psychology and human geography. *Society and Natural Resources* 9: 507–21.

4

From Disease to Desire
The Afflicted Amalgamation of Music and Nostalgia

MICKEY VALLEE

Despite its original diagnosis as an "afflicted imagination" enkindling despair and death in its victims, nostalgia was adopted as a musical device in Classical, Romantic, and early popular music. In this chapter, I trace nostalgia's migration from its diagnosis as a crippling disease to its paradoxical incorporation into musical composition.

It Isn't What It Was

Contemporary conjectures about nostalgia describe the emotion as an empowering state of self-awareness that dissociates the past from the pain of its historical consequences. But the definition of nostalgia isn't what it used to be. Where once nostalgia was diagnosed as an "afflicted imagination" (Hofer 1934, 381) associated with displacement and depression, it has recently been portrayed as a technology that weaves disparate historical moments within a singular narrative.

Because nostalgia is so wholly subjective, it is tactless to venture into objectivist descriptions—indeed, we have all suffered from nostalgia, yet we may find that defining it is an arduous task. An affective state entwined somewhere between emotion, memory, and identity, nostalgia is less a direct psychological referent to the totality of a past experience than a series of faded snapshots that project full features of one's self within the bygone event's imaginary space. Such a space, in turn, reassembles the image of the self in the present. According to Davis's (1979) pioneering sociological study, while nostalgia resembles the optimistic fantasy of a better time,

> it is a time we have already known. It reassures us of past happiness and accomplishment and, since these still remain on deposit, as it were, in the bank of our memory, it simultaneously bestows upon us a certain current worth, however much present circumstances may obscure it or make it suspect. (34)

Nostalgia, as Davis has it, alienates us from the present by way of an intensified extraction of affects from our past, but such alienation contributes toward identity preservation. Nostalgia doesn't cause us to suffer, Davis says, but rather enables us to overcome our current social discontinuities with an adherence to the self's superior ability at surviving past experiences; nostalgia, in other words, weaves an optimistic thread of continuity throughout the experiential disruptions of identity. It allows us to interrogate the past, not as a repository of veridical events, but as memorial planes of certain affectual transcendence: an assurance that I was "thereness" on the "beachness." Davis justifies his sanguine approach to alienation with the triumph of the self, which guarantees the protraction of identity and, as a corollary of protraction, prepares identity to overcome prospective disruptions in peaceful harmony between the self and world. By armouring the self with a vision of its own history without consequence, nostalgia is the cognitive technology that empowers the self as the triumphant autonomous figure unaffected by its social ground.

Davis designates the autonomous figure as the "secret self," which "gives testimony to one's prescience, to a heightened sensitivity and oneness with the deepest impulses of an age" (34). And since this "secret self" is also a social being (if we agree that keeping a secret anticipates the social art of confession), it will inevitably encounter other secret selves and share with them their secret spaces in present time. The exposing of the secret self to another person occurs within what Davis calls a "nostalgic memory exchange," which discloses the "wonderment of the revelation of how much more alike than different our 'secret' pasts are" so that we experience multiple shared memories "ad infinitum in paradoxical regress" (134). Nostalgia, according to Davis, exhibits a constructive social function. It allows us to regress into the fantasy of our past, yet it is a regression that causes us to resurface and share our memory with other people. Simply, as much as nostalgia is an always-already of the human condition, as much as we are interpellated as the subject of our own past, we find points of articulation in these subjective regressions to connect with others based on the mutual affects we share. We can, as perhaps a cultural apologist would argue, model a community through the ostensible alienation.

Indeed, music appears as the commensurate cultural alignment with nostalgia because either can be approached as the affective movement of pure memory. In other words, because music can relay the historical instance without the burden of its consequence, and because music circumvents the world of objects through its technology of signification, it has been generally taken as pure memory and an expressive tool for the becoming of pastness. It seems appropriate, if we are to talk about pastness (or regression for that matter) and music, to turn our attention briefly to Adorno. Adorno (1941), in a generous donation to the cultural apologist artillery, argued that music (through the unvarying modern edifice that constitutes the nostalgic subject) manipulates consciousness by evoking the past, employing formulae that follow the listener's first experiences with music in early childhood. Popular music and neoclassicism, in particular, confine listeners to the inescapable bassinet of regression. Adorno writes, "popular music is the sum total of all the conventions and material formulas in music to which he [the listener] is accustomed and which he regards as the inherent, simple language of music itself, no matter how late the development might be which produced this natural language" (444).

Adorno declares that popular music fails the progressive mobility of consciousness on account of the fact that its minimum compositional convention serves fantastic regression. The regressive listener embodies an optimistic mirage of awareness that lifts consciousness away from the here and now, evidenced by the fact that popular music's communicative function is (yes) "baby talk," or the "unabating repetition of some particular musical formula comparable to the attitude of a child incessantly uttering the same demand," accompanied by "the limitation of many melodies to very few tones, comparable to the way in which a small child speaks before he has the full alphabet at his disposal" (450). So the regression facilitated by popular music is a regression into a world wherein which events are no longer subject to their consequences; the listener is "stupefied" through infant listening habits.

Cultural apologists have had adverse reactions to such modernist condemnations of mass culture. Maurey (2009), for instance, takes nostalgia as a necessary tool for navigating the historical instances of popular music and for assembling a tonal palette of past performances; nostalgia is an essential thread for the postmodern flow between styles in its ironic distancing from historical certitude. Further, if music signifies nostalgia in place of modernity's interrogation of universal truth, it does so to the benefit of multivocality and multiplicity, and as a powerful deconstructive tool, a "device to unsettle and question received truths" (100). Likewise, Plastino (2007) takes nostalgia, even in its most nationalist contexts, as a personal and reflective nostalgia, a "continual interrogation of time and becoming" in musical affect (439). Because music can play out the sounds of history, or rather can mimic the affect associated with events in one's history, it can relay the affects of those events with its own certitude. Music allows the nostalgic a powerful route of access into the most certifiable mien of the self as coalesced into a temporal-experiential continuum.

Nostalgia scholarship proposes that the affect is personally and/or politically empowering, discerning a difference between reflective nostalgia, which empowers the self by placing dominant historical narratives at a distance for ironic appropriation, and restorative nostalgia, a nationalist attempt to reconstruct the lost past through national monuments and icons. And it is precisely this kind of split that affords the currency of empowerment theses when the topic of nostalgia arises. The distinction comes from Boym's (2002) lauded cultural history:

> For restorative nostalgia, the past is a value for the present; the past is not duration, but instantaneous perfection. The past, furthermore, shows no sign of decadence: it must be freshly depicted in its original image and remain eternally young. Reflective nostalgia is centered on historical and individual time, on the irrevocability of the past and on human finiteness.... Restorative nostalgia evokes a national past and future. Reflective nostalgia contemplates rather individual and cultural memory.... It reveals that fervent desire and critical thought are not opposed, and that memory and emotion don't preclude reason, critical judgment, and compassion. Reflective nostalgia does not seek to restore that mythical place called home. (59–60)

Restorative nostalgia removes an object from its pastness and represents it in the present to elevate the greatness of a nation. By contrast, reflective nostalgia interrogates the certitude of the past in an optimistic imaginary plane; it is the individualist inward fold of nostalgia, the suffering nostalgic, the sentimental nostalgic. A reflective nostalgic accepts the loss and makes no attempt to reconnect except through memory. Restorative nostalgia operates at the level of the nation, while reflective nostalgia functions at the level of the individual.

Studies of music's restorative nostalgic power read music as part of an attempt to manufacture authenticity and tradition (see Brennan 1999; Sant

Cassia 2000). But these studies, as cautious as they are of celebrating the nostalgic affect as self-adulation, are focused less on the specificities of a musical language than on the socio-historical framework within which musical processes transpire. Restorative nostalgia, in other words, requires an elaborate display of cultural artifacts that seek to reconstruct a sense of pastness, built into modern history to repeat what was once revolutionary in hopes of sustaining the spirit of an age.

Reflective musical nostalgia, on the other hand, refers to the ostensible constitution of and complications within the self. Jankélevitc (1992) provides a more refined understanding of the nostalgic listener as afflicted by the irremediable: "To say that nostalgia consists wholly of the bitterness of what has been is equivalent to saying ... that the object of nostalgia is the pain of the irreversible" (140). The nostalgic embarkment preludes an impossible reunion between the subject and the lost object because the latter fills the former with the enjoyment of loss. Music, as Jankélevitc has it, is the equally irreversible art of iteration, but its linear processes can be re-experienced at any point, and so it has a central role in nostalgic affect as the guarantee that the past unfolded in just such a manner. Music, simply, allows access to the affects associated with the bygone.

Through his examination of "old-timey" music such as hillbilly and blues, Middleton (2006) undertakes a musico-psychoanalytic approach to nostalgia as a "romanticized memory" (54), designating the moment as one of compulsive repetition:

> Densely layered, without clear origin, or else with an origin repressed from view, the nostalgic moment in its typical obsessive repetition may be identified, using Freudian-Lacanian terminology, as a species of fantasy, its object located within the "acting out" of a fantasy scene. In this sense, nostalgia is actually emblematic of modernity, for it is the fracturing of tradition that brings forth this particular figuring of loss—even though ... the effect when it emerges, as part of the psychoanalytic excavation of the modern subject, is to reveal what was always already there: a structure built around a lost object, which is in one form or another a human constant. (57)

For Middleton, nostalgia is built directly into old-timey music as the interpenetrative dialectic of tradition and modernity, constituting an object that is feared yet desired. In an idiosyncratic Lacanian formula that fundamentally favours nostalgic empowerment, Middleton describes modern musical nostalgia as that which bars the subject from encountering the traumas of personal or collective historical consequence. Nostalgia extends into the mirror of the bygone to reconnect with the whole complete self; for Middleton, nostalgia marks an attempt to sustain the imago of the mirror stage before it was breached by the symbolic order (60). Blues nostalgia does not simply sing of loss, but does so with a resilient character, "a particular inscription of absence in a present that will, at all costs, be survived" (61), lending listeners their existential consistency. And so we return full circle to the paradox of nostalgia: it is a deceptive but necessary component of modern subjectivity. The self must be continually interrogated as units of experience in order to remain whole. My question now turns to the original diagnosis of the disease in order to historicize select discourses that accommodated music and nostalgia's aesthetic amalgamation.

The "Afflicted Imagination"

In his 1688 dissertation, Johannes Hofer described nostalgia as an "afflicted imagination," a peculiar form of homesickness that plagued the minds of students and servants who studied or worked abroad but who had not properly adjusted to the foreign customs of their current surroundings. According to Hofer, who fused the Greek *nosos* (return to Native Land) with *algos* (suffering or grief), nostalgia was the cause of panic attacks, shortness of breath, anxiety, anorexia, suicide, despair, heart palpation, and, in its final stages, fever and death. Such existing terms as the German *Heimweh* (homesick) or the French *maladie du pays* (sickness for/in the country) did not indicate the idiosyncrasy of the disease's despair.

Despite the proclivity to classify nostalgia as longing for lost time, Hofer specified that it wasted away the consciousness of youth who in their travels abroad were either "abandoned by the pleasant breeze of their Native Land" or imagined "themselves enjoying this more." Nostalgia invaded consciousness with a singular idea, facilitated by a constellation of cathectic objects: a cool breeze, a familiar taste, a recognizable melody, any phenomena with the slightest reminiscence of home, which cast the Native Land in new lights of fantastic regression. Not age, but place, yet more properly displacement, incited the afflicted imagination (Hofer 1934, 380).

Hofer's primary case study, a student from Berne, had moved to study in Basel, and, "suffering from sadness for a considerable time, finally fell victim to this disease; [saying] that he was attended by a continual ... fever, that he had concocted these desires of the heart himself, and that worse symptoms had developed daily" (380). The student's housemates expected death at his door and prayed for his soul after a doctor had given him an enema and had taken several other measures to purify the body otherwise invaded by "animal spirits." Hofer, faced with what he considered to be the student's inevitable demise, prescribed to him nostalgia's cure: hope. According to Hofer, the student's breathing became more regular and he returned to his "whole sane self" when promised that he would return home, long before he even embarked on his journey.

The painstaking list of explicit diagnostics that a victim of nostalgia suffered is a far more monstrous account than most contemporary descriptions. According to Hofer, victims of nostalgia could be identified by their "wandering about sad," a tendency to "scorn foreign manners," a "distaste of strange conversations," an inclination "by nature to melancholy," to "bear jokes or the slightest injuries to other petty inconveniences in the most unhealthy frame of mind" while they "frequently make a show of the delights of the Fatherland and prefer them to all foreign things." Finally, nostalgics would find one another: "if they get together to endure their injuries, if they are afflicted by some disease or another and thence sad and thoughtful and breathe out in the atmosphere of the Fatherland" (386). Patients who exceeded these rather preliminary diagnostics were fully consumed by the disease in its late stages. Hofer wrote that if individuals meditate unusually upon the Fatherland, portray unrecoverable sadness, cannot sleep (or sleep too much), exhibit a physical weakening, are chronically hungry and thirsty, experience sensory deprivation, worry about their heart condition, suffer from heart palpitations, chronically sigh, become "stupid" by not entertaining anything but the object of their loss, and finally succumb to fever ... then they are likely suffering the full effects of nostalgia. And if the fever was not treated in a timely manner, nostalgia would devour the body in death.

In order for the patients to amass their own willpower to return home, the body had to be purged of animal spirits by way of administering cephalicum, mercury, powder, and medicated wine directly into the brachial vein. Purging the body of blocked substances allowed consciousness to remain in the current environment. No matter the developmental stage of nostalgia, recovery would occur at the mention of returning home. Only at the end of his dissertation does Hofer witness the miracle of hope occurring before his very eyes in the body language of a servant:

> [N]ot long since it was told me by a Parisian that he himself had an Helvetian bound servant who was sad and melancholy at all times so that he began to work with lessened desire; finally, he came to him and sought dismissal with insistent entreaties, of which he could have no hope beyond him. When the merchant granted this immediately, the servant changed from sudden joy, excused from his mind these phantasma for

several days, and after a while remained in Paris, broken up no longer by this disease. (390)

The first reprint of the dissertation appeared in 1710, part of Zwinger's "Fasciculus Dissertatiunum Medicarum Selectorium," which included a relatively insolent rephrasing, as well as a replacement of the term *nostalgia* with *pothopatriadalgia*, some other case histories, and an introduction to what he considered a culprit facilitator for the disease, a "sweet melody of Switzerland" that produced homesickness in those who heard it—he called it a "pathological air," or a *Kuhe-Reyen*. This air was also known as a *Ranz des vaches*, a Swiss mountain song, which Rousseau (1975) describes as an example of that which is not music but rather a "memorative sign" (267). While music was described as the "art of combining ... sounds in a manner pleasing to the ear," a profound "art of the beautiful," the *Ranz des vaches* was a style of music "so generally beloved among the Swiss, that it was forbidden to be played in their troops under pain of death, because it made them burst into tears, desert, or die, whoever heard it; too great a desire did it excite in them of returning to their country" (266–67). But it did not produce a longing in people who were not Swiss.

The remaining discussion pivots on nostalgia's incorporation into Classical, Romantic, and popular music as an aesthetic nexus for the subject to experience the loss of an object of which they were never in possession.

Haydn's Farewell: A Case of Expunging Nostalgia

Students, servants, and the military longed for home especially when returning home appeared impossible. As they faced harrowing battles, unhealthy living conditions, foreign customs, and imminent injury, victims would understandably imagine and idealize the comforts of home. Indeed, musicians stood on equal footing with other servants under their employers and suffered similar ailments of displacement. We will recall Hofer's closing remarks on the state of the servant, because they bear relevance to the story of a group of classical musicians serving under Joseph Haydn (1732–1809).

As court composer, Haydn was required to write numerous compositions weekly ranging from string quartets to operas, concerti, symphonies, and keyboard sonatas all for the court's entertainment. Prince Nicholas Esterhazy himself was devoted to music, having designated a concert hall and two opera houses on his property to be used solely for the performances of Haydn's compositions. Haydn's popularity resulted from both his talents and the providence of working for an appreciative employer. One autumn, while under the strict regimen of entertaining those at the Esterhaza estate, Haydn's musicians, on the brink of suffering from nostalgia, had requested that Haydn expedite their return home.

Their schedule was so exhaustive that musicians employed by Esterhazy were required to live on distant estate properties during summer months in barracks, where they adopted a regimen of intense rehearsals and flawless performances; when they could return to their families was a decision entirely left to the prince (Green 1997, 158–89). In 1772 Esterhazy hadn't given word to his musicians regarding their anticipated and due return home, and so the musicians became restless. Haydn and Esterhazy had a healthy working relationship, but Haydn recognized his role as servant and could see that his musicians were anxiously awaiting the official cue to return home.

Haydn composed a solution that conveyed the longing musicians were suffering in their desperate situation. His composition became known as the "Farewell Symphony" in F-sharp minor (no. 45), a typical symphony for his *Sturm und Drang* period but one with an unusual ending. The final movement, which was generally expected to be an exciting *Allegro Assai* or *Vivace*, took a delicately lyrical detour before its conclusion. At its performance Esterhazy was subjected to a simple soft theme across the entire orchestra, which each musician gradually ceased performing, extinguishing his candle and leaving the stage with his instrument, leaving an empty and dark place behind. The gesture was repeated sequentially until Haydn, as conductor and first violinist, was left only with the second violinist playing in the centre of a vacant hole once composed of musicians whose spirits were slowly dissipating, letting sounds swell in the augmentation of pleasurable emptiness. Once they concluded, they too left the stage in complete darkness. Esterhazy let them return home immediately. As Haydn's biographer confirms:

> One year, against his usual custom, the prince determined to extend his stay in Esterhaza for several weeks. The ardent married men, thrown into utter consternation, turned to Haydn and asked him to help. Haydn hit upon the idea of writing a symphony in which, one after the other, the instruments fall silent. At the first opportunity, this symphony was performed in the prince's presence. Each of the musicians was instructed that, as soon as his part had come to an end, he should extinguish his light, pack up his music, and leave with his instrument under his arm. The prince and the audience at once understood the point of this pantomime; the next day came the order for the departure from Esterhaza. Thus Haydn related the occasion for the Farewell Symphony to me; the other version, that Haydn thereby dissuaded the prince from his intention to dissolve the entire

Kapelle ... is to be sure more poetic, but not historically correct. (quoted in Webster 1991, 1)

According to Webster, the "Farewell" is unusual not only for its program but also for its tonality, standing as the only F-sharp minor symphony in the eighteenth century. In typical symphonic form of this pre-Classical period, the piece should end in the key in which it began, in this case in F-sharp minor. But the farewell section of the final movement deviates from the tonal centre of the work by way of a deceptive cadence to (its relative) A major. The farewell theme, which unfolds as a minuet in a binary sonata form, modulates to its own recapitulation in F-sharp major. In other words, it fantasizes its own home key into a modulated return to its parallel major. It does not long for home as a lost object and hold it at an idealized distance. It uplifts the hollowed sound of F-sharp minor into its parallel home key, as if home was found through the straightforward solution of hope, which was in the previous century the prescribed medical cure for nostalgia.

The central governing principle of the work is the hope to return home, represented by the symphony's program as well as its tonality. F-sharp minor was a relatively unheard of key to perform in (minus the rare exceptions by Haydn), and an especially difficult one to tune brass instruments in. As Webster interprets it, "F-sharp minor thus represents a remote and inhospitable part of the musical universe—just as Esterhaza lay in a remote and inhospitable district" (116). When home is finally reached in the resolved parallel F-sharp major, the instruments are performing in an even more distant domain. Indeed, in orchestral music of the eighteenth century we see little that goes well into the sharp keys, and horns could be played in keys sharper than E major only with significant difficulty, which would prove to be especially laborious given the final movement's move toward F-sharp major.

Rather than idealizing its lost object, the "Farewell" facilitates a symbolic return toward it; it illustrates an arising consciousness concerning nostalgia and its negotiability through creative forms such as musical composition. Indeed, nostalgia was a grave enough illness for a group of performers to unite and execute an act of symbolic resistance (since Haydn had responded directly to his musicians' requests for a solution to their problem), employing the technical language of tonality to annex the possibility of nostalgia—the musicians were longing for their homes, their wives, their families. They were not yet fixated on home enough to communicate a melancholic yearning for what was lost (that was up to the Romantics).

Thus, I am not suggesting that the "Farewell" is an example of "musical nostalgia," but rather that it was the cure for nostalgia (at least according to Hofer's dissertation): hope.

If the potential for an afflicted imagination facilitated an act of resistance, it's little wonder that nostalgia in the military was forcefully discouraged! Military forces in various European nations, specifically France and Russia, reported that their soldiers suffered an equally intense homesickness abroad. Meanwhile, however, military personnel in the United States boasted that they had found the cure for nostalgia. According to Boym (2002), American physician Theodore Calhoun "proposed as treatment public ridicule and bullying by fellow soldiers, an increased number of manly marches and battles and improvement in personal hygiene that would make soldiers' living conditions more modern" (6). In other words, nostalgia translated into weakness, which was properly cured through discipline. In these cases, however, the nostalgic was encouraged not to return home, but instead to remain broken through self-discipline.

Romantic Distance and the Loss of Loss

By the early nineteenth century, composers had exhausted "absolute music" (i.e., symphonies and concerti containing autonomous relations of motifs bearing little extramusical association), seeking instead as sources their own vernacular traditions, ones with which members of the nation could have a rapport. Operas were consummate vehicles to express music of the people because the people were easily translated into characters on stage. For instance, as Dahlhaus (1991) argues,

> folk melodies resist symphonic manipulation (it is rarely possible to break down the lines of a song into motivic particles capable of undergoing a Beethovenian process of development without seeming willful and heavy-handed), whereas they can easily be incorporated into an opera, where the resultant unavoidable fractures in style can be justified as fulfilling dramaturgical functions in the plot. (218)

Such an example reflects a restorative nostalgia: the active reconstitution of an object purporting the ideal image of the nation. But a reflective nostalgia was expressed through the melancholy of Romanticism, and in social philosophic terms, this translated into the rise of the subject at the expense of humanism. According to Rosen (1998), both the Classical and the Romantic styles worked according to the logic of memory. Classical memory would reminisce about bygone happiness (such as the innocence of youth), while the Romantic memory recalled a period within which hope was still a possibility, memories "of absence, of that which never was" (175). Yet Romanticism expresses more of a melancholy than it does a nostalgia. Romanticism suffers loss without attempts at unification. Simply, the Classical style longs for that which one may repossess, such as the homes of those musicians in Esterhazy's court, while Romanticism longs for that which was never possessed. Romanticism expresses less its fixation on the lost object than its loss for something that it never possessed. In general, the Romantic aesthetic was marked by a contemplative and poetic distance facilitated by the very embrace of loss. For instance, take Robert Schumann's letter to his mother as he left home for his studies in Leipzig at age eighteen:

> I left on the 21st. With a melancholy heart, I took leave of the whole precious home with a long, silent look down from Mosler mountain; the autumnal morning was shining like a mild day in spring, and the illuminated world was tenderly and cheerfully smiling on my beautiful, lonely wandering. The moment of separation from loved ones, and of farewell, gives our soul the gentle melancholic minor chord, which is seldom heard. All the bells of past childhood, the present, and the future flow into one chord—the shining future would like to drive out the past, and so tender, undefined feelings are gently fighting in our breast.... The evening was wonderful, and the soul was as it is on a still Friday; before Altenburg I sat down for a few hours and rested peacefully, and followed the setting sun with my eyes, and the image of the *sfie Heimath* [sweet home] appeared shy and tender before my eyes and sank like the parting and reddening sun, like its last ray, still and stiller into the graves of the past. Therese stood before me and sang softly: sweet home. And while I was dozing off in the evening, every minute of the day and of the past was darkly wafting by again, and like the gentle echo of the soul, I heard the sounds melting and dying away and the last one trembling softly: sweet home. (quoted in Hoekner 2002, 72)

According to Hoekner, the literary descriptions here distance Schumann from his directly inhabited world and turn toward an embrace of loss itself as the catalyst for creativity, and this distance summons the distant sounds of music. This notion of distance was particularly influential on Schumann's early work *Papillons*, Op. 2, based on his own reading of Jean Paul's Flegeljahre, where Walt and Vult, the novel's two protagonists, attend a ball with a woman whom they are both in love with. When the woman settles with Walt (a poet), Vult (a musician) wanders off into a void, and as the brother walks away, the final sentences of the novel ring out into romantic distance: "Enchanted, Walt heard the vanishing sounds still speaking from afar: for he did not notice his brother vanishing with them" (quoted in Hoekner 2002, 57). Indeed, loss itself was extolled within Romantic aesthetics.

Nostalgia is the irrevocable symptom of the subject. Rather than expressing the loss of something in the concrete world, nostalgia is the psyche's means of coping with the trauma of a primordial loss by imagining a utopian historical certitude of total union. In short, nostalgia in music was a connotative form of signification that signified not the loss of a particular object, but the inherent affect of loss embedded in an object its listener may never have been in possession of; or if they had suffered a real loss, at least the musical connotations were a shadowy manifestation of the object's absence. To allude briefly to psychoanalytic terminology, Romanticism marks a transition from the humanist age of the whole self to the modern age of the split subject. Žižek (1992, 1997), for instance, argues that four configurations around this loss are central to subject/object relations in the post-humanist age of subjectivity: (1) the object-cause of desire creates the inability to attain it; (2) the object is immovable unless its exchange can be expunged from its motion in contemporary reality; (3) the object emerges as a means for us to return to the quest to attain it; and (4) the more horrifying the libidinal impact the object has once its material property is diminished from our grasp, the more increasingly it facilitates an enjoyable pursuit. These are, Žižek (1992) writes, perfectly valid paradoxes, as "the domain of the subject's impossible relation to the object-cause of its desire, the domain of the drive that circulates endlessly around it" (6). Nostalgia denies the subject the nostalgic object, which is precisely what constitutes its enjoyment factor. And, indeed, the enjoyment of loss is what leads us to our final example: the sentimental ballad.

After the Ball Was Over: The Nostalgic Fold of the Tin Pan Alley

If music under the Romantic aesthetic portrayed loss as a creative force, the popular music industry doubled over on loss as the foremost component of music's commodified condition; Tin Pan Alley songwriters explicitly evoked nostalgia as a requisite to selling songs to a newly emerging mass market (Shepherd 1982). Under a rising modern edifice, home was a precarious concept to the nostalgic subject. The popular music industry engendered a parallax shift in the attitude toward nostalgia by turning the listener's experience directly toward it in the most paradoxical of consumption spaces: the home.

Stephen Foster was the first songwriter to incorporate nostalgia as a central compositional device in his sentimental ballads. His songs communicated in simple and effective folk-like melodies representing the heterogeneous nationalities of nineteenth-century American heritage (his use of step-wise and pentatonic melodies was characteristic of Scottish and English folk music, for example). According to Key (1995), alluding to the past in the context of the present has further implications in Foster's use of the chorus: "The chorus brings the past into the present and achieves a nostalgic, rather than dramatic, goal. One might look at this structure as an 'interrupted narrative' where progress is inevitably interrupted by backward glances" (160).

If Foster established the techniques of popular music composition, then Tin Pan Alley made it accessible to the public. Tin Pan Alley refers to a New York neighbourhood of music publishers that employed songwriting teams in the late nineteenth century, producing popular songs on sheet music for vocal and simple instrumental accompaniment. Charles K. Harris in 1892 published the first hit of the music industry, a ballad entitled "After the Ball," the first mass consumed hit as it sold a prodigious 10 million copies, generating $25,000 per week (approximately $600,000 per week by today's standard). Following the song's initial success, Harris moved to New York and published compositional methods in his instruction booklet, *How to Write a Popular Song* (1906). The proven success of the sentimental ballad, according to Harris, rested on the criteria that it was written in a "fashionable musical style" while either appearing topical or appealing to mass emotion, using such a sentiment as nostalgia for its emotional basis. The lyrics to "After the Ball" describe a conversation between youth and age in order to prescribe the preventative measures for avoiding a life of regret:

> *Verse:* A little maiden climbed an old man's knee
> Begged for a story, "Do, uncle, please!
> Why are you single? Why live alone?
> Have you no babies? Have you no home?"
> "I had a sweetheart, years, years ago
> Where she is now, pet, you will soon know.
> List to the story, I'll tell it all
> I believ'd her faithless, after the ball."
> *Chorus:* After the ball is over,
> After the break of morn,
> After the dancers' leaving

After the stars are gone;
Many a heart is aching
If you could read them all
Many the hopes that have vanished
After the ball.
Verse: Bright lights were flashing in the grand ballroom
Softly the music playing sweet tunes;
There came my sweetheart, my love, my own,
"I wish some water, leave me alone."
When I returned, dear, there stood a man
Kissing my sweetheart, as lovers can.
Down fell the glass, pet, broken, that's all
Just as my heart was, after the ball.
Verse: Long years have passed, child, I've never wed
True to my lost love, though she is dead.
She tried to tell me, tried to explain
I would not listen, pleadings were vain.
One day a letter came from that man,
He was her brother, the letter ran;
That's why I'm lonely, no home at all
I broke her heart, pet, after the ball.

Consumers embodied the synecdoche of modern nostalgia by yearning for the ideals of a lost home from within the domestic space; the compositional method for ballads was designed, as Key (1995) writes, to "offer fertile ground on which to express feelings of loss and alienation" while living in the experience of the present, allowing the listener, the performer, and (however at a distance) the author to experience contemporaneous "throes of nostalgia" (149). The transformation should be evident at this point: where once the nostalgic suffered for home in its absence, the modern nostalgic enjoyably suffered for home in its presence.

"After the Ball" is a calculated fantasy that concomitantly mourns and celebrates loss through the optimistic momentum of a waltz (a mid- to late-nineteenth-century dance that was especially popular with youth). While we hear the waltz at a distance, it is not a Romantic distance; we are not inclined to dance a waltz so much as experience its sounds that cradle the impossible dialogue between age and youth. "After the Ball" does not seek to recover from loss by summoning hope, as was the case with Haydn's symphony, nor does it luxuriate in Romantic melancholy. In the sentimental ballad, we are witness to a nostalgic confrontation with a lost object on the grounds of unobtainable reconciliation. The sentimental ballad succeeded by tickling the subject with an emotion common to all subjects under the edifice of modernity. The sentimental ballad thus represents the fall from grace every listening subject suffers on his or her interpellation into the listening experience—it assumes that every listener has somewhere within a broken heart that can sympathize with the characters in "After the Ball," a scenario that sanitizes the moment after the fall. While the sentimental ballad implies the very framework within which the loss eventuated, we are hidden from it. In the case of "After the Ball," nostalgia pleads to an Other who cannot fathom the depth of regret, a child.

Conclusion

I do not intend for this chapter to conclude with the usual devices of nostalgic scholarship, to either prescribe a political empowerment or denounce its alienating consequences. I merely suggest that further analytic work is required if we are to unravel the properties of an emotion that is so intimately entwined with music and the culture industry more broadly. Indeed, if nostalgia is "a feeling of sadness and longing that is not akin to pain, and resembles sorrow only as the mist resembles the rain" (Longfellow 1886, 87), then paying heed to its historical appearances rather than succumbing to its seductive affect is a more sensible than sentimental form of interrogation.

References

Adorno, T. W. 1941. On popular music [with the assistance of George Simpson]. In *Essays on music / Theodor W. Adorno*, ed. R. Leppert, 437–69. Berkeley; Los Angeles: University of California Press.

Boym, S. 2002. *The future of nostalgia*. New York: Basic Books.

Brennan, V. L. 1999. Chamber music in the barn: Tourism, nostalgia, and the reproduction of social class. *World of Music* 41: 11–29.

Dahlhaus, C. 1991. *Nineteenth-century music*. Berkeley: University of California Press.

Davis, F. 1979. *Yearning for yesterday: A sociology of nostalgia*. New York: Free Press.

Green, R. 1997. Representing the aristocracy: The operatic Haydn and Le Pescatrici. In *Haydn and his world*, ed. E. Sisman, 140–60. Princeton, NJ: Princeton University Press.

Hoekner, B. 2002. *Programming the absolute: Nineteenth-century German music and the hermeneutics of the moment*. Princeton, NJ: Princeton University Press.

Hofer, J. 1934. Medical dissertation on nostalgia, trans. C. Kiser Anspach. *Bulletin of the Institute of the History of Medicine* (August): 376–91.

Jankélevitc, V. 1992. La nostalgia. In *Nostalgia. Storia di un sentimento*, ed. A. Prete, 119–76. Milan: Raffaello Cortina Editore.

Key, S. 1995. Sound and sentimentality: Nostalgia in the songs of Stephen Foster. *American Music* 13 (2): 145–66.

Longfellow, H. W. 1886. *The poetical works of Henry Wadsworth Longfellow*. Boston; New York: Houghton, Mifflin and Co.

Maurey, Y. 2009. Dana International and the politics of nostalgia. *Popular Music* 28 (1): 85–103.

Middleton, R. 2006. *Voicing the popular: On the subjects of popular music*. New York: Routledge.

Plastino, G. 2007. *Lazzari felici*: Neapolitan song and/as nostalgia. *Popular Music* 26 (3): 429–40.

Rosen, C. 1998. *The romantic generation*. Cambridge, MA: Harvard University Press.

Rousseau, J.-J. 1975. *A complete dictionary of music; consisting of a copious explanation of all words necessary to a true knowledge and understanding of music*, trans. W. Waring. New York: AMS Press.

Sant Cassia, P. 2000. Exoticising discoveries and extraordinary experiences: "Traditional" music, modernity and nostalgia in Malta and other Mediterranean societies. *Ethnomusicology* 44: 281–301.

Shepherd, J. 1982. *Tin Pan Alley*. New York: Routledge.

Webster, J. 1991. *Haydn's "Farewell" symphony and the idea of classical style: Through-composition and cyclic integration in his instrumental music*. New York: Cambridge University Press.

Žižek, S. 1992. *Looking awry: An introduction to Jacques Lacan through popular culture*. London: MIT Press.

———. 1997. *The plague of fantasies*. New York: Verso.

Section II: Desire

5

The Tourist Affect
Escape and Syncresis
on the Las Vegas Strip

ROB SHIELDS

How does one understand an isolated desert city devoted to gambling and
leisure escapes such as Las Vegas? How does one understand the place, an
urban environment like the four miles of The Strip, or the casino resorts
and hotels along it such as the Belaggio? Is The Strip just a design icon (cf.
Barbour 2000; Dannatt 2002; Gendall 2006; Irazabal 2007) or is it a trench-
ant social lesson? A key point of this chapter is that such places must be
analyzed in relation to other places. They are all embedded in a network or
spatialization that casts places in a qualitative light. This "topology" positions
sites and regions as "places for this and places for that" (see Shields 1991;
Shields forthcoming). In the spatialization of North American and global
neo-liberal jouissance and accumulation, Las Vegas's place is secured by its
famous reputation. These places must be understood in a wider cultural
context and their qualities probed to reveal how pleasure in the spatialization of neo-liberalism is actualized, even in the face of inequalities and
exploitation. In the urban studies literature in general and the literature on
Las Vegas in particular, the focus is on political economy and sociology, in
particular of its immigrants (Baird et al. 2008) and tourists (Gladstone
1998). Even its impossible sustainability in the middle of the desert tends
to be ignored (Poyner 1998), trumped by its status as a neo-liberal "camp-
out" for globalized capital and its labourers. Its image and the meanings of
its facades have elicited some critique (Gottdiener, Collins, and Dickens
1999; Raento 2009), partly in relation to the enormous journalistic literature on contemporary urban consumption culture in the United States.

However, the political economy of The Strip turns on another, affective, economy (Bataille 1988) that provides the opportunity to produce The Strip as well as driving its psychosocial and economic processes.

Can attention to affect offer a level of social analysis relevant to critical topology and social geography? Although it has been the topic of a recent surge in geographers' attention, notably from proponents of "non-representational theory" (cf. Thrift 2008),[1] affect appears in many guises in social science research—in discussions of expectation, of fear, or of hope, as well as studies of attachment to place (cf. McCormack 2003). Flickering back and forth between actual and virtual moments of embodiment and emotion, what I will refer to as the "syncresis" of affect can be illustrated as the relation between rising or falling "capacity for action" as a disposition or outlook and material comportment and psychological states (Shields 2003; Citton and Lordon 2008).

Las Vegas's Strip presents itself as a street of dreams outside of normal jurisdictions and offers holiday experiences cut loose from the everyday lives of its mostly North American clientele. While foreigners do visit, they often do so for conferences and trade shows rather than to take part in the hotel and casino business that has made The Strip infamous.[2] From the 1980s, neo-conservative policies encouraged public-private partnerships to develop cities, which converged with an "entertainment economy" predicated on consumption-oriented culture. These policies brought about investment in entertainment and sports venues, resorts, stadiums, and casinos (Hannigan 1998, 61–62). Las Vegas's "Strip" of casino resorts sought to realize the entrepreneurial aura of a swashbuckling "casino capitalism" of *la fin du vingtième*, celebrating the spatial fix of capitalism's new globalization in the form of simulated versions of the most famous landmarks and world cities, reproducing pyramids (the Luxor), Paris (Paris-Las-Vegas, see Lampert-Greaux 2000), art deco architecture (the Belaggio)—anything but the desert. Vegas became the most famous exemplar of the excesses of commercial culture in America (cf. Venturi, Izenour, and Scott Brown 1977). The synergy of the commercialization of popular culture with landed and financial capital meant that property speculation on new consumption sites such as malls, hotels, casinos, and theme parks was one important element driving the economy (see A. Scott 1980; A. J. Scott 1997, 2006). Places such as Atlantic City, Reno, and Las Vegas were

> the temple[s] not only of gambling or greed, but of the very creed and faith that represent the underlying values of the neoliberal USA. Entrepreneurs like Donald Trump and Steve Wynn, just a step ahead of bankruptcy and

floating on junk bonds, are its high priests; the players at the blackjack tables are its acolytes, but so too are the shoppers in its malls, the audiences at its clubs and stages, and the real-estate speculators buying up its properties. All are players in the game of casino capitalism, and now so too are the local governments that place their bets on casinos as the saviours of their tax-base and regional economy. (Sheller 2008, 109; see also Goux 1998)

Between 2002 and 2007, the volume of visitors to Las Vegas grew almost 9 percent from about 35 million to peak at just fewer than 39.2 million before declining about 4 percent in 2008 due to the U.S. recession.[3] Convention attendance in Las Vegas accounts for about one-sixth of this volume, with tourism accounting for the majority of this growth. The bulk of the roughly 142,000 hotel rooms are in large hotels on The Strip. The concentration of accommodation on The Strip leads to large crowds inside and outside of the hotels; despite the pretensions to exclusiveness, this is a mass holiday destination.[4]

The Strip is more than an urban form—a boulevard that serves both automobiles and pedestrians—it is also a social form: its laminar flows consist of the strolling crowd flanked by an automobile crowd who are en route to join this fluid pedestrian mass at some further point (for few would choose the congested boulevard as an efficient route). It is a linear stage on which to see and be seen. The crowds are thus heterogeneous but still conjoined mobilities and *consumption publics* (see also Shields 1997). They are quite different from past publics of civil society that built many other North American cities. The resort-like casino hotels are performative actualizations of a commercialized model of structured, guided, and monetized play and gaming with money, which produces profits and whose winnings can be taxed. Casino hotels are a material and semiotic infrastructure that serves the interests of interlocked sets of developers, investors, legislators, consumers, and gamblers as a built form. Local citizens are perhaps least well served, other than as employees. Local civic culture is repressed (Sheller 2008, 124). During the recession, the mid-2009 unemployment rates in Las Vegas had grown to 12.3 percent, up from 3.8 percent in 2006 (Stein 2009, 26); residential foreclosure rates were nearly 18 percent in January 2010, the highest in the United States and four times the national average at 1 in every 95 housing units foreclosed (as reported by RealtyTrac, http://www.realty trac.com; see KIVI-TV 2010).

Not surprisingly, a stereotype persists of the gambling holiday where people are wooed to spend their savings and their attention is kept on the casino and other diversions on the property, with cut-price food and hotel

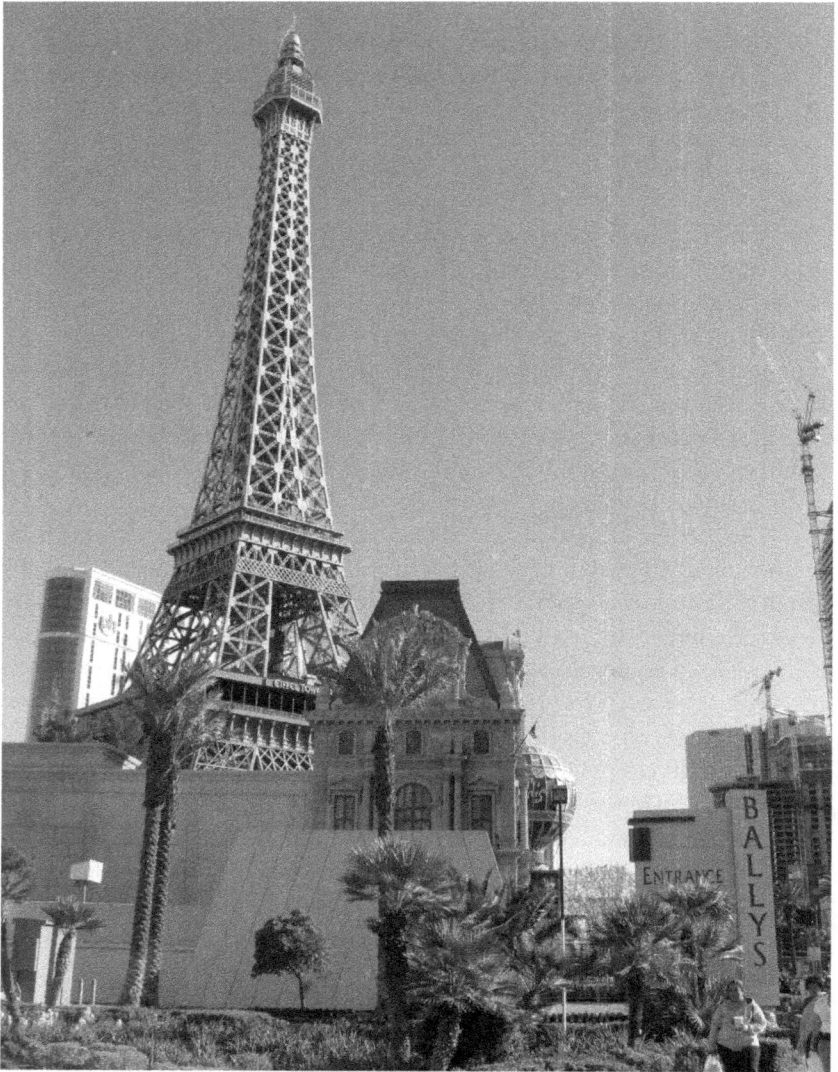

Figure 5.1 The Strip, Las Vegas. (Photo credit: R. Shields)

accommodation. The redevelopment of Las Vegas has fed on a nostalgia for a purified moment of desire and an image of the entrepreneurial gambler as poised, elegant, and retro-fashionable, incarnated by the late 1950s and early 1960s Hollywood screen and recording stars retrospectively known as the "Rat Pack."⁵ The historical vernacular of casino cities is "spectacle and speculation, the 'fantasy city'" (Sheller 2008, 117; Binkowski 2008). With the collapse of the global speculative economy of the United States in 2008, these historical ideal moments and sites remain as ghostly presences in the new casinos and in the few remaining casino hotels of The Strip's older sections, and as haunting absences in the form of cleared sections and abandoned construction sites for ever-larger, multi-billion-dollar real estate wagers made by developers, planners, and pension funds, as well as by venture capitalists who counted on the continued flows of spendthrift patrons (on the dynamics of Las Vegas real estate values see Zhou and Sornette 2008; see also note 4). This is literally what James Kunstler (1993) called an empty "geography of nowhere" of highway strips, parking lots, mega-malls, and junked cities (Sheller 2008, 114).

Escape Attempts

A more extensive version of this place myth (see Shields 1991) is of Las Vegas as an "escape" holiday destination. Escape from weather, rain, and snow, into the interiors of hotel casinos and onto the mile or so of The Strip, which leads nowhere other than to other hotel casinos (see Figure 5.2). Escape from responsibility to abandon and self-indulgence. Escape from work and seriousness to play and frivolity. Escape from thrift and planning to expenditure and an endless present of slot machines and the speeded-up time of video lottery terminal betting cycles.

"Escape attempts" have been defined as practices of resistance and retreat from paramount reality. These might include the "activity enclaves" of hobbies or gambling, the "new landscapes" of holidays, or even the "mindscapes" of drugs (Cohen and Taylor 1976). To a certain extent, the escape holiday is implicit rather than explicit. However, it is often referenced in promotional materials and in media reports of Las Vegas hotels and the overall tourist experience of the isolated city. Crawford (1992) notes that people are now accustomed to understanding shopping as diversion and pleasure (28; Junemo 2004; Schmid 2006; Shih-Diing 2008; Yeung, Lee, and Kee 2008). Could one feel homesick in the artificial world of the resort hotel? (See Vallee on nostalgia in this volume.) The airplane flight—which is the means of travel for the vast majority of visitors—marks the transition from everyday life, with its anticipation on the way. The return flight is a coming down from the gambler's high, the embarrassment of a partier's drunken self-revelations in front of friends, or preparation for returning to the responsibilities of work, family, or home life.

Although isolated by distance and its desert setting, Vegas is also tied to and dependent on the social, economic, and cultural conditions of the

Figure 5.2 Casino gambling hall, Las Vegas. (Photo credit: R. Shields)

everyday life it offers an escape from. As a destination, it purports to offer attractions unavailable elsewhere or on a grander scale than anywhere that might compete. Circuses, wild-animal shows, entertainers, and prostitutes complement the casinos. They lend the image and the expense, although rarely the reality, of high class and taste. In actuality, refinement, excitement, and the extraordinary are more likely to be found in large metropolitan centres. The high-rolling gamblers are few, and local casinos are now an almost ubiquitous strategy, at least in Canada, for supplementing government tax coffers. Now, the singers and the circuses all tour, and tourists are likely to travel to see wild animals more impressive behaviour in either nature park settings or in exotic countries where they herd together on a scale beyond even the imaginations of Vegas entertainment "imagineers."

> The economy of spectacle and speculation thoroughly permeates the civic realm, the state realm, the economic realm, and even the past. We live and work to spend on this crass entertainment, to gamble it away, to shop until we drop, to party all night, to sink it into flimsy buildings ... participation in this charade of wealth is a kind of liberation, and an escape; it is perhaps the best our culture has to offer, and many certainly experience it as such. (Sheller 2008, 124)

If Vegas is not unique by most standards, it follows that its attraction to visitors lies elsewhere. Rather than being a singular destination in the sense of uniqueness, it is a particular line of flight and escape from everyday life. Its particularity lies in its differentiation from the weave of everyday duties, routines, and patterns. Its position in the geography of nowhere is accomplished by spatial distance more than separation and by monopolizing visitors' attention during their stay via the all-encompassing theme environment of the casino hotel. The monotonously glitzy attention economy of the individual establishments and of The Strip creates a texture that is unbroken by the demands of community or household operation. In the artificially lit and poorly signed casino hotel interiors, it is difficult to mark time and the succession of day and night, or to differentiate location and orientation in a forest of slot machines and a maze of endless gambling halls or "floors."

The banal quality of the Las Vegas experience—including the repetitiveness of casting bets—is reinforced by the high number of repeat visitors: almost 4 out of 5 tourists have been to Las Vegas before. Predictability is a virtue. "Escape" is thus part of a routine cycle of vacations. Canadians make up less than 6 percent of visitors but exemplify the seasonal escape by plane. Notably in late February or March, Vegas offers an early annual taste of spring, an affordable mass destination one charter flight away from suburban family routine. The respondents' maps in Dorow and Dogu (in this volume) demonstrate how escape destinations such as Vegas appear as a line of flight for workers and residents of northern resource cities and towns, while tourists from colder areas of North America experience a haven from weather inside the casino resorts and on The Strip itself. For example, for tourists from the oil sands centre of Fort McMurray Alberta, Vegas is the alter ego to shift work and the boreal forest.

However, the economics of the casino resorts depend on a flexiblized, often visibly subaltern workforce imported into the area (Debouzy 2006). The low-wage positions are dominated by immigrant populations such as Hispanics. These jobs are often female positions, which are socially marginalized by the dominant society and vulnerable (Whitfield et al. 2004). Most workers are on permanent casual contracts, precluding them from the benefits of full-time wage earners, and are tightly interpellated into a hierarchical system of seniority and ranks among, for example, chambermaids in a given hotel. Tens of thousands of waiters, cleaners, salespersons, security guards, croupiers, groundskeepers, and maintenance personnel are employed, as well as taxi drivers, sex workers, and transportation and supply workers who have immigrated from other parts of the United States, Mexico, Central and Latin America, Korea, the Philippines, Vietnam, and elsewhere.

With strict work regimes and protocols for interacting with patrons, casino hotel workers are compelled to wear uniforms that pay little regard to their ethnic, gender, or religious differences. Diversity is flattened to create standardized representatives of the casino's brand name. After work hours, these workers are supported by ethnic services and patronize neighbourhood specialty stores. The largest union, Unite-Hire, represents 60,000 culinary and hotel workers in Las Vegas. Other groups of workers such as casino dealers have unionized more recently and have attempted to negotiate first contracts for over a year in the "Right to Work" State. In studies of Las Vegas, the hospitality management literature tends to view with alarm the social solidarity of Hispanic social networks, which they see as augmenting workers' respect for strike picket lines.

Vegas combines different forms of consumption around a routine script similar to an annual vacation at an isolated resort or on a cruise ship. By concatenating convention and business trade show meetings with the leisure holiday model, and with illicit and escape holiday models, Vegas entrepreneurs have innovated and expanded the appeal of the city as a tourist destination as well as broadened their clientele from adult gambling to family vacationers. For visitors from smaller centres, Las Vegas may represent a family shopping trip to well-known chain stores that are available only in the shopping malls of larger cities—the place affords simple consumption but also satisfies needs and allows people to achieve goals.

Diversion is solace to some and is harnessed in complex ways to compensate, confirm, reinforce, and amplify tourists' own sense of accomplishment, power, and/or sense of self. That is, they may feel that they "ticked off" a site to be seen once in one's life, or that they got the best of an unequal bargain by walking away from the slot machines. They may feel amplified and confirmed by their ability to perform on the various stage sets, to be glamorous in their own eyes, to run with crowds imagined to be well off, to put on a swagger, "live larger," or just wear or do something more daring than they would at home. This is a potent economic product in high demand. But what is it; what is the product? Las Vegas deals in mixtures of affect and affords stage sets such as the Strip for experimenting with or enacting affective experiences, small and large. This product is virtual: the momentary as-if-ness of a life not actually lived, of a standard of living not actually possessed.

Rather than being a geography of nowhere, Las Vegas nihilism is hardly empty—nor is it destructive in a simple manner, as comments about wealth "going up in smoke" imply. It is clearly located and spatialized not as "nowhere" but as an "elsewhere" in contrast to its clientele's everyday lives.

To properly understand it, the Las Vegas Strip has to be analyzed in conjunction with tourists' places of origin, not as an isolated entity. Both workers' and tourists' hometowns are related to The Strip within an overarching spatialization. This cultural formation makes sense of what people actually do in these different locations (Shields 1991). The uncomfortable truth is that it evidently satisfies some need or provides an outlet for desires not satisfied at home. Perhaps this is the more significant nihilism of North American life?

The affect of escape to these sites is couched in the naturalization of service workers as part of the background decor of casinos and selective acknowledgment of the participants in the street life of The Strip. Not everyone present in these scenes is indulging in a temporary utopia of personal consumption. The play of surfaces and decor which distracts from a systematic inspection of the situation in, for example, a resort casino's gambling halls, gives rise to an economy of attention in which affect is separated from ethics. That is, the emotive and imagined is disconnected from action and from embodiment. A commonly reported feeling is that one tends to be numbed or guided in relation to the periodic shouts of winners or sports-channel fans watching on large televisions in adjoining areas. Expressions of emotion don't appear to have the social import and effect on others that they might in other settings. While noticed, they become merely an "acting out" of the pent-up emotions of players and of spectators. Meanwhile, slot machines require repeated actions over long spans of time and attention to rapid displays of results and minor choices among options. Analysis is repressed in favour of distraction and the mechanical gestures of gross muscles. This is an ecology of repressed affects, equally as nihilistic an environment as those of single-industry resource towns in which people are encouraged to exist only to work (see Dorow and Dogu in this volume).

On The Strip, hope is entirely individualized and couched in the future as a misplaced desire for miracles: winning big rather than actualizing a talent or a latent capacity in oneself or one's environment. This entails more than a calculated bet on probabilities (actual possibles) that can be realized as a windfall. It involves a suspension of calculation and a hope that abstracted, not real, not actual fantasy objects will be somehow realized. Vegas itself is desired as a line of flight from the actual—that is, as an escape from the realities of everyday life and even a denial of the probabilities of the betting and gambling industry. Nostalgia is similarly related to those who may once have realized their hopes via gambling in this place—a realization that seems improbable and impossible in the now-time of consumption and chance.

Tourist Affect

In any description of Las Vegas, affect abounds: desire or fear, loathing or delight. Vegas realizes hopes for better climate but also entertains hopes for a liberation from cares and from the economic constraints of wages that never seem to stretch far enough to cover the costs of participation in North American consumer society. Its desires are represented in the media or enforced through suburban home ownership, which in turn may require automobiles and so on. There is even a faint, almost indiscernible quality of nostalgia for earlier times of 1960s popular entertainment and "great" gamblers, but this is muted, and few cues are preserved in Las Vegas's ongoing self-consumption as older hotels are detonated to make way for ever newer constructions.

Affect is most easily identified as the sensation of an anticipated encounter, positive (rising, joy) or negative (falling, sadness, dread, and a sense of anticlimax). It is the preconscious nascence of responses to stimuli (see Introduction in this volume). An environment such as the Las Vegas Strip offers a stage set that simulates rising affect through a fantasy of wealth and status, glamour and esteem—an illusion of individual differentiation, social recognition, positive reinforcement, and enhanced capacities: the "states of a body by which its power of acting is increased or lessened, helped or hindered, and also the ideas of these states" (Spinoza 2004, 51: Part 3, Def. 3). There is a constant flow or variation of the logical content of our consciousness but also perpetual change in our state or sentiments as we react to our surroundings. This does not depend on a comparative evaluation of ideas or states (Spinoza 2004). The mind does not "have" ideas but *is* "its" flux of ideas, each of which has its affective aspect. While Spinoza's rationalism and geometricism is often given pride of place as a critique of religious superstition, affect also welds the operations of imagination into his theoretical understanding of the individual actor in a double-edged manner. Spinoza attempts to contextualize the Cartesian body, which is the limit to and other of reason. Thus, imagination and the nonrational are acknowledged and integrated (see Gatens and Lloyd 1999, 27). Imagination is not merely a source of distorting illusion but a politically and intellectually essential resource to remedy a deficiency in reason itself. "The stimulation of the 'imagination' leads to a higher performance of adequate thought through ... the innate power of thinking. This transition is the source of active joy ... and ... adequate thought" (Schrijvers 2001, 77).

What makes Spinoza a useful ally in an analysis of The Strip is not just his integration of passion or some form of drives, but also his insight that imagination plays a powerful role in binding together humans into groups and into complex communities. Mimesis and identification between individuals opens up a space of intersubjectivity. Affect is therefore central to any social science; indeed, it is the foundational requirement on which any "sociological imagination" might be built.

Like a gambler realizing he or she is out of money to continue to bet, sadness or "unpleasure is a passage to a lesser perfection" of our capacity to act (Spinoza 2004, 111: Part 4, Prop. 64, Demonstr.). However, the more adequate our ideas and our related actions, the more considered our relationship to our world, the more we are free from the arbitrary flux of affect (Yovel 2001, 51). Affect itself is *animi pathema*, the "lived passage from one degree of perfection to another" (Deleuze 1978: n.p.). Spinoza uses *passio* for passion (Spinoza 2004, 51: Part 3, Def. 3), which he criticizes as involving inadequate ideas and as typifying unreflected-upon and passively experienced situations. Both passions and affect are a natural aspect of the body[6] and its practical interactions and its striving to exist (*conatus*)—but Spinoza advocated that passions should be turned actively toward the pursuit of self-enlightenment via rationality and self-awareness. Spinoza makes critical use of the distinction between active and passive, advocating understanding and Reason as the path to self-understanding and active affective engagement so that one enters intentionally rather than passively into relations with other bodies, objects, and the environment.

The Strip

Consider, in this context of escape, affect, and virtuality, The Strip. Four miles long, six and more lanes wide, The Strip brings car mobility to the heart of most tourists' Las Vegas experience, as well as being a line of casino resorts. For North American English speakers, "The Strip" connotes the commercial quality of developments along it, as well as illicit qualities associated with sex, money, and exploitation. "Strip" also suggests the cartoon quality of its simulations and architectural caricatures, and more subtly, the play of surface and glimpses of a veiled depth, of appearance and reality—the tease of a nightclub stripper's routine. It is not truly a boulevard, an avenue, or a promenade. Nor is The Strip a "street" like others in an urban grid or even a highway departing it. Instead, it appears as its own line of flight, arrowing out of the city centre of Las Vegas in curious proximity to the airport. It is almost a parallel runway, but apparently leads to no destination.

While the sidewalks are relatively wide, The Strip is a pedestrian environment where crossing the street is impossible mid-block and involves a perceptible trek across asphalt at intersections. If the roadbed affords little to the pedestrian, automobiles dominate, whether as individual cars or as a mass of creeping and idling traffic (see Tiessen in this volume).[7] While they have the option of taking relatively expensive double-decker buses, and decidedly expensive taxis, most tourists walk The Strip either as purely touristic flâneurs or en route to destinations such as the Venetian Hotel's architectural simulacra of the Doge's Palace and the Eiffel Tower, or the evening spectacle of fountains with music and lights outside the Belaggio. Some go to specific shops, and a smaller number seek out the restaurants or attractions of other hotels. One could transport Deleuze's spatial illustration of affect:

> I walk down a street where I know people....
>
> I run into Pierre [or to unwelcome Others], for whom I feel hostility, I pass by and say hello to Pierre, or perhaps I am afraid of him, and then I suddenly see Paul [or a sight which attracts my amazed attention] who is very very charming, and I say hello to Paul re-assuredly and contentedly.... In part, succession of two ideas, the idea of Pierre and the idea of Paul; but there is something else: a variation also operates in me.... When the idea of Paul succeeds the idea of Pierre, it is agreeable to say that my force of existing or my power of acting is increased or improved.... This representation of existence already isn't bad, it really is existence in the street, it's necessary to imagine Spinoza strolling about. (Deleuze 1978)

Spinoza foreshadows the sense of The Strip as a space of adventure and encounter. Deleuze foregrounds Spinoza's ethics as a proto-geopolitics of everyday affect. Queasy or overjoyed, affect names the colours of our social spaces. *Social space* and mobile, interacting *bodies* are central to Spinoza's psychological ethics and essential mediators between Spinoza and Deleuze. This allows the latter to appropriate and reread the former's *Ethics* for contemporary purposes. In his *Lecture*, Deleuze draws out the meaning of affect through socio-spatial scenarios such as walking, which are very similar to the experience of mixed encounters on The Strip. I compose myself with the traffic and with others of the crowd of strollers, leisure-seekers, and tourists.

Not only do hotels attempt to keep visitors within the casino resort, but inquiries about walking are dampened with advice that empty areas between hotels are dangerous and unpleasant. These places are mostly just empty and unaesthetic (see Figure 5.3); thus most visitors are unaware of the smaller motels and facilities in between big hotels or just off The Strip

Figure 5.3 Abandoned lots and construction projects along The Strip. (Photo credit: R. Shields)

and are not affected by hawkers or called back to critical consciousness. Learning about the city is frustrated by the relative isolation of The Strip as a self-contained leisure space that takes its cue from other totally designed environments such as malls and from the facilities management practices of other built retail environments. While urban- or tropical-themed resorts abound on The Strip, even the acoustic and olfactory qualities of each casino resort are engineered to distinguish it from others. Thus MGM Grand smells quite distinct from other gambling floors. "Music-theming" is carried to its apogee at the Hard Rock Hotel and Casino (see also Johnson 1998; Patridge 2004).

Liminal Passage: The Space of Affect

On The Strip, a new form of group hawking has emerged. The hawkers form a line that melds with the crowd (and can scatter quickly). Characteristically flicking decks of cards or handbills to make an audible raffling noise, they appeal for custom and push brothels' calling cards into the unsuspecting and often surprised hands of passing pedestrians who are novices to the Strip. They have no choice but to run the gauntlet of the line. The bodies of these hawkers are distinct from those of the overfed but able-bodied tourists; they are marked by their race (for the crowd is *so* white), dress, language, body size, and youth, and by their knowing comportment based on the reality of casino economics, not the fantasy. Finally, they stand out as a result of their diverging affect: they are working in a team rather than at leisure as individuals or in groups of friends or family. This encounter with desperation, racialization, and class distinction detonates the illusion of a momentary utopia where chance favours all. *Fortuna!* Ambushed, one is called back to critical consciousness in the form of a struggle to only selectively relate to Others and to the environment of The Strip by careful vigilance—who approaches now? This is not a call to revolution or even enlightenment; it is more likely to spark a re-engagement in the micro politics of the lumpen crowd practice by raising one's guard. Regardless, group hawking stands as the most critical intervention to take on the affective economy of The Strip. How might we understand this? Deleuze (1978) advances a striking reading of the ethics of encounter:

> Spinoza, in the *Ethics,* uses the Latin term: *occursus* ... the encounter. I encounter bodies, my body never stops encountering bodies. The bodies that he encounters sometimes have relations which compose, sometimes have relations which don't compose with his. What happens when I encounter a body whose relation doesn't compose with mine?... [A] phenomenon happens which is like a kind of fixation.... That is, a part of my power is entirely devoted to investing and to isolating the trace, on me, of the object which doesn't agree with me. It is as if I tense my muscles ... in other words I devote a part of my power to investing the trace of the thing ... to put it at a distance, to avert it.... [T]his quantity of power [force] that I've devoted to investing the trace of the disagreeable thing ... is no longer at my disposal. This is the tonality [of] affective sadness: a part of my power serves this unworthy need ... Spinoza said: like lost time, like it would have been more valuable to avoid this situation.

As a public space, the fantasy urbanism of the Strip is not simply an inclusive street and sidewalk. Its success is partly related to its ability to stage a public performance of elitism, that is, of exclusion of the poor (Blumenberg and Ehrenfeucht 2008), of racial dominance whereby ethnic Others (Hispanics, Asians, and Blacks) appear mostly as service workers (Davis 1992). It is a drama of "conspicuous consumption, class leveling and social climbing" (Simon 2004, 7). Policy rhetorically dehumanizes the poor by alluding to "Don't feed the animals" posters found in zoos with the slogan "Don't feed the homeless" (Jost 2006). The result of these and other ordinances to forbid the sharing of food or feeding of the poor in public (or via mobile soup kitchens), supposedly in the name of public health, "sends the message in each city that implements them that those in need are not seen as part of the 'public' of public space" by impinging on the rights and attempting to channel the congregation of the homeless and indigent (England 2008). Encounter and avoidance, even exclusion, are the tangible forms of the intangible flux of affect.

Flickering Syncresis of Affect

As a lived transition, affect is liminoid[8] in its spatiality. It is an interaction and communication between bodies. While it is experienced by a body, it is the experience of another and is a property of the interaction, properly speaking. It is not reducible to either party, nor to a response to a stimulus. In its temporality, affect figures change (between states over time). The difficulty of affect lies in reifying it as an apperception or emotion. Affect thus defies the symbolic order. It is sub-symbolic, a-signifying. "Affect is the 'inter' of feeling as such: binding dynamism of the in-between" (Massumi 2002, 27). If affect is always the flow in between crystallized states that are more easily characterized, it defies theory, which depends upon static, representational building blocks. Syncresis names the flickering in-between-ness of affect.

Its liminoid qualities mean that there is a vagrancy or mobility to affect. It is not only fleeting but its character is fluid, and it has no fixed address. Its suspended, in-between-ness, hints at the radical ambivalence of affect where transition does not necessarily determine an end state. Affect is not teleological (Jarret 2001; Rice 2001; Ben-Ze'ev 2001), but radically cast between, a metric of the capacity to act in relation to a particular context, encounter, and a particular Other. It is thus a calculus of the adequacy or "perfection" of one's humanity—that is, species-being understood as one's capabilities—at any given moment. Affect is a space in time, a spatio-temporal moment where conflicts can appear—conflicts involving not only representations but also affects (Bertrand 1983, 84). If the temporality of affect is duration, the spatiality of affect is the interval, "cut," or interstice betwixt and between emotional state and dispositions.

Rather than a world of subjects, syncresis delivers us into a world of bodies, or embodiments and interactions between specifically localized bodies, objects, and environments as lived passage—*duration concretized*, embodied. Where opportunities arise to enter into alternative relations and assemblages for purposes other than those legitimated by dominant forces—such as the lines of group hawkers—the space itself is reconfigured. This links Spinoza's *Ethics* to what de Certeau (1985) refers to as tactics of space, in contrast to dominant strategic control of social spaces and environments. Affect is not a geometrical relation between subjects, but rather is the very constitution of modulating subjectivities and our sense of ourselves as capable beings in relation to a context. The Strip is less a boulevard in which things happen than a syncretic affective and material space of flows in which affect is a part of spatial relations among subjects and the environment.

Affect recasts monadic encounters as subliminal exchanges and power relations between emotionally charged and motivated bodies. It churns what Spinoza calls *occursus*, the encounter and concrete "occurrence," into the liminal time-space of passage; it allows contingently performed subjectivities to be understood as immanent to their interactions and to The Strip. In its syncresis, affect recasts the event of meeting into a flow or durée of momentary states and dispositions of the self—a process that involves both virtualization and actualization. That is, it involves both a virtualization of the embodied encounter and an actualization of capacities. Affect has not only an internal dynamism as passage between crystallized (emotional) states but also a flickering quality between the virtual and the concrete. *Syncresis* designates this exchange or mobility between the ideal and actual as continuous actualization and virtualization. Syncresis is a porous, incomplete merging of different elements which preserves enough of the originals' identities to not fully subsume them into a new synthesis. Affect is both virtual and material, straddling the divide between actual and ideal. While it is known through its effects (a classic definition of the virtual), it exists as an interface between material states and bodies (Shields 2003).

The spatiality of affect means that it could be understood as the relational intersection of the potentialities of objects and bodies—their range of capacities (acknowledged or not, actualized or not) to combine synergistically or to resist and remain distinct. It is not just bodies that interact but the capacities of bodies are in brought into communication. They can be exchanged, join and supplement each other, or diffract and negate each other's potential. That is, this is not a mere discussion of physics or mechanics as when billiard balls collide. Thus in the case of the "thing whose relations don't agree with mine, why does it affect me with sadness, that is decrease my power of acting" (Deleuze 1978)? Because power involves limiting others' capacity to act, this allows Spinoza to pose the exercise of power in ethical terms. Whether the sadness of time lost or the joy of time gained, affect is space-time. Duration stabilizes what might otherwise be a merely analytical element. In as much as it "takes place," in both the temporal and spatial senses of the phrase, affect is actualized in a continuous, syncretic oscillation between the virtual and material.

The Strip is the inverse of what is usually meant by territorialization, which is often used to designate a form of actualization of a virtuality such as "society" which takes specific local form in a time and place. But affect as a time-space of lived syncresis accomplishes a *displacement* from land into meaning-laden landscape via the mediating capacity of the virtual "space-between" these two states. The process of syncresis accomplishes a socialization of time and space at the same time as the social is spatialized. Affect brings space into the realm of the social in the sense of a microgeography of territories and assembled interfacing bodies and objects. Affect is a liminoid break in any attempt to homogenize space. Spaces themselves create affect, and the management of space and spatialization amounts to the management of affect, of the power of actions to be efficacious and to be understood in their full significance. Thus affects fit closely with spaces: they do not seem to be easily separated from context but unite body, mind (imagination), ideas, and interaction by transcending each of these. To give a simple example, we often recall emotions and experiences not even by a name but in relation to places and situations. But the brute landscape in which we live takes on personal and collective sense. It is recollected not as a terrain or sites of this or that emotion. Rather it is a different topology, a translated or syncretic geography that is not simply physical but very much "of affects." The Strip's secret formula is that it doesn't have sense as, for example, a site of some past happiness where that single happiness is re-experienced. Rather it is recollected or encountered within a broader spatialization as a site of the passive affect of "joy," where the affect of a past experience of increased potential, self-affirmation, or capacity can be relived as an affect brought into the present moment.

Notes

1 Affect is central to understanding "non-representational theory," for although this misnomer obscures the fact that all theory is representation, non-representational mental activity and thought—for example, sentiments such as love—are precisely examples of the affects these theories attempt to grapple with. The distinction between the idea of an emotion and an affect is one between conceptual thought, which represents something, and non-representational thought such as hope, pain, or love, which, strictly speaking, represent nothing beyond themselves even though they presuppose an idea, such as an idea of what is loved (see Frijda 2001). In a similar manner, cultural geographers have parsed shifts in advertising and retail theory to think in terms of a "libidinal economy"

of desire and away from Freudian understandings of motivation, structured around absence and lack. In post-structural theories of the libidinal as a productive motivator, desire is understood as productive, as a vitalistic forward-driving impulse, closely tied to affect.

2   For example, in 2004 about 392,000 people visited Las Vegas from Great Britain, Las Vegas's largest overseas market, which amounts to just over 1 percent of the total 38,566,717 visitors that year. Also that year, Japan, the number two overseas market for Las Vegas, sent 217,000 travellers to Las Vegas (U.S. Department of Commerce Office of Travel and Tourism Industries cited in Velotta 2005; CBER 2008). In 2007, only 12 percent of Las Vegas's tourists had an international origin; 79 percent of foreign visitors were married. In 2003, 79 percent were repeat visitors with an average stay of 3.7 days. In 2007 Canada, Mexico, Great Britain, Japan, and Germany represented about 76 percent of foreign visits.

3   Statistics for 2002 are as follows: visitor volume 35,071,504; hotel rooms 126,787 (84 percent occupancy); airline passengers 35,009,011; conventioneers 5,105,450. For 2007: visitor volume 39,196,761; hotel rooms 132,947 (90.4 percent occupancy); airline passengers 47,728,414; conventioneers 6,209,253 (CBER, 2008).

4   Las Vegas was strongly affected by the economic recession of 2008–09, with occupancy rates at Wynn hotels quoted by *Time* magazine as hitting a low of 72 percent (Stein 2009, 23), leading to reductions in costs and a halt to construction. Without paying customers, the formula for financing the expansion of gambling collapsed, resulting in foreclosures and bankruptcies. The financing for Las Vegas is intertwined with that of the expansion of Dubai as a global tourism destination, financed by Dubai World and other banks that are active in real estate speculation globally (for example, in Macao and Singapore; see Stein 2009, 26, 29). By the summer of 2009, idled construction projects lined one side of The Strip in particular and included the Hilton Grand, a time-share condominium, Boyd Gaming Corp.'s $4.8 billion Echelon, the bankrupt Fontainebleau casino hotel, Trump Towers second tower, Las Vegas Sands Corp.'s St. Regis condominium, and Harrah's Entertainment's $1 billion expansion of Caesars Palace, leaving only MGM Mirage's $8.4 billion City Centre project underway. This amounts to over $9 billion in cancelled or delayed construction, with major impacts on Las Vegas households and thus on the residential real estate market, where houses are worth less than buyers paid for them. Nevada's foreclosure rate in 2008 was highest in the United States, at 72.9 per 1000 homes.

5   The all-male Rat Pack included Sammy Davis, Jr., Frank Sinatra, Peter Lawford, Dean Martin, and Joey Bishop. Lesser known as members were actresses Shirley MacLaine, Lauren Bacall, and Judy Garland.

6   See the debates between Misrahi and Beyssade over whether or not "affect" should be reserved for "the realities that refer to the mind" (see Revault d'Allones 2001; compare Beyssade 2001 versus Misrahi 1990). There appears to be a tendency among North American theorists to turn the discussion toward psychoanalytic theories of the unconscious (see Davidson 2001), to which Spinoza's concept of "imagination" seems very comparable.

7 Affect is the change in capacities of bodies in context whereas affordances are, in a similar sense, specifically the capacities of objects and environments to allow bodies to enter into certain combinations or assemblages with each other and to rule out other combinations. However, affect is dynamic and responsive, whereas affordances have been theorized to be simply either present or latent unless objects are transformed to realize new possibilities (see Gibson 1982 and Tiessen in this volume).

8 In the anthropology of performance, *limen* or threshold designates social spaces and moments held apart from everyday life, often for rites of passage or ritual dramas which are 'betwixt and between' different social states or statuses (Turner 1969). As such, liminality is characterized by suspension rather than inversion of social codes, symbols, and norms (Shields 1991).

References

Baird, J., R. M. Adelman, L. W. Reid, and C. Jaret. 2008. Immigrant settlement patterns: The role of metropolitan characteristics. *Sociological Inquiry* 78 (3): 310–34.

Barbour, D. 2000. Las Vegas: The new showrooms. *Entertainment Design* 34 (2): 43–45.

Bataille, G. 1988. *The accursed share: An essay on general economy*. New York: Zone Books.

Ben-Ze'ev, A. 2001. Emotions and change: A Spinozistic Account. In *Desire and affect: Spinoza as psychologist*, ed. Y. Yovel, 129–38. New York: Little Room Press.

Bertrand, M. 1983. *Spinoza et l'imaginaire, Philosophie d'aujourd'hui*. Paris: Presses universitaires de France.

Beyssade, J. M. 2001. *Nostri corporis affectus*: Can an affect in Spinoza be "of the body"? In *Desire and affect: Spinoza as psychologist,* ed. Y. Yovel, 113–28. New York: Little Room Press.

Binkowski, C. J. 2008. Review of *Candy Barr: The small-town Texas runaway who became a darling of the mob and the Queen of Las Vegas burlesque*. *Library Journal* 133 (11): 70.

Blumenberg, E., and R. Ehrenfeucht. 2008. Civil liberties and the regulation of public space: The case of sidewalks in Las Vegas. *Environment and Planning A* 40 (2): 303–22.

CBER (Center for Business and Economic Research). 2008. Metropolitan Las Vegas tourism statistics. Las Vegas: University of Nevada. http://cber.unlv .edu/tour.html (accessed April 29, 2009).

Citton, Y., and F. Lordon. 2008. *Spinoza et les sciences sociales*. Paris: Editions Amsterdam.

Cohen, S., and L. Taylor. 1976. *Escape attempts: The theory and practice of resistance to everyday life*. London: Allen Lane.

Crawford, M. 1992. The world in a shopping mall. In *Variations on a theme park: The new American City and the end of public space*, ed. M. Sorkin, 3–30. New York: Hill and Wang.

Dannatt, A. 2002. Learning from Las Vegas: New Guggenheim Museum in the Venetian Resort-Hotel-Casino, Las Vegas—Rem Koolhaas architect. *Connaissance Des Arts* (590): 100–107.

Davidson, D. 2001. Spinoza's Causal Theory of the Affects. In *Desire and affect: Spinoza as psychologist*, ed. Y. Yovel, 95–112. New York: Little Room Press.

Davis, M. 1992. Blacks are dealt out—racial caldron in Las Vegas. *Nation* 255 (1): 7–10.

Debouzy, M. 2006. Service workers in Las Vegas since the 1980s. *Mouvement Social* (216): 75–76.

de Certeau, M. 1985. Practices of Space. In *On signs*, ed. M. Blonsky, 122–45. Baltimore, MD: Johns Hopkins University Press.

Deleuze, G. 1978. *Lecture transcripts on Spinoza's concept of affect (Cours Vincennes 24 January 1978)*. http://www.webdeleuze.com/php/sommaire.html (accessed May 25, 2010).

England, M. R. 2008. "No soup for you": Public space and food provision ordinances. *Critical Geography* 08, Ohio University. http://www.as.phy.ohiou.edu/Departments/Geography/critical_geog_conference_files/Crit-Geog08_Presenter_Abstracts_and_Bios.pdf.

Frijda, N. H. 2001. The self and emotions. In *Identity and emotion*, ed. H. A. Bosma and E. S. Kunnen, 39–57. Paris: Cambridge University Press.

Gatens, M., and G. Lloyd. 1999. *Collective imaginings: Spinoza, past and present*. London; New York: Routledge.

Gendall, J. 2006. Architecture's claim to fame (Las Vegas). *Architectural Record* 194 (10): 272.

Gibson, J. J. 1982. *Reasons for realism: Selected essays of James J. Gibson*. Hillsdale, NJ: Lawrence Earlbaum and Assoc.

Gladstone, D. L. 1998. Tourism urbanization in the United States. *Urban Affairs Review* 34 (1): 3–27.

Gottdiener, M., C. Collins, and D. Dickens. 1999. *Las Vegas: The production of an all-American city*. London: Wiley-Blackwell.

Goux, J. J. 1998. General economics and postmodern capitalism. In *Bataille: A critical reader*, ed. F. Botting and S. Wilson, 196–213. Oxford: Blackwell.

Hannigan, J. 1998. *Fantasy city: Pleasure and profit in the postmodern metropolis*. London: Routledge.

Irazabal, C. 2007. Kitsch is dead, long live kitsch: The production of hyperkitsch in Las Vegas. *Journal of Architectural and Planning Research* 24 (3): 199–223.

Jarret, C. 2001. Teleology and Spinoza's doctrine of final causes. In *Desire and affect: Spinoza as psychologist*, ed. Y. Yovel, 3–24. New York: Little Room Press.

Johnson, D. 1998. Sound like an Egyptian (Sound designer Mike Cusick worked closely with the architect of the new performance space at the Luxor-Hotel-&-Casino in Las-Vegas). *Tci* 32 (2): 13–15.

Jost, D. 2006. Don't feed the homeless (Las Vegas strategy to discourage indigents from using city parks). *Landscape Architecture* 96 (11): 147–48.

Junemo, M. 2004. "Let's build a palm island!": Playfulness in complex times. In *Tourism mobilities: Places to play, places in play*, ed. M. Sheller and J. Urry, 181–91. London: Routledge.

KIVI-TV. 2010. U.S. foreclosures fall 10%, Idaho among highest foreclosure rates, February 11. *Today's 6 News*, Boise, Idaho (ABC Television affiliate). http://www.kivitv.com/global/story.asp?s=11968878 (accessed February 27, 2010).

Kunstler, J. 1993. *The geography of nowhere: The rise and decline of America's man-made landscape*. New York: Simon and Schuster.

Lampert-Greaux, E. 2000. A tale of two cities—the theming of the Strip continues with Paris-Las-Vegas and the Venetian. *Entertainment Design* 34 (2): 40–43.

Massumi, B. 2002. *Parables for the virtual*. Durham, NC: Duke University Press.

McCormack, D. P. 2003. An event of geographical ethics in spaces of affect. *Transactions of the Institute of British Geographers* 28 (4): 488–507.

Misrahi, R. 1990. *Ethique*. Paris: Presses universitaires de France.

Patridge, D. 2004. Listening in Las Vegas—as musical theatre takes hold of Sin City, audio pros are heading West. (There is a synergy of elements that come together to make up the landscape of shows in the Las Vegas valley.) *Entertainment Design* 38 (10): 36–37.

Poyner, A. M. 1998. Watering Las Vegas. *Geography* 83 (358): 37–45.

Raento, P. 2009. Las Vegas: Media and myth. *Urban Studies* 46 (4): 969–70.

Revault d'Allones, M. 2001. Affect of the body and socialization. *Desire and affect: Spinoza as psychologist*, ed. Y. Yovel, 183–90. New York: Little Room Press.

Rice, L. 2001. Action in Spinoza's account of affectivity. In *Desire and affect: Spinoza as psychologist*, ed. Y. Yovel, 155–68. New York: Little Room Press.

Schmid, H. 2006. Economy of fascination: Dubai and Las Vegas as examples of themed urban landscapes. *Erdkunde* 60 (4): 346–61.

Schrijvers, M. 2001. The *conatus* and the mutual relationship between active and passive affects in Spinoza. In *Desire and affect: Spinoza as psychologist*, ed. Y. Yovel, 63–80. New York: Little Room Press.

Scott, A. 1980. *The urban land nexus and the state*. London: Pion.

Scott, A. J. 1997. The cultural economy of cities. *International Journal of Urban and Regional Research* 21 (2): 323–39.

———. 2006. *Geography and economy: Three lectures*. Oxford; New York: Oxford University Press; Clarendon Press.

Sheller, M. 2008. Always turned on: Atlantic City as America's accursed share. In *Consuming the entrepreneurial city*, ed. K. Hetherington and A. Cronin, 107–26. London: Routledge.

Shields, R. 1991. *Places on the margin*. London: Routledge.

———. 1997. Ethnography in the crowd: The body, sociality and globalization in Seoul. *Focaal: Tijdschrift voor Antropologie* 30/31: 23–38.

———. 2003. *The virtual*. London: Routledge.

———. forthcoming. *Topologies of space*. London: Sage.

Shih-Diing, L. 2008. Casino colony (Reprinted). *New Left Review* (50): 109–24.

Simon, B. 2004. *Boardwalk of dreams: Atlantic City and the fate of urban America*. New York: Oxford University Press.

Spinoza, B. 2004. *Ethics demonstrated in geometrical order*, trans. S. Shirley, updated by J. Bennett. http://www.earlymoderntexts.com/pdf/spinoza.pdf (accessed April 30, 2010).

Stein, J. 2009. Less Vegas, August 24. *Time* 174 (7): 22–29.

Stychin, C. F. 2006. "Las Vegas is not where we are": Queer readings of the Civil Partnership Act. *Political Geography* 25 (8): 899–920.

Thrift, N. J. 2008. *Non-representational theory: Space, politics, affect*. London; New York: Routledge.

Turner, V. 1969. *The ritual process: Structure and anti-structure*. Chicago: Aldine.

Velotta, R. 2005. Getting a handle on international tourism, October 18. *Las Vegas Sun*. http://www.lasvegassun.com/news/2005/oct/18/getting-a-handle-on-international-tourism/ (accessed April 29, 2009).

Venturi, R., S. Izenour, and D. Scott Brown. 1977. *Learning from Las Vegas*. Cambridge, MA: MIT Press.

Whitfield, S., D. Miller, P. Wagner, K. A. Edmundson, and L. Stanfill. 2004. Unsung heroes of Las Vegas. (Backstage mavens who keep Vegas entertainment running smoothly). *Entertainment Design* 38 (11): 8–9.

Yeung, Y., J. Lee, and G. Kee. 2008. Hong Kong and Macao under Chinese sovereignty. *Eurasian Geography and Economics* 49 (3): 304–25.

Yovel, Y. 2001. Transcending mere survival: From *conatus* to *conatus intelligendi*. In *Desire and affect: Spionoza as psychologist*, ed. Y. Yovel, 45–62. New York: Little Room Press.

Zhou, W. X., and D. Sornette. 2008. Analysis of the real estate market in Las Vegas: Bubble, seasonal patterns, and prediction of the CSW indices. *Physica A: Statistical Mechanics and Its Applications* 387 (1): 243–60.

6

(In)Human Desiring and Extended Agency

MATTHEW TIESSEN

In order to relate everything to oneself, one must first of all be this Self to whom everything is related.... I am indeed myself, but I am not brought to myself in this me that I am. I am given to myself, but it is not me myself who gives me to me. (Henry 2003, 104)

In this chapter I will explore how desire, hope, and place can be rethought by rethinking the role of relationship. My observation is that relationships are not a product of the meeting of definable entities or concepts, but rather themselves constitute and determine what we—in retrospect—later come to identify as singular or seemingly independent "individuals." When understood this way, individual *things* become *products* of the relationships that bring them into being.

My interest in the significance of relationships for the constitution of objects derives from my work on "desire lines" (Tiessen 2007), which in turn derives from my enthusiasm for the sport of mountain biking—for flying along narrow and technically challenging ribbons of dirt on two human-powered (and sometimes, hill-powered) wheels. These two-wheeled trajectories are routinely expressed in the form of desire lines (see Figure 6.1).

Desire Lines

Although *desire line* is not the most common of terms, desire lines are ubiquitous in our everyday lives. Desire lines are identified by architects or urban

Figure 6.1 Accepting the desire line's invitation on two wheels. (Photo credit: M. Tiessen)

planners as those footpaths we all contribute to when our strolling deviates from preplanned directional imperatives such as paved walkways. A desire line can cut across a field on a university campus or weave among flowers in a forest. Often desire lines are regarded by planners as problems—as muddy scars on the landscape—and are sometimes blocked with barriers or "made official" by being paved over. Desire lines can be inaugurated by us— by, for example, forging a footpath through newly fallen snow—or can be offered to us fully formed.

The term itself—*desire line*—is, not unlike the term *inhuman*, an anthropocentric one, suggesting that the paths *we* trace through the dirt are or were willed into being by *our* all-too-human desires. However, as Maurice Merleau-Ponty (1968) has described using his concept "Flesh" or "chiasm," and as Deleuze and Guattari (1987) have suggested with their concepts "assemblage" and "machinic phylum," what we perceive as human agency when we think of people forging paths is more complex than the simple image the desire line might suggest. By studying how desire lines come into being we can begin to observe why it is not merely the human who can be described as "agential." This is the case because human beings act, make decisions, and pursue pathways in response to and in relation to the actions—indeed, invitations—of their environment and, ultimately, of the panoply of forces, dispositions, and limitations that constitutes that especially large prosthetic appendage that envelops us all—the earth. My suggestion is that reflecting upon how desire lines come into being—upon the conditions of their emergence—can provide us with a way to understand the degree to which humans (and human "desires," etc.) are interpenetrated, riven, and always already mediated— and even determined—by relationships with human and nonhuman "objects" that might not conventionally be thought to have agency of their own.

Mountain Bikers and Relation

Mountain bikers look for, respond to, and create lines of desire; they seek out challenging trails that enable them to achieve maximum "flow," that enable them to respond and interact with the earth's offerings. They thereby become a sort of bio-techno-human-hybrid—the Mountain Biker—that generates euphoria, thrills, and adrenaline. The earth, in turn, insofar as it affords these abilities to the biker-hybrid, actualizes one of *its* capacities— the capacity to afford fun, to provide us with thrills and spills. This intra-action—this affecting and being affected—is achieved, it should be noted, with less impact on the earth than more destructive, motorized forms of deep-woods entertainment (see Figure 6.2).

Figure 6.2 Carving a desired line. (Photo credit: M. Tiessen)

When out biking or walking, we might find that we are compelled to follow particular trajectories that seem as though they've been laid out before
us as a sort of invitation; indeed, we could even think of these earthly offerings beckoning to us (in the form of a clearing, a splendid view, a geographical formation, etc.) as gifts (and even as gifted—like a child with surprising
abilities). My suggestion, then, is that desire lines can be thought of as being
offered up to us, like a present, like an invitation to become part of something larger—a relationship. The gap in the trees, for example, can be thought
of as literally inviting us in, urging us to explore, to uncover its offerings
and, in turn, to uncover ourselves. Desire lines are *made available* by the
ground itself before we accept the invitation to follow them. The gap in the
trees, the edge of a hill, and the beauty of a landscape all have particular
abilities—or affordances—that beckon to us. By accepting the desire line's
invitation, we, to paraphrase Spinoza, contribute to the actualization of what
we and a gap in the trees "can do."

Techno-theorist Manuel DeLanda (2003) urges us to "not privilege the
viewpoint of the human observer" (n.p.), suggesting instead that matter,
both organic and inorganic, is active and has its own sort of agency that
accords with its propensities and range of capabilities. The desire path, then,
is a product of a relationship, a reciprocal relationship of offering (by the top-
ographical context) and acceptance (by you or me); in turn, we contribute
our own range of capabilities or effects to the environment—and the loop
continues. (Of course, the relationship between entities within environments can also be destructive and annihilating, but these types of relations,
insofar as they are not sustainable, are of little interest to self-preservatory
desires.) What desire lines have the potential to reveal is the degree to which
the "humanistic" boundaries that have defined us have been a *conceptual*
reality rather than one that adequately describes the relationship between
us and the world around us. As Katherine Hayles (2002) observes, beginning "with relation rather than preexisting entities changes everything,"
enabling us to observe how "embodied experience" is in constant dialogue
with the environment (298–99).

Privileging the role of relationships when thinking about agency has the
potential to call into question our understanding of our own independence,
subsuming what we regard as our "will" beneath an extended field of nonhuman but actively emergent forces. Reframing our desires and hopes as
expressions not of ourselves alone, but of relationships, intertwinings, and
interdependent becomings has the potential to alter significantly our understanding of the world around us. It also has the potential to redefine how we
understand ourselves and our situatedness in an interdependent world. If

we see ourselves, for example, as consisting of the elements of various relationships rather than as discrete individuals, or as collective enunciations or expressions of environments, then our actions—our expressions of agency—become not so much instances of our own picking and choosing, but rather examples of our propensity to act and react in accordance with both our inherent capacities to act and be acted upon and our environment's capacity to act and, more importantly, to act upon us.

Existence, when conceived as an expression of extended agential capacities, becomes an ongoing unfolding of interdependent relationships where the actions of one entity depend on the ability of another entity to be acted upon, and where the capacities of one entity are enabled by the capacities of another. That is, no act is possible without there first being a relationship from which the act can issue forth. The human no more creates something than she or he is granted this ability to "create" by the capacities and affordances of the materials (etc.) from which this creation is composed.

You could say, then, that in such an environment humans can be thought of not as individuals, agents, actors, subjects, or creators, but as articulations and expressions of their environments. Each of us is a site-in-process, a crossing, where forces come to play. Theorists Deleuze and Guattari (1987) describe such a site as a "haecceity": a singular set of relations, an individual multiplicity.[1] We are an expression of forces, a consequence and product of unpredictable and novel—though determined—capacities to affect and to be affected, as Spinoza would say. The human here is, significantly, not a person or a subject, but, as Deleuze and Guattari put it, the product of "relations of movement and rest between molecules or particles, capacities to affect and be affected" (261). In other words, it is incorrect to imagine that we are agents/subjects that interact/exist distinct from our environments—distinct from sets of relations. Deleuze and Guattari would warn us that we "must avoid an oversimplified consciliation"—that there exists on one side "formed subjects," and on the other, "spatiotemporal coordinates of the haecceity type":

> For you will yield nothing to haecceities unless you realize that that is what you are, and that you are nothing but that.... You are longitude and latitude, a set of speeds and slownesses between unformed particles, a set of non-subjectified affects. You have the individuality of a day, a season, a year, a life (regardless of its duration) a climate, a wind, a fog, a swarm, a pack (regardless of its regularity). Or at least you can have it, you can reach it. (Ibid.)[2]

We might imagine that things—including us—exist as components within a haecceity, as agents within a field of agent-like actors whose agency is not so much determined by their ability to avoid danger or pursue pleasure as it is by the capacities, affordances,[3] propensities,[4] and dispositions[5] that permit them, in a world of flux and change, to maintain—for a time— material (and immaterial) coherence and cohesion. The nature and extent of our intra-relationships[6] are not always apparent; further, we are too often compelled to focus on the (rather limited) sets of habits and clichés that derive from the all-too-human limitations of our language, epistemes, quantitative "data," etc. As Deleuze and Guattari (1987) write, "Movements, becomings [and] pure relations of speed and slowness ... are below and above the threshold of perception" (281).

On the matter of intra-relationships, Alfred North Whitehead's (1861–1947) writings precede Deleuze's by decades, yet his thought complements Deleuze's insofar as he regards becoming as issuing forth from complex sets of relationships, from a chaotic, unactualized field of process and potential. Whitehead's process ontology—a philosophy of organism[7]— attempts to take seriously the interconnected relationships between thought, the environment, causal forces, and the creation of change. Observing that the "complexity of nature is inexhaustible" (1978, 106), Whitehead attempts to reveal the teleological and anthropocentric prejudices that have defined, thus far, great swaths of Western philosophical tradition. He suggests that our subjectivity and values are too often defined by abstraction, having little to do with the world's causal processes. Whitehead observes too that our preference for teleological narratives—for conclusions, answers, finality, closure (whether in religious, political, or philosophical thought)—reveals the degree to which we cling to the "prevalent fallacy" that all forms of seriality "necessarily involve terminal instances" (111).

In *What Is Philosophy?* Deleuze and Guattari remind us, "Every territory, every habitat, joins up not only its spatiotemporal but its qualitative planes or sections," and that "every territory encompasses or cuts across the territories of other species ... forming *interspecies junction points*" (1994, 185). Here again they are describing the interwoven relationships among things—things organic and inorganic, material and immaterial, actual and virtual. They suggest that the world is an expression of relationships; they use the musical term *counterpoint* to describe the interconnected relationship of things. The capacities of habitats to support and produce "interspecies" results in what they describe as "melodic" relationships, reinforcing relationships that are not teleological but reciprocal. The relationships of counterpoint described by Deleuze and Guattari are at once determined and determining by their constitutive components, capacities, and dispositions. Deleuze and Guattari (1994) observe that these contrapuntal relationships "join planes together, form compounds of sensations ... and *determine* becomings" (185). These *determined* becomings—what they call "determinate melodic compounds"—are, in turn, expressions of those forces that support their existence, that enable them to exist upon an infinite "symphonic plane of composition" (185). Environments, habitats, and territories—haecceities—are themselves open to the outside, open to what they describe as the "cosmic forces that arise from within or come from outside" (185). These "cosmic forces," in turn, are sometimes "selected" by territories; at other times they call out to the inhabitants of a territory and launch the inhabitants "on an irresistible voyage" (185).

Reciprocity

More recently, theorist Karen Barad (2007) has described these reciprocal relationships that constitute our everyday lives (and everything else, for that matter) as relationships of "intra-action." Existence, she writes, "is not an individual affair"; individuals, she notes, "do not preexist their intra-relating" (ix). Barad, extending her work in theoretical physics, states that "time and space, like matter and meaning, come into existence [...] through each intra-action, thereby making it impossible to differentiate in any absolute sense between creation and renewal, beginning and returning, continuity and discontinuity, here and there, past and future" (ix). Barad's observations are only among the most recent to grapple with the consequences of thinking about what it means to be human within a wider landscape of entities upon which we are dependent.

It is worth acknowledging here that agency occupies somewhat uncomfortable terrain when applied to entities that are not, at the very least, "alive" in some form or other. Kauffman and Clayton (2006), for example, attempt to limit agency—that is, "minimal biological agency"—to beings that manifest certain basic physical conditions. We could say, however, that agency and what is counted as agency will be different depending on who is doing the counting. It seems too that denying agency to, for example, nonliving beings functions, at the very least, to bolster certain claims about human exceptionalism while reinforcing myths of independent action within an intradependent world. The question of agency is made more problematic by subsuming it (or disavowing it) as, at best, a misidentified fantasy where behaviour brought about by certain capacities, propensities, dispositions, or sets of affordances is understood to issue forth from a being who, despite the forces in play around it, can somehow make choices that are, in some sense, its alone.

The rest of this chapter will examine the theoretical and ethical significance of an ontology wherein human agent is decentred and resituated within an extended field of human and nonhuman "agencies." I suggest that such a decentring invites us to cultivate what I call a "modest ontology," grounded in an acknowledgment that our human capacity to act is not our own but is, in a very real sense, gifted to us by the affordances provided to us by nonhuman environments.

Affordances

To build an ontological position upon an understanding that relations come first is to recognize that the capacities inherent to what we conventionally might describe as "individuals" rely, in full, on the existence of other so-called individuals. That is, to be able to *do*, entities must not merely *be*, but *be-with* (Nancy 2000). Action implies and requires relation. *Individuals do not exist*, since individuals (were there to be such things) would have no capacities. Rather, humans and nonhuman agents alike rely on the *affordances afforded* by—constituted by—relationships.

Affordances and their ontological, psychological, and biological import are central, most famously, in the work of James Jerome Gibson (1986). For Gibson, affordances were the capacities of things—whether human or unhuman. As Gibson explains, "The verb *to afford* is found in the dictionary, but the noun *affordance* is not. I have made it up"; Gibson describes an affordance as something "that refers to both the environment and the animal in a way that no existing term does. It implies the complementarity of the animal and the environment" (127). Affordances are actionable possibilities of things that can be mobilized differently relative to different relationships, stimuli, contexts.[8]

For DeLanda, affordances distinguish something beyond the quantifiable qualities of a thing, gesturing instead toward what a thing is capable of in relation to other things. DeLanda (2002b) explains:

> A piece of ground does have its own intrinsic properties determining, for example, how horizontal or slanted, how flat, concave or convex, and how rigid it is. But to be capable of affording support to a walking animal is not just another intrinsic property; it is a capacity which may not be exercised if there are no animals around. Given that capacities are relational in this sense, what an individual affords another may depend on factors like their

relative spatial scales: the surface of a pond or lake may not afford a large animal a walking medium, but it does to a small insect which can walk on it because it is not heavy enough to break through the surface tension of the water. (72)

DeLanda (2002a) notes also that affordances are "symmetric"—involving both the Spinozist capacities to affect and to be affected: "Thus the assemblages 'walking animal-solid ground-gravity' or 'predator-prey-hole in the ground' reveal capacities which are dependent on, but not reducible to, the assemblage components' properties" (n.p.).

The affordances of things are differently determined by the relationships involved. A paintbrush and canvas and pigment afford artmaking to the artist, but do not afford artmaking to the bird, the infant, or the stone. Gibson points out that affordances can be described using the -able suffix.[9] Gibson (1986) explains, for example, that if a horizontal surface is basically flat, sufficiently extended, and fairly rigid, the surface will afford support: "It is stand-on-able, permitting an upright posture for quadrupeds and bipeds. It is therefore walk-on-able and run-over-able. It is not sink-into-able like a surface of water or a swamp, that is, not for heavy terrestrial animals" (127). He goes on to note that if we were to use the scales and standard units of physics to measure the characteristics and qualities of things, we would be able to discern particular, relatively stable relationships or ratios; this would be to measure the object's physical properties: "an affordance of support for a species of animal, however, they have to be measured *relative to the animal*. They are unique for that animal. They are not just abstract physical properties. They have unity relative to the posture and behaviour of the animal being considered. So an affordance cannot be measured as we measure in physics" (127). Of course, we can also think of desirable things or circumstances as affording us the opportunity to desire, etc.

To think of the capacities of objects, contexts, humans according to affordances is, at once, to recognize the infinite number of permutations available to us and the things of this world; we are also compelled to recognize, however, that all the options available to "things" are limited by the specific relationships in which they find themselves and the specific affordances these relationships allow. Understanding the fluctuations of existence as products of the affordances granted by relationships serves to dissolve reductive subject–object distinctions. We are left having to grapple with an awareness that an object's or an environment's affordances—its particular characteristics and abilities—exist only relative to something or someone to which these affordances are offered and then, effectively, accepted. There-

fore, insofar as an entity can be said to be composed of its respective qualities and capabilities—by what it can do—these qualities and capabilities
themselves depend on the existence of something upon which these capabilities can be exercised. So, for example, a mountain biker *becomes* a mountain biker only by responding to the invitations of the trail, the rocks, the roots,
and the trees. Similarly, for an artist, the paintbrush's "paintbrushability"
comes into existence only thanks to the generosity of the flat surface's being
paint-able.

Human beings, according to such an ontological framework, can be
thought of as *inhuman* hybrids in that our capacities are effectively determined and delimited not merely by us—by our bodies, our willpower, our
desire—but by the nonhuman agents (at both micro and macro scales—see
Hroch in this volume for more on the significance of scale) that grant us
and afford us existence. As philosopher Ansell-Pearson (1999) observes,
human behaviour "can no longer be localized in individuals …; but has to be
treated … as a function of complex material systems which cut across individuals (assemblages) and which transverse … organismic boundaries (rhizomes)"; this requires, Ansell-Pearson suggests, "the articulation of a
distributed conception of agency. The challenge is to show that nature
consists of a field of multiplicities, assemblages of heterogeneous components
(human, animal, viral, molecular, etc.) in which 'creative evolution' can be
shown to involve blocks of becoming" (171).

The affordances of things and of relationships—what things can do,
can be made to do, can do for others—is limited only by the number of combinations available to the entities involved. But while affordances may differ "from species to species and from context to context," they can't be
regarded as "freely variable" since, as theorist Ian Hutchby (2001) reminds
us, while a tree "offers an enormous range of affordances for a vast variety
of species, there are things a river can afford which the tree cannot, and vice
versa" (447). If the mountain biker, for example, is interested in exploring
new lines (new "lines of flight")—in being "cyclically-creative"—it falls to him
or her to seek out the not-yet-perceived affordances or invitations offered
by his or her environmental encounters. This requires a concerted attempt
to attune ourselves to the world around us. As Hutchby (2001) argues, we
need to pay more attention to "the material substratum" that undergirds
"the very possibility of different courses of action" (450).

We are left then with environments, entities, and individuals that
express and are expressions of a profound reciprocity. Taking this reciprocity seriously, in turn, might compel us to cling less vigorously to anthropocentric perspectives about what is and is not an agent, or what does or does

not merit ethical consideration. Further, to the extent that the world around us can be regarded as beneficial to us, we can interpret this beneficence as an expression of generosity and openness, as an open invitation to accept its gifts and to reciprocate in kind.

Additionally, and further decentring the human as the arbiter of what does or does not exist (and as modestly equipped), it's worth pointing out that most affordances exist without our being conscious of them, without their being thought. Rather, affordances can emerge only out of contexts that are adequate to their emergence (whether we're aware of it or not). Alphonso Lingis (1998) affirms this position when he observes that not only do objects "make thought do-able," but they also very often make thought possible. In a sense, then, "as parts of networks of effectivity," objects think (99).

What becomes significant, when we attune ourselves to the world of affording affordances, to a Spinozist world of affecting and being affected are the ontologically derived ethical implications of a world in which all constituents are defined by co-creative expression—of a contrapuntal world wherein entities depend on one another to bring one another into being, and where one entity cannot be valued over another out of hand since any relative value *exists* relative to and because of interconnected and dependent relationships. Deleuze and Guattari (1994) objectify the interdependent world of affordances using a tick as an example. The tick, they explain, is "organically constructed in such a way that it finds its counterpoint in any mammal whatever that passes below its branch, as oak leaves arranged in the form of tiles find their counterpoint in the raindrops that stream over them. This," they posit, "is not a teleological conception but a melodic one in which we no longer know what is art and what nature" (185). Deleuze and Guattari's is an ontology that recognizes the interconnected interaction of the world's constitutive parts, the variegated resonances that vibrate across immanence. A world of complementarity (Scarantino 2003, 950), mutual beneficence, co-generosity.

I'd like to suggest that such an ontological logic—one wherein the human is at once creative, decentred, determined, and dependent—demands an ethical stance responsive to the reciprocal nature of all relationships. Such an ethical stance, I suggest, would respond to an ontology made modest by affordances, a modest ontology that recognizes that the role of the human is currently, and has always been, subsumed within a field of cosmic forces generous enough to grant us existence and gracious enough to provide for us—to respond to our desires. Such an ontological position could challenge, for instance, ecologically destructive understandings of the non-human world as available to us merely to be used and exhausted.

By modest ontology, I am proposing a schema wherein the human inhabits the world as an experimenter and problem solver, working *with* the materials and immaterial qualities that have been afforded in pursuit of mutually beneficial—and ultimately sustainable—ends. The nonhuman world is at once integral to and integrated into human functioning and must be considered if the human is to exist successfully in perpetuity, as an organism within extended affecting and affectable environments. This, we must keep in mind, is an emergent world of *limits* insofar as it is an immanent realm of mutual reliance; indeed, we could go further in our dehumanization of the human by observing that frankly, in many respects the life-world, the cosmos, could and would get along fabulously without us. I will close with Michel Serres (1995), who reflects on the conditions under which a more modest ontology might be appropriate: "If winds, currents, glaciers, volcanoes, etc., carry subtle messages that are so difficult to read that it takes us absolutely ages trying to decipher them, wouldn't it be appropriate to call them intelligent? How would it be if it turned out that we were only the slowest and least intelligent beings in the world?" (30).

Notes

1   Deleuze and Guattari's (1987) description of haecceities recalls Spinoza's pantheism, but without God as substance:

> There are only haecceities, affects, subjectless individuations that constitute collective assemblages. Nothing develops, but things arrive late or early, and form this or that assemblage depending on their compositions of speed. Nothing subjectifies, but haecceities form according to compositions of nonsubjectified powers or affects. We call this plane, which knows only longitudes and latitudes, speeds and haecceities, the plane of consistency or composition (as opposed to the plan[e] of organization or development). It is necessarily a plane of immanence and univocality. We therefore call it the plane of Nature, although nature has nothing to do with it, since on this plane there is no distinction between the natural and the artificial. However many dimensions it may have, it never has a supplementary dimension to that which transpires upon it. That alone makes it natural and immanent. The same goes for the principle of contradiction: this plane could also be called the plane of noncontradiction. The plane of consistency could be called the plane of nonconsistency. (266)

2   Deleuze and Guattari (1987) continue:

> It should not be thought that a haecceity consists simply of a decor or backdrop that situates subjects, or of appendages that hold things and people to the ground. It is the entire assemblage in its individuated aggregate that is a haecceity; it is this assemblage that is defined by a longitude and a latitude, by speeds and affects, independently of forms and subjects, which belong to another plane. (261)

3   Gibson (1986) suggests that an affordance is whatever one entity allows another entity to do. For example, I might perceive that one of the affordances of viscous pigment (i.e., paint) is that it can be smeared onto a canvas (it is smearable), or diluted (it is dilute-able), or mixed with a different pigment (it is mix-able). Similarly, individuals manifest affordances; events and contexts manifest affordances; ideas, ideologies, and concepts manifest affordances.

4   Jullien (1995) describes how things and circumstances have their own sets of inclinations or "propensities."

5   Sometimes referred to as a "power," or "propensity," a disposition is the ability of an object to bring about some state of affairs (its "manifestation") when met with the appropriate stimulus. This stimulus (typically) consists in an arrangement of other objects; the other objects being such that they too have dispositions, and it is owing to the complementary dispositions of the objects involved that they mutually produce their manifestation. Dispositions are characterized by the manifestations they produce, and hence are for that manifestation. For example, the disposition fragility has as its manifestation a shattering or breaking of the fragile object, so fragility is a disposition for shattering or breaking. "Dispositional realism" refers to any theory of dispositions that claims that an object has a disposition in virtue of some state or property of the object. Characteristic of the realist position is the belief that objects are capable of manifestations that might never obtain. If an object has some disposition, it has it in virtue of the way (state) that the object presently is, and not because of some situation that might obtain in the future, or some behaviour exhibited in the past. (Borghini and Williams 2008, 23)

6   Karen Barad (2007) describes the reciprocal relationships that constitute our everyday lives (and everything else) as relationships of "intra-action."

7   "The aim of the philosophy of organism is to express a coherent cosmology based upon the notions of 'system,' 'process,' 'creative advance into novelty,' 'res vera' (in Descartes' sense), 'stubborn fact,' 'individual unity of experience,' 'feeling,' 'time as perpetual perishing,' 'endurance as re-creation,' 'purpose,' 'universals as forms of definiteness,' 'particulars—i.e., *res verae*—as ultimate agents of stubborn fact" (Whitehead 1978, 128).

8   An affordance, to use the term coined by the perceptual psychologist Gibson, is a perceived feature of the environment which indicates a possible action in the environment for the perceiver. Whereas affordances have been discussed before in this context, no one has to my knowledge successfully argued that they can be both representational and nonconceptual (Almäng 2008, 161–62).

9   Gibson sometimes used a characteristic linguistic construct to refer to affordances, namely, [verb phrase]-able. For example, he described a surface such as the brink of a cliff as fall-off- able, a substance such as an apple as eat-able, an object such as a stone as throw-able, an animal as copulate-with-able, and an event such as a burning fire as cook-with-able. In each case, the affordance property is possessed by a bearer relative to a specific organism or class of organisms (Scarantino 2003, 950).

References

Almäng, J. 2008. Affordances and the nature of perceptual content. *International Journal of Philosophical Studies* 16 (2): 161.

Ansell-Pearson, K. 1999. *Germinal life: The difference and repetition of Deleuze.* London; New York: Routledge.

Barad, K. M. 2007. *Meeting the universe halfway.* Durham, NC: Duke University Press.

Borghini, A., and N. E. Williams. 2008. A dispositional theory of possibility. *Dialectica* 62 (1): 21–41.

DeLanda, M.. 2002a. Deleuzian ontology: A sketch. Presented at New Ontologies: Transdisciplinary Objects, March 30, University of Illinois. http://www2.uiuc.edu/unit/STIM/ontologies/delanda2b.pdf (accessed April 8, 2009).

———. 2002b. *Intensive science and virtual philosophy.* London; New York: Continuum.

———. 2003. 1000 years of war: CTheory interview with Manuel De Landa. *CTheory.* http://www.ctheory.net/articles.aspx?id=383 (accessed April 8, 2009).

Deleuze, G., and F. Guattari. 1987. *A thousand plateaus: Capitalism and schizophrenia.* Minneapolis: University of Minnesota Press.

———. 1994. *What is philosophy?* New York: Columbia University Press.

Gibson, J. J. 1986. *The ecological approach to visual perception.* Hillsdale, NJ: Lawrence Erlbaum Associates.

Hayles, N. K. 1999. *How we became posthuman: Virtual bodies in cybernetics, literature, and informatics.* Chicago: University of Chicago Press.

———. 2002. Flesh and metal: Reconfiguring the mindbody in virtual environments. *Configurations* 10 (2): 297–320.

Henry, M. 2003. Phenomenology of life. *Angelaki* 8 (2): 97–110.

Hutchby, I. 2001. Technologies, texts and affordances. *Sociology* 35 (2): 441–56.

Jullien, F. 1995. *The propensity of things: Toward a history of efficacy in China.* New York; Cambridge, MA: Zone Books.

Kauffman, S. 2007. Beyond reductionism: Reinventing the sacred. *Zygon* 42 (4): 903–14.

Kauffman, S., and P. Clayton. 2006. On emergence, agency, and organization. *Biology and Philosophy* 21 (4): 501–21.

Lingis, A. 1998. *The imperative.* Bloomington: Indiana University Press.

Merleau-Ponty, M. 1968. *The visible and the invisible: Followed by working notes.* Evanston, IL: Northwestern University Press.

Nancy, J.-L. 2000. *Being singular plural.* Stanford, CA: Stanford University Press.

Scarantino, A. 2003. Affordances explained. *Philosophy of Science* 70 (5): 949–61.

Serres, M. 1995. *Angels: A modern myth.* Paris: Flammarion.

Tiessen, M. P. 2007. Accepting invitations: Desire lines as earthly offerings. *Rhizomes: Cultural Studies in Emerging Knowledge* 15. http://www.rhizomes .net (accessed April 8, 2009).

Whitehead, A. N. 1978. *Process and reality: An essay in cosmology.* New York: Free Press.

7

Cityscapes of Desire
Urban Change in Post-Soviet Russia

OLGA PAK

*I was standing in one of Moscow's streets in the summer of 2007, gaz-
ing at old and new buildings. A man came up to me and asked: "Do
you like how this city is changing?" "Why do you ask?" I replied. "I
personally don't like this new city. I was born here ... quite a while
ago. Now I can't even say 'it is my city' anymore. It ceased being
built for people. It used to be spacious and welcoming. Now it's
cramped and unkind. I just wanted to let you know that it used to
be better," the man explained to me and continued his way along
the street.*[1]

Varying from glorification to aversion, sentiments about post-Soviet
cityscapes fuse affective perceptions of rearranged spaces, imaginaries of
desirable living, and aspirations and disappointments associated with political change, as well as persistent references to the Soviet past. It is this nexus
that I interrogate in this chapter. I discuss how post-Soviet urban space is
contested in the overlapping domains of desire and affect and how these
contestations result in reimagining the Soviet city, as well as in its transformation into an idealized space of both nostalgia and hope.

Post-Soviet urban "transition" (the term widely employed in post-
socialist studies) has been explored from different perspectives: physical
restructuring of cities, their market saturation and economic growth, changes
in social groupings and policies, social and political controversies, urban
art, etc. (e.g., Alexander, Buchli, and Humphrey 2007; Andrusz, Harloe,

and Szelenyi 1996; Brade, Axenov, and Bondarchuk 2006; Czepczynski 2008; Ioffe and Nefedova 1998; Iyer 2003; Leskin 2008; Pivovarov 2003; Stanilov 2007; Tsenkova and Nedovic-Budic 2006; Yurasovsky and Ovenden 1994). I attend to the changes in how people imagine the transforming post-Soviet and disappearing Soviet urbanity rooted in people's everyday experiences, perceptions, and symbolic conceptualization of various city spaces. I argue that not only the visible, tangible, and countable metamorphoses (re)shape the concept of the post-Soviet city, but these changes also transform the understandings developed by city dwellers about their cities. I discuss a post-Soviet "transition" through exploring the social imagination of the post-Soviet "transition" reflected in city spaces.

Soja (2000) describes the "urban imaginary" as "a mental or ideational field, conceptualized in imagery, reflexive thought, and symbolic representation, a conceived space of the imagination" (11). Shields (2005) argues that the urban is the city's virtuality, which is "as much imagined as it is lived," "the naming and characterization of the world as a space of significant objects and processes" (383). Following these ideas, I view urban imaginaries characterizing the Soviet and post-Soviet city as virtualities—a lived reality, the imagined "truth" about people's encounters with the city. I discuss the city's virtual dimension as the domain where responses to existing and existed materiality of the city and ideas about the city's future are constructed and contested in relation to people's experiences, desires, hopes, and notions of the good life (see Park in this volume). This chapter is focused on the moments of such contestation in the context of post-Soviet transformation of cities. My analysis is a further explication, complication, and contextualized illustration of the idea that "[u]nlike the concrete physicality of the city, the intangibility of the virtual makes it a domain open to intervention, *métisage* and experimentation by those with less power and resources, despite being resistant to immediate change through merely material interventions. Thus spaces may be appropriated and events hijacked for new ends" (Shields 2005, 384).

I start with a case of an ambitious project called Okhta Centre in the Russian city of Saint Petersburg to discuss (1) how contested desires motivate reconfiguration of the urban symbolism that thus becomes the domain where the right to the city is articulated; (2) how regardless of its origin and history, existing materiality of the city is idealized in popular imagination and thus serves to contest current undesirable physical and ideational transformations; and (3) how, when challenged, people's aspirations for desirable change can motivate reimagining the Soviet city. Building on this case and presenting other examples of popular responses to post-Soviet city (re)making, I further discuss how the post-Soviet city, imagined as the space of wasted hopes, allows the Soviet city to be reimagined today as a deterritorialized virtual location of desire suggesting the potential for resistance to current tendencies.

Contested Desires and Urban Symbolism: A Tower of Discord

> *It's like wearing pink briefs on a head [sic]: Why should clothing be good-looking? The whole point is that I stand out and am notable from afar! (commentary to a blog post about ambitious high-rises shaping post-Soviet cityscapes, 2007)*[2]

The project Okhta Centre (initially called Gazprom City) was proposed for the city of St. Petersburg, Russia, in 2005 by Gazprom Neft (a daughter company of Gazprom Group, the largest oil and gas producer in Russia). The centre, a large-scale business and social district, is scheduled to be completed by 2016 in an area near the historic centre, particularly close to the renowned Smolny Cathedral. The mayor of the city, Valentina Matvienko, was motivated by the desire to secure the corporation's revenues for the city's budget and to attract other big investors. Gazprom Neft aspires not only to locate its headquarters in the second capital city of Russia, but, as the promotion puts it, "to deliver the city's modern architectural symbol" (Gazprom Neft, n.d.).

The project stirred up considerable resentment, engaging various publics for various reasons.[3] I will focus on a particular issue—the symbolism of the city. The tension among the intended, emerging, and already established symbolic meanings involves both ideational speculations and the affective dimension of the urban imaginary. Giving my own spin to Donald's (2006) ideas about the branding of cities, I argue that the visual identification for St. Petersburg that is promoted by the corporation intervenes in and alters the popular "structures of feeling" theorized by Williams as "affective elements of consciousness and relationships" that motivate people's feelings and thoughts about their places (Williams 1977, cited in Donald 2006, 66). The corporation aims to replace these popular structures of feeling with "structures of attention" that would determine "how people produce and consume the idea of the city by paying emotional attention to it" (Donald 2006, 65–66). Thus, while the corporation offers its own emotional template for the city dwellers' identification with the city, resentful city dwellers confront corporate intentions to modify existing urban symbolism and the way people identify with it. In this confrontation, the established structures of feeling activated by popular memories, experiences, and vernacular ideas about city space are opposed to the structures of attention that involve a rather abstract "wow"-affect (as a result of the project's extravagant features), downplaying other forms of ideational and emotional engagement. The new symbolism interacting with these structures of attention accentuates the project's potential to impress and to be visually memorable. However, the popular struggle to uphold another deeply rooted set of structures of feeling undermines the corporation's superficial structures of attention and reveals and resists a more complex symbolism embedded in the project.

Gazprom's idea of architectural symbolism rather trivially follows the framework of international corporate modernism—the erection of the tallest tower, or one that is iconic, designed by a star architect.[4] From this viewpoint, St. Petersburg can simply provide an advantageous spot because it is a flat city: the horizontally oriented skyline of its historic centre has been preserved for about three hundred years (and is the reason for its UNESCO protection). Few contemporary projects have actually been approved by the city. The architectural competition for the Okhta Centre project neglected the city's height regulation restricting buildings potentially affecting the valuable skyline to the height of no more than 42 metres or, with approval of expert assessment, 48 metres.[5] The design chosen for Okhta Centre (proposed by British architectural firm RMJM) envisioned the Gazprom Tower to be 396 metres high. Apparently, the corporation's desire for a tower in a certain location and of outstanding height plays with the imagery of a low skyline, which would emphasize the tower's height and visualize its absolute power over that skyline. This conception assumes the Gazprom Tower proudly standing alone with no other high-rises to challenge its dominance. Ironically, if the structure is indeed built, the contestation of publics clamouring to save the skyline may help to prevent the appearance of other high-rise competitors.

Discussing the Okhta project, various experts, cultural workers, and city dwellers argued that a skyscraper was by no means an option for a city like St. Petersburg. The St. Petersburg Union of Architects vetoed the competition and wrote open letters to attract attention to the issue. UNESCO expressed a strong concern with the project; Europa Nostra appealed to Russian president Vladimir Putin asking him to safeguard the delicate silhouette of St. Petersburg from being "forever ruined" (Europa Nostra 2007, n.p.). "Starchitect" Kisho Kurokawa resigned from the jury of the architectural competition, claiming that none of the six proposals were relevant for the city. Norman Foster and Rafael Viñoly left the jury, indignant about the pressure of the city administration lobbying for the RMJM design. City dwellers criticized the blatant simulation of "public choice": the initial task for the architects was never publicly discussed. All the finalists centred on high towers, yet public voting did not provide the option "against all projects."

Arguably the most spectacular simulation of democratic procedures and of public choice occurred in the public hearings on Okhta Centre held on January 14 and June 27, 2008. People's reactions to those events qualified them as a "shameless farce." The mass media reported on supporters of the project being paid by the administration and a scandalous intrusion of OMON (police special forces) into the hearings to confront protesters.[6] The administration was also accused of misinforming the public, with the incompleteness and inaccuracies of the documentation presented and deliberate silencing of such a critical issue as the project's height, which was missing from the agenda in both hearings. According to activists, detailed and argued criticism of the project and of new construction regulations in the designated area were ignored. Finally, although the height regulations could be lawfully changed only by the city parliament and after public hearings, they were altered overnight by the city administration. According to the new regulations, the height of buildings in the area allocated for Okhta Centre was restricted to one hundred metres, with a provision for exclusions in "unique" cases—the loophole for Gazprom.[7] As Colin Amery (2006), a renowned architectural critic, regretted beforehand, "It is sad that the city of St. Petersburg's enthusiasm for the offices of the world's largest natural-gas producer could mean the abandonment of the careful regulations that make the city so agreeable and unlike other cities."

These and other controversial and scandalous episodes in the Okhta Centre story, encompassing legal, financial, social, and promotional issues, gradually supplemented people's initial protest against the height of the tower with their indignation about the crude omnipotence of corporate and administrative powers. Such a context encouraged abundant caustic interpretations of the tower's symbolism in unofficial discourse on the project.

Puzzles of Symbolism

The symbol of Petersburg is the soaring angel, not the burning flare.
(Tatiana Krasavina, the leader of the NGO Okhtinskaya Duga)[8]

The Okhta Centre controversy is not outstanding in terms of administrative manipulation. Nor is it unique in terms of the attempts of capital to reshape the cityscapes regardless of both the consequences of the engendered changes and the feelings of publics about them. For people in Russia, this case is just one among many. Still, it is somewhat specific. Reshaping space to fit its needs, Gazprom intervenes into the cityscape with the desire to dominate it symbolically (of note, the tower is described as the new "dominant vertical" of the skyline) and to become the new symbol of the city that plays such a big role in the Russian nation-building imaginary. It is common for corporations to desire recognizable and symbolically loaded headquarters (King 2004; Lindner 2006). But Gazprom's will to "deliver a new symbol to the city" collides, in an intriguing way, with St. Petersburg's history and the rich and persistent discourse on the city's symbolism engaging the notions of "freedom," "power," and an "ordinary/insignificant person"—a classical theme in Russian literature and politics. Let me discuss some symbolic collisions resulting from the intersection of the Okhta project with St. Petersburg's existing genius loci.

Today's popular symbolism of St. Petersburg's skyline is mostly indebted to the writings of renowned historian of Russian literature and culture Dmitry Likhachev. He borrowed the notion of a "skyline" from the English-language descriptions of Manhattan and applied it to the interpretation of the symbolism of St. Petersburg in his essay "Nebesnaya liniya goroda na Neve" (Skyline of the City on the Neva River, 1989). He developed the theme further in other essays and public speeches, such as "Gradostroitelnye zavety Petra Velikogo" (Town-Planning Legacy of Peter the Great, 2006a) and "Zapiski ob arhitekture" (Notes on Architecture, 2006b). In the 1990s, Likhachev's ideas about the city's symbolism were employed to prevent the building of the 130-metre-tall Tower of Peter the Great in St. Petersburg, a successful case of public struggle against a commercial skyscraper. Other contributions to the popular symbolism of the city include recognized cultural theorist Yuriy Lotman's essay "Simvolika Peterburga i problemy semiotiki goroda" (Symbolism of Petersburg and the Problems of Semiotics of the City, 1984), architect and architectural theorist Grigoriy Kaganov's book *St. Petersburg: Obrazy prostranstva* (*St. Petersburg: Images of Space*, 1995), and philosopher Boris Markov's book *Khram i rynok* (*The Temple and the Market*, 1999).

Likhachev's interpretation suggests that the rare and delicate verticals of St. Petersburg are especially prominent in juxtaposition to the structural horizontals of the city: the river, the flat relief of its banks and embankments, and a slightly cogged, low skyline. Significance of the verticals for the city's ideology emerges from the functional aspects of those buildings: spires and domes of cathedrals assume the dominance of the spiritual care for the soul over the material care for wealth and power. As Likhachev put it in his interview to *Sankt-Peterburgskie Vedomosti*, "Verticals of cathedrals and of the Admiralty have a certain ideological meaning. The fact that the Isakiy [Isakievskiy Cathedral] has been so far the highest building in the city means the priority of the spiritual. So, why should the business center be higher than the Isakiy?"[9] Today, this interpretation of St. Petersburg's skyline is a significant part of the urban imaginary and provides a highly evocative discursive and emotional context for any new "vertical" in the cityscape, let alone "dominant verticals."

In this framework, the outstanding verticality of the Gazprom Tower (396 metres tall) facing the Smolny Cathedral (94 metres tall) across the Neva River and well superseding the height of the other domes and spires of the skyline inverts the existing urban symbolism. The inversion suggests that the power of wealth and the desire for power suppress the striving for spirituality, whereas the hierarchical subordination displaces the horizontal social ties (managerial hierarchy of office space vs. cathedral space of brotherhood/sisterhood). This new symbolism is further complicated by the notion of the merged power of the state and capital—suggested by the zealous administrative backing for the project and by the fact that 50.002 percent of Gazprom belongs to the state. Discussions of the emerging symbolism of Okhta are abundant in mass media, blogs, forums, etc. Some sarcastic interpretations elaborate on the idea of a new religion worshipping Mammon, of which Gazprom seems to be the perfect embodiment in today's Russia, where wealth is so dependent on oil and gas.

In the popular vision, inverting or transgressing the symbolism of the ethically loaded skyline points to an existing but uncomfortable, improper ethos. An affective aspect of such an iconography seems to evoke the uncanny, in the Freudian sense: something at once familiar and alien, what has been repressed and now recurs, inciting uncomfortable feelings (Freud 2003, 147–48). The origin and the history of St. Petersburg reveal that the conception of horizontal democracy and the priority of the spiritual are beautiful ideals rather than a reflection of the actual practices and ideologies that generated the city: despotism (of the tsars and of the state), longing for wealth (the state's imperial ambitions), and insignificance of human life

Figure 7.1 Okhta Centre: a widely circulated representation of the tower's positioning in regards to the city from a publicity booklet of the project. (Credit: Okhta Cultural and Business Center Public Corporation, http://www.ohta-center.ru/en/official/)

against the background of big ideas and desires (as the marshlands of the Neva were drained by the forced labour of the local population). The new tower is a visualization of the uncanny in the new imagery of St. Petersburg's skyline. It contradicts the desirable paradigm of the popular urban symbolism that prioritizes the idealized, empowering interpretation. Notably, it seems crucial to city dwellers that the imagery of St. Petersburg's silhouette not be allowed to solidify undesirable reminiscences, but rather invest the urban imaginary with hopes for the ideal. To be welcoming and inspiring, the city's skyline was reimagined not to represent past or existing power relations, but to mythologize empowering ideals as a part of the city's history and a token of its liberating spatial ideology.[10]

Paradoxical Space: Popular Semiotics vs. the City's Uncanny

To situate Gazprom's architectural ambitions within a historic tradition, proponents of Okhta Centre claim that although St. Petersburg's skyline is horizontally oriented, the primary intention of the architects who created its vertical focal points was to reach the sky. Hence, the new project would in some way accomplish the dream of the architects and Peter the Great (the founder of the city), as well as of his successors. This "dream" fits the symbolism of innovation and progress and contextualizes it within Russia's centuries-long striving for modernization and global significance. The figure of the first Russian emperor and the founder of the city, Peter the Great, is actively exploited by the Okhta Centre promotion. Peter's mythologized persona embodies the fulfilled imperial ambitions, the desire for modernization of the country, the obsession with innovation and technology, democratism in relations with lower classes, and the commitment to meritocracy. The expression "Nebyvaloe byvaet!" ("The impossible is possible!"), used as the Okhta project's motto, was attributed to Peter, implying his belief in human abilities, which, under the reasonable and inspiring leadership, could result in a rapid modernization and enlightenment of the country and its rise in the global arena. Such an image of Peter the Great had become promoted under Stalin[11] when that mythology was employed for the propaganda of Soviet "miraculous" industrialization/modernization and the cult of a personified leadership.

However, Peter the Great is an ambivalent figure in Russian history and is central to another kind of social mythology. In certain contexts, and with references to both Russian classical and Soviet literature,[12] Peter's persona alludes to despotism. This despotism is reflected, among other notorious cases, in the origin of the city of St. Petersburg. A result of Peter's imperial aspirations, St. Petersburg was conceived as the metropolitan city to match and supersede, in beauty and power, European imperial cities. St. Petersburg was an outcome of the sovereign's immediate will and a huge sacrifice of bare-life-bodies that built the city at a fast pace in the midst of swamps and a harsh climate. The city's origin and imagery, and the life of the common man in this city, are among the most developed themes in Russian literature since Pushkin and thanks to Gogol and Dostoevsky. As Berman (1983) comments about Pushkin's poem "The Copper Horseman,"[13] "St. Petersburg's whole life story is here, brilliantly crystallized and compressed: a vision of the city's grandeur and magnificence, and a vision of the madness on which it is based" (188).

Paradoxically, the geopolitical and economic pragmatism of the state (to build a gateway into Europe) and personal aesthetic preferences of the sovereigns[14] shaped the new city that later became imagined through the symbolism of spirituality and freedom,[15] and as a space proportionate to an ordinary individual, opposed to the gigantism of embodiments of imperial power. In this context, the promoted symbolism of Okhta Centre (somehow recurrent to the Soviet propaganda but with new pragmatics) becomes complicated. The visual impression of the massive tower dominating the skyline summons supplementary allusions to the tyranny of the state and the dominance of economic interest and sovereigns' desires over the lives of "insignificant people." This effect is intensified with the very manner of the project's execution—namely, the numerous examples of administrative and corporate omnipotence compared to people's feeling of powerlessness and insignificance.[16] Apparently, glorification of such a symbol as the Gazprom Tower seems to city dwellers absurd. It is resisted because, in popular imagination, it would be a crude and obtrusive embodiment of what has been negated and reimagined as a result of the popular desire to live in a symbolically inspiring city. The imperial desire of the corporation to subordinate the city's skyline and the mercantilist administration's desire to represent the wealth of the city collide with the desire of city dwellers to protect the empowering structures of feeling against the structures of attention that propose an impressive spectacle but sublimate the disempowering imagery and imaginary of the city.

This case illuminates how popular urban symbolism can be activated by the desire for inspiring city spaces and can reframe the ideologies inscribed in the origin and materiality of these spaces. Spatializations of the past that are the outcomes of certain histories and ideologies can be reimagined in an idealized way to produce empowering urban imaginaries and to confront the undesirable present transformations. Referring to Lefebvre's renowned concept (Lefebvre 1996, 147–59), such symbolism claims the "right to the city" in the realm of urban imaginary and becomes the means of resistance to undesirable interventions into both the city's virtuality and materiality. In what follows, I will show how people's perceptions and conceptions of ongoing post-Soviet transformation lead to reimagining of the Soviet city in an idealized and nostalgic way. I will argue that this reimagined Soviet space becomes a virtual location where blocked hopes for change and frustrated desires for livable and inspiring cities interact with a deterritorialized affective space of reimagined Soviet experiences.

Reimagining the Soviet Urban Space: "Lost Views" and Wasted Hopes

> *"What have you done to my city?"—this is the phrase that everybody repeats today. (David Sarkisyan, director of the State Museum of Architecture, Moscow, TV talk show* Shkola Zlosloviya, *2006)*[17]

It's a beautiful, spacious, considered city. Beautiful in its simplicity, modesty, and self-restraint. It used to be such. And now all what have not yet been demolished in order to build supermarkets and casinos is filled up with cars, covered with commercial banners or turned into shop-windows. (commentary on photos of Soviet Moscow at "NoNaMe," an Internet photo depository, 2009)[18]

Let me relay an anecdotal story published in the popular nationwide Russian newspaper *Izvestia* (Davydova 2007, n.p.). By assignment of the mayor of Moscow, Yurii Luzhkov, Moskomarchitectura (the Moscow Architecture Board) nominated about two hundred and fifty valuable panoramic views of Moscow that were "worth preserving." However, it happened that almost all of them became so seriously affected by newer construction projects that their preservation no longer made sense. Of the nine views still left for consideration, one was later removed from the list because its protection would conflict with the ongoing construction of Moscow City (the major business district in Moscow). Eventually, none of the views were given the special protection that would prevent the undesirable interventions of developers into those cityscapes.

Another story that received a great deal of public attention was of a journalistic investigation by Andrey Loshak produced for TV but spread mostly via the Internet under the rubric of being prohibited for TV broadcasting.[19] The story, titled "Here Is Office Now," tells about the forceful and often violent displacement of dwellers from, and destruction of, historical buildings in locations attractive for developers because of the potential price of office and retail space there. The journalist showcases how such desirable locations are prone to "accidental" fires, commonly viewed as deliberate arsons, which immediately resolve problematic situations if they occur. Destruction due to fire makes contestation over the buildings, protected by resisting dwellers or understood as "cultural heritage," irrelevant. As a result of this and similar practices, the report concludes, people lose their homes while the city loses its heritage, its beauty, and its unique "aura."

The first story provides an illustration of the most common commentary on Moscow's changing cityscapes: Moscow has become "ugly"; it is losing its charm and beauty. The second example, while discussing contested transformations of city spaces, articulates aloud one of the "shared secrets" about the cynical and brutal means of those transformations. It reiterates a pervasive urban imaginary about the inability of city dwellers to confront the developers' greed for big money and to prevent "fire" (both real and metaphorical) that epitomizes an irreversible destruction of city spaces.

Excitement with the political change in Soviet Russia of the late 1980s (e.g., see Holdsworth 2003) invigorated various popular hopes, including those about the revitalization of cities. A new rhetoric of democratic partic- ipation promised that diverse private interests (as opposed to discredited sub- jectless "public" or "communal" interests) would drive changes within Soviet cities in a way satisfying the needs and wants of all and everybody. Accord- ing to another common belief, the "invisible hand" of free capitalism would generously provide the financial means to fulfill people's desire for beauti- ful and comfortable city spaces. Those aspirations were soon challenged. Private interest was not considerable in any individual case, but when backed by financial and administrative resources, capital appeared not so demo- cratic in its subordinating and discriminating gestures. As for cities, they indeed have changed; however, they have not become viewed as satisfying, let alone inspiring.

Post-Soviet cityscapes embody many people's upset hopes and feed a desire for yet more change. The "lost views" of Moscow and St. Petersburg, widely discussed in mass media and in public conversation, became espe- cially emblematic. It is noteworthy that the semantics of "loss" (not, for example, of "enhancement" or "revival") is so recurrent in the characteriza- tion of the changing cityscapes. Suggested by the contexts in which "loss" is associated with city views, this notion assumes people's emotional responses not only to physical transformations of city spaces, but to certain post-Soviet processes in general.

The imagery of "lost city views" visualizes for city dwellers aestheti- cally unpleasing outcomes of "infill" and "point" construction[20] that have become common practices in post-Soviet cities. Both approaches are premised on the idea that land in Soviet city centres is underused (e.g., see Bertaud and Renaud 1997). Encouraged by the market economy, the required (that is, desirable by investors owing to a high demand and value of central loca- tions) density of construction can be achieved by building new structures where it is technically possible. An ideologically discredited practice of city planning cannot control or confront developers' rush for quick profits. As Iyer (2003) observes,

> The collapse of what local planners refer to as "vertical control" has impacted attitudes towards planning, plans, and planners themselves. Considered the hallmark of the previous regime, planning faces a tenuous fate because of its perceived incompatibility with progress towards a dem- ocratic, market-based society. (202; see also Nedovic-Budic 2001; Shove and Anderson 1997)

Diverging interests of chief architects, mayors, and developers, as well as the disrepute of city planning, have resulted in haphazard architectural interventions into city spaces that often occur regardless of technical restrictions, let alone such considerations as visual intrusions into cityscapes.

Besides, the negative reaction to the aesthetics of "infilled" ("lost") cityscapes and of new architectural structures is often motivated by the emotional response to the associated loss of communities, public spaces, and green areas; the loss of certain valued everyday practices and experiences in reconfigured places; and the loss of "auratic" qualities of the city in general. "Lost city views" also symbolize the unrestricted power of capital and administrative willfulness, as, for example, in the case of Okhta Centre, and allude to the cynicism and brutality of current approaches to the city spaces and to their inhabitants, as in the story about arsons and forceful displacements of people. Thus, in the social imaginary, the emerging cityscapes signify the loss of the conditions for a good life, the loss of the city's beauty and authenticity, the loss of the right to the city (articulated in early years of post-Soviet transition), and the loss of "order" dismantled by new power relations.

Unlike the imaginary of disciplined and orderly spaces of Western capitalism, with their grids, excessive rationality, and zoning, the post-Soviet production of space is viewed as haphazard and arbitrary, and as deregulating the course of everyday life. The imagery of gated and guarded communities, elite complexes intruding in the midst of decaying neighbourhoods, manifestations of the unrestricted arbitrariness of developers and their wealthy clients, public secrets of legal and moral violations, and an increasingly visible contrast between wealth and impoverishment are all viewed as symptoms of the re-feudalization[21] of post-Soviet spaces. This re-feudalization is reflected in the oft-cited "vulgar eclecticism" of emerging cityscapes and in the deterioration of inherited ones. Terms like *feudalism* or *barbarism* that people frequently use to characterize the current state of affairs assume a step back in historic continuity of modernity, or demodernization. "Unfortunately, our cities started to die. We are savages yet. Already savages!" as the director of the State Museum of Architecture in Moscow, David Sarkisyan, commented on the ongoing processes in Russian architecture (quoted in "Arkhitektura" 2006, n.p.). Summing up opinions of provincial city planners, Iyer (2003) states, "For the first time in Russian planning history, planners in stagnating cities need to plan for decline" (215).

My observations of the popular perceptions of post-Soviet city making add to the phenomenon also illustrated by other examples in post-socialist studies[22] swapping Soviet and post-Soviet definitions of modernization and demodernization. Competing socialist and capitalist versions of modernity (Bauman 1991; Buck-Morss 2002; Hoffmann 2003) collided in the post-Soviet reality, turning it into a space of ambivalence. Brandtstädter (2007) articulated this phenomenon very well:

> Postsocialism not only replaced one type of modernity with another, but it also replaced a socialist modernity, which used to define the capitalist project as backward and flawed, with a capitalist modernity, which now defines everything socialist as unmodern. This opposition itself creates room for cultural struggles: as capitalist "dream worlds" created spaces from which to criticize flawed socialist realities (see Yurchak 2003), socialist ideas of the modern can, today, inspire resistance to a "transition" that is, ironically, more often than not experienced as a de-modernization. (134)

In the case of post-Soviet urban changes as they are reflected in the social imagination, the ambivalence of these liminal spaces of "transition"—aspiring to the ideals of modernization and accommodating experiences of demodernization—makes the capitalist project contested and resisted, whereas the socialist one is reimagined and reconsidered, as I will show later.

The imagery and imaginary of "lost cityscapes" can be understood as affective constructions that reveal people's general frustration from wasted hopes for inspiring and welcoming city spaces. In the beginning of post-Soviet transformation, the market economy, liberalization, and democratization were imagined as promising the opportunities for architectural revival. Apparently, the notion of "lost" cities is indicative of the more general "loss"—of hopes for the advent of democracy and for positive consequences of financial freedom and private property rights. I began this part with media stories, and I will end it with a few exemplary citations from interviews with renowned Russian architects:

> Administrative pressure and market pressure are unbearable! We should regulate those "market laws." The city which we've been building for people has become hostile to people. (Yuriy Sdobnov, vice president of the Union of Architects of Russia)[23]

> Recently we made a film. Andrey Gozak [architect and critic] and I attached video cameras to our heads and walked around the whole Ostozhenka [a gentrified district in Moscow known as the most successful example of post-Soviet Moscow's reconstruction]. It's a ghetto. No people. Only security in black suits and with wires in their ears—only they are visible. Rich people buy realty just to invest profitably their money; they employ guards but they don't live there. This is not a city; this is a kind of bank cells where money is protected from inflation. What is all that architecture for then?

Instead of a district having its own face, its own life, there is nothing. Just an empty space that is expensive.... The city is vanishing. And I don't want to speculate about architectural problems against such a background of a city life. It turned out that we destroyed life and, instead, we learned how to make roof boarding more or less straight.... This is incommensurate. (Alexandr Skokan, architect, who participated in the reconstruction of Ostozhenka)[24]

Today skyscrapers have grown over Moscow.... The whole Moscow is seen from the top. Our city looks awful. One can see how they started some new garden and then filled it all up with garbage.... Boxes, boxes—they filled up the space, like tossed-away packages from an eaten life. (Michail Philippov, architect)[25]

Deterritorialized Land of Desire: Reimagining the Soviet Urban Space

Oh ... I'm looking at the old photos and think: what a bad luck that I was born in 1993, not earlier. I wish those old times could return. (a comment to the photo show "Retro Moscow of 1970s" on YouTube, 2008)[26]

The lived materiality of the Soviet urban space was a poor competitor of the imagined capitalist environments represented in the colourful imagery of Hollywood cinema and in seductive tales of the Soviet citizens who had a chance to travel abroad.[27] Yurchak (2005) shows how the idea of the Imaginary West that imbued late socialism had little to do with the actual reality of the Western countries (158–206). Regardless of its ontological status, however, this mythological West provided a vivid imagery for late Soviet and early post-Soviet comparisons.

I suppose that this imagined foreign land became a virtual location of desire from which Soviet people started to observe their Soviet cityscapes and city spaces. Viewed from within, these cityscapes seemed acceptable as signifying certain optimization of mass construction, with its promises of increasing volume of housing for masses whose major aspiration was to have the waiting list for apartment distribution somehow shortened. At least, I shall note, this is how it is being remembered by people today. From the viewpoint located in the Imaginary West, the uniform Soviet cityscapes could not sustain their "modern charm" and appeared simply grey, dull, and lacking care for imagination. Emotional response to this gaze pre-empted somewhat more balanced critical assessments of both the pros and cons of socialist city planning and shifted attention toward the emerging possibilities of radical change—a generalized hope for the new and better. In this affective context, what had appeared before as colourful and bright became commonly perceived as grey and depressing. I remember how people, my neighbours in a newly built "micro-rayon" (neighbourhood) of a Siberian city, liked their local apartment houses for being of different colours. The inhabitants used to make endless jokes about the overall uniformity of their buildings, but those jokes did not convey distaste for the built environments, probably because the improvement of living conditions took priority. Later, in the 1990s, the notion of "colourful buildings" became viewed as totally inappropriate in relation to the same cityscapes, while their uniformity became detested.

Changed attitudes toward Soviet-built environments manifested popular hope that political change would result in necessarily positive spatial expressions. There was no looking back in search of anything valuable in the ways the Soviet space used to be produced and experienced. The aspirations for new spaces were quite in spirit with the modern project: the drive to obliterate the past and the belief in the progressive/positive course of a new history. Hence the disgust for Soviet spatiality and anticipation of its (miraculous) transfiguration from uniform, grey, and poor into diverse, colourful, and wealthy. These attitudes remind the utopian aspirations of the early post-revolutionary Soviet period, when space appeared reclaimed and full of transformative potential (e.g., see Stites 1988), and when red communist flags coloured "grey" streets while amateur political posters displaced commercials. This time, ironically, it was the red Coca-Cola tents that coloured "grey" Soviet environments and amateur advertisements that replaced already trivial slogans.

In 2002 a young man from a Siberian city told me in an interview that he liked how bright and eye-catching advertising had changed the "grey and boring streets," filling them with colours. A few years later, in 2008, I noted the assertion of a young urbanite that "easily ignorable" Soviet visual propaganda with its routine "Slava trudu!" ("Glory to Labour!") would be preferable to the "irritatingly obtrusive" and "brainwashing" post-Soviet advertising. Ubiquitous commercials on the buildings spoiling the views of fine facades and creating overwhelming visual noise stopped being viewed as the colours of urban revival. In both cases the sentiments were not exceptional, as I infer from other opinions expressed on the Internet, in media, and in private conversations. A similar tendency reappears in attitudes toward the first new "rich" buildings, which initially "brightened up" post-Soviet cities and which became viewed later as the "irritating" and "shameful" kitschy exhibitionism of their owners.

Earlier I suggested that certain affective and ideational responses of city dwellers to post-Soviet transformation of cities created the possibility for the reappearance of the Soviet urban space as an imagined space of desire and nostalgia. This Soviet space may have little to do with the actual space of Soviet experiences (especially in imaginaries of post-Soviet generations), but its implications for contemporary evaluations of urban transformations and new aspirations about change cannot be dismissed as insignificant. Like the Soviet comparisons of a Soviet life to a life in the Imaginary West described by Yurchak, the post-Soviet city spaces are viewed and criticized today in relation to the Imaginary Soviet Space.

As the idealized symbolization of St. Petersburg's skyline demonstrates, popular imagination can produce an inspiring conception of a city space regardless of the politics and histories that determined the materiality of that space, but using the potential for a good life that this materiality offers. Commentaries of city dwellers and architects on the ideas behind Soviet spatializations reveal that today the Soviet materiality appears to have such a potential in comparison to newly built environments and the forms of urban life they engender. This discourse disassociates Soviet structures of power and the "good intentions" of people such as architects and city planners who, although functioning within these structures, were motivated by certain ideas and ideals about social well-being in cities. What at some point was devalued as empty signifiers of Soviet official rhetoric reappears today as filled with the ideals that used to influence certain practices of Soviet urbanism. In the nostalgic discourse on the Soviet city, the failures of implementation (for various reasons, including notorious stylistic preferences of the party leaders or shortages of construction materials) are separated from the ideals and intentions of the professionals who attempted to address the needs of common people and to create the city for a good life. To exemplify such discourse, I would like to cite the architects who could hardly be called the apologists of the Soviet regime and who are popular and successful practitioners in today's Russia. Their opinions convey nostalgic sentiments similar to that of city dwellers:

> Attitudes toward this [Soviet] architecture may be different but, doubtlessly, it was made for common people. Unlike today's. (commentary on photos of Soviet Moscow posted on the Internet, 2009)[28]

> Then [in 1984], it was possible to make pedestrian areas. It was possible to make a city for people. But all these died. What pedestrian zones when

there are continuous fences; every plot is being gated from the city? The problem of Ostozhenka is that it was conceived as the city for people but works as the city for [private] property. In this sense, the "milieu" is dying.... The soviet city was indeed projected for the good of people—there were streets, courtyards, public buildings ...; ground floors used to open into the city.... But in 1990s, we somehow enthusiastically decided to build up the areas, which by soviet city planners were designated for public uses.... Today we cannot return to city planning for a human being. (Sergey Tkachenko, director of the Institute of the General Plan of Moscow)[29]

[In Soviet times,] we used to serve 99, 100 per cent of the population, didn't we? [Refers to another architect Mikhail Khazanov, who nods in reply.] We worked for Muscovites; we built [enumerates some well-known places in Moscow].... Maybe not in the best way but ... honestly. Our creative intentions were oriented in a very specific way: they were aimed at social tasks, at resolution of social problems.... I would, with pleasure, make a project of a rural hospital, for example, or of a rural school. But I cannot imagine that I can get such a commission today.... A rural school! That is "social policy"! But our today's architecture is driven by [the task] to glorify the power or to glorify money. (Evgeniy Asse, architect and educator at Moscow Institute of Architecture)[30]

Connection of architects with that society [communities engaged in planning] was then, in 1984, much stronger than it is now. (Yurii Avvakumov, architect, educator, and founder of conceptual "paper architecture" in the Soviet times, 2006)[31]

Here is a commentary on the collisions of the public with power structures in the case of Okhta Centre:

Anything is done to push the irresponsible project of the skyscraper of Okhta Center.... The powers absolutely ignore the public. This did not happen even in Soviet times. Various dubious ideas occurred to Grigoriy Romanov [First Secretary of the Communist Party Committee of the Leningrad Region] too, but he used to consider opinions of city dwellers and the arguments of specialists. Off the cuff I can recall a couple of occasions. Grigoriy Vasil'evich wanted, for example, to demolish the Apraksin Dvor and to erect in the Nevskiy [Prospect] a memorial with flashing lights designating Lenin's route at the eve of the Revolution of 1917. But many people opposed these ideas; they explained why these must not happen in the historic part of the city.... And the first secretary of obkom drew back. And today, it is a complete inconsideration [of the public opinion]. Everything is decided by people who do not understand the facts of the matter and simply blatantly push the desirable decisions through. (Boris Niko-

Iashchenko, head of the Architecture and Planning office; Scientific, Research and Project Centre of Saint-Petersburg's Master Plan, 2008)[32]

This comparison of the Soviet and post-Soviet episodes is predicated on the presupposition of taken-for-granted arbitrariness, absurdity, and nondemocratic nature of Soviet power structures and thus the expected superiority of the post-Soviet situation. But the proposition prioritizes the Soviet reality as more acceptable. Such a reference to the Soviet structures of power coded in post-Soviet discourse as "totalitarian" undermines the "democratic" claims of post-Soviet reality. This opinion does not convey nostalgic longing for the return of the Soviet past, but its recollection confronts the undesirable features of the present. Interestingly, the notion of ideal-type democracy is not used for the evaluation of its current abuses, but rather an instantiation of the supposedly nondemocratic Soviet regime. Moreover, it is not the worst facets of the Soviet past that are actualized to belittle the present imperfections, but instead the examples that define present flaws as degradation and call for change.

Popular recollections of the Soviet city have a similar function: they call for change. But they also become a repository of ideas of what a good city shall provide for its inhabitants. Abstract futuristic fantasizing may lack practical credibility; the idealized imaginary West does not seduce as it used to. Hence, the ideational and affective resources for the current resistance to undesirable transformations are found in the best examples of Soviet spatializations. Unlike the popular interpretation of St. Petersburg's skyline that required reimagining of the actual city's materiality, the imagined Soviet city deals with vanishing materiality, obliterated or decaying. The imagery of the Soviet city space is being reconstructed in numerous websites, discussed in web posts and offline conversations, visualized in photographic slide shows on YouTube and in blogs, and animated in old films. Thus, the Soviet city is becoming a deterritorialized virtual space constructed from memories (sometimes also reimagined in new contexts) and evocative visual signifiers (such as photos, films, or postcards) with open possibilities for the production of meaning. The emerging popular (re)imaginary of the Soviet city space as a city-for-common-people provides the context in which current spatializations of greed-driven desires and discriminating power relations seem inappropriate violations of normality. Viewed in contrast to actually experienced post-Soviet spatiality and its demodernizing modernization, the Soviet imaginary city becomes one of the locations from which capitalist modernity is contested and undesirable spatial transformations are resisted.

Final Remarks

My argument deals with certain people's perceptions that reflect how, regardless of any ideal conceptions of capitalism and socialism, the post-Soviet "transition," its point of departure and the presumed destination, used to be imagined and are now reimagined by people in Russia. I have dealt with how these imaginaries are implicated in nostalgic views of the recent past, and also in an ongoing desire for change and new aspirations. The widely used term *transition* implies a certain model of transformation that, on the one hand, is politically loaded and assumes the adjustment of the Soviet structures, practices, and institutions to the requirements of the market economy. On the other hand, it is invested with emotionally charged expectations that the transition means the progression from the undesirable reality toward a better life. For many people, this affective meaning of *transition* became the legitimization and the driving force of the transition in its political meaning. Therefore, the popular hope for a better life implied in the conception of post-Soviet transformation should not be downplayed in discussions of outcomes of the transition. In my view, the assessment of post-Soviet change in Russia should take into account, in addition to other indicators, the affective and ideational dimensions of people's feelings and thoughts about the point of departure from the Soviet and the point of arrival to the post-Soviet as they are viewed at the current moment. This is crucial because social imaginaries, engaging conceptual and emotional responses to the lived and remembered realities, motivate a further desire for change and the vision of the nature of that change.

Notes

I thank my colleagues for their support and the editors for their careful editing of this chapter.

1 All translations from Russian are by the author.
2 "Contemporary Moscow," blog post, Sept. 23, 2007, http://zharkov.livejournal .com/334142.html (accessed May 15, 2008).
3 Among the discontented publics are city dwellers, the St. Petersburg Union of Architects, NGOs, organizations for city planning and heritage preservation, deputies and advisers of the mayor, journalists and cultural workers (including the director of the Hermitage Museum, Michail Piotrovsky), UNESCO, and Europa Nostra (the pan-European Federation for Heritage). Mass media continuously attend to this case and mostly support the outraged public. For example, the Russian web portal on architecture (http://www.archi.ru) collected more than two hundred media publications on Okhta Centre; such archives are also available on the web portal Gazprom City (http://www.gazprom-city .spb.ru) and the Internet newspaper sites Fontanka.ru (http://www.fontanka .ru/gpcity/) and ZakS.ru (http://www.zaks.ru/new/archive/view/47141/).

4 The architectural competition considered six projects proposed by Jean Nou-
   vel, Rem Koolhaas, Jacques Herzog and Pierre de Meuron, Masseimiliano Fuk-
   sas, Daniel Libeskind, and the company RMJM London Ltd.
5 These numbers are well known by city dwellers and are widely discussed in
   mass media (e.g., T. Likhanova, "Zabeg v vysotu," *NovayaGazeta.SPb.Ru*,
   November 16–19, 2006).
6 For example, see B. Vishnevskiy, "Govorit i pokazyvaet OMON," *Novaya
   Gazeta SPb*, June 30, 2008; M. Mikhailova, "Okhta Centr teper's proektom,
   no po-prezhnemu bez vysoty," *ZAKS.Ru*, April 1, 2009; B. Vishnevskiy,
   "Razreshite otklonit'sya," *Novaya Gazeta SPb*, April 6, 2009.
7 For example, see "Peterburgskiy deputat: Izmeneniya v vysotnyi reglament
   goroda prinyaty nezakonno," *IA REGNUM*, January 23, 2008, http://www
   .regnum.ru/news/946255.html (accessed February 10, 2008); I. Kravtsova,
   "Vysotnyi reglament nad Okhtoy probili," *IA Rosbalt-Petersburg*, January 25,
   2008.
8 Here, she is referring to the shape of Okhta Centre's tower, which alludes to a
   flame. The flame is also the key element of Gazprom's logo. Quoted in B.Vish-
   nevskiy, "Govorit i pokazyvaet OMON," *Novaya Gazeta SPb*, June 30, 2008.
9 The interview with D. S. Likhachev for *Sankt Peterburgskie Vedomosti* on his
   resistance to the project of the Tower of Peter the Great was first published in
   1994; the newspaper reprinted it (posthumously) on November 11, 2006, in
   relation to the Gazprom City (Okhta Centre) case.
10 For example, unlike the critique of the American disciplining urban grid, the
   regularity and linearity of St. Petersburg's main streets (prospects) are viewed
   by both critics and city dwellers as opening up the space and thus liberating gaze,
   movement, and navigation of the body.
11 Examples of such mythologizing include a popular film, *Peter the First* (1937–39,
   director V. Petrov); a novel by Alexey Tolstoy, *Peter the First* (1945); and specific attention paid to this period of Russian history in Soviet school textbooks
   on history and literature.
12 For example, Alexey Tolstoy did not idealize Peter the Great in his novel *Peter
   the First*. On the contrary, the novel is driven by the complexity of this rather
   evil character, whose despotism and cruelty are, nonetheless, justified in a historic perspective and in relation to the interests of the state and nation.
13 Alexandr Pushkin's poem "Mednyi Vsadnik" ("The Copper Horseman") explores
   the complex relations between the despotic power (embodied in the monumental figure of the Copper Horseman—Peter the Great) and the life of an
   "insignificant" common man (the protagonist). The protagonist's tragedy—the
   death of his fiancée and his own insanity and death—is viewed by Pushkin to
   be the outcome of madness that characterizes the city of St. Petersburg, founded
   by the "Copper Horseman."
14 Peter the Great and his successors personally decided what and how to build
   in the city.
15 The notion of freedom and, associated with it, the notion of resistance are also
   grounded in certain facts of the city's history, such as the revolutions taking
   place in St. Petersburg, the nine-hundred-day siege during the Second World
   War that the city endured, and dissident resistance during late socialism. These

events were not formative of the skyline, but they contributed to the popular urban imaginary.

16 Expressions like "we can't change a thing," "struggle is pointless," "administrative power and money will do what they want anyway" are recurrent in people's opinions on the situation. Nonetheless, this general feeling of powerlessness does not prevent many of these people from being engaged in the confrontation.

17 Arkhitektura" (Architecture), *Shkola Zlosloviya*, NTV TV, Moscow, August 1, 2006, http://www.etvnet.ca (accessed November 20, 2008).

18 "Architecture of the USSR, part 1," Photo depositary "NoNaMe," January 2009, http://fototeka.nnm.ru/arhitektura_sssr (accessed February 16, 2009).

19 For example, Loshak's report was posted and discussed on YouTube (http://www.youtube.com/watch?v=3Wk215HVzwk; accessed August 17, 2008) and on a website of the social movement "Archnadzor" (http://www.archnadzor.ru/?p=1145; accessed August 17, 2008). Both sources emphasized that its TV broadcast was prohibited.

20 *Zapolnyayuschaya zastroyka* ("infill construction") is the term used in St. Petersburg; *tochechnaya zastroika* ("point construction") refers to the practice employed in Moscow. Both terms are used in other Russian cities.

21 City dwellers' characterization of post-Soviet urban transformation as feudalization resonates with the academic paper of Ryabov (2008) analyzing the reappearance of feudal elements in social institutions and practices of contemporary Russia.

22 For example, see the issue of *Critique of Anthropology* 27 (2), 2007.

23 Quoted in "Sovremennaya gradostroitel'naya praktika i genplan Moskvy," *Arkhitekturnyi Vestnik*, April 10, 2007.

24 Alexandr Skokan, interview by Grigoriy Revzin, *Agency of Architectural News*, September 3, 2008, http://agency.archi.ru/news_current.html?nid=8527 (accessed November 10, 2008).

25 Mikhail Philippov, interview by Grigoriy Revzin, *Agency of Architectural News*, September 6, 2008, http://agency.archi.ru/news_current.html?nid=8539 (accessed November 10, 2008).

26 CyrillosRussian, comment on "Retro Moscow (Moscow of the 1970s)" photo show, http://www.youtube.com/watch?v=nOMmgSqBrNo (accessed March 20, 2009).

27 Travelling abroad was highly restricted and controlled in the Soviet Union. Those who visited foreign countries often portrayed them in the best colours and in extreme contrast to the Soviet reality (e.g., see Yurchak 2005, 158–206).

28 "Architecture of the USSR, part 3," photo depositary "NoNaMe," January 2009, http://nnm.ru/blogs/sexy_baby/arhitektura_sssr_chast_3/ (accessed February 16, 2009).

29 Sergey Tkachenko, interview by Grogoriy Revzin, *Agency of Architectural News*, August 27, 2008, http://agency.archi.ru/news_current.html?nid=8428 (accessed November 10, 2008).

30 "Sovremennaya arkhitektura: Gradostroitel'noe tvorchestvo ili bumazhnaya igra?" Tem vremenem, TV "Kul'tura," Moscow, October 30, 2006, http://www.etvnet.ca (accessed November 20, 2008). The same idea was expressed by

Evgeniy Asse in his interview "Sel'skaya shkola i drugie mechty arkhitektora," *Nezavisimaya Gazeta,* February 8, 2008.
31 "Sovremennaya arkhitektura ..."
32 T.Likhanova, "Vysochaishaya nizost," *Novaya Gazeta SPb*, January 21, 2008.

References

Alexander, C., V. Buchli, and C. Humphrey, eds. 2007. *Urban life in post-Soviet Central Asia*. Gleich-Lesen: UCL Press.
Amery, C. 2006. Gazprom Tower will blight St. Petersburg skyline. *Bloomberg News*, January 7.
Andrusz, G., M. Harloe, and I. Szelenyi, eds. 1996. *Cities after socialism: Urban and regional change and conflict in post-socialist societies*. Oxford: Wiley-Blackwell.
"Arkhitektura." 2006. August 1. *Shkola Zlosloviya*, NTV TV, Moscow. http://www.etvnet.ca (accessed November 20, 2008).
Bauman, Z. 1991. *Modernity and ambivalence*. Oxford: Polity Press.
Berman, M. 1983. *All that is solid melts into air*. London; New York: Verso.
Bertaud, A., and B. Renaud. 1997. Socialist cities without land markets. *Journal of Urban Economics* 41 (1): 137–51.
Brade, I., K. Axenov, and E. Bondarchuk. 2006. *The transformation of urban space in post-Soviet Russia*. New York: Routledge.
Brandtstädter, S. 2007. Transitional spaces: Postsocialism as a cultural process. *Critique of Anthropology* 27 (2): 131–45.
Buck-Morss, S. 2002. *Dreamworld and catastrophe: The passing of mass utopia in East and West*. Cambridge, MA: MIT Press.
Czepczynski, M. 2008. *Cultural landscapes of post-socialist cities*. Aldershot, UK: Ashgate.
Davydova, N. 2007. Bashni moskovskogo City brosayut vyzov bashnyam Kremlya, February 16. *Izvestia*.
Donald, S. 2006. The idea of Hong Kong: Structures of attention in the City of Life. In *Urban space and cityscapes: Perspectives from modern and contemporary culture*, ed. C. Lindner, 63–73. London; New York: Routledge.
Europa Nostra. 2007. Europa Nostra appeals to President Putin: Stop Gazprom from devastating the world heritage skyline of St. Petersburg! December 7. *Agency of Architectural News*. http://agency.archi.ru/news_current.html?nid=4834 (accessed January 2, 2008).
Freud, S. 2003. *The uncanny*. New York: Penguin Classics.
Gazprom Neft Press-Center. n.d. http://www.gazprom-neft.com/okhta-center/ (accessed November 23, 2008).
Hann, C., ed. 2002. *Postsocialism: Ideals, ideologies and practices in Eurasia*. London: Routledge.

Hoffmann, D. L. 2003. *Stalinist values: The cultural norms of Soviet modernity, 1917–1941*. Ithaca, NY: Cornell University Press.

Holdsworth, N. 2003. *Moscow: The beautiful and the damned: Life in Russia in transition*. London: André Deutsch.

Ioffe, G., and T. Nefedova. 1998. Environs of Russian cities: A case study of Moscow. *Europe-Asia Studies* 50 (8): 13–25.

Iyer, S. D. 2003. The urban context for adjustments to the planning process in post-soviet Russia: Responses from local planners in Siberia. *International Planning Studies* 8 (3): 201–23.

Kaganov, G. Z. 1995. *St. Petersburg: Obrazy prostranstva*. Moscow: Indrik.

King, A. D. 2004. *Spaces of global cultures: Architecture, urbanism, identity*. New York: Routledge.

Lefebvre, H. 1996. The right to the city. In *Writings on cities*, ed. E. Kofman and E. Lebas, 147–59. Oxford: Wiley-Blackwell.

Leksin, V. 2008. Regional economic centers and social life of Russia. *Russian Social Science Review* 49 (3): 26–34.

Likhachev, D. 1989. Nebesnaya liniya goroda na Neve. *Nashe nasledie* 1: 8–13.

———. 2006a. Gradostroitelnye zavety Petra Velikogo. In *Vospominaniya. Razmyshleniya. Raboty raznyh let, vol. 2*, D. Likhachev, 227–35. St. Petersburg: ARS.

———. 2006b. Zapiski ob arhitekture. In *Vospominaniya. Razmyshleniya. Raboty raznyh let, vol. 2*, D. Likhachev, 239–47. St. Petersburg: ARS.

Lindner, C. 2006. The death and return of the New York skyscraper: Cather, Libeskind, and verticality. In *Urban space and cityscapes: Perspectives from modern and contemporary culture*, ed. C. Lindner, 122–33. London; New York: Routledge.

Lotman, Y. 1984. Simvolika Peterburga i problemy semiotiki goroda. *Uchonye Zapiski Tartusskogo Gos. Universityeta* 664: 30–45.

Markov, B. V. 1999. *Khram i rynok*. St. Petersburg: Aleteïia.

Nedovic-Budic, Z. 2001. Adjustment of planning practice to the new Eastern and Central European context. *Journal of the American Planning Association* 67 (1): 38–52.

Pivovarov, I. L. 2003. The urbanization of Russia in the twentieth century. *Sociological Research* 42 (2): 45–65.

Ryabov, A. 2008. *Vozrozhdenie "feodalnoi" arkhaiki v sovremennoi Rossii: Praktika i idei*. Working Papers 4. Moscow: Carnegie Moscow Center.

Shields, R. 2005. The virtuality of urban culture: Blanks, dark moments and blind fields. *Soziale Welt* 56: 377–86.

Shove, C., and R. Anderson. 1997. Russian city planning, democratic reform, and privatization: Emerging trends. *Journal of Planning Education and Research* 16: 212–21.

Soja, E. W. 2000. *Postmetropolis: Critical studies of cities and regions*. Oxford: Wiley-Blackwell.

Stanilov, K., ed. 2007. *The post-socialist city: Urban form and space transfor-mations in Central and Eastern Europe after socialism.* Berlin: Springer-Verlag.

Stites, R. 1988. *Revolutionary dreams: Utopian vision and experimental life in the Russian revolution.* Oxford: Oxford University Press.

Tsenkova, S., and Z. Nedovic-Budic, eds. 2006. *The urban mosaic of post-social-ist Europe: Space, institutions and policy.* Heidelberg: Physica-Verlag.

Williams, R. 1977. *Marxism and literature.* Oxford: Oxford University Press.

Yurasovsky, A., and S. Ovenden, eds. 1994. *Post-Soviet art and architecture.* New York: Academy Editions.

Yurchak, A. 2003. Soviet hegemony of form: Everything was forever, until it was no more. *Comparative Studies in Society and History* 45 (3): 480–510.

———. 2005. *Everything was forever, until it was no more: The last Soviet gen-eration.* Princeton, NJ: Princeton University Press.

8

Illustrating Desires
The Idea and the Promise of the Suburb in Two Children's Books

ONDINE PARK

Introduction

In this chapter, I consider the idea and the promise of the suburbs.[1] I do this by looking at how they are imagined in two children's picture books about young kids newly encountering the suburban landscape. *The City Kid and the Suburb Kid* (2008, written by Deb Pilutti and illustrated by Linda Bleck) and *On Meadowview Street* (2007, written and illustrated by Henry Cole) are as much about suburbs as they are set in them. Each, in its own way, mobilizes familiar cultural imaginaries, representing the suburb as a recognizable, taken-for-granted place while enabling the reader to consider suburbia anew as the young characters explore the possibilities it offers. I take up these highly acclaimed picture books (Chicago Public Library 2009; Mattson 2007; Whalin 2007) as illustrative of broader, shared imaginaries of the idea of the suburb and its promise to provide a much-desired good life.

As tools for enculturation and as demonstrations of cultural assumptions, these children's books gesture vigorously toward dominant, normative cultural meanings, values, and ideals. In particular, they affirm the "dominant and effective" (Williams 2005a) notion that the suburban place is a landscape that promises and provides for the good life, which is, above all, for young children. These books show suburbia as seeming to offer itself up ever to be rediscovered, waiting to reveal the surprising wonders of a pleasant nature, and as an alternative, self-contained whole world in contrast to the other world of the city. *The City Kid and the Suburb Kid* considers the suburb in direct comparison to the city, celebrating the different possibilities of everyday life afforded by the suburb versus the city. In this semi-nostalgic portrayal of the suburban good life, with its imperative to enjoy (Žižek 2006), suburbia appears as a vibrant, nurturing, inspiring, and abundantly natural place. In contrast, in *On Meadowview Street*, the suburb appears (at least initially) as a bland, alienating, conformist, and artificial space in the gently persuasive depiction of an individual actualizing the suburban promise through transformative intervention. With an ethical enjoiner to act, it demonstrates a rehabilitation of the relationship between suburbia and nature and considers the suburb primarily in this relation to nature. Although the images of suburbia presented by the two books differ, both are common suburban tropes, and, ultimately, their superficial divergence gives way to a similar desire for what the suburb can offer and what it might mean. In this wish image, suburbia appears as a nurturing environment that is an extension of the private, interiorized home, encompassing a benevolent nature and supported by family life. The suburb in this image is a conceptual and material space to express and actualize one's supposed most interior and desired self.

   On Meadowview Street and *The City Kid and the Suburb Kid* do challenge the normative suburban imaginaries somewhat. As picture books for and about young children encountering suburbia, these books juxtapose multiple liminalities (that of the picture book as medium, the child as audience and story character, and the suburb as subject, as I discuss further in the conclusion). They bear the potential to open up subversive "liminoid" gaps

Figure 8.1 Suburbia as a paper doll chain: a suburban ideal-type? (Photo credit: O. Park)

in the meaning and interpretation of the shared cultural imaginaries of the suburban good life. Yet despite this potent conjunction of liminalities, ultimately, the limits of the familiar, dominant imaginary are reinscribed, and the hegemonic tropes are reaffirmed and naturalized. My purpose is not, of course, to point an accusing finger at these particular children's books for failing to offer a more profound and radical critique of suburbia in their attempt to show children the suburban good life. It is rather to point precisely at these ideals and values, tropes and imaginaries, that are so deeply entrenched, ideological, and "normal" as to be invisible and, if made visible, seemingly intractable.

Representing Suburbia

There is a vast multiplicity of expressions of the suburban. Indeed, the suburb might be seen to act as "an open text—an endlessly interpretable landscape" (Knox 2005, 33). As a result, what "suburban" might mean specifically, or to what it should refer, seems ever contingent and undecidable. This leads many contemporary critical suburban scholars to contend that it is no longer a relevant category, especially when set in a binary against the city (Harris 2004; Nicolaides and Wiese 2006, 8). Despite this, however, there is an ongoing production of suburban images and representations that continue to have cultural resonance, as in the two books at hand. I suggest the "open text" of the suburb is closed when the "central system of practices, meanings and values, which we can properly call dominant and effective," is recognized (Williams 2005a, 38). This system is "a whole body of practices and expectations; our assignments of energy, our ordinary understanding of the nature of man [*sic*] and of his world. It is a set of meanings and values which as they are experienced as practices appear as reciprocally confirming. It thus constitutes a sense of reality for most people in the society" (Williams 2005a, 38). It is my contention that such a dominant and effective idea of suburbia operates in any representation of suburbia in which it is recognizable as such. This dominant and effective idea, then, can be gleaned from our two representative books.

Suburbs, like "the city" or other such places, "are not only the subject of representation but are 'objects' in representations" (Shields 1996, 228). Representations, then, make the suburb

> available for analysis and replay. Their strange effect is that, like the snow falling in a souvenir snow-bubble, representations blanket the city [and also the suburb], changing the way it appears to us. In Marxist terms,

> reality is obscured by ideology, which furthermore affects how we see our-
> selves and understand our actions.... In everyday life, we fashion and receive
> countless representations. Of course we all realize that a totally accurate rep-
> resentation—a perfect copy—is impossible. We are happy to settle for a good
> likeness. (Shields 1996, 228)

This ideologically interpreted good likeness is perhaps closer to any so-
called reality of the suburb than any ostensibly "real" suburb: an actually existing suburb looks "like" a suburb only inasmuch as the suburb that it looks
like is an idea—specifically, an ideal-type: a conceptual construct (*Gedanken-
bild*) to which an approximation might be made but which can never be
realized (Weber 2006, 264).[2] Representations of suburbia, then, "achieve the
appearance of reality to the extent that they conform to our preexisting conceptions of the suburb, which ... is a social image,[3] a state of mind" (Muzzio
and Halper 2002, 547–48)—an ideal-type. Inasmuch as any representation or any actually existing suburb more or less closely approaches this
ideal-type, it is a good likeness.

The ideal-type "is neither historical reality nor even the 'true' reality....
It has the significance of a purely ideal limiting concept with which the real
situation or action is compared and surveyed for the explication of certain
of its significant components" (Weber 2006, 266). This always contingent,
but seemingly fixed, conceptual construct is one that is built up through,
for example, an accretion of social, cultural, and personal experiences, images
provided by cultural encounters (mass media, hearsay, art, these children's
books, etc.) and by ideological and personal expectations. Subject to change
and reinterpretation, past and imaginable future encounters are used to
evaluate and make meaning of the ideal-types while they are simultaneously reevaluated and reinterpreted. There is, then, a web of reciprocal relations among the representations of the suburb, the built forms of the suburb,
and the idea of the suburb. Works about suburbia, such as *The City Kid and
the Suburb Kid* and *On Meadowview Street*, illustrate our already existing
presumptions and expectations of suburbia, and in turn render suburbia as
a particular thing, orientation, or image. These, then, are applied to subsequent encounters with suburbia, illustrating what a suburb ought to be or
how it shall be recognized.

The Suburban Place in Picture Books

On Meadowview Street and *The City Kid and the Suburb Kid* are two
examples of picture books that take suburbia as the focus of the story

Figure 8.2 Suburbia glimpsed through the back window of a moving vehicle. A child's-eye view of the suburbs? (Photo credit: O. Park)

(and not simply a background setting). Rather than depicting everyday life, these stories take as their problem exceptional, liminal engagements with the suburbs—how children are to make sense of, make home in, and find a good life in the suburban place with which they are newly presented. They demonstrate the possibilities and promises offered by suburbia. In *On Meadowview Street*, the young Caroline and her parents move to the distinctly misnamed Meadowview Street. Far from having a meadow view or being meadow-like, the neighbourhood consists of rows of repetitive, nearly identical houses on flat plots of lawn, fenced into cubicles. (One might be reminded of the tragic joke that suburbs are named after what they destroy and replace.)[4] Eventually, Caroline transforms her lawn, with the help of her parents, into a lush, variegated garden, attracting many living creatures. The neighbours soon follow suit, resulting in a transformed neighbourhood teeming with diverse flora and fauna. In *The City Kid and the Suburb Kid*, city kid Jack spends a week visiting his suburban cousin Adam. The two boys enjoy the fun and cozy offerings of this verdant suburban neighbourhood. Adam also spends a week visiting Jack in his bustling city neighbourhood. Initially excited to visit his cousin's place, which he idealizes, each boy eventually decides his favourite place is home.

Figure 8.3 Ubiquitous suburbanization? (Photo credit: O. Park)

These two books are among only a handful of North American, English-language children's books explicitly about (and not simply set in) the suburbs.[5] This is surprising given that in the English-speaking world, and especially in North America, suburbia is deeply culturally entrenched and nearly ubiquitous. In the United States, the suburban population equalled the combined populations of rural and urban dwellers by 2000 (Nicolaides and Wiese 2006, 1), and Canada had become a "suburban nation" by the 1960s, according to Richard Harris (2004). With this being the case, stories placing the suburb at the fore provide an opportunity for children to see themselves reflected in stories that make sense of their familiar setting and the everyday lived landscape shared by ever-growing numbers of children in North America. Moreover, the status of the suburban landscape continues to be contentious in the North American imaginary.[6] Despite strong dominant images and normative tropes, there is, nevertheless, an ideological battle over the interpretation of the desirability and affective meaning of suburbia, oscillating between such extremes as seeing suburbia as the embodiment and pinnacle of the "American dream" and viewing it as a "nowhere" threatening to make a vast wasteland of North America (if not also the rest of the world) and devastating sociality and community (e.g., Thompson 2006; Kunstler 1993). As such, one might expect to see some of this working out in stories about suburbia. In view of the limited number of such books and the contestation over what suburbia *should* mean, it is perhaps not entirely surprising that the few picture books about the sub-urbs imagine exceptional, *liminal* engagements with the suburbs rather than everyday life.

The liminal is an indeterminate time and space "neither here nor there," but rather "betwixt and between" (Turner 1969, 95), in which the ordinary, day-to-day social norms and order, space and time are suspended, allowing antisocial expression not tolerable in the everyday workings of society.[7] Although the term *liminal* tends to be used generically to mean sim-ply a time or space out of the ordinary and unbeholden to it, there is an important distinction between the *liminal* and a second term: the *limi-noid*. Liminoid times and spaces are similar moments of freedom from the ordinary constraints of society (examples include theatre, children's play, and sports). Whereas the liminal is a characteristic confined and restrained by the structure of ritual, the liminoid carries a potential for radical liber-ation. The liminal is a moment that ultimately serves to conserve and renew the existing social order, reasserting and strengthening its totality, and absorbing those who have transitioned back into community. The limi-noid, unconstrained by a ritual order, offers a potentially revolutionary break with social rules and responsibilities, and may induce a lasting inno-vative (anti-conservative) change in society (Turner 1987, 1982, and 1969; Shields 1991, and in this volume).

The qualities of liminality and possibility are characteristic of picture books as a genre, holding open the possibility of subversive, even revolu-tionary critique of everyday life.[8] Not exclusively a children's medium (e.g., Huizenga 2006; Kandinsky 1981; Masereel 1972, 1988; Tan 2008), picture books have "the power to provide insight into the 'changing terms of our world'" (Johnston and Mangat 2003, 203, quoting Birkerts). What is impor-tant about picture books, whoever the audience, is that one must read between and across co-present texts. The visual text of images is more than merely illustrative of or supplementary to the lexical text (if there are any words present at all). These texts do different work. They are read inde-pendently or interdependently; "their relationship is contrapuntal" (Shule-vitz 1996, 240). They can complement or complete one another, each helping to provide a fuller sense of the story (ibid.), but they may also be at odds with each other, opening up "liminal spaces" (Johnston and Mangat 2003, 203) of incommensurability and illegibility—or of possibility. In addition to the words and images, there are often additional significant *paratextual* elements to consider, such as the physical construction of the book or per-formative interactions with the book. Untypical of other written genres, pic-ture books, particularly ones intended for young children, can be multimedia performances when they are read to (or along with) children. The visual, aural, haptic, and even oral capacities of the child as reader-audience might all be engaged as the child looks at the images, listens to the words, feels the book and the presence of co-readers, and joins in the performance (or the undoing of the performance, such as by interrupting or losing attention).

Reading picture books is a process of active meaning-making intratextually within and across media, and intertextually across social, cultural, and experiential texts (cf. Crawford and Hade 2000). This reading across and between texts disturbs and subverts the usually "relatively stable interpersonal system" between writers and readers rendering visible the interstices between text and reader (Lewis 1996, 268), between performer and audience, and between texts. In such readings, the reader-audience is dramaturgically immersed into an alternative inchoate world where limits and boundaries push into and out of the texts, enveloping the reader in an "interstitial" (Lewis 1996, 260) world of potentiality. This immersion is sanctioned, even enforced, by the person in authority who performs the reading, possibly by the conditions through which the book was acquired, and perhaps by the very givenness of the book itself. With all of these overlapping modes of interpretation, children may, and often do, interpret picture books in multiple, highly idiosyncratic, and seemingly inconsistent ways, particularly when they encounter something that is unfamiliar or out of their experience (Crawford and Hade 2000).

However, for all this liminoid possibility, picture books often render complexities (such as, in our two books, the idea of the suburb, the city, family, community, or nature) into a thing that is knowable and to-be-taken-for-granted by visually and lexically codifying and contextualizing "explanations of items foreign to the viewer ... in order to expedite the meaning-making process" (Trifonas 2002, 191). In this way, potentially radical, creative, liminoid readings that this medium makes possible are ideologically subdued and recaptured. In particular, by illustrating what is presupposed to be easily recognizable as suburban, *The City Kid and the Suburb Kid* and *On Meadowview Street* key into and reify dominant cultural imaginaries of the suburban ideal-type, presenting a good likeness that is (meant to be) obvious and that children either already recognize as a "normal" place or presumably should learn in order to get to know their everyday world. Both books show the suburbs as consisting of relatively large single-family detached houses on large, private plots of land, covered in lawn, and surrounded by mostly self-contained neighbours with similar residential arrangements, all situated within an exclusively residential neighbourhood. Both books also highlight an imminent relationship to a benign (rather than malevolent) nature. They assert (by taking as given) the primacy of the Romantic family unit (i.e., a heteronormative, nuclear family in which emotional relations are primary), demonstrate the apolitical interiority of the private home dwelling, and hint at the dependence of these suburbs on automobile transportation. As "a place apart, the suburb offers a space of freedom, imagination, escape and fantasy" (King 2004, 106) that is at the same time far removed from the incursions of other people, "culture," and a sense of liveliness. For the most part, then, the subversive potential of these books is absorbed by their stronger normative pedagogical aims into a reaffirmation of the dominant and effective suburban imaginary.

The Suburban–Urban Dichotomy in Three Variations in *The City Kid and the Suburb Kid*

The City Kid and the Suburb Kid is a vibrantly illustrated, simply told, two-part story in the form of a "flip-over" book: the reader reads one story and at the end of it physically flips the book over to read the other story. One side is the story of the city kid Jack visiting his suburban cousin Adam for a week. The other side is the story of Adam visiting Jack in the city for a week. Each story begins with the boy reading an invitation from his cousin to visit. The invited boy is full of hope as he looks forward to leaving behind his everyday routines and annoyances (in particular, the tiresomeness of domestic suburban life for Adam and the invasiveness of crowded city life for Jack) to join his cousin in what he imagines to be "the perfect life" in an ideal place. This hopeful anticipation is reversed toward the end of the stories, with the visiting boy nostalgically thinking about home and the familiar things he originally couldn't wait to leave behind. The two stories follow an arc of shifting desires: anticipation of leaving home, enjoyment of the new place, longing for home, and a happy return.[9] Both stories end with each boy concluding that his cousin had a nice life, but that home is his favourite place. The last image is the boy writing a postcard inviting his cousin to visit, leading into the other story. The stories thus form a continuous loop.

Aside from the two moments of anticipation (of leaving and returning home), author Deb Pilutti's lexical narrative of how the cousins spend their time in the two places is paralleled almost verbatim in each story. The particularities of place are marked almost exclusively by illustrator Linda Bleck's pictures, which tell the story of the differences in the boys' experiences. For example, when, on each visit, they "took a ride downtown and explored the shops" (n.p.), in the suburb they are shown eating ice cream in the outside courtyard of a mall complex, whereas in the city they eat ice cream in an open downtown square amid buildings, traffic, and a throng of people feeding pigeons, playing basketball, taking in the sights, and more. The words graphically curling across each of the pictures suggest that in the suburb Adam's mom drove the two to the mall, while in the city Jake's mom and baby brother accompanied their ride on the subway or bus. On another day, when the boys "played in the water," in the city they can be seen playing in a public water park with many other children of various races, surrounded by tall buildings; in the suburb they play in Adam's grassy backyard, surrounded by trees, fences, and neighbouring houses, supervised by his older sister. This book pushes the possibilities offered by the multitextual picture book genre and plays on the tension in the gap between the sameness of the words and the difference of the images. The reader is required to interpret multiple simultaneous and consecutive texts: the words, the pictures and *sequences* of pictures, the relationship between the words and pictures, and the performance of reading these books. The reader then must make (or unmake) sense of all of these elements together. It is amid all this work of reading the many overlapping, competing, and separate elements that the book's three representations of the relationship between the city and the suburb can be seen to emerge. One version imagines that the suburbs and the city are fundamentally the same, differing only in minor specificities. Another shows the suburb and city to be complementary extensions of each other. The third variation shows the city and suburb to be diametrically opposed.

In the first variation of the suburb–city relationship, just as each lexical story is the extension of the other, and both stories are contained in the same book, the city and suburb can also be understood to be extensions of each other—each a different iteration of the urban (as compared, perhaps, to the unmentioned rural or wild). As Richard Harris (2004) notes, "Their very name, 'sub-urbs,' implies that they exist, function, and should be seen primarily in relation to the city." They function "primarily as adjuncts to the city.... The character of suburbs then is fundamentally urban" (48–49). Among the similarities are the types of fun and play opportunities available: going to a park, the movies, shopping, etc. The overall effect of this reading of the story suggests that fundamentally, people, whether urban or suburban, have similar desires and experiences, that the particularities of their dwellings are not sufficiently significant to suggest different modes of being, and that differences between the city and suburb are only superficial— indeed, they are barely worth noting.

These differences *are* noted, however, in the important opening and closing pages that act both to frame and to marginalize these considerations.

These few words that differ between the two stories (although still structurally parallel) bear significant assumptions about the city and suburb. For example, in looking forward to his impending vacation, Jack anticipates, "No more honking horns!" while Adam thinks, "No more lawns to mow!" Jack is eager to leaving behind hot waits for noisy subways, while Adam is glad not to have to wait for his mother to drive him everywhere. Jack thinks about his cousin's "huge yard with a big oak tree," while Adam thinks about the tall buildings surrounding his cousin's apartment. These differences, while otherwise unidentified in the central portion of the lexical story, are reiterated to fuller effect in the visual story and underscore a second vision of the relationship between the city and suburb, suggesting that the suburb and city are defined in their contrasting, perhaps complementary, relation to each other—each offers what the other cannot. The visual story depicts a stereotyped difference between the two places: the city is marked by diversity of activities and a background of culture (architectural buildings, people reading books and newspapers, ads for the zoo); the suburb is marked by nuclear family togetherness (Miller 1995) and neighbours, and a background of "nature"[10] (a pleasant, almost cute nature marked by trees, shrubs, flowers, and seemingly friendly little animals).[11] The city is a bustling mix of work, shopping, and leisure; the suburb is a place of recreation and home. The city features an elision between inside and outside, private and public, with many social and physical interdependencies and hybridities (e.g., eating restaurant food at home, watching a movie at an outdoor theatre in a park that is nestled among towering buildings), and many public places but little private space (Jack has to share his apartment bedroom with his baby brother). The suburb, by contrast, features relatively rigid demarcations between inside and outside, private and public (e.g., watching a movie in a movie theatre, going shopping at a mall rather than in a mixed-use neighbourhood, eating homemade food in the backyard), with vast domestic private places but little public space, and characterized by familiarity and an apparent independence from others beyond the immediate family, at least in the context of the neighbourhood. Whereas in the city there is an intensity of relations among strangers of various socio-economic positions mixing in a contracted space (cf. Simmel 1997), in this nearly ideal-typical suburb, there is an intensity of middle-class familial relations (Archer 1983; Fishman 1987; Miller 1995) and an expansiveness of space in which to do a narrower range of activities.[12]

The material construction of the book (that is, that one must physically flip the book upside down between stories) suggests, most extremely, that the suburb and the city are oppositional and incommensurate with each

Figure 8.4 Rectilinear suburbia. (Photo credit: O. Park)

other. In this reading, the suburb is the obverse or inverse of the city: they are worlds apart. One must literally turn the city on its head to reach or have a proper perspective of the suburbs, and vice versa. Like Alice, who famously visits a topsy-turvy, mirror-image world in Lewis Carroll's *Through the Looking-Glass*, Adam and Jack visit worlds turned upside down, where what is said and what is seen do not align, creating an uneasy breach in meaning. Jack's experience of the suburb and Adam's experience of the city unfold like a classic tale of voyage: the protagonist adventurously discovers the place of the story and finds it to be uncanny in its strange familiarity but ultimately alienating otherness. Initially marvelling at the newness, the protagonist (and reader), through the course of the adventure, becomes familiar with the surroundings, but always fundamentally remains a stranger who eventually leaves the place. Both Jack and Adam have an experience of the strange familiarity but abiding and unassimilable otherness of that fantasy ("perfect") world of his cousin.

The suburban good life offered in this book *becomes meaningful* only when juxtaposed to the good life of the city through the cousins' experiences of each other's place. Whereas Adam starts off understanding his life in the suburbs to be unhappily dominated by his responsibility to contribute to maintaining private property, by tolerance of and dependence on his family, and by boredom, he later is able to appreciate these as providing for a distinctly suburban good life: one marked by safety, recreation, and privacy. The comparison between the city experience and the suburban experience reiterates the dichotomization of *urban* experience into these two manifestations, with each offering a different fulfillment of the desire for a good life. Because they form a symbiotic binary, however, the suburb and the city are rendered mutually defining by their mutual exclusion: "In dualisms like urban-rural or public-private, each term is dependent on the other for its distinctness and definition.... In this system of meaning, the definition of terms and concepts ultimately is circular" (Shields 1996, 232). And we see this circularity rendered literally and haptically as, at the end of each story, the reader is enjoined to flip the book over and read the next story. Again and again, Adam and Jack are constantly leaving and entering that uneasy place. They never cease desiring, hopefully and nostalgically. They never feel satisfied at home, never come to feel at home in the new environment, and never return home for good. Jack's and Adam's desires for the perfect place wax and wane endlessly. Yet, in the face of all this unsatisfied desire, hope, and nostalgia, and despite the uncanniness across the two sides of the stories, neither the city nor the suburb is disrupted. Each is left to be exactly as it was: "perfect" and flawed in its own way. For all the tension between the words and pictures and the need for the reader to make active interpretations, Jack and Adam never get to fulfill their desires or resolve their misgivings in a final way.

It is not insignificant that Jack is in the suburbs exceptionally: he is there for a short-term visit with no expectation that he will stay and fit into an ordinary rhythm of life. While the place of suburbia is presented as normal and quotidian, both Jack's and Adam's experience of it is liminal: their everyday concerns (such as Jack having to share his room with his brother or Adam having to mow the lawn) are suspended in deference to constant enjoyment; their usual social identities of brother or son are disrupted and recast as special guest and generous host. And although the suburb Jack comes to discover is a world that is a known, pre-existing place in which enactment of desire unfolds, through the liminoid processes of play and discovery, the suburb is detached from its broader context and reshaped as a liminal space in which the extraordinary is possible. Ultimately, each boy emerges from his visit with a new sense of his social identity and a strengthened desire for his own community: whereas before the visit, each boy may not have seen himself as a suburb kid or city kid, by the end, each boy has an affirmed sense of his identity and of what place counts as home.

For Jack and Adam, the already burgeoning suburban conditions of home, nurturing nature, and close family life are simply waiting to be discovered and mobilized through playful engagement. *The City Kid and the Suburb Kid*, by opening up spaces between texts, holds open possibilities for imagining new orientations and new understandings of the suburb. But, ultimately, these texts, by playing on (and playing up) normative variations of the urban–suburban dichotomy, render these pre-scribed imaginaries as the only possibilities to be enjoyed. For Caroline, on the other hand, the latent potential of the suburban promise is recognized and actualized only through her transformative intervention, guided by her desire for a home in beautiful nature. Whereas Jack and Adam inherit existing worlds into which they must fit, Caroline acts to create a world of her own making and her own desiring.

The Nature of Suburbia: *On Meadowview Street*

On Meadowview Street opens with an image of an austere row of three identical detached houses, fronted by flat, rectangular lawns and prominent driveways. These configurations are separated by tall fences. Like figures in a paper doll chain, each house-lawn-driveway-fence configuration is identical to the next, with only minor passing differences: the lawn of the middle house sports a realtor's "For Sale" sign, and another features an adult pushing (or chasing) a lawn mower in seemingly frantic labour. The uniformity, blandness, and consistent rectilinearity of the features and lay-out of the built environment suggest an unimaginative, artificial, and alien-ating suburban landscape. Perhaps it is one that might be familiar to the reader. Caroline and her parents arrive (from where or why, we don't know), and as their moving truck is unloaded, curious, if rather undifferentiated, neighbours look on as they walk by with dogs and children, or simply watch at a distance.

Soon after unpacking, Caroline sets about "to explore the new street to see if there *was* a meadow on Meadowview Street" (n.p., emphasis in orig-inal). Before she gets very far, she notices a small flower in the yard and convinces her dad, who was about to cut the grass, to mow around it. She sets up stakes and string to form a "small wildflower preserve." As she notices more and more flowers, Caroline claims more and more of the lawn for her preserve. Eventually, the preserve of flowers and tall grass encompasses a large portion of the yard and her father sells off the lawnmower. With her parents, Caroline plants trees, creates ponds, and installs homemade bird-houses. In time, the yard becomes "a home to many things" as insects, birds, and other creatures move in, and children come over to picnic. One by one, the neighbours follow Caroline's lead, re-landscaping their lawns and sell-ing their mowers. By the end of the story, and answering the initial curios-ity with the same words, "there really *was* a meadow on Meadowview Street" (emphasis in original) and, finally, "a home for everyone." Under these last words, Caroline stands with watering jug and trowel in hand, watching birds gathered around a birdhouse. Here, "everyone" appears to refer to the birds,

Figure 8.5 "Cookie cutter" suburb. (Photo Credit: O. Park)

the transformed garden, and Caroline herself. Caroline has created a home for herself. The final image of the book parallels the first image: the three houses in a row. Now, instead of the bland, rectilinear house-lawn-driveway-fence configurations, birds are seen flying over the lush, verdant gardens replete with trees, flowers, animals, and ponds that front and visually link together these same houses. Caroline is no longer seen in this last image; one might guess that, having finished her heroic labour in making this place home, she has finally gone inside to dwell.

In this book, the suburb as a context for a relationship to nature and a place for home is primary. It is problematized inasmuch as the suburb in which Caroline initially arrives seems merely to simulate nature and home (and a home in nature), displaying isolated elements of natureness or homeness, or hinting at abstract ideas rather than realizing them. The fundamental questions of whether a home in nature or a home in suburbia is desirable or good remain unasked; indeed these are taken for granted as desirable. This image of suburbia as a home in nature (which, of course, we also see in *The City Kid and the Suburb Kid*) echoes early and still dominant ideals of the modern suburb as a marriage of city and nature, town and country. In the nineteenth century,

> the ideal of suburbia as a place of quiet, beauty, wealth, and Arcadian [i.e., pastoral] delights became a powerful and influential new paradigm. It represented the spatial expression of a new value system that emerged out of broad changes in society, economy, religion, and culture. Rooted deeply in

the history of the eighteenth and nineteenth centuries—across national boundaries—the elite suburb came to express a new bourgeois conception of the world. (Nicolaides and Wiese 2006, 14. See also Archer 1983; Howard 1965; Loudon 2006)

This suburban ideal is based on Romantic ideas of nature. With its origins in eighteenth-century Europe, Romanticism was both a backlash to and an outgrowth of Enlightenment rationalist philosophy (Berlin 1999). In this view, nature is interpreted to be "a realm of general perfection both morally above and ontologically prior to the corruptions and vices of human society" (Archer 2005, 158) particularly concentrated in the cities. Appearing in the nineteenth century in the United States and redefining "nature as benign and virtuous—rather than dangerous or threatening," the Romantics "emphasized the value of nature as a vehicle for human perfection and a source of contact with the divine" (Nicolaides and Wiese 2006, 14). Guiding the exercise toward human perfection is "the indomitable will," one of the central elements of Romanticism (Berlin 1999). That is,

> you create your own vision of the universe, exactly as artists create works of art—and before the artist has created a work of art, it does not exist, it is not anywhere.... The heart of the entire process is invention, creation, making, out of literally nothing, or out of any materials that may be to hand. The most central aspect of this view is that your universe is as you choose to make it, to some degree at any rate. (Berlin 1999, 119)

In this view, "the universe is a process of perpetual forward self-thrusting, perpetual self-creation" (ibid.). If one is able to recognize that the creative force of the universe is also in oneself, then the universe, that is, the natural world, appears *friendly* and one will "at last be free" (Berlin 1999, 120). Much in this way, it is through Caroline's labour that the potential for the ideals of a home in nature and a self agentically produced through the placing of home are finally actualized. Like the Romantics' redefined relationship to nature, the revised promise of the suburban good life that *On Meadowview Street* offers is one that embraces a benign, co-creative nature. This promise replaces the one with which Caroline's family is initially confronted, a place that struggles against an unruly nature that must constantly be confronted and overwhelmed. Caroline shows that instead of taming nature, suburbanites can foster it, repurposing existing suburban spaces into ones that might sustain the flourishing of an abundance of life.

Figure 8.6 Suburban encroachment on green field. Suburbia versus "nature"? (Photo credit: O. Park)

The book's implicit critique of the alienated conditions of suburban living and the failure of mass-produced built environments to fulfill the promise of and desire for suburbia is an important one. More vociferous detractors of suburbia argue that it is a failure aesthetically and ethically: that it is uninspiring, unimaginative, and inauthentic, harbouring conformity, complacency, and isolation—it "actively erodes the interactive social foundations of everyday life" (Thompson 2006, 35). They decry the failure in imagination that reproduce such a suburbia, and which exploits the signs of a good life in a good place but ultimately does not deliver upon it (e.g., Duany, Plater-Zyberk, and Speck 2003; Knox 2005; Kunstler 1993; Thompson 2006). *On Meadowview Street* illustrates an ecological, and thus more holistic, orientation to understanding a system of nature, showing that the suburban yard might be transformed from a monocultural lawn into a place hosting a diversity of flora and fauna. It offers what seems to be a *return* to a more natural nature—it seems when the lawn stops being mowed that the always-already present wild nature can self-actualize without the destructive interference of constant human activity. The book shows the wasteland version of suburbia—or "soulless suburbia and its faux-bucolic trappings" (Mattson 2007, 70)—then challenges the image, showing that care and effort, and expression of desire, can create a vital and sustaining place. In this way, the story quietly and gently offers solutions to a few major critiques of suburbia: by showing the transformation of possibility (Meadow-*view*) to actuality (a supposedly more natural nature), the story seems to suggest that suburbia need not be an artificial, barren, and utilitarian agglomeration of tract housing that destroys and wastes natural spaces for singular human use. Caroline's heroic efforts, supported by her parents and reaffirmed by her neighbours' efforts, suggest that the promise of the good life lying dormant in the suburban landscape can be vitalized with some agentic intervention. In the end, however, it does not fundamentally challenge the dominant promise or desire of an isolated and privately owned, single-family home. It goes only so far as to offer a way of abiding in these conditions alongside a less-reified version of an idea of nature.[13]

This narrative of recovering the real promise of the suburbs accepts an ideal of the suburban good life that relies on premises of a separate domestic space—the home as an expression and extension of one's self (Archer 2005; Bachelard 1964; Benjamin 1999; Csikszentmihalyi and Rochberg-Halton 1981), and privately owned property as a necessary sanctuary for the middle-class, heteronormative family (Fishman 1987); suburbia as a marriage of city and nature; and nature as an aestheticized ethical experience (Duncan and Duncan 2001; see also Olmstead 1968). Thus, rather than overturning those ideals, the story reproduces a fetishization of nature and romanticizes a narrative of mastery and perfection. It is the story of a single, heroic, self-actualizing and world-actualizing individual actively changing the environmental place and (perhaps) the social culture of her new community. Through her perfection of place and expression of will, she actualizes herself and places herself. In Caroline's relentless effort to create a meadow in her backyard, the story reaffirms the promise that home can indeed be a reflection and extension of the interiorized self, and that making home is an act of agentic self-actualization. That the neighbourhood is made a meadow entirely through actions on discrete household properties by individual families, rather than, for example, through a coordinated community effort, further suggests that home should be seen not only as a reflection of self, but also as an expression of private, bounded, *family* life. The neighbourhood is united aesthetically in nature-like beauty, rather than ethically in community. When it comes to their own family, however, Caroline's parents' quiet and active support re-enforces the ideal of the heteronormative family as a nurturing, emotional unit, grounded in the guarantee of nature itself (Fishman 1987). This nature they create is an aesthetic and ethical nature: one that extends caring, by being "home," to other living creatures.

Despite *On Meadowview Street*'s apparent critique against it, the ideal-type suburb of its opening pages, characterized by uniformity and conformity, is not ultimately challenged. By the end of the book, the uniformity of

Figure 8.7 Reformed suburbia? (Photo credit: O. Park)

the houses is again re-established, if revised aesthetically and with the possibility that the street might be more environmentally sustainable. Conformity, too, is reasserted. Although Caroline expresses her own desires in her
labouring, when the neighbours follow suit, they seem merely to imitate Caroline's aesthetic example. Whereas she processually responds to the affordances of the garden with no apparent master plan except to rescue and fulfill
the meadowness of her suburban space,[14] the neighbours reproduce her final
outcome. The book illustrates a movement toward a different sort of sameness despite its apparent attempt to show fulfillment of one's desires through
the enactment of one's capacity.

Conclusion

In this chapter, I have looked at the idea and the promise of the suburbs as
illustrated in two recent picture books about the suburban landscape. Both
of these books respond to a shared desire for a pleasant, mutually generous, and mutually nurturing relationship with nature, a place that supports
the protective and loving sphere of family togetherness, a place for kids to
be kids unassaulted by the woes of urban life,[15] and all of these combining
to make home. In their respective articulations, they affirm that suburbia is
desirable and a good life is supported by it. In *The City Kid and the Suburb*

Kid, the good life of suburbia is simply waiting to be appreciated (acknowledging that this version of the good life does not appeal to everyone, as eventually "the city kid" discovers). In *On Meadowview Street*, the good life and good home lying in potential in the suburbs must be actualized through active intervention.

In these books, the liminality and marginality of the child, the picture book genre, and suburbia come together to a potentially radical conjunction. Young children, both the intended audience and the represented suburbanites of these particular picture books, are liminal, occupying a marginal, at times invisible, social status in a world dominated by adults. Typically seen to be in a process of becoming, they are understood to be full of a future-oriented potential to be, but are ever not-yet. Yet, while socially marginal, they are, simultaneously and paradoxically, also culturally central (if fetishized) in justifications of suburbia. The picture book is also liminal as a marginal literary genre in which ambivalences within and between the multiple co-present texts can proliferate irreconcilable readings, opening up fecund gaps of meaning. This exceptionally flexible and "unconventional" medium "frequently possess[es] a playful and subversive quality" and may be (and quite often is) used for challenging, ridiculing, and subverting dominant, normative perspectives (Lewis 1996, 260). The suburb, too, is liminal, in no small part because it continues to be at least partially disavowed, contested, and misrecognized in its multiplexity, while also being the primary imagined space of home and the family. Spatially peripheral and culturally marginal (that is, rarely understood to be the site of "culture"), the suburbs form the expansive perimeters of the city and of the urban imaginary. Suburbia is also interstitial: imagined to be not quite urban and not quite rural, suburbs always seem, moreover, to be in the process of development yet remaining perpetually incomplete. This proliferation of liminalities holds open the possibility of transforming these containable *liminal* eruptions into a radical *liminoid* break, which might surpass merely reappropriating the promise of suburbia to radically recast the desire for a good life in a revelatory and liberating imaginary.

Both books do challenge some conventions, with Caroline creating a renewed vision of nature in suburbia, and Jack and Adam venturing through multiple overlapping and at times incongruent relationships between the suburb and the city. But in the end, for all their possibilities, their liminoid potential subsides into a bounded liminal eruption. Thus, the story of *The City Kid and the Suburb Kid* unfolds as an endless transition: with Jack and Adam coming and going, visiting but never staying. And Caroline, too, is seen only in transition as she moves to her new suburban place

Figure 8.8 Suburban home in nature? (Photo credit: O. Park)

on Meadowview Street, and then works to transform it into a home. Once she has successfully made the place her home, she is no longer visible to the reader. The books become tools for re-enforcing and displaying hegemonic ethical, aesthetic, and practical bases for judgments, illustrating recognizable and reiterated cultural imaginaries. The imaginaries reify the suburb as a familiar place that fulfills normative desires for an ideologically appropriate home in a safe place imbued with nature and family. It is a place that fulfills the desire for a limited and present-oriented conception of a good, happy, and well-placed life in which to raise young children. With both books, the idea of suburbia and the desire for the suburban good life are explored but remain fundamentally unchallenged.

Notes

Sincere thanks to Rob Shields, Olga Pak, and Alissa Overend for feedback on earlier versions, and especially to Heidi Bickis, Tonya Davidson, and Barret Weber for ongoing feedback. Any faults, of course, remain my own. This chapter builds on research supported in part by a Queen Elizabeth II Scholarship granted by the Government of Alberta.

1   In this chapter, I use the terms *suburb*, *the suburbs*, *suburbia*, and *the suburban* more or less interchangeably, recognizing that these designations have distinct implications. Common usage is not so rigorously delineated as in academic use, and the elisions between the different terms allow for a useful flexibility in considering the multiplexity of the suburban. Here, I am adapting the

notion of the multiplex suburb from Amin and Graham's (1997) discussion of the multiplex city.

2 See also De Certeau (1984) on the city as a concept, rather than an actually existing reality, and Amin and Graham (1997) on the ordinary city.

3 See Cambre in this volume for more on the image.

4 See King (2004) for a discussion of the work that is done by the names of suburbs.

5 A search of the electronic catalogues of the U.S. Library of Congress produces only twenty-one books for children and juveniles with any variation of the word *suburb* tagged as a subject heading. Four of these, including *On Meadowview Street* and *The City Kid and the Suburb Kid*, are fictional books for younger children (eight years and under). All four are picture books, published within the last few years (Robey and MacDougall 2006, and Ziefert and Cohen 2004). There is, in fact, a much larger number of children's books, both contemporary and older, set in suburbs (the popular Arthur series by Marc Brown, the mid-twentieth-century Dick and Jane series, and so forth), but, because the suburban setting in these stories is taken for granted as an ordinary, unremarkable place, it is not explicitly tagged in the keywords. As a result, such books remain unnumbered. Regardless of how many suburban-set books there may be, there is a notable dearth of children's books that put the focus on suburbia itself. See Muzzio and Halper (2002) on the difference between suburban-set and suburban-centred narratives (specifically movies).

6 See Pak, in this volume, for more on the "imaginary."

7 According to Arnold van Gennep (1960), this ambiguous status is associated with the middle stage of the three-part rite of passage ritual in which individuals or communities shift from one significant social category to another through the stages of separation, transition, and reincorporation. These rites may be linear (as in an individual's rite of passage to a new social status) or cyclical in nature (in which a community phases through different stages of seasonal change, for example).

8 See Hroch, in this volume, on puppetry. Puppetry's similar "minor art" form status affords it the freedom to critique radically.

9 Compare this to Hui's discussion in this volume of the role of the *virtual* home in actually making, leaving, and returning home.

10 To be clear, the word *nature* is never used in either this book or *On Meadowview Street*.

11 Buffam (this volume) finds a more extreme version of this urban–suburban dichotomy mobilized in his study.

12 It is worth nothing that both this and the suburban neighbourhood in *On Meadowview Street* do not reproduce the racial homogeneity that significantly prevails in other versions of the dominant image of suburbia. In addition, the main characters' racialization seem indeterminate in both books, but especially so in the case of Caroline.

13 On the "idea" of nature, see Williams (2005b). Duncan and Duncan (2001) show the hidden work that the idea of wild nature is made to do to protect socio-economic privilege and exclusion.

14 See Tiessen in this volume on affordances and capacities.

15 See Buffam in this volume for a discussion of the ideal of innocent childhood.

References

Amin, A., and S. Graham. 1997. The ordinary city. *Transcriptions of the Institute of British Geographers*, New Series 22 (4): 411–29.

Archer, J. 1983. Country and city in the American romantic suburb. *The Journal of the Society of Architectural Historians* 42 (2): 139–56.

———. 2005. *Architecture and suburbia: From English villa to American dream house, 1690–2000*. Minneapolis; London: University of Minnesota Press.

Bachelard, G. 1964. *The poetics of space*, trans. M. Jolas. Boston: Beacon Press.

Benjamin. W. 1999. *The arcades project*, trans. H. Eiland and K. McLaughlin. Cambridge, MA: Belknap Press.

Berlin, I. 1999. *The roots of Romanticism*, ed. H. Hardy. Princeton, NJ: Princeton University Press.

Chicago Public Library. 2009. Best of the best. http://www.chipublib.org/dir_documents/bob_09.pdf (accessed June 7, 2010).

Cole, H. 2007. *On Meadowview Street*. New York: Greenwillow Books.

Crawford, P. A., and D. D. Hade. 2000. Inside the picture, outside the frame: Semiotics and the reading of wordless picture books. *Journal of Research in Childhood Education* 15 (1): 66–80.

Csikszentmihalyi, M., and E. Rochberg-Halton. 1981. *The meaning of things: Domestic symbols and the self*. Cambridge, UK; New York: Cambridge University Press.

De Certeau, M. 1984. *The practice of everyday life*. Berkeley: University of California Press.

Duany, A., E. Plater-Zyberk, and J. Speck. 2000. *Suburban nation: The rise of sprawl and the decline of the American Dream*. New York: North Point Press.

Duncan, J. S., and N. G. Duncan. 2001. The aestheticization of the politics of landscape preservation. *Annals of the Association of American Geographers* 91 (2): 387–409.

Fishman, R. 1987. *Bourgeois utopias: The rise and fall of suburbia*. New York: Basic Books.

Harris, R. 2004. *Creeping conformity: How Canada became suburban, 1900–1960*. Toronto: University of Toronto Press.

Howard, E. 1965. *Garden cities of to-morrow*. Cambridge, MA: MIT Press.

Huizenga, K. 2006. *Curses*. Montreal: Drawn & Quarterly.

Johnston, I., and J. Mangat. 2003. Cultural encounters in the liminal spaces of Canadian picture books. *Changing English* 10 (2): 199–204.

Kandinsky, W. 1981. *Sounds*, trans. E. R. Napier. New Haven; London: Yale University Press.

King, A. D. 2004. Suburb/ethnoburb/globurb: The making of contemporary modernities. In *Spaces of global cultures: Architecture, urbanism, identity*, 97–110. London; New York: Routledge.

Knox, P. 2005. Vulgaria: The re-enchantment of suburbia. *Opolis: An International Journal of Suburban and Metropolitan Studies* 1 (2): 33–46.

Kunstler, J. H. 1993. *The geography of nowhere: The rise and decline of America's man-made landscape.* New York: Simon & Schuster.

Lewis, D. 1996. The constructedness of texts: Picture books and the metafictive. In *Only Connect: Readings on Children's Literature*, 3rd ed., ed. S. Egoff, G. Stubbs, R. Ashley, and W. Sutton, 259–75. Toronto; New York: Oxford University Press.

Loudon, J. C. 2006. *The suburban gardener and villa companion* excerpt. In *The suburb reader*, ed. B. M. Nicolaides and A. Wiese, 16–18. New York; London: Routledge.

Masereel, F. 1972. *The city. Die Stadt; 100 woodcuts.* New York: Dover Publications.

———. 1988. *Passionate journey: A novel told in 165 woodcuts*, trans. J. M. Bernstein. Harmondsworth: Penguin.

Mattson, J. 2007. Review of *On Meadowview Street*, by Henry Cole. *Booklist* 103 (19/20): 70.

Miller, L. J. 1995. Family togetherness and the suburban ideal. *Sociological Forum* 10 (3): 393–418.

Muzzio, D., and T. Halper. 2002. Pleasantville? The suburb and its representation in American movies. *Urban Affairs Review* 37 (4): 543–74.

Nicolaides, B. M., and A. Wiese, ed. 2006. *The suburb reader.* New York; London: Routledge.

Olmstead, F. L. 1968. The city beautiful: Trees, parks, and other open spaces. In *The American city: A sourcebook of urban imagery*, ed. A. L. Strauss, 456–62. Chicago: Aldine.

Pilutti, D., and L. Bleck. 2008. *The city kid and the suburb kid.* New York: Sterling.

Robey, K., and L. MacDougall. 2006. *Hare and the big green lawn.* Flagstaff, AZ: Rising Moon.

Shields, R. 1991. *Places on the margin: Alternative geographies of modernity.* London: Routledge.

———. 1996. A guide to urban representation and what to do about it: Alternative traditions of urban theory. In *Re-presenting the city: Ethnicity, capital and culture in the 21st-century metropolis*, ed. A. King, 227–52. New York: New York University Press.

Shulevitz, U. 1996. What is a picture book? In *Only connect: Readings on children's literature*, 3rd ed., ed. S. Egoff, G. Stubbs, R. Ashley, and W. Sutton, 238–41. Toronto; New York: Oxford University Press.

Simmel, G. 1997. The metropolis and mental life. In *Simmel on Culture*, ed. D. Frisby and M. Featherstone, 174–86. London: Sage.

Tan, S. 2008. *Tales from outer suburbia.* Toronto: Tundra Books.

Thompson, M. J. 2006. How suburbs destroy democracy. *MONU* 4: 35–37.

Trifonas, P. P. 2002. Semiosis and the picture-book: On method and the cross-medial relation of lexical and visual narrative texts. *Applied Semiotics/Sémiotique Appliquée* 4 (11/12): 181–202.

Turner, V. 1969. *The ritual process: Structure and anti-structure*. Chicago: Aldine.

———. 1982. Liminal to liminoid, in play, flow, and ritual: An essay in comparative symbology. In *From ritual to theatre: The human seriousness of play*, 20–60. New York: Performing Arts Journal Publications.

———. 1987. Betwixt and between: The liminal period in rites of passage. In *Betwixt and between: Patterns of masculine and feminine initiation*, ed. L. C. Mahdi, S. Foster, and M. Little, 3–19. La Salle, IL: Open Court.

U.S. Library of Congress. n.d. On-line catalogue. http://catalog.loc.gov (accessed April 15, 2009).

van Gennep, A. 1960. *The rites of passage*, trans. M. B. Vizedom and G. L. Caffee. Chicago: University of Chicago Press.

Weber, M. 2006. Ideal-type constructs, trans. E. A. Shils and H. A. Finch. In *Sociological Writings*, ed. W. Heydebrand, 262–75. New York: Continuum.

Whalin, K. 2007. Review of *On Meadowview Street*, by Henry Cole. *School Library Journal* 53 (9): 161.

Williams, R. 2005a. Base and superstructure in Marxist cultural theory. In *Culture and materialism: Selected essays*, 31–49. London; New York: Verso.

———. 2005b. Ideas of nature. In *Culture and materialism: Selected essays*, 67–85. London; New York: Verso.

Ziefert, H., and S. Cohen. 2004. One smart skunk. Maplewood, NJ: Blue Apple Books.

Žižek, S. 2006. Freud lives! *London Review of Books* 28 (10). http://www.lrb.co.uk/v28/n10/zize01_.html (accessed August 29, 2009).

Section III: Hope

9

The Virtual Places of Childhood
Hope and the Micro-Politics of Race at an Inner-City Youth Centre

BONAR BUFFAM

In cities across Canada and the United States, recreational youth centres have become politically popular antidotes to the crime, poverty, and hopelessness that are thought to pervade "inner-city," ghettoized spaces (Kelley 1997). In Edmonton, Alberta, the Eaglewood Community Youth Centre[1] was created to combat this "deleterious" influence of the street. This chapter draws on ethnographic fieldwork I undertook there to illustrate how the safe place *desired* by the centre organizers was intended to act upon and transform the otherwise hopeless futurities of inner-city youth. As centre staff worked to materialize this place of hope, the relations between youth, staff, and the material space of the centre surged with fleeting but effectual images and ideals of what childhood could and should entail. Occasionally, when youth flouted these virtualities, the *ecology of affect* that composed these relations intensified, registering different material and psychic displacements from and within the space of the centre.

On one afternoon during my fieldwork, the relational landscape of the centre was transformed by an argument between two centre staff and a nine-year-old boy named Ricky, who stormed out of the building as one of the staff shouted after him, "... and don't even think about coming back here for at least two weeks!" Jenny, one of the staff involved in the altercation, explained how the episode began earlier that day after she learned that Ricky had sworn at a cashier at the pawnshop next door. Upon confronting Ricky about his behaviour, the supervisors decided he should write a letter of apology to the cashier or face expulsion from the centre. Suspecting that Ricky could not fulfill this task, Jenny insisted she would help him write the letter, an offer he refused by yelling, "Fuck you, bitch! I don't need your help!" Although swearing was commonplace at the centre, it was rare to hear youth swear directly at staff; yet, in recreating the altercation, Jenny seemed less troubled by Ricky's aggressive, misogynist language than by his refusal to accept her seemingly benevolent offer of help. In fact, as her narration of the event came to an end, she let go a deep sigh and explained bewilderedly, "It just upsets me when they won't let me help them help themselves out of all this."

During my fieldwork, I often observed staff discipline or even eject youth for their "misbehaviour" or "lack of respect for others." These interventions into the place of the centre were typically animated by desires to help youth actualize particular idealizations of childhood, variously imagined by staff as a state of innocence, purity, or, in the case of Jenny, incompetence and dependence. In this chapter I conceive of these idealizations as virtualities of childhood that are neither simply abstract nor illusory. Rather, as they affect different practices of exclusion and displacement, these virtualities of childhood acquire fleeting, immaterial, but effectual presence in the place of the centre. Following Shields (2003), I conceive of these modalities of the virtual as "placeholders for different forms of reality that are not tangible even though they are essential and necessary and productive" (19). Premised on particular desired futures for youth, virtualities of childhood animate the place of childhood sought by centre organizers. Like Hui, who theorizes a distinction between space and place, I differentiate the place of childhood promise sought by the centre staff from the material space of the centre itself, upon which they try to superimpose this desired place.[2]

As staff worked to open the "present" to the distant, suppressed potential of childhood, their practices of hope transformed the "ecology of affect" through which bodies and objects were related in and *to* the material space of the centre. Rather than simply defer change to an uncertain future, as accounts of hope often suggest (Anderson and Fenton 2008), these practices of hope affect the surveillance and displacement of perceived attachments to the inner city, which might otherwise endanger the promise of childhood. Following Anderson and Fenton (2008), I attend to how "hopes provisionally emerge from within the sets of relations and encounters that make up processes of hoping" (78). In this vein, I document how practices of hope are imbricated with racial modes of identification that apprehend Aboriginality as a symptom of anachronism and criminality (Blomley 2003; Razack 2002a). Attempts to materialize this place of hope through the centre sanction a distinctly racial politics of ambivalent inclusion whereby its accessibility is circumscribed to actors who disavow, sublate, or excise the imagined racial differences of Aboriginality (Bhabha 1994; Goldberg 2002; Hesse 2007). Before I explicate the historical and geographical locations of the centre in the inner city of Edmonton, I must first discuss the centre as an ethnographic site suitable to an analysis of how virtualities of childhood inform the distinctly "racial" production of place.

Methodological Interlude

The Eaglewood Community Youth Centre is a drop-in recreational centre open to all youth between the ages of seven and seventeen from 3 p.m. to 8 p.m., Monday through Saturday. During an average five-hour shift, its facilities are used by approximately seventy youth, roughly half of whom frequent the centre daily. While inhabiting this space, youth are expected to participate in the different recreational activities provided by staff, including basketball, soccer, video games, billiards, and air hockey. In order to provide these services, centre organizers receive funding from local and provincial state agencies, in addition to the donations they solicit from local businesses and the broader public. During my tenure there, the centre was staffed by eight people: the executive director, the assistant to the director, the floor supervisor, and five other floor staff, including myself, all of whom lived outside the neighbourhood. Although one staff member occasionally referred to his Aboriginal heritage, at other times explicitly referencing his whiteness, the centre staff typically identified themselves as working-class white men and women.

I acquired research access to the centre through my participation in their fledgling hip-hop program.[3] For five weeks in the summer of 2005, older Aboriginal youth taught kids at the centre about the four primary elements of hip-hop: breakdancing, rapping, graffiti-art, and turntablism (Lashua 2005). During this time I served as the resource coordinator for the instructors, ensuring they had access to all the materials and instructional support necessary to run the program effectively. Yet, because the program ran for only two hours each day, I was often at the centre outside the bounds of the program in order to immerse myself in the daily relations between staff, youth, and the space of the centre. As I spent more time there, staff came to approach me as a volunteer capable of performing different supervisory tasks. These added responsibilities provided me with additional insight into how staff laboured to create a place hospitable to particular virtualities of childhood, allowing me to more fully engage in and understand the relations between staff, youth, and the material space of the centre. Overall, I undertook six weeks of intensive fieldwork at the centre, during which time I went there five hours a day, six days a week. Once the program concluded, the executive director hired me as part-time floor staff for another four months, with only one five-hour shift a week. This prolonged ethnographic immersion in the space of the centre has allowed me to explicate the ambivalent, even contradictory ways in which the "micro-politics" of race organize the relations of this place.

The "Hopeless" Place of the Inner City

The Eaglewood Community Youth Centre is located on the northeast periphery of downtown Edmonton, a major metropolitan centre in the Canadian province of Alberta. Although this area is three kilometres northeast of the main commercial sector of the city, its reputation as a local hub for illicit economies of sex and narcotics has led both state and public actors to characterize it as "the inner city" of Edmonton. Before I illustrate how this pejorative imaginary suffuses the relations of the centre, this section will sketch the distinctly racial contours of the inner city. This will allow me to show how racial modes of identification intersect with and inject the practices of hope that guide attempts to materialize a place for childhood promise. Urban sociologist Loïc Wacquant (2002) is right to warn of the analytical problems that arise when scholars appropriate folk concepts like "the inner city" from their circulation in policy and media discourses. Yet, as both Park and Jackson and della Dora illustrate (in this volume), mobile imaginaries of places like "the suburb," "the island," and "the inner city" cultivate affective attachments to and displacements from particular places and spaces. For example, the perception of this Edmonton neighbourhood as a crucible of crime and immorality is productive of different state and legal interventions into the area, a phenomenon that complicates tidy distinctions between the concrete space of the inner city and its discursive iterations (Keith 2005). When referring to this area as the "inner city" of Edmonton, I intend to evoke the multiple psychic, material, and discursive geographies that mediate how this neighbourhood is racially imagined, governed, and inhabited.

Like most other inner cities across Canada and the United States, this impoverished Edmonton neighbourhood is a distinctly racialized space, partitioned by boundaries that affect its differentiation from the rest of the city (Starchenko and Peters 2008; Keith 2005; Blomley 2003). Although Aboriginal people constituted only 5 percent of the city's total population in 2006 (Statistics Canada 2006), centre organizers typically estimated that at least 60 percent of their clientele are of some Aboriginal descent. The relegation of indigenous peoples to inner-city spaces has become a common process in Canadian cities with sizable Aboriginal populations, particularly Winnipeg, Regina, Vancouver, and Edmonton[4] (Ratner 1996; Starchenko and Peters 2008). Having endured centuries of colonial subjugation, indigenous peoples are more likely to experience the multiple dimensions of poverty than any other demographic group in Canada (Driedger 1999). To understand the distinctly racial efficacy of the inner city, as well as how the "benevolent" interventions of the centre intersect with colonial legacies of power, "the inner city" must be approached as an artifact of colonial desires to exclude indigenous bodies from the symbolic space of the Canadian body politic (Razack 2002a).

Colonial authorities first claimed the land now mapped as Canada by declaring it *terra nullius*, "uninhabited earth" or "nobody's land"[5] (Blomley 2003). By proclaiming the land previously uninhabited, authorities legally disavowed the historic and enduring presence of indigenous peoples on this territory, regarding their patterns of land use and ownership as uncivilized (Razack 2002b). To maintain the imaginative geography of this declaration, legal authorities across the emergent Canadian nation-state worked to expel indigenous bodies to spaces of peripheral visibility to white settler populations (Blomley 2003; Mawani 2003; Razack 2002a). Aboriginal title was thereafter consolidated to swaths of land known in Canada as "reserves," the majority of which were geographically distant from emergent urban centres of trade and commerce (Mawani 2003). On reserves, indigenous bodies have been subject to different tactics of surveillance and moral regulation that work to police and restrict their movement across the racial boundaries of the reserve (Mawani 2000, 2009). As the impoverishment of reserves intensified, indigenous peoples started migrating en masse to urban centres in search of employment and affordable housing (Ratner 1996). Once there, they are often subject to colonial geographies of containment and segregation that circumscribe their habitations of the city to impoverished, "inner-city" spaces (Blomley 2003; Ratner 1996).

Akin to well-documented "ghettos" in Chicago and Los Angeles, these inner-city spaces function as mechanisms of "ethno-racial" control wherein putatively undesirable populations are confined to peripheral areas of the city (Davis 2006; Keith 2005; Wacquant 2001, 2008). Yet, social scientists typically reserve the term *ghetto* for areas characterized by a stable, homogenous population, wherein the infrastructure of the city is mirrored by a duplicate set of institutions to ensure few people move across its boundaries (Wacquant 2001, 2008). Despite its disproportionately indigenous population, the inner city of Edmonton is characterized by a more heterogeneous population than most ghettoized areas, a phenomena that Driedger (1999) attributes to the smaller size of most urban Aboriginal populations. Regarded as the local epicentre of illicit urban economies, the inner city of Edmonton is often feared for the criminal proclivities or "criminogenic capacities" of its inhabitants. Outside the boundaries of the inner city, residents of this neighbourhood are routinely subject to practices of surveillance that conflate visible Aboriginality with criminality and danger. In fact, indigenous youth who frequented the centre recalled many instances when they were excluded from public transit; made the target of racial epithets by strangers; and temporarily detained by police officers, a phenomenon a number of them called "walking while native." These practices of racial subjection configure Aboriginal difference as a metonym for all the disreputable, criminal activities that are thought to pervade the inner city (Bhabha 1994; Keith 2005).

In these racial representations of the inner city, its inhabitants are divested of hope as they are consigned to phantasmic futures of criminality. Concerns about the hopelessness of "inner-city" populations have spawned a variety of state and public responses, including routines of avoidance, revanchist police suppression, and charitable public action (Kelley 1997; Wacquant 2008; Zukin 1996). It is these last, more "benevolent" interventions into the inner city, often spawned by public campaigns to ameliorate poverty, that have received the least academic scrutiny. Yet, since the late 1960s, recreational youth centres have proliferated in inner-city spaces as various social actors work to counter the "criminogenic" influence(s) of the inner city (Kelley 1997). In Edmonton, a group of senior citizens created Eaglewood Community Youth Centre as a corrective to the hopeless futurities faced by Aboriginal youth. According to the centre's promotional literature, these local residents desired a more socially productive alternative to "life on the street," which they cast as a place overrun by "an ever-presence of drugs, alcohol and prostitution." In the next section, I document how the place of hope desired by centre organizers is imagined and crafted in direct opposition to these phantasmic racial dangers of the inner city.

Hope and the "Latent" Potentiality of Inner-City Childhood

Since 1997 Eaglewood Community Youth Centre has offered youth in the "inner city" of Edmonton a place to participate in supervised recreational activities. According to its mission statement, the centre is intended to "give inner city youth *a better chance* by providing recreational activities in a safe environment" (italics added). In this articulation of its purpose, the beleaguered futures of inner-city youth figure as the objects of intervention for centre staff. By creating a place that is divorced from the perceived exigencies of the street, centre organizers intend to attenuate its criminogenic influence and return a sense of hope to the futures of inner-city youth. In this sense, my chapter is concerned with more determinate practices and processes of hope than Hroch and Jackson and della Dora (in this volume), whose contributions attend to hope as an affective state elicited by modalities of fear and surprise. Like Dorow and Dogu (in this volume), I explicate how quotidian practices of hope, which are oriented to more specifically parametered objects and futures, however immaterial, compose and transform the places imagined by social actors. As I illustrate in this section, the place sought by centre organizers hinges on particular virtualities of childhood that acquire fleeting, immaterial, but effectual presence in the relations between youth and staff.

   Sociologists and geographers alike evince how childhood acquires its semantic coherence through discursive processes of Othering and normalization (Hogeveen 2005; Kelly 2003; Kraftl 2008; Valentine 1997). Understood in opposition to the "fully developed" capacities of adults, children are often regarded as beacons of hope that possess "an immutable and assured futurity" (Kraftl 2008, 82). To the actors who organize and maintain the centre, it is precisely these futurities of neighbourhood youth that have been stifled and suppressed by the inner city. For instance, in a brochure intended to solicit public donations, the centre is lauded for "allowing these young people to be children, which is in sharp contrast to their lives outside of the Centre." Here, childhood is differentiated from the lived realities of inner-city youth, casting it as a capacity for potential that has become latent following their prolonged exposure to the dangers of the street. In this sense, the acts of hope practised by staff are more akin to its Latin derivation as *potentia*. Whereas *dunamis* refers to hope as it is situated in actual capacities, *potentia* denotes a form of hope rooted in a latent capacity or potency, one that is "distant in time and space but nonetheless not severed from the activities of the present" (Shields 2008, 129–30). Michael, the executive director of the centre, also conjured this virtuality of childhood after overhearing a young woman complain that she had to miss an activity planned by the staff to work at the local carnival. "You're thirteen!" he blurted with feigned joviality. "You shouldn't be working! The only thing you should have to worry about is having fun here!" For Michael, the true meaning of childhood, conceived here as a state of unrestrained play, is perverted by the exigent circumstances of life in the inner city.

Posters and plaques visible on the walls of the centre also cast child-hood as a capacity that can be retrieved from the dangers of the inner city. These material objects figure as constituent components of the centre's representational spaces, conceived by Henri Lefebvre (1991) as space as it is "experienced through the complex symbols and images of its 'inhabi-tants' and 'users'" (172). For instance, one week into my fieldwork, staff taped a poster about safe needle deposit to one of the building's front win-dows, making it immediately visible to the youth who use the billiards table in the foyer. Sponsored by the Alberta Street Safety Campaign, an initiative of the provincial government, the poster featured an image of a young girl staring intently at the viewer as she crouches next to an intravenous nee-dle, which she is ineffectually poking with a stick. The image is anchored by the question "What would you do if you found a needle?" Next to this question is a block of text that instructs children to notify the nearest adult of the needle's location without touching it. Positioned near a symbol of the inner-city drug trade, the young girl's image communicates that child-hood innocence is in danger of corruption by the street. Through its pre-scribed response, the poster imagines childhood as a potential that can and *must* be retrieved through strategic intervention into the inner city. As Kelly (2006) documents, this elision of childhood with potentiality war-rants practices of surveillance and intervention to help "immiserated" youth actualize particular futures.

The youth who used the centre were by no means passive recipients of these imposed virtualities, bringing different modes of apprehension to the consumption of images and symbols of childhood. During a routine game of pool, a sarcastic remark about this poster incited three adolescent boys to recall their encounters with intravenous needles. With each passing story, the details of how each of them overcame the "danger" posed by the needle became more heroic and fantastical, until one eleven-year-old bragged of using a needle to ward off an older "banger," a term the youth used to describe older "gangster wannabes." By performing their competence for others, these youth subverted and satirized the normative idealization of childhood prescribed by the centre organizers. Yet, as I document in the final section of this chapter, youth were typically forced to hide, silence, or disavow such competing articulations of childhood or risk being disciplined or expelled from the centre.

The physical exterior of the centre also differentiated its space from the surrounding area. In fact, the building itself had been recently painted bright blue and white, setting it apart from the worn aesthetic of the other businesses on the avenue. When graffiti occasionally appeared on the outside walls, staff ensured it was immediately painted over, preserving its differentiation from the boarded-up building next door that was marked by different graffiti tags. Upon entering the centre for the first time, one adolescent boy even remarked, "Wow, this is like the only place on the street that isn't ghetto! Everywhere else is like boarded up or burned down."

The entrance to the centre is framed by two plaques that distinguish its interior from the imagined dangers of the inner city. Engraved on the plaque to the left of the entrance is the declaration, "Hope for the future for Eaglewood Kids." Through this commemoration, the futures of youth are again made the loci of psychic attachment and affective investment for the actors who sustain this space. Yet, according to this commemoration, it is only youth who participate in this social space that can activate their latent potential, consigning others to the hopeless futurities of the street. The plaque to the right is engraved with the words "Through these doors our promise for tomorrow." The polysemic connotations of this declaration facilitate a number of readings of exactly what is entailed by the "promise" of the centre. Children are oft-imagined as agents of change and transformation (Hogeveen 2005; Kelly 2000; Kraftl 2008). By nurturing their latent potential, centre organizers hope to fashion youth who are capable of change and promise. Yet, if we think of centre organizers as the authors of this enunciative act, "the promise" of the centre might be understood differently. It can be read as a declaration that, like its clientele, all marginalized populations will eventually be granted inclusion in secure spaces of the city. In deferring this inclusion to an uncertain future, the temporality of this promise parallels the historic promise of colonial modernity.

Since at least the nineteenth century, the benefits or "promise" of democratic citizenship have appeared to "non-Western" populations as the instruction to await inclusion in the discursive and governmental horizons of modernity (Chakrabarty 2007; Goldberg 2002). To rid these populations of their "anachronistic," "uncivilized" habits, vast governmental apparatuses have been elaborated to administer the entrance of racial difference into the symbolic space of Euro-colonial modernity[6] (Hesse 2007; Mawani 2009). Inclusion in this space of desired universality has typically been contingent on the violent erasure of peoples' perceived particularities, especially their "different" cultural, religious, and economic practices (Goldberg 2002). In Canada, the project of "modernizing" indigenous peoples involved the proscription and suppression of cultural and spiritual events, the forcible re-education of children in residential schools, and the imposition of capitalist modes of land usage and economic interaction (Blomley 2003; Mawani 2009; Razack 2002a).

Conceived as a universal state of becoming, childhood is frequently conceived as a vector of transcendent potentiality (Kelly 2003; Kraftl 2008). In the social imaginary of the centre staff, the modalities of racial and cultural difference through which indigenous peoples have been excluded from the white body politic can be erased or sublated into this universalized, "presocial" state of becoming. Yet, during their daily provision of safe space, staff regularly apprehend modalities of Aboriginal "difference" as evidence of some attachment to the "particularities" of inner-city spaces. For Homi Bhabha (1994), this vacillation between the disavowal and recognition of "difference" is characteristic of the ambivalent force of colonial racisms, which is encapsulated by the title of Fanon's canonical book, *Black Skin White Masks*. In the racial ontology that undergirds and animates Canadian social spaces, urban Aboriginality references both the fabricated differences that legitimized their colonization, as well as the phantasmic depravities of the inner city that have become part of the public imaginary (Keith 2005; Razack 2002a; Wacquant 2002). As these differences threaten to fracture the desired universality of childhood, staff work vigilantly to mute, suppress, and excise their different iterations from the material space of the centre. In fact, as I document in the last section of this chapter, access to this place of hope is spatially administered through the ambivalent recognition and disavowal of inner-city, Aboriginal difference.

Administering a Space of Childhood Promise

Practices of surveillance have long been integral to the racial governance of urban spaces, facilitating the production and maintenance of different segregating boundaries and topographies (Razack 2002a; Staples 2000). Even as they elaborate a discursive space through which subject populations can be more effectively known and governed, these practices of disciplinary observation can affect peoples' conformity to certain prescribed modes of being (Bhabha 1994; Foucault 1977; Haggerty and Ericson 2000). In this last section of the chapter, I consider how the centre staff deploy different tactics of surveillance to superimpose a place of childhood hope upon the material space of the centre. Centre organizers intend these practices of observation to interpellate youth who can properly manage and overcome their attachments to the inner city, especially the drugs, sex, and violence that staff treat as symptomatic of this place. Yet, in practice, these tactics of surveillance materialize processes of racial identification that isolate Aboriginal difference as a sign and symptom of inner-city danger.

"In or Out": Practices of Differentiation

Through their routine practices of supervision, centre staff work to differentiate the space inside the centre from the phantasmic dangers of the inner city
outside. As the only point at which people can enter the building, the front
foyer figures as the primary site of disciplinary observation. Regardless of how
many staff are working at any one time, one person is always stationed in the
front foyer to police the movement of bodies in and out of the building. Aid-
ing this task of surveillance is an alarm bell that sounds every time the entrance
door is opened. Youth absorbed in their routine activities typically take no
notice of the alarm; yet, for staff, the muted tone of this bell serves an integral
role in maintaining the boundaries of place at the centre. Upon hearing it
sound, staff are expected to determine exactly who has entered or exited the
building. During a bimonthly staff meeting, the floor supervisor, who is responsible for the daily coordination of other staff, instructed everyone that "no
matter where you are on the floor, you should be able to hear the alarm and
see who's coming. If you can't, you better move to somewhere you can."

Staff supervising the front foyer are also expected to ensure that all
youth entering the building immediately "sign in" to the centre by recording their contact information in a binder located in the front foyer. Youth who
frequent the centre obey this rule with relative frequency, as deviations from
this routine attract the attention of staff, who I often heard yell, "Sign in!"
at errant youth. Although the instrumental purpose of the log is to track
how many youth use the centre each month, the practice of signing in works
to symbolically inculcate youth into the social space of the centre.

This boundary between the street and the centre is also reinforced
through the stipulation that youth are not allowed to leave and re-enter the
building on the same day. During my fieldwork I regularly heard staff bark
the injunction "in or out!" at youth moving toward the exit. Tired of youth
pleading ignorance about the rule, the floor supervisor eventually posted a
sign on the exit which informed kids that if they leave the centre they will
not be allowed back that day. The enforcement of this rule, which was
intended to curb teenagers' smoking habits, mitigates contact between the
centre and the street outside. It is against this putatively ordered backdrop
of the centre that staff try to identify and isolate signs of inner-city danger
as they circulate through this space.

Practices of Excision and Expulsion

Once inside the centre, youth are subjected to the surveillant optics of staff.
Here, their bodies figure as sites of scrutiny while staff work to identify

perceptible attachments to the inner-city streets. More specifically, during their daily supervisory tasks, staff survey the landscape of the centre for *signs* of the drug use, sexuality, and violence that metonymize the imagined dangers of the street. It was to mute, oppose, or cast out these phantasmic "vices" that virtualities of childhood acquired presence in the space of the centre. That "vice" is an antonym of virtue, out of which the concepts virtual and virtuality are derived (Shields 2003), gestures to how these processes of hope intersect with and are propelled by desires for the moral transformation of the inner city as well.

Signs of drug use, for instance, regularly attracted the disciplinary ire of staff. Youth wearing clothing with marijuana insignia were told to remove the article of clothing, turn it inside out, or go home to change their clothing entirely. Staff occasionally instructed teenage boys to remove cigarettes from behind their ears out of concern that it might send a bad message to the younger kids.[7] To keep the centre free of the influence of *illegal* drugs, staff honed a surveillant optic to help them determine whether a particular child had recently used drugs. After hearing from one of the staff that a teenager was behaving erratically, the floor supervisor instructed her to stare closely at the boy's eyes to determine whether he had recently smoked marijuana. "If his pupils are dilated or the whites of his eyes are too red," he explained, "he's high. Boot 'em!"

Overt displays of sexuality were also rigorously surveilled and suppressed by centre staff. Although the computers available to youth were equipped with filters that restricted the consumption of pornography, adolescent boys regularly perused sexually explicit material, particularly on social networking platforms and websites for men's magazines like *Maxim*, *Stuff*, and *FHM*. When caught looking at "inappropriate" material, they were typically banned from the centre for the day and suspended from the computer lab for at least a week. Of greater concern to staff, however, were perceived displays of sexual desire. Young women exposing "too much skin" were told to cover up their bodies or go home to change. For instance, a fourteen-year-old wearing a low-cut tank top was instructed to put on a sweater after a number of boys were spotted trying to look down her shirt. Subject to a distinctly gendered form of responsibility, this young woman was held to account for the violence that might be visited upon her body by the *imagined* sexual desires of her male peers. To the staff, she was rendered visible through "the only form of capital young women can trade on ... their body, their sexuality, and their fertility" (Bullen and Kenway 2004, 148).

These distinctly moral virtualities of childhood also manifested during a meeting about the hip-hop program. As it wrapped up, Michael, the executive director, informed us that a previous dance program had failed after the instructor refused to wear "age-appropriate" clothing to her lessons. Recreating his confrontation with the instructor, Michael explained that

> she would come in all scantily clad and we'd tell her [intimating an overtly patient, rational tone that was belied by his infamously short temper], "You know, you need to dress differently." Then she was like [mimicking the tone and mannerisms of a petulant young woman], "Well, that is what I wear at the club." So I just finally told her, "Yeah, but this is a bunch of thirteen-year-olds. Many of these kids see their moms, cousins, and sisters dress like this when they go out for a night on the town."

Behind closed doors, Michael was prone to employ racial tropes to characterize the family lives of the centre clientele. Here, the ambiguous turn of phrase "go out for a night on the town" conjures more innocuous images of urban nightlife even as it purposefully evokes the phantasmic depravities of (Aboriginal) women working inner-city strolls. In so doing, Michael casts the familial realm of inner-city youth as a place overwrought by the excessive sexual desires of women, a perception that demands the creation of a public space devoid of sexual desire. Looming over this benevolent prescription is the trope of the sexually wanton Aboriginal woman, whose excessive sexual desires have long been a figment of the Canadian colonial imagination (Pratt 2005; Razack 2002a).

Of particular concern to staff was the seemingly ubiquitous threat of violence in the centre. To most of them, gangs were the most *perceptible* catalyst of violence. As a result, presumed symbols of gang affiliation were always intensely surveilled by staff. A staff meeting was derailed when the assistant director recalled seeing the words "Indian Posse" scrawled on a nearby bus stop, only to have the threat dissipate when the floor supervisor insisted that the graffiti actually said "Indian Pussy." "Oh, okay," the executive director explained, conveying his relief. "If it had said 'Indian Posse' I would have to report it to the police." Gang colours, in particular, were the signs of inner-city danger most rigorously policed by the staff. Although they never had exact specifications of what constituted a display of colours, black, red, and white bandanas were effectively banned from the centre, particularly when worn by young Aboriginal men. During my second week of fieldwork I watched the floor supervisor admonish a teenage Aboriginal boy for wearing a black bandana around his head. "I've told you time and again, no colours in the centre!" he barked, the tenor of his voice communicating an urgency rarely expressed by someone so acclimatized to the antics of youth.

Bulletins about trends in gang dress released by the Edmonton Police Service informed how staff identified gang colours. In the update issued in fall 2005, a battery of similarities in dress were catalogued as signs of potential participation in gangs, including groups of youth wearing the same colour of bandanas, baseball hats, shoelaces, and bands of tape worn over the arm; the same earrings; and sloppily tied shoelaces. When viewed through this legal optic of surveillance, otherwise mundane objects of clothing acquired a menacing potential for violence. That two Aboriginal gangs, Indian Posse and Red Nation, were the only gangs mentioned in the update affixes a violent potentiality to Aboriginal-looking bodies with perceptible attachments to the inner city. In this sense, the phenotypical markers through which Aboriginal "racial" difference is projected onto the body serve as semiotic tools in the identification of "gang" affiliations. As Goldberg and Hristova (2007) more poetically explain, "Skin situates its bearers in racially predicated societies. It sites and restricts, it announces and delimits, it allows and disables, it fixes relation and relates fixations, orders belief and anchors belief in order" (n.p.).

The manner in which staff responded to these signs of inner-city danger varied according to the perceived "hopelessness" of the youth in question. During their daily practices of supervision, staff differentiated between clientele who could escape "the street" and those who would succumb to its hopeless futurities. This was made especially evident after the only time I ejected someone from the centre. That afternoon I had repeatedly warned a white eight-year-old boy named Charlie to stop interfering with the other kids, a number of whom had complained of his aggressive behaviour. Finally, after being told that he had shoved and hit someone, I told Charlie that he was banned from the centre for the day. Ten minutes later, I was approached by one of the staff, who told me that, unlike the other youth his age, Charlie was not to be kicked out. "With Charlie," he explained, patiently, "you have to find some other way to discipline him 'cause there's no point in booting out the few ones who have a shot." While younger kids were often treated more leniently than teenagers, no one was given the same leeway as this young white boy. For staff, the perceived fragility of his future required a different, more "strategic" response than other youth his age, who they felt did not have the same "shot" at escaping the phantasmic influence of the street.

The Dangers Outside

The surveillance practices of staff were not limited to the material space of the centre itself;the zone immediately outside the building was subject to rigorous observation as well. Of particular concern to staff was the abandoned building next to the centre, which they suspected was being used to distribute marijuana and "crystal meth." To manage the danger it posed, one of the floor staff used her fifteen-minute smoke breaks to monitor activity in and around the building. Upon completing these "perimeter sweeps," she would then record the licence plate numbers of any cars observed outside the building in a binder that she later turned over to a community police officer.

Concern about this alleged drug house was magnified after Trisha, one of the floor supervisors, noticed a woman "tweaking out" in the alley behind the centre. After police detained and removed her from the area, the executive director of the centre called an impromptu staff meeting, which he started by informing everyone that "a Native woman had been coming down off of crystal meth right out back." "Yeah, she was shaking and stuff," Tasha interjected, gesturing to the apparent gravity of the situation, "so who knows what she'll do! I mean do whatever, but this is a youth centre for god sakes!" For Trisha, the apparent addiction of this woman recapitulated the imagined unpredictability and disorder of her explicitly *cited* racial difference. Although this woman had not tried to interact with youth or even enter the centre, her mere proximity to it demanded her immediate ejection from the area.

The corner across from the centre, which was reputed to function as a stroll for the solicitation of sex, also attracted the surveillant optic(s) of staff. In fact, the sight of an Aboriginal-looking woman standing on the corner frequently drew the attention of staff, a number of whom would call police to move the woman from the area. On only my third visit to the centre, my meeting with Michael, the executive director, was interrupted by the sight of a woman waiting at the corner. Once at the window, Michael peered through a crack in the blinds to discern the plate number of a truck that was idling by the woman. Leaning back, he remarked to me, "It's a full-time job, you know." "What, prostitution?" I asked, thinking he was referring to the work of the woman he was surveilling. "No, no," he replied, "taking down the licence plates." Already lost to the criminogenic futurities of the street, women working in the sex trade were consigned by staff to a place beyond the ambit of hope, their promise deemed no longer retrievable from the street. To staff, their bodies figured as contagions from which youth must be vigilantly protected, a task that Michael thought required "full-time" surveillance.

Conclusion

Six months after completing my fieldwork, I ran into one of the staff who still worked at the centre. After some initial small talk, I asked after a number of the youth who used to frequent the centre, including an eleven-year-old boy named Dale, with whom I had established a good rapport. During my last month there, staff had grown concerned that Dale was being "unduly" influenced by his older cousin, a fourteen-year-old named Clayton, who occasionally inhabited the centre with a group of older Aboriginal boys. "Dale doesn't come around much anymore," she explained, "and when he does it's usually with those other boys with mile-long rap sheets. At this point, we're all pretty sure we've lost him." In my experience, staff differed in how they characterized the threat this group of young men posed to the other youth at the centre; while the floor supervisor dismissed Clayton and his friends as "posers," regarding their aggressive behaviour as mere posturing, a number of the staff appeared more troubled by their presence there, becoming enraged at their slightest deviation from the rules. To them, Clayton and his friends metonymized the racial force of the street to which the centre was opposed in a phantasmic conflict over the futures of inner-city youth. In this sense, Dale's absence from the centre signified that he had been enveloped by the racial place of the street to which these older boys were already "lost."

During earlier phases of colonization in Canada, familial ties were oft-regarded as an impediment to the effective "modernization" of indigenous youth, a perception that sanctioned their removal from the domestic sphere and forced enrolment in residential schools. In their quest to combat the force of the street, the social actors who maintain the centre recapitulate these racial modes of identification by casting older Aboriginal relatives as criminogenic influences that endanger the promise or potential of youth. To retrieve this promise, centre staff work to create a place that is radically extricated from the fabricated dangers of the inner city. Yet, in striving to materialize this place, they gave rise to a particular "ecology of affect" in which the iterative differences registered by Aboriginality elicit processes of surveillance and exclusion. By documenting the different "micro-political" fissures, (dis)placements, and (dis)associations that are engendered by the spatialization of childhood promise, this chapter has shown how different practices and processes of hope intersect with and propel specifically racial assemblages of power. In circumscribing the accessibility of its space, the centre organizers exclude the very people they want to help, displacing, or by the logic of their own imaginary, re-placing them in the space of the inner city.

Notes

The research upon which this chapter builds was generously supported by a Canadian Graduate Scholarship from the Social Sciences and Humanities Research Council of Canada. I am indebted to the editors and other collaborators for their feedback on this chapter, as well as to Bryan Hogeveen, George Pavlich, Karen Fox, and Renisa Mawani for their guidance on earlier drafts of this work.

1 To maintain the anonymity of my research subjects I have changed the names of the youth centre, the centre staff and all of the youth who attend the centre. When necessary I have also changed certain identifying details of the centre's location and history without, however, modifying the substantive features of its functions.
2 I do not, however, have room to fully explicate the dimensions of place that emerge from the relations between staff, youth, and the material space(s) of the centre, focusing instead on the iterations of place desired by the staff in particular. For more on the theorization of place, see Davidson, Hui, and Park in this volume.
3 Started by a leisure studies doctoral candidate, the hip-hop program was originally a recreation-based music course for students at a charter school in downtown Edmonton (see Lashua 2005).
4 Studies of urban Aboriginal populations in Canadian cities show that segregation intensifies as the size of local Aboriginal populations increases. For instance, Winnipeg, the largest city in the Prairie province of Manitoba, has both the largest urban Aboriginal population of any metropolitan centre in Canada and the most intensified segregation (Driedger 1999; Starchenko and Peters 2008).
5 By the standards of international law, land can be claimed only through war, cessation, or if the land is previously uninhabited, *terra nullius* (Razack 2002b).
6 Critical race theorist Barnor Hesse (2007) uses the term "Euro-colonial modernity" to denote the historical agglomeration of ideational, material, and juridical apparatuses that are organized to assert the natural and historical superiority of European populations, whose qualities are displaced onto different whiteness, Christianity, and secularity.
7 That three of the staff regularly smoked in front of and behind the building, in plain view of the youth, seemed to have no bearing on this practice.

References

Anderson, B., and J. Fenton. 2008. Editorial introduction: Spaces of hope. *Space and Culture* 11 (2): 76–80.

Anderson, B., and A. Holden. 2008. Affective urbanism and the event of hope. *Space and Culture* 11 (2): 125–141.

Bhabha, H. K. 1994. *The location of culture*. New York: Routledge.

Blomley, N. K. 2003. *Unsettling the city: Urban land and the politics of property*. New York: Routledge.

Bullen, E., and J. Kenway. 2004. Subcultural capital and the female underclass? A feminist response to an underclass discourse. *Journal of Youth Studies* 7 (2): 141–53.

Chakrabarty, D. 2007. *Provincializing Europe: Postcolonial thought and historical difference.* Princeton, NJ: Princeton University Press.

Davis, M. 2006. City of Quartz. New York: Verso Press.

Driedger, L. 1999. Immigrant/ethnic/racial segregation: Canadian big three and Prairie metropolitan comparisons. *Canadian Journal of Sociology* 24 (4): 485–509.

Fanon, F. 1967. *The wretched of the earth.* New York: Grove Press.

Foucault, M. 1977. *Discipline and punish: The birth of the prison.* New York: Vintage.

Goldberg, D. T. 2002. *The racial state.* New York: Blackwell.

Goldberg, D. T., and S. Hristova. 2007. Blue velvet. *Vectors: Journal of Culture and Technology in a Dynamic Vernacular* 3 (1): n.p.

Haggerty, K. D., and R. Ericson. 2000. The surveillant assemblage. *British Journal of Sociology* 51 (4): 605–22.

Hesse, B. 2007. Racialized modernity: An analytics of white mythologies. *Ethnic and Racial Studies* 30 (4): 643–63.

Hogeveen, B. 2005. Toward "safer" and "better" communities? Canada's Youth Criminal Justice Act, Aboriginal youth and the processes of exclusion. *Critical Criminology: An International Journal* 13 (3): 287–305.

———. 2006. Unsettling youth justice and cultural norms: The youth restorative action project. *Journal of Youth Studies* 9 (1): 47–66.

Keith, M. 2005. *After the cosmopolitan? Multicultural cities and the future of racism.* New York: Routledge.

Kelley, R. D. G. 1997. *Yo' mama's disfunktional! Fighting the culture wars in urban America.* Boston: Beacon Press.

Kelly, P. 2000. Youth as an artefact of expertise: Problematizing the practice of youth studies in the age of uncertainty. *Journal of Youth Studies* 3 (3): 301–15.

———. 2003. Growing up as risky business? Risks, surveillance and the institutionalized mistrust of youth. *Journal of Youth Studies* 6 (2): 165–80.

———. 2006. The entrepreneurial self and youth-at-risk: Exploring the horizons of identity in the twenty-first century. *Journal of Youth Studies* 9 (1): 17–32.

Kraftl, P. 2008. Young people, hope and childhood. *Space and Culture* 11 (2): 81–92.

Lashua, B. D. 2005. Making music, re-making leisure in the beat of Boyle Street. Doctoral dissertation, University of Alberta.

Lefebvre, H. 1991. *The production of space.* Malden: Blackwell.

Mawani, R. 2000. In between and out of place: Racial hybridity, liquor and the law in late nineteenth and early twentieth century British Columbia. *Canadian Journal of Law and Society* 15 (2): 9–38.

———. 2003. Legal geographies of Aboriginal segregation in British Columbia: The making and unmaking of the Songhees Reserve. In *Isolation:*

Places and practices of exclusion, ed. C. Strange and A. Bashford, 173–90. London: Routledge.

———. 2009. *Colonial proximities: Crossracial encounters and juridicial truths in British Columbia, 1871–1921.* Vancouver: University of British Columbia Press.

Pratt, G. 2005. Abandoned women and the spaces of the exception. *Antipode* 37 (5): 1058–72.

Ratner, R. S. 1996. In cultural limbo: Adolescent Aboriginals in the urban life-world. In *Not a kid anymore: Canadian youth, crime and subculture*, ed. G. O'Bireck, 185–202. Toronto: Nelson Canada.

Razack, S. H. 2002a. Gendered racialized violence and spacialized justice. In *Race, space and the law: Unmapping a white settler society*, ed. S. H. Razack, 121–56. Toronto: Between the Lines.

———. 2002b. When place becomes race. In *Race, space and the law: Unmapping a white settler society*, ed. S. H. Razack, 1–20. Toronto: Between the Lines.

Shields, R. 2003. *The virtual.* New York: Routledge.

———. 2008. Hope and fear in biotechnology: The space-times of hope and affect. *Space and Culture* 11 (2): 125–41.

Staples, W. G. 2000. *Everyday surveillance: Vigilance and visibility in postmodern life.* London: Rowman and Littlefield.

Starchenko, O., and E. J. Peters. 2008. Aboriginal settlement patterns in Canadian cities: Does a classic index-based approach apply? *Environment and Planning A* 40 (3): 676–95.

Statistics Canada. 2006. *2006 Edmonton community profile—Census metropolitan area/census agglomeration.* Ottawa: Statistics Canada, Government of Canada.

Stoler, A. L. 1995. *Race and the education of desire: Foucault's history of sexuality and the colonial order of things.* Durham, NC: Duke University Press.

Valentine, G. 1997. Oh no you can't: Children and parents' understanding of kids' competence to negotiate public space safely. *Antipode* 29 (1): 65–90.

Wacquant, L. 2001. Deadly symbiosis: When ghetto and prison meet and mesh. *Punishment and Society* 3 (1): 95–134.

———. 2002. Scrutinizing the street. *American Journal of Sociology* 107 (6): 1468–1532.

———. 2008. *Urban outcasts: A comparative sociology of advanced marginality.* London: Polity Press.

Zukin, S. 1996. *The cultures of cities.* Malden, MA: Broadview Press.

10

Virtual Resurrections
Che Guevara's Image as Place of Hope

MARIA-CAROLINA CAMBRE

Thus a window is a window because a region of light opens out beyond it; hence, the window giving this light is not itself "like" the light, nor is it subjectively linked in our imagination with our ideas of light—but the window is that very light itself, in its ontological self-identity, that very light which, undivided-in-itself and thus inseparable from the sun. But the window all by itself —i.e., apart from its relationship to the light, beyond its function as carrier of light —is no longer a window but dead wood and mere glass. (Florensky 1996, 65)

Looking is also an action that confirms or modifies ... "interpreting the world" is already a means of transforming it. (Rancière 2007, 277)

Introduction

In 2006, while reading news on the Internet, I came across an image of Hindu women demonstrating in the streets of Tamil Nadu, Chennai.[1] The special correspondent describes the crowd and its demographic composition under the banner "Expressing Solidarity" and reports on the reasons they have publicly gathered to protest. The caption under the photograph reads, "Student activists from Assam taking part in the procession to mark the beginning of the national conference of the AISF in Chennai on Tuesday." I read on in an effort to better comprehend this image:

They came from Andhra Pradesh, Assam, Bihar, Karnataka, Kerala, Maharashtra, Orissa, West Bengal and different parts of Tamil Nadu. And they marched along Anna Salai and Wallajah Road on Tuesday in traditional costumes, raising slogans in different languages.

But the young girls and boys, who participated in the procession to mark the beginning of the 26th national conference of the All-India Students Federation (AISF), had a common mission: oppose "all attempts to commercialise or communalise education." ("26th AISF National Conference Begins" 2006, n.p.)

Questions boomeranging in my head, I peered at the image and hunted through the text while conscious that I was not exempt from what Jacques Rancière tells us in the second epigraph: each time we witness we know *something*; when we try to think of what that might be, we are transforming it by interpreting it. Confirmation that I was seeing what I thought I was seeing came in the form of the correspondent's descriptive note: "The activists, carrying AISF flags and portraits of *Che Guevara* and freedom fighters Bhagat Singh, P. Jeevanantham and K. Baladhandayutham, raised slogans ... [and] called for effective measures to stop collection of capitation fee in schools and colleges" (my emphasis). Odd but true, in ancient Tamil territory, southern India, near the Bay of Bengal, it *is* Che Guevara's posterized face (multiple copies) born aloft by sari-clad women. I cannot discern other "freedom fighters" in the photograph, and it really looks like Che alone is accompanying these protesters. The textual confirmation serves only to make the image that much more bizarre: Why Che and not Gandhi or someone local, or perhaps a more relevant figure? Why here, and what is the link with India or any issue in Hindu education? The sight of Che's posterized face in this photograph was like an inexplicable anomaly, compelling my disoriented eyes to contemplate it.

This image has not only appeared in Chennai: in countless situations and places around the world, Cuban photographer Alberto Korda's iconic face of Che Guevara is an image that goes beyond T-shirts, key chains, and other knick-knacks, beyond being a brand appropriated by one or another movement, and beyond being a symbol of some type of rebellion.

The demonstrators in Figure 10.1 have a dream not just for themselves but for a better education for their community; it is a hope in the sense that it is not a case of "us" or "them," but "we." My wonderings about this and other such experiences led me to a phenomenological approach. Phenomenology enables me to conjecture why *this* image accompanies the people in the photograph. Why here? Why now?[2] How is it being experienced? In the spirit

Figure 10.1 "26th AISF national conference begins." (Photo credit: R. Shivaji Rao, *The Hindu: Online edition of India's National Newspaper*, January 4, 2006)

of Gabriel Marcel's method of concrete description and personal invocation, I adopt an approach or "methodology that has been called *d'après Heidegger*, ontological-phenomenology" (Grady 1970, 56). While mindful that particular lived-experience anecdotes may provide *reflective* understandings of phenomenological topics, I study them "as a concrete example of a possible phenomenological topic" (Max van Manen 2008, personal communication). Thus, this process is not methodologically objective; rather, it is open at every turn through "heuristic attentiveness, creative insight, interpretive sensibility, and scholarly preparedness" (Max van Manen 2008, personal communication).

In the first epigraph Florensky cautions that ontologically, windows are not *like* the light but rather are inseparable from it, as inseparable as light is from the sun in our experience. Without light no *window* really exists, just wood and glass. Like windows, images can be conceived of as structural possibilities, although they are not limited to that alone. Without the viewer looking, it is not an image, just paint or pixels on a surface. So how can we know when an image is imaging?

Roland Barthes (1982) offers us the concepts of the *studium* and *punctum*. Although Barthes is generally regarded as a structuralist, in *Camera Lucida* he provides notions that are more fluid and transitive in that they exist in a relation and move back and forth without being synthesized. The *studium*, for example, functions to inform, to represent, to cause to signify, to provoke desire. In contrast, the *punctum* is of the order not of form but of intensity—not the "detail" but "time." It is uncoded and unnameable; it *acts*. The *punctum* speaks more to the limits and contradictions missed when we assume visual representation is made up of legible signs that scholarly systems can classify. When people describe their experiences of this image of Che Guevara, we can ask if they felt a *punctum*. Did the image act; was it imaging with/for them, as wood and glass become a window when the light shines through?

In the following experiential account, a Lebanese student is "stopped dead" when she encounters a graffiti version of the Korda photograph.[3] The anecdote was a response to a widely distributed request for experiential accounts about confronting the image of Che. Abbey[4] describes her experience of this image transfiguring the "apartheid" wall in Palestine:

> When I saw the image on the walls that enclose Ramallah and Bethlehem, I was stopped dead in my tracks. I mean, I'd already seen it on key rings and T-shirts in the markets, but this was different.
>
> Bigger than life and almost bigger than the wall—looking out at a future—a possibility—over the wall and beyond the occupation. At least that is what it felt like to me. And this image, offering solidarity—not just his own—but reminding Palestinians living under military occupation that they are not alone in either their suffering or their resistance. Reminding Palestinians imprisoned behind those walls that there are people beyond who are working and struggling in solidarity—reminding them that there is a global structure that is oppressing them, that this is not a tribal war but a war that feeds on patriarchy and capitalism. That there are millions who are imprisoned behind walls. The wall is an oppression and is guarded and watched all the time. To manage to get an image on the wall is, in itself, an act of subversion and resistance. His image there speaks to the meaning embedded in that iconic gaze and face.

Does the image somehow displace or dissolve a wall built to divide, demarcate, and decide territorial boundaries in Abbey's eyes? She was able to see beyond the wall, not physically but temporally. The coordinates of the place have been revised; no longer is the painted area simply part of the wall. It reconfigures that physical place as well as the lived experience of the beholder. Recognizing its very presence as transgressive, she wonders how an image like that came to be painted on the ever-watched wall. This is the aspect that grabs hold of her, that strikes her. On this wall that seems to never end and reaches forbidding heights, the image seems to override rather than be overwhelmed. Its presence demonstrates that, though watched,

Figure 10.2 West Bank barrier Che Guevara. (Photo credit: http://www.heyche.com; used with permission of the webmaster. Image is no longer at the site but is available at Wikimedia Commons)

the artists created their graffiti unseen. Just as the vision through a window can be larger than the wall in which it is embedded, her sense of solidarity and the possibilities of resistance seem to "outsize" the oppression. Does the image bring those "beyond" into contact with those others trapped behind the wall? Does it act as a "reminder," making present those invisible allies and reinforcements who seem to be at hand? If the image transforms that which is empirically already there with an almost alchemical "as-if-ness," it is not because of some projection of political allies but rather for the unseen act of imagining an *other* future. Abbey expresses the hope of seeing a barrier become a bridge through the image.

Viewing the image not only brings about the effect of displacing the wall, but also helps Abbey relocate herself in relation to that place, and become other than who/what she was. Martin Heidegger (1962) tells us the *phainomenon* is that which shows itself, and through logos "that" is made manifest, so with the aim of letting "that which shows itself be seen from itself in the very way in which it shows itself from itself" (58). But that which shows itself can also hide itself and can be dynamic, flickering between visibility and invisibility, transparency and opacity, legibility and indecipherability. This goes to the very nature of the image as such. Philosopher Jean-Luc Nancy (2005) coincides when he writes, "[T]he image is a thing that is not a thing; it distinguishes itself from it, essentially" (2). As in Abbey's account, her experience of the image actively altered her sense of time and space as she lived it. The wall was made present and at the same time withdrawn by the image in the moment of her being "stopped dead" in her tracks. The metaphorical figure of being "stopped dead" hints at how dangerous it is for her to imagine the future. Was she the walking dead in that place under the shadow of the wall, until Che stood in for the future?

In that moment the image brought with it another dimension, it *became* the thing that is not a thing. In both places, Chennai and Ramallah, the image of Che Guevara's face had more than informational value. It also had agency in the sense that it was not merely the communication of a thing that can be known, the portrait of an Argentine-Cuban revolutionary (Che-*studium*), it is a thing that makes things happen or at least somehow anchors a hope that something, a change, will happen (or Che-*punctum*). At this point some questions arise regarding the nature of this hope that seems to translate to any language, time, or place and the quality of its relationship to this image.

At the same time, although we have witnessed the forceful impact of the image of Che's face on the mural in Ramallah, and there are many such examples, we cannot ignore one of the most ubiquitous mediums for presenting this image, the humble T-shirt. Does the visual effect when we see someone wearing a Che shirt parallel what we have heard thus far? When we see someone wearing a Che shirt, is it a sign of hope or merely desire? What is the difference?

How Is Hope Experienced?

When a couple finally buys the house they had been saving their money for, when a professional gets the promotion she or he had been working toward, when people achieve significant successes in their lives, as soon as these "hopes" are satisfied, we realize they were not much more than desires or lesser hopes. Benedict XVI (2007) gives us a more nuanced understanding of hope than the standard dictionary definition of an expectation or wish by helping us distinguish between lesser hopes and greater hopes. Though these lesser hopes can keep us going, they are not enough. Once satisfied, they reveal themselves as meagre and misplaced, failing thus to qualify as true hope and being, rather, "hope for myself alone, which is not true hope since it forgets and overlooks others" (28).[5]

In Gabriel Marcel's comprehensive and rich doctrine of hope published in *Homo Viator*, he takes great care to distinguish between hope and desire. Joseph Godfrey (1987) explains, "Marcel insists that to hope is not to desire: desiring is essentially insistent, fixated and covetous or self-centered, while hoping is none of these" (235). He adds, it is not that all wanting is like this, but there is a difference in the *"quality* of the wanting" (236). With Marcel, then, I take one of hope's definitions to be

> essentially the availability [*disponibilité*] of a soul which has entered [*engagée*] intimately enough into the experience of communion to accomplish in the teeth of will and knowledge [*à l'opposition du vouloir et du connaître*] the transcendent act—the act establishing the vital regeneration [*par lequel elle affirm la pérennité vivante*] of which this experience affords both the pledge and the first fruits. (quoted in Godfrey 1987, 235)

Vital to this understanding of hope is recognizing its essence as both act and attitude. In other words, hope is performative in that taking the attitude of opening one's soul to the "experience" *is* at the same time an opening to that experience. And it is not just any experience but one of "communion," that is, in unity or close relationship with others. Hope is necessarily social. Thus Marcel emphasizes "the difference between essentially material results and those that engender true human community" (Godfrey 1987, 236).

Hope invites our participation in the experience of this communion that, while including human others and human community, is conceived of much more broadly. Marcel's conception of the "intersubjective" dynamic of hope is core. To elaborate on the concept, Godfrey draws on Martin Buber's doctrine of the I-Thou as a complementary parallel to Marcel's work to reveal how these intersubjective relationships extend to nature, texts, artworks, and other things. Although the absolute hope for, Marcel claims, "beyond all data, beyond all inventories and calculations, a mysterious principle which is in connivance with me" (Godfrey 1987, 238), it does not dissolve in abstraction, but instead is always empirically mediated. Thus "a person does not hope in God without some relation to something experiential" (238–39). So the question remains, what are the vehicles opening experiences by which we can be called to participate in hope?

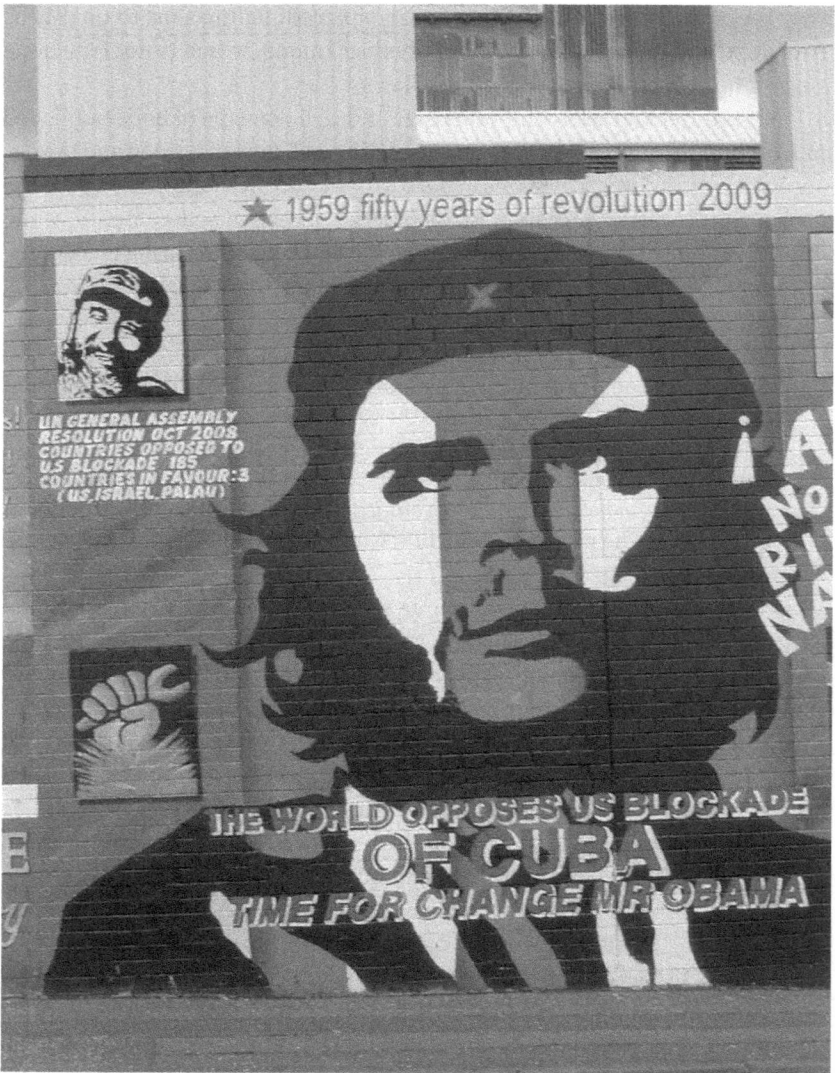

Figure 10.3 Mural, Belfast, Ireland, 2009. (Photo credit Anna McClean)

Representing Hope

Anchors are the most ancient symbols for hope and were used by the early Christians to signify the cross in disguise, thus elevating the safety represented therein to an image of eternal salvation. Yet long before this use of the anchor-as-cross, the anchor was seen as a sailor's last chance to steady his vessel in a deadly storm, intimately connecting it to the notion of hope. In the biblical Epistle to the Hebrews, the writer describes "Hope" set before us "as an anchor of the soul, sure and firm" (Hebrews 6:19–20, New International Version). Metaphorically, hope is a ground. It is the particular ground we need in times of overwhelming struggle or when in danger of despair.

Opposing conventional ways of taking hope as something that can be aimed—"Hope has a target" (Godfrey 1987, 239)—Marcel's analysis coincides with early understandings that "hope is precisely the holding off from despair when I'm sorely tempted to say: All is lost. Hope is 'the act by which this temptation [to despair] is actively or victoriously overcome'" (ibid.). It is no surprise that places where people endure the direst conditions are also the places where the most resolute hope actively and visibly manifests itself. Thus, we find hope in Pandora's box with all the evils and wherever there is a temptation to despair.

Returning to Marcel, hope "unites the human being, not to the world in general, which would mean nothing, but to a certain determinate ambiance which is as concrete as a cocoon or a nest. [Thus the] linkage is determinate, concrete to the point of being nest-like, conferring a sense of at-home and nurturing" (Godfrey 1987, 238). Using the localized image of an intimate home, a point of safety and trust, prompts Godfrey (1987) to write: "This seems a very fruitful way of imagining the strong hoping of finite people in finite situations, without requiring some sort of idolizing or absolutizing of the finite term of hope" (239). Building on these understandings of hope, we can turn back to the image of Che and wonder: If we can hope in the anchor for stability in the storm, does the action of this image resemble a kind of phenomenological anchor in a storm? Can this image function as a vehicle, or refuge, enabling that transcendent act of defying will and knowledge in opening one's self in hope?

Hope vs. Desire: Just Another T-shirt?

The Che phenomenon is challenging because its role in popular culture in terms of differentiating between its appearance as a form of "designer rebellion"[6] on the T-shirts of youth and tourist key chains, for example, co-exists with its ability to act as an anchor of hope, as in Abbey's case and the image from Chennai. While recognizing the number of arguments on both sides of the problematic nature of the status Che's image, Gabriel Marcel's and Roland Barthes' frameworks help engage the debate between those who hold that it is an either/or. Let's examine the following anecdotes related by three people.

> When I was in high-school, my observational skills could not help but notice this image everywhere. Already developing an obsession with T-shirt designs, I had to hunt one down for my wearable collection. A family visit to T— finally gave me this opportunity. (Anna)

An almost immediate response in the impulse to "collect" a T-shirt with this "design" on it leads to a "hunt." From what we have understood through Marcel's distinctions between hope and desire, we can see there is desire in this case to possess one of these shirts. But Anna's "obsession with T-shirt designs," made her feel she "had" to have this one. In a sense, it was essential to the collection, creating a more intense wanting, a need. Why is it such an essential item to include in the collection?

> The image makes me think about high school, when I just moved to Canada. A lot of teenagers seem to like wearing T-shirts with the simplified silkscreened photo of Che. Not that I've never seen this photo, it's just that where I come from it's not that fashionable. (Julia)

Julia is relocated to another time and place when she looks at the image. She attributes the popularity of the T-shirt to fashion, and it becomes a marker for her of the difference between Canadian society and her original society, as well as signifying youth. It stands out for her as difference and she is highly aware of its presence, and yet it is significantly powerless, almost uninteresting.

> When I see/saw Che on the T-shirts in Ramallah and Jerusalem, I chuckled and passed by—went on looking for Za'atar and olives. The T-shirt Che is just a marketing tool—it doesn't elicit any thoughts of resistance or activism. It's just a T-shirt with an image. (Abbey)

Again, the image on the T-shirt calls one's attention to it. In this case, Abbey, who had been so affected by the image on the "apartheid" wall, is prompted to chuckle and shrug off the image because "it's just a T-shirt." As a shirt, then, it does not have the *punctum* it had for her when it was on the separation wall. It is therefore easy to disregard.

The ubiquitous presence of the image of Che Guevara as a two-tone print on T-shirts has made it a cultural phenomenon. Frequently it is associated with the colour red, but all colours and sizes of shirts carry this reproduction of Che's face. Most often it is accompanied by slogans such as, "Hasta la victoria siempre" or "Patria o muerte," or by even the slogans of bands such as Rage Against the Machine. Generally, these slogans indicate rebellion,

Figure 10.4 Palestine Nakba Commemoration, May 2008. (Photocredit: Amber Hussein)

violence, or resistance against the institutionalized dominant order. The image is more widely known than the history of the man. It has become a popular culture icon, and yet calling it either an icon or a symbol does not satisfy it. In fact, Cuban exiles who call him a mass murderer,and speak against Guevara's philosophies and policies, and Leftists who imitate Che or use him as an example, as well as politicians such as Hugo Chavez and Evo Morales all refer to the same image. Both sides argue against the fashion-centred uses of the image, insisting there is more to it (though for different reasons). Yet, as we have seen, this alone is not enough to endow the image with *punctum*, although the possibility of its transfiguration haunts it constantly. In this sense, Ariel Dorfman (1999) is able to look at the T-shirt and say, "Deep inside that T-shirt where we have tried to trap him, the eyes of Che are still burning with impatience" (1). Exceeding their medium, the eyes punch through the T-shirt from elsewhere. Possibly there is an expectation of something to come:

> Just a sense of determination and focus. (Michael)

The gaze sometimes described as defiant, sometimes as pensive, leaves us feeling that there is a future anticipated. When people are asked about the image, they most often speak of rebellion, even if they are unfamiliar with the historical figure of Che Guevara himself. Words like *intense/passionate*,

Figure 10.5 Athens, Greece. (Photo credit: Indymedia, Copyleft)[a]

bravery, inspired, determination/defiance, Cuba, sight into the future, group and belonging, and *confidence* often come up.

> Che was all about change. (David)

Many people wear these T-shirts and carry memorabilia, but the image is often disconnected from memory. Do they understand or share his cause, or are they romanticizing the idea of revolution? A great deal of debate seems to exist, at least in North America, around the person, as well as the image.

No matter the degree of visual abstraction, this image still seems to have the ability to attract or *arrest* so many viewers. Barthes would say it is "without a code," but it might be more fruitful to think of it as a code that devours any medium. Although we immediately decipher posture, such as rebellion, or socio-political context, such as 1960s Cuban revolution, or what Barthes would refer to as the *studium*, often something is still there that we cannot name. Barthes (1981) writes:

> What I cannot name cannot really prick me. The incapacity to name is a good symptom of disturbance ... [it] *holds* me, though I cannot say why, *i.e.*, say *where*: is it the eyes, the skin.... The effect is certain but unlocatable, it

---

[a] Copyleft. Unless otherwise stated, all Indymedia contributions are considered available for use without the permission of the author, as long as those who use the contributions allow further free use of the work. This form of licensing is known as Copyleft. Though the system varies from one Indymedia base to another, some specify the terms of publication from a range of off-the-shelf licences, including Creative Commons' ShareAlike licence and the GNU Free Documentation licences. Indymedia is a messy but beautiful thing.

does not find its sign, its name; it is sharp and yet lands in a vague zone of myself; it is acute yet muffled, it cries out in silence. Odd contradiction: a floating flash. (53)

This acute yet muffled paradoxical floating flash or *punctum* performs. The following anecdote illuminates the *punctum*'s operation by reflecting on a common reaction to buying the T-shirt:

> Walking home from the pub, my eyes are caught by a mannequin in the window. Not unusual for this street designed to sell, the central hub of the latest trends, but unusual for me. Though in my years living here, out of self-preservation I have developed the ability of letting my eyes slide over the windows without seeing what lies beyond them. So today is different; my eyes slide right through the window, unusually drawn to this figure and the shirt she wears. It is red, silk-screened with the face of Che Guevara. I instantly recognize the face. The moment I see it I want it. I want that shirt. I think of going in, trying it on, buying it—but no!—I stop myself. I don't want that shirt, I tell myself, though my desire for it still flutters in my chest. I don't want that shirt. Think about it, my brain argues. I'm saddened, no; I suppose I don't want it. My desire gives its last few futile flutters and lies still, now heavy in my chest. This all in the minute it takes me to walk past the store. (Ed)

The inner tug-of-war Ed experienced in that moment of passing the shop window seems like a manifestation of the innate ability he had to differentiate between hope and desire. The wanting was there, but resistance was stronger. Like Barthes, he cannot immediately name his disturbance; we do not know why he resisted buying the shirt, but we do know his eyes were "unusually drawn" to the shirt with its image. Perhaps this experience gestures toward the *punctum* of this image for Ed because his eyes were simply unable to slide over that particular window. He had another experience:

> Wandering through the streets of Venice, I am annoyed. The Biennale is on and the artists have taken over the city. Entire blocks are excluded to normal foot traffic (unless you pay to see the exhibits), and the canals prevent jay-walking to one's destination. I am lost somewhere in the back alleys, trying to find my way back to something recognizable.
>
> The walls around me are high, old, growing moss, and periodically revealing a residence behind them. I see ahead of me a poster pasted on the alley wall, and, by sheer dint of there being nothing else to look at, my eyes are drawn to it. As I approach, I make out a recognizable face, a black-and-white photo, with text above and below. As I get closer, the face isn't quite as recognizable

as I thought. No, something is definitely off. It is not the face I know, but an imitation of it. An identical imitation, if there can be any such thing. My eyes scan the text for some clue—Italian, which I don't read, but I can fathom the poster's purpose. An exhibit, by the woman who has put herself in Che's place. I am angered by the artist, by her nerve. Spitefully, however, I think "she's behind the times. That's been done. She'll never win." (Ed)

The replacing of the original facial features with those of the artist angers Ed; he is jolted and disappointed. Although he assesses and processes information from the poster, the *studium*, he still experiences something powerful from the present absence of the face he expected (it is there evoked in him by its deferral by an imitation, but it is not concretely there). The comment "No something is definitely off" alerts us to the existence of the *punctum*. Although the original face is not concretely there, it is still virtually acting. Paradoxically, acting becomes other than being. From Elvis to Madonna, and even George Bush, almost every face imaginable has been substituted in to the frame provided by the silhouette of Che Guevara's long hair and starred beret. It is a kind of invasion of a territory, an assumption of a shared space, provoking indignation in those who might feel that place is not to be shared. For Bachelard (1958), looking and knowing are not separated, but the knowing of looking is of an altogether different order: "to specify that the image comes before thought, we should have to say that poetry, [or the visual image] rather than being a phenomenology of the mind, is a phenomenology of the soul" (xix–xx).

Where Is the "Here" of the Image?

Deleuze and Guattari's notion of territory is described by Grossberg (1997) as "a consolidation across contexts, a holding together of heterogeneity by the expression of a rhythm among the elements" (20). It helps us describe what is happening when someone locates or is relocated by looking at any rendering of Che Guevara's face taken from the matrix photograph, however indirectly. The dynamic mode of existence that Deleuze and Guattari call "territory" can be imagined as a moment where all the lines of context converge—from the medium (T-shirt or other) onto which the image is rendered, to what an individual is thinking in the moment of detecting the image, to the colours and shapes, and how these strike that particular eye in that particular sighting, and any other thing that contributes the rhythm or "refrain"—allowing the "expression" of that rhythm to open up an inside of an outside and an outside of an inside of that experience, "a way of constantly holding back and opening up to the chaos, which is never only chaotic"

Figure 10.6 School mural in Gonzales Catán, Buenos Aires, Argentina. (Photo credit: M.-C. Cambre)

(Grossberg 1997, 20). In this regard the experiences can be seen as places ("you had to be there") that are neither geocentric nor anthropocentric. Thus, they are free to be mobile and intersubjective and open any passages and conduits matching the rhythm of expression. For example, when Turkish singer/songwriter Sezen Aksu (2005) sings, "Acinin yuzolcumu yeryuzunden cokmus aslinda," or "The surface area of pain is (actually) greater than the surface area of the earth," she reveals this kind of deterritorialization. Although we are bound to the earth and have an innate sense of "territoriality," we are called to recognize and tap our universal and boundless extraterritorial dimensions (dreams, hopes, and emotions). Consequently, to be able to respond appropriately to affective phenomena, we require philosophically deterritorialized ways of thinking, with all their complexity and ambiguity.

The dynamic of the construction of place, if we look at it in this way, has a great affinity for how places of hope do their "becoming." However, we need to differentiate how the place of hope is experienced differently, how it "folds out of revelations of renewal in our being ... at once a return to our authentic being as ex-istence (standing-out radiating) and the burgeoning of uniqueness" (Grady 1970, 61). Or, in Marcel's words, "as before, but differently and better than before" (in Grady 1970, 61): revived, resurrected, and yet transfigured.

Fittingly, this particular image authorizes a link to a similar rhythm when given the possibility of expression. In other words, the anchor does not become a place of hope until there is a terrifying storm, just as the face of "Che" does not become a place of hope until contexts converge. This is the link Marcel talks about whereby we are always already involved in every act of hope. The force of the convergence creating this experiential anchor or territory of hope can be life-altering, as this next account vividly depicts.

> My first encounter with Che took place in the aftermath of a bloody student confrontation with the police at the University of Nairobi. Some protest leaders had used some Che portraits in the protest and this had greatly incensed the government. One of my friends on campus had smuggled a Che portrait into his room, and he was so proud showing it to us behind closed doors: a huge risk. I mean, associating with Che meant days and nights in a police dungeon; people perceived as having "Marxist/revolutionary" leanings were routinely tortured in Kenya in the '80s. Having a portrait of Che would be considered sufficient association to warrant a visit to the dungeons. I remember vaguely admiring the man, Che. How could a portrait be so powerful, how could it make a government run scared? But I guess I feared Che more than I admired him. Knowing him could mean the end of my university education, and possible detention. The fear pervading the country, then, was that bad. I have hardly "interacted" with Che since, but any mention or even the sight of his portrait reminds me of those dark, oppressive days in Kenya. I think Che was part of the oppression. Che was a household name, in the list of banned personalities. (Paul)

The fear Paul experienced resulted in part from his knowledge of the likely government reaction to finding the image of "Che" in a student bedroom, and yet testifies to the hope of those who were willing to risk "a visit to the dungeons," as well as to the government's phobic relationship, "running scared" with it. Through the alchemy of the image, a bedroom becomes a lair of resistance. An image that permits and incites police brutality against students transfigures a place of learning into a place of punishment, encouragement into reprimand. Paul remembers those days as dark ones, his fear linking Che's image to them irretrievably.

A thread connects the life of the man represented in the image to its presence in the minds of students, but for Paul's testimony, it accrues the additional history of being an image that did not ward off oppression but rather brought it on. Those accepting the likely possibility of detention, torture, and an end to their lives as they know them understand the risk; perhaps the hope they hold out is seen as something greater than their own individual lives. Or they may be engaging the fearful aspects of resistance that are usually left unsaid—that death is as likely an outcome as victory. An image takes the shape of the hope it's invested with through a process of inter-animation. We animate the image, and in turn it animates us, renewing our vision as we look.

The Historical Image of Che

To understand how this image is always becoming an anchor for diverse people globally, it is important to reflect on its sheer status and popularity, as well as some of the reactions evoked by it. It is almost always the same face gazing, unsatisfied, from flags, banners, murals, posters, and T-shirts. All the usual features, eyes, ears, nose, and mouth, appear, depicting a man's face, Caucasian, thirty-two or thirty-three years old, in two tones. It is devoid of background; a clear, cloudless sky behind the figure is virtually blank: nothing special about this empty space. These endless repetitions of Guevara's face, sometimes printed and at times hand drawn, are the progeny of the original photograph whose publication rocked the world of photography like an explosion, as its author once observed. Somehow it became the most reproduced photograph in the world. Is it simply a matter of the subject, the man himself? Yet he appears in countless other photos unremarked. What is so special about the moment of looking at this image, and being seen by it?

The rough, roguish, unkempt hair and beard, a Robin Hood–esque tilted cap, eyes gazing up and into the distance, suggestive, and simultaneously expressive. We are constantly bombarded with images of aesthetically beckoning, evocative faces, and yet this one stands out. Some say it is famous because of the timing of its publication: it appeared just as he himself disappeared—a mysterious kind of aura clings to it. Perhaps this image, this face, is not *just* there, but is actively showing itself, calling the viewer to confront it, to respond, to *see* otherwise. And viewers do respond:

> The star. It shines so bright in the sky and so does he, he stands out from the crowd; he's so different. His hair, so long, experienced and gone through many struggles and life-threatening events, just like his soul, his body, his life. His eyes, sees everything, happiness, sadness around the world and tries to change it in some form of way. His nose smelt [*sic*] all different kinds of dirt, the smell of death, the smell of victory, the smell of change. His voice, persuaded many people, changed many lives with the interaction and his presence. The voice of many people. His face, everyone knows it's just you which describes it. (John)

And:

> Revolution, romance, rugged lifestyle, protest, "fighting the man," erotic feeling. Makes me tingle, feel fierce, and it makes me feel powerful. I think that's what makes me tingle. Makes me nervous/uncomfortable. (Natasha)

John and Natasha have textured, affective experiences of this image. Ernesto Guevara was an individual who lived a unique and brief historical moment, and yet the face is one that "everyone knows." A presence that causes tingling, is energizing, and gives discomfort, and yet a "star" to be followed. Many people feel the reverberations and respond to this portrait of Che Guevara. It repeatedly emerges in the midst of social protests and demonstrations and gazes out from placards and banners. Masked participants protecting their identities make Guevara's image more conspicuous through the contrast. The visual outcome is, in effect, a face for the faceless.

The phenomenon does not pass unobserved, and poets, songwriters, and novelists attempt to capture it. Uruguayan writer Eduardo Galeano poetically writes of Che as "el nacedor"[7] which translates roughly to "the one who tends to be born" or "the one who keeps being born." In the poem he asks why it is that Che has this dangerous habit of repeatedly being born. Perversely, the more he is insulted, manipulated, betrayed, the more he keeps being born through the image—a movement remarkably like that of hope itself. "In fact, we could characterize the essence of hope as 'the very movement by which it challenges the evidence upon which men claim to challenge it itself'" (Grady 1970, 60). On another occasion, Galeano comments that Che is resurrected in each one who believes in what Guevara believed in, and is resurrected in the great popular liberation movements of these lands that were not condemned by any gods to the disgrace that they endure. Rebirth and hope are intimately linked.

Theorizing the Image: The Punctum and Access to the Virtual

Georges Didi-Huberman (2005) points out that the "relation of the soul to the world of the eye" is none other than the *not-synthesis* of an instance that is itself torn between consciousness and unconsciousness, and of a world that coheres only up to a point (141). So the structure is open in the sense that it will be breached at its centre—and in the eyes of the beholder it is ignescent, capable of bursting into flame. Just as an actor's performance achieves its best result from the "polarity of the opposition between the mental representation evoked by the text and the action performed by the actors—it's all about that disparity the gap, that is where it all happens, it is one of the underlying bases ... the opposition is a basic prerequisite—synthesized in the spectator's act of interpretation which transforms both the representation and the reality in a flash of emotionally charged 'seeing'" (Honzl 1976, 88).

In the original photograph, Che's gaze does not engage us—we are positioned below, and he is unaware and lost in thought. Raw documentary feel transmits in black and white, but also in the seriousness and unposed quality of the figure. In discussing such "fugitive testimony" in the case of photography, Barthes (1981, 93) elaborates on *studium* and *punctum* writing. "It is not possible to posit a rule of connection between the *studium* and the *punctum* (when it happens to be there). It is a matter of co-presence" (Barthes 1981, 42). Che, the historical personage, is the *studium*. But simultaneously the image has become something else, more than just a rendering of a man, not Che but a *punctum* we might also recognize as the talismanic "Che," Mireya Castañeda (1997) writes, "The photo is converted into myth ... revealed in his look is the super-concentrated rage for those deaths, there is an impactful force/strength in his expression" (para. 3).

Is that it? Is concentrated rage over injustice the *punctum* that makes this photographic image immortal and uncrushable by the fetishistic commodity sphere selling "designer rebellion?" An elusive essence, it somehow can transmit regardless of the varying media sporting the image. For Barthes (1981), "the Photograph sometimes makes appear what we never see in a real face" (103). It is what Didi-Huberman (2005) termed "visual."

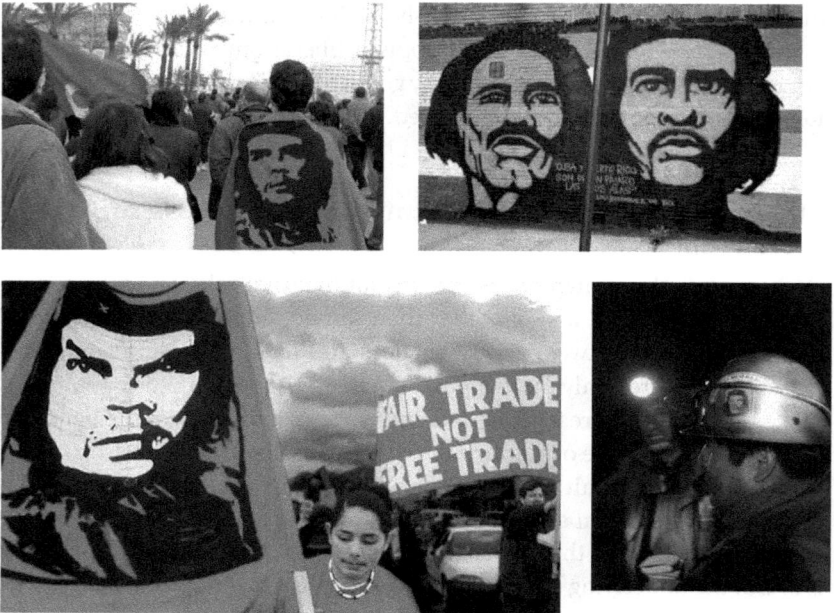

Figure 10.7 Top left: Barcelona (photo credit: Indymedia, Copyleft); top right: New York mural (photo credit: Indymedia, Copyleft); bottom left: Honduras (photo credit: Indymedia, Copyleft); bottom right: Bolivian miners (photo credit: Indymedia, Copyleft)

Where the *visible* is all that is seen on the surface of the image, the *visual* is all those things seen but not apparent, such as the "mother's eyes" in the daughter, or whatever the viewer brings, but it also includes indexical features; for example, hair blowing would be the *visible* indication of wind, which would then be the *visual* element. However, the alchemy of the photograph of Che Guevara is not just that it is *visible*, or *visual*, but that it also provides a space for the Barthesian *punctum* to act, or in Didi-Huberman's terminology, the *virtual*.

Didi-Huberman (2005) writes:

> The word *virtual* is meant to suggest how the regime of the visual tends to loosen our grip on the "normal" (let's say rather: habitually adopted) conditions of visible knowledge.... The event of *virtus*; that which is in power, that which is power, never gives a direction of the eye to follow, or a univocal sense of reading.... It is irrefutable and simple as event; it is situated at the junction of a proliferation of possible meanings, whence it draws its necessity, which it condenses, displaces, and transfigures. (18–19)

Figure 10.8 Top left: Tehuacán, Mexico, and Marcos (photo credit: Indymedia, Copyleft); top right: Brussels, 2004 (photo credit: Indymedia, Copyleft); bottom left: Spanish protest (photo credit: Indymedia, Copyleft); bottom right: Protest rally, London, England, May 17, 2003 (photo credit: Indymedia, Copyleft)

This image provokes, holds a possible future, an almost-legible-yet-escaping-expression sense of a frontier or horizon that presents itself and yet withdraws in the sheer rawness of the image despite, or rather precisely because, it is delinked from the actual human being whose figure once deflected light onto the film. Although the Bolivian miner has only a small sticker on his helmet, the original is invoked, and the image is no less effective as an amulet, a much-hoped-for protection in the lethal context of the Bolivian mine.

The Likeness: A Face in Time

John Berger offers the notion of "the likeness" to provide perspectives for approaching some of the elusive elements of the experience of this image, while they fall short of explaining the unique impact of this specific photograph. We might accept that the photo's experience is something perhaps out of reach of the merely explanatory and take what we can from what they offer. Berger believes the transcendent qualities manifested through, but not necessarily on, the human face are the key to the mystery of the Other, both in art and in daily encounters.

As Berger (1980) discusses photographs of people experiencing terror, pain, and grief, he observes "these moments are in reality utterly discontinuous with normal time." Later, he reiterates, "such moments, whether photographed or not, are discontinuous with all other moments. They exist by themselves" (39). He recognizes first, that time can be interrupted by raw emotion, and second, that this ruptured moment can create a place in and through a photograph. Susan Sontag also defines the photograph as "a trace, something directly stenciled off the real, like a footprint or a deathmask" (in Berger 1980: 50). Digital photography and reproduction, far from doing away with this imprint of the subject, has actually absorbed it. The affective force, the feeling of witnessing, and that someone was there is still evoked; even with all the savvy photo-editing techniques available, there is still a possibility of a Barthesian *punctum*.

Berger aptly describes our media environment surrounding us as one where the volume of images, as in quantity and also as in noise, is unprecedented. In addition, a great number of these images are faces that "harangue ceaselessly by provoking envy, new appetites, ambition or, occasionally pity combined with a sense of impotence" (Berger 2001, 58). Not all of these faces represent the "likeness" of the person pictured; indeed, the opposite is true. For Berger, a "likeness" is characterized more by the absence than by the presence of a person and requires one to have somehow experienced the person him- or herself before a "likeness" is possible. He explains:

> When a person dies they leave behind, for those who knew them, an emptiness, a space: the space has contours and is different for each person mourned. This space with its contours is the person's likeness and is what the artist searches for when making a living portrait. A likeness is something left behind invisibly. (19)

What does the eye perceive that the microscope cannot reveal? Berger would say, a "likeness." He illustrates this concept by narrating his attempts to draw the face of a friend. He drew her face many times in her presence but was unsatisfied because he could not capture the aspect he sought. Later, he redrew the picture from memory and found the remembered face had the missing essentials: it was a "likeness." Somehow, via memory, essences animating, giving life to a person's face can be envisioned. Berger and Benjamin use the metaphor of a broken jar lovingly reassembled, thus becoming "both flawed and more precious" to compare to the "image of a loved place or a loved person when kept in the memory after separation" (Berger 2001, 59).

The likeness cannot materialize without the artist,and the emotions the memory of the Other serve to trigger in the artist, who then seeks to transmit them, to become a medium for this contour, or space, noticed but not understood. A "likeness" cannot exist independently of the interaction between one and the Other; the resonance or vibration occurring in the human relation makes the "likeness" possible. For Berger, the eyes of the viewer are essential, but the eyes cannot be looking in an indifferent way.

In *About Looking*, Berger's theory of the likeness is still undeveloped, but its root can be detected when he writes, "A person loved is recognized not by attainments but by the verbs which can satisfy that person" and thus "their contour or shape is not a surface encountered but an horizon which borders" (1980, 130). A horizon (the idea of the horizon in me?) can be understood as something not visible, but visual, always receding, present and absent. Berger ends *The Shape of a Pocket* (2001) with a reference to Alberto Korda's photograph of Che:

> A likeness is a gift and remains unmistakable—even when hidden behind a mask.
> A likeness can be effaced. Today Che Guevara sells T-shirt, that's all that's left of his likeness.
> Are you sure? (258)

"The face speaks. The manifestation of the face is already discourse"[8]

In Davis's *Levinas: An Introduction*, we learn, "the encounter is not an event that can be situated in time; it is rather a structural possibility that precedes and makes possible all subsequent experience" (1996, 45). It is a space, and it is the kind of space where hope's manifestation is possible. For Berger, this time-transcendent element can be transmitted, but not tamed, in images of the Other. And for Barthes, the photograph itself is invisible yet provides a vehicle for the image, just as the physical face provides a mobile map, features, and contours, for emotional expression. In either case, the "epiphany" or "revelation" is located not inside but between the Other and the Same. Or as Levinas tells us, "the face of the other at each moment destroys and over-flows the plastic image it leaves me" (Levinas in Davis 1996, 133).

Although the face is present to our vision, at all times we see the "plastic" image, yet there is always more. In a parallel comment Derrida (1978) states, "[T]he face is not in the world because it breaches and exceeds total-ity" (134). Faces are profoundly communicative, and we need no lessons in how to decipher the myriad expressions that can manifest themselves on such a mobile surface. The face's expression is also key as it "expresses the expression itself, it always remains master of the meaning which it delivers. 'Pure act' in its way, it [il] refuses to be assigned an identity, cannot be reduced to what is already known, brings help to itself,... speaks" (Levinas in Davis 1996, 132). If the expression is present, communicating, and "act-ing," the way Levinas believes, it can permit/authorize the emotionally charged "look" to penetrate the medium of the picture. This is a new space. Yet the dependency on inter-animation with the viewer also can facilitate com-modification of the image, and consequently indifference. This possibility is exploited by popular culture continuously. Nevertheless, enormous numbers of receptive viewers continue to be "arrested" by the image today.

Overflowing its medium via the expression, the "Che" image is always beyond reach as Other. At the same time, the look on Guevara's face turns the receptive viewer into Other. Since the expression of intense emotion can invoke a facial response—for example, we may grimace or frown when we see someone experiencing a tragic moment, or we may smile when we see someone having a particularly joyful moment—we have the capacity to mir-ror what we see. This photo can other us because the expression recreates and dislocates.

Conclusion

The "likeness" left behind by Ernesto Guevara is invisible but perceptible in the matrix photograph taken by Korda, or virtual but not visible. This pho-tograph authorizes, for individuals who are inclined to the experience, the gift of the Benjaminian jar to reassemble for themselves, to *renew* the jar, so that it is the same as before, flawed but better. Thus the image, as jar, becomes an intersubjective place. Witnessing the image sanctions relocation: we can thus reassemble a more precious place in and through it, though imperfect, because as relationship it now includes the viewer.

The exceptional possibility offered by the matrix image of Che Gue-vara is of an expression of a rhythm matching the dynamic of hope whose essence is movement challenging the ground upon which claims "to challenge it itself" (Grady 1970, 60) are made. Whenever/wherever despair rears its head, hope is reborn, resurrected anew. Those who see hope in the image are perceiving the light that makes a window *happen*.

Notes

This chapter builds on research supported in part by a Queen Elizabeth II Scholarship granted by the Government of Alberta. Additionally, I am grateful to Ondine Park and Tonya Davidson for all the brainstorming sessions. I am also indebted to Dr. Rob Shields, Dr. Max van Manen, Dr. John Plews (St. Mary's University), and Leticia Cambre for their insightful feedback and guidance on earlier drafts of this work.

1   Note on photographs: Every reasonable effort has been made to trace and acknowledge the ownership of the copyrighted material. Any errors that may have occurred are inadvertent and will be corrected in subsequent editions, provided notification is sent to the author. Because I have been collecting photographs in which Guevara's face appears since 2004, many of the Internet sites that once featured them are no longer available. Regardless, I downloaded only images that were designated "in the public domain," and the primary source for these has been the Indymedia network.

2   I am grateful to Dr. Magda Lewis of the Faculty of Education at Queen's University for her guidance. She helped me first frame this enquiry so long ago when it began as a paper in her class. She would always ask: Why this? Why here? Why now? She has provided a fruitful springboard indeed.

3   I use the term *image* to designate all derived versions of the original matrix photograph of Che Guevara's face taken by Alberto Korda. Thus, they can be in different mediums, colours, and sizes, and by various authors, but they always recognizably refer back to the original.

4   In order to preserve the anonymity of participants, some proper names, places, and circumstances have been changed.

5   Benedict XVI has written an extremely thorough encyclical on hope in the Christian context. The encyclical does not reference the work of Gabriel Marcel, whose doctrine on hope was written much earlier, but the definitions and concepts are complementary. Similarly, Martin Buber's work within the Judaic tradition is in harmony with the Christian understanding. In comparison to other philosophical concepts, there is comparatively scarce literature on hope; however, Marcel's *Homo Viator: Introduction to a Metaphysic of Hope* is widely regarded as a seminal text.

6   "Designer rebellion" is a term coined and used by Dr. jan jagodzinski, Department of Secondary Education, University of Alberta (personal communication).

7   All translations are the author's unless otherwise indicated. Original: "¿Por qué será que el Che tiene esta peligrosa costumbre de seguir naciendo? Cuánto más lo insultan, lo manipulan, lo traicionan, Más nace," by E. Galeano, available at http://eddafediz.blogspot.com/2008/06/che-en-su-80-renacimiento.html.

8   Levinas 1979, 66.

References

Bachelard, G. 1958. *The poetics of space*. Boston: Beacon Press.

Barthes, R. 1981. *Camera lucida*. New York: Hill and Wang.

————. 1982. *Mythologies*. New York: Granada Books.

Benedict XVI. 2007. Encyclical letter, evangelium vitae. In *On Christan hope*. Rome: Libreria Editrice Vaticana.

Benso, S. 2000. *The face of things: A different side of ethics*. New York: State University of New York Press.

Berger, J. 1980. Uses of photography. In *About looking*, 52–71. New York: Pantheon.

————. 2001. *The shape of a pocket*. New York: Vintage International.

Burnett, R. 2004. *Camera lucida: Roland Barthes, Jean-Paul Sartre and the photographic image*. http://www.eciad.bc.ca/~rburnett/COV.htm (accessed July 15, 2004).

Castañeda, M. 1997. La más famosa foto del Che. In *Granma Internacional 1997*. La Habana, Cuba: Edicion Digital. http://www.granma.cu/che/korda .html (accessed November 15, 2006).

Davis, C. 1996. *Levinas: An introduction*. Notre Dame, IN: Notre Dame Press.

Derrida, J. 1978. *Writing and difference*, trans. A. Bass. London; New York: Routledge.

Didi-Huberman, G. 2005. *Confronting images: Questioning the ends of a certain history of art*. University Park, PA: Pennsylvania State University Press.

Dorfman, A. 1999. Heroes and icons, June 14. *The Time*. http://205.188.238 .181/time/time100/heroes/profile/guevara01.html (accessed November 15, 2007).

Dorfman, A., and F. Jameson. 1990. *The legacy of Che Guevara 40 years on*. http://amorworld.blogspot.com/ (accessed October 9, 2007).

Florensky, P. 1996. *Iconostasis*, trans. D. Sheehan and O. Andrejev. Crestwood, NY: St. Vladimir's Seminary Press.

Galeano, E. 1996. *Querido Che*. Interview by Iosu Perales. *Bolivianet*. http://www .stormpages.com/marting/queridoche.htm (accessed November 15, 2003).

————. 2001. Rule of the few. *The Progressive*. http://www.thirdworld traveler.com/Global_Economy/Rule_of_Few.html (accessed March 3, 2005).

Godfrey, J. J. 1987. Appraising Marcel on hope. *Philosophy Today* 31 (3): 234–41.

Grady, J. E. 1970. Marcel: Hope and ethics. *The Journal of Value Inquiry* 4 (1): 56–64.

Grossberg, L. 1997. Re-con(fig)uring space. *Space and Culture* 4 (5): 13–22. (Revised version of a paper first published in *Unmapping the Earth, Kwangju Biennale, Kwangju Korea*. Durham, NC: Duke University.)

Hassett, M. 1907. The anchor (as symbol). In *The Catholic Encyclopedia*. New York: Robert Appleton Company. *New Advent*. http://www.newadvent .org/cathen/01462a.htm (accessed April 13, 2009).

Heidegger, M. 1962. *Being and time*, trans. J. Macquarrie and E. Robinson. New York: Harper & Row.

Honzl, J. 1976. *Dynamics of the sign in the theater*, trans. I. R. Titunik. In *Semiotics of art*, ed. L. Matejka and I. R. Titunik, 74–94. Cambridge, MA; London: MIT Press.

Levinas, E. 1979. *Totality and infinity: An essay on exteriority*, trans. A. Lingis. The Hague; Boston: M. Nijhoff.

Löwy, M. 1997. Che Guevara 1967–1997: La chispa que no se extingue. In *Seminario Internacional "Ernesto Che Guevara—30 años,"* October 2–5. http://home.swipnet.se/~w64823/int/archivos/Che%20Guevara1.html.

Merleau-Ponty, M. 1993. Eye and mind. In *Merleau-Ponty aesthetics reader: Philosophy and painting*, ed. A. Johnson Galen and M. B. Smith, 121–49. Evanston, IL: Northwestern University Press.

Nancy, J.-L. 2005. *The ground of the image.* New York: Fordham University Press.

Rancière, J. 2007. The emancipated spectator. *Artforum* (March): 270–341.

26th AISF national conference begins. 2006. January 4. In *The Hindu: Online edition of India's National Newspaper*. http://www.hindu.com/2006/01/04/stories/2006010408920400.htm (accessed February 12, 2006).

11

Performing Spaces of Hope
Street Puppetry and the
Aesthetics of Scale

PETRA HROCH

Imagine a four-storey elephant moving slowly toward you in the city street. Imagine a giant "little" girl inhabiting the streets where you live for a few days and performing ordinary daily rituals—showering, dressing, eating, sleeping, and going for a walk—on an extraordinary scale. If Royal de Luxe recently visited your city or town, such sights would not be mere figments of the imagination, but rather real events that actualize worlds one might never have imagined possible.

The significance of scale in our everyday lives and on our experience of the places we inhabit is often overlooked and undertheorized.[1] This chapter emphasizes the significance of scale on human experience in and of space by focusing on Royal de Luxe, a street puppet theatre company based in France, in the city of Nantes, whose mechanical players' gigantic size relative to their audience is a defining characteristic of their performances. The company was founded in 1979 by Jean-Luc Courcoult and has since its inception created theatre in public spaces in Europe, Asia, Africa, and South America (Harris 2007a, 1).[2] In this chapter I suggest that differences in scale contribute to more than merely a *quantitatively* different spatial register; they create a *qualitatively* other—an aesthetically and affectively other— experience of space. The gigantic scale and resulting slow-motion mobility of the puppet performances Royal de Luxe creates in cities and towns around the world physically transform the everyday urban spaces we inhabit and bring into being an alternative affective dimension that audiences describe as feeling full of hope.

Setting the Scene: Puppet History

Puppetry is what Deleuze and Guattari describe as a "minor" art form (1986, 16). "Minor" arts, according to these theorists, are always "political" and "collective" enunciations (17); they exist within and alongside "major" art forms but are less static (16). In other words, puppetry, like other "minor" arts, is not only materially but also institutionally more mobile. In this chapter I argue that *mobility* and *scale* are two of puppetry's most socio-politically relevant attributes. The mobility and scale of puppets relative to the human body enable this performance art form to create alternative aesthetic and affective spaces within "everyday life"—spaces wherein convention can be challenged, the power of authority can be subverted, new sets of social relations can proliferate, and indeed, a hopeful atmosphere can be felt (Lefebvre 2002).

Puppets have a long history of intervening in the social and political sphere. Puppetry is one of the most ancient forms of theatre; historians suspect that this form of performance art originated as part of religious rites before the world's earliest written records (Baird 1965, 35). Puppetry is also perhaps the most geographically widespread form of theatrical performance (7). From their earliest known beginnings, puppets have been used to tell stories that supported the didactic religious, educative, and political ends of those in power (10). However, their physical versatility made puppets perfect vehicles for not only prescribing but also critically reflecting upon social or political states of affairs. In fact, although puppetry has had moments in history during which it was considered to be "high art," its propensity for parody, profanity, bawdy comedy, caricature, and satire has classed it principally, at least among Western theatrical traditions, as a form of popular entertainment. The status of puppetry as a popular, folk, "low" art has contributed, in turn, to puppeteers' ongoing freedom to subvert canonical aesthetic standards as well as to take certain social and political liberties.[3]

To describe puppetry as a "minor" art is, of course, not necessarily a comment on puppets' often small size. In fact, although the history of smaller-than-human-sized puppets, figures, or dolls extends back tens of thousands of years into the history of art (e.g., the small limestone statuette of the Woman from Willendorf from around 33 000 BCE), large-scale "puppet" figures such as ancient effigies also have a long history in communal rituals, festivals, and spectacles. In an issue of *Puppetry International* devoted to "mega-puppets," American puppeteer and puppet historian John Bell (2007) points out that an "interesting aspect of giant puppets" is that they are "often absent from lists of various forms of puppetry throughout the world" (26).

He notes that often in historical records, "the focus is wholly on smaller-than-life puppetry; there is no sense of giant puppets as a pre-twentieth century tradition" (ibid.). Paradoxically, then, gigantic puppets might be described as belonging to more of a "minor" art tradition than puppets of the more common, miniature variety: "Although giant puppets would seem to be naturally included in almost any general definition of puppetry ... there is something about them that places them outside the minds of many who think of puppets. In a way, giant puppets are the 'elephant in a room' of puppetry—an undeniably huge presence, yet somehow difficult for us to deal with. Why might this be so?" (ibid.).

Royal de Luxe mobilizes gigantic puppets to create an alternative dimension in public spaces—one that I will go on to suggest functions as a "critical utopia" (Gardiner 1993, 179). The gigantic performances of Royal de Luxe change, and thus challenge our world as it currently exists and present us with ways that our spaces and experiences could be different from what we know. In this chapter I ask: How do varying scales (and consequently different mobilities) of puppets contribute to the creation of alternative spaces? How do the size and movement of puppets in relation to the human body put into relief the reality we know? How do these elements evoke or exemplify other ways of being—and being affected—in the world?

Puppet Potential

In his guidebook *Puppetry: The Ultimate Disguise*, twentieth-century American puppeteer George Latshaw provides an abbreviated list of puppet potentialities entitled "reasons for being a puppeteer" (1978, 28). Latshaw's purpose in enumerating these "reasons" is not to convince us all to take up puppeteering; rather, his interest is to emphasize that puppets should be used not as mere replacements for human actors, but as entities with their own unique capacities. The reasons Latshaw gives for "being a puppeteer" (in other words, for choosing a puppet over a human actor) highlight two sets of characteristics specific to puppets: their "appearance" and their capacity for "action" (ibid.). Latshaw delights in puppets' extraordinary range of performance potential when he notes:

> Reasons for being a puppeteer based on the puppet's appearance include:
> 1) The puppet provides the "ideal" appearance for a role; it projects the visual "essence" of the character
> 2) A puppet can appear to be smaller than human size (a dwarf, an elf, a gnome, a fairy, a troll, a goblin, a leprechaun)

3) A puppet allows you to appear larger than life—a giant, a monster, an ogre, a dragon, a towering grotesque

4) An extreme distortion of proportions is possible

5) A puppet can be an inanimate object or even an abstract shape that moves. A variety of nonhuman forms can spring to life to become the players.

Reasons for being a puppeteer based on action include:

1) The puppet is an alternative anatomy for acting and does not have to be constructed following the human skeletal system. The design, construction, and substance of the puppet can allow it to move in novel and wondrous ways

2) Some puppets can say "Good-bye Gravity." They can float, rise, fly, or walk on air, defying the natural laws that keep the actor earthbound

3) Puppets can play tricks with time—slow motion on the ground, a languid leap in the air, and what goes up can take its own time coming down. A puppet can streak across the scene with almost blurred speed. (ibid.)

Latshaw's lists highlight the possibilities available to puppets relative to human actors. Clearly, puppets can exceed human bounds in terms of the scale of their construction (their size relative to the human) and the potential mobility in their performance (their manoeuvrability, portability, and transportability). These particular capacities, I argue here, have historically contributed to puppets' usefulness as an apparatus in a unique creative and socio-politically critical theatrical form.

Historically, the freedom to be had for small puppets acting out in socially or politically subversive ways was twofold: first, to be able to *do* anything (aesthetically) by exceeding the physical constraints to which human actors are typically bound, and second, to potentially get away with their actions (politically) by being able to say and do things that humans could not. After "acting out," a small puppet actor could, at least in theory, be hidden, whisked away, or left behind at the first sign of trouble. In reality, puppeteers have historically been only moderately successful in this regard. In the medieval era, for example, puppeteers were often on the run from the authorities for the biting critique they levelled at official religious and state structures. Sometimes, they escaped successfully by abandoning their little actors at the scene, or, in the case of one Czech puppeteer, by using his puppets as an alibi: "It wasn't me: the puppets did it!" (quoted in Blumenthal 2005, 7). Indeed, it is precisely the assemblage created by the interaction of the human actor with the puppet actor that allows for a degree of slippage as to who is the agent responsible for "speaking" or "acting" (and consequently what is and is not allowed to be said or done). When this limit was crossed, however, puppeteers could not always outmanoeuvre the authorities: as Bell (2000) interestingly points out, the best place for historians to research puppet theatres is in police records (18).

If the more conventional small-scale puppets have particular capabilities because of their diminutive size, what are the potential aesthetic and political capacities of gigantic puppets such as Royal de Luxe's larger-than-life performing machines? What is the effect of giant figures and humans sharing the same space? If miniature puppets are portable and thus more "mobile," what kind of mobility do gigantic puppets perform? And how do the combined effects of such relative differences in scale and mobility alter our experience of a space?

Puppetry, like other performing arts, puts physical movement on display. As audience members watching a puppet performance, we encounter movement or "mobility" in a number of ways: we perceive the movement of *objects*, we participate in a kind of *imaginative* travel, and in some instances we might ourselves even engage in *corporeal* travel (all types of "travel" referred to by Urry 2002, 256). Indeed, particularly when watching a gigantic puppet performance in a street, we may be required to move our own bodies in order to follow the puppet bodies that transform the city into a stage for a larger-than-life drama. Giant puppets present an alternative dimension to everyday life by virtue of their scale. Experiencing ourselves in relation to the gigantic means experiencing ourselves and our world from another perspective—we are made miniature, and our mundane cityscape is transformed into a set for the puppet players in motion.

Royal de Luxe Comes to Town

In May 2006 London became the stage for the first performance by Royal de Luxe in the English-speaking world. Londoners and visitors to the city travelled both physically and imaginatively as they followed an enormous "Little Girl Giant" and an even larger elephant when *The Sultan's Elephant*, the latest episode of the ongoing epic entitled *Saga of the Giants*, took place there. The gigantic "little" girl and the elephant puppet—measuring twenty and forty feet in height, respectively—were created by François Delarozière, and the production was directed by Jean-Luc Courcoult (Harris 2007a, 1). (See Figure 11.1.)

During their visit to London, a site (for Londoners, at least) of work and routine, Royal de Luxe transformed the city into a place of spectacle and adventure. Although the performances are "rigorously choreographed"

Figure 11.1 The Little Girl Giant meets the Sultan's Elephant. (Photo credit: Simon Crubellier)

(Jahnke 2007, 1), Royal de Luxe creates what feel like very spontaneous, or what Urry (2002) calls "inadvertent," meetings—informal encounters in "certain parts of towns or cities" (260). Royal de Luxe keeps the details regarding the exact time and location of each performance secret until the last moment in order to heighten the effect—for those lucky enough to be present—of having accidentally come across an extraordinary event. Elatia Harris (2007a), describing what was then the puppet company's upcoming visit to Reykjavik, explains that

> no one there but the functionaries who must know them shall have all the details in advance. The venue is simply the streets and open spaces of the city—by the lake, by the harbor and in the city centre. Admission is not only free, but accidental, since the show may begin anywhere, even in two places at once, and will overtake its audience bit by bit, for they shall not have known where to assemble and wait for it. Once it begins, it will keep moving, and people will follow it or even try to run a little ahead of it en route to the next corner it seems bound for, where others shall have started to hear things and look up. No member of that audience, not even the most avid, will see the show in its entirety—like the London event, it will be structured to make that impossible. (1)

The secrecy surrounding the exact time and location of Royal de Luxe events means that audiences experience a "live" event that generates "intense moments of co-presence" (Urry 2002, 261): "live" events are events that "cannot be 'missed'" and "set up enormous demands for mobility at very specific moments" (262). As one Londoner put it, "If you didn't go, then you'd miss out on a life-altering event, a barriers-down experience you'd share with one million other people" (quoted in Harris 2007a, 12. See Figure 11.2).[4]

Figure 11.2 The Sultan's Elephant in the streets of London. (Photo credit: Corentin Cremet, ORKA communications)

Royal de Luxe creates site-specific performances insofar as the puppets respond very directly to their location, their landscape—the urban streetscape—and the time of day.[5] Each time Royal de Luxe performs in a particular city, Courcoult creates a story specific to the people living there— he endeavours to write a "simple story" that reaches "deeply into the trove of archetypes" and yet can be understood by young children (Harris 2007b, 1). For the duration of the visit to a city or town, the gigantic puppets live in the open spaces of the street:

> Each [story] is enacted over several days, nights included, it being of the utmost importance that the Giant [the Little Girl Giant's father] abide with the town. During that entire time, the Giant is out in the open, his hair and face getting wet in the rain, sleeping by night in a chair the size of a cantilever bridge, breathing always—and dreaming. (Harris 2007a, 2)

Often, extensive arrangements must be made in order for the city streets to accommodate the puppets. In London, for example, critic Robert Eaglestone (2006) called the co-operation between Royal de Luxe and the mayor of London, the Arts Council, Artichoke (the UK producers), the police, the media, and other stakeholders involved in preparing the performance "extremely impressive" (524). In her reflection on the impact of Royal de Luxe's large-scale performance on the city, Dorothy Max Prior (2006) noted, for example, that much of central London was closed down during the event to "make way" for the "extraordinary piece of outdoor art" (1). She remarked that the producers of the London event had "pulled off miracles" such as the "exclusion of cars from Trafalgar Square and The Mall" (an honour usually reserved for the Queen) and the "removal of traffic lights along the main routes" (ibid.).

These alterations to the physical London streetscape allowed much more intangible transformations of the city to take place. Because London made room for Royal de Luxe's gigantic puppets, the puppets were able to make themselves "at home" in the city and perform their everyday routines in the city's public spaces and according to the city's daily and nightly rhythms (see Figure 11.3). By residing in the city spaces and becoming a part of city life, the puppets in turn transformed the city from an ordinary place of work and routine to a space of other potentials and new possibilities. By becoming "at home" within the city's spaces, the gigantic figures had the effect of dis-locating them—that is, the presence of the figures made these spaces instantly appear less "fixed" in relation to their usual meaning and in terms of the potential affective experience they could offer.

Figure 11.3 The Little Girl Giant takes an afternoon nap in St. James's Park, London. (Photo credit: Dave Chiu)

Royal de Luxe's large-scale puppets create both an alternative space and an alternative pace of life in the cities they inhabit. The size of the puppets demands that they be moved with the help of anywhere from eight to thirty puppeteers, sometimes using wheels, pulleys, levers, and trucks, and usually very slowly. In comparison with a miniature puppet show, in which a series of events is often condensed into five to forty-five minutes, Royal de Luxe's gigantic puppet performances unfold over four to eight days.[6] Unlike the typically speedy movements of busy Londoners and city dwellers around the world, the gigantic puppets' movements take place at a slow pace. The puppets' actions—each blink of an eye, each footstep, and each gesture—take far longer than is typically "human." But no matter how slow the action, Harris (2007a) remarks that, because of the puppets' sheer size, "I still can't take it in. And that, I came to understand, is precisely the point" (1). Harris suggests that because of the radically different sense of space and pace Royal de Luxe creates during their stay, by the time the giant puppets leave, "the village is ensorcelled" and their interlude is "likened by everyone to a dream" (ibid.).

Sizing Up Spaces

How, specifically, does the scale of these puppets relative to the city spaces they inhabit and the people they encounter contribute to this sense of a "dreamlike" interlude? As I have already discussed, the giants create an experience of "co-presence" because of the uniqueness of the live event. In part, as Royal de Luxe elucidates, a shared experience is made possible by virtue of the puppets' sheer size and thus the large numbers of people being able to view the performance at the same time. Further, people may experience a Royal de Luxe performance as a "collective" experience in part due to an understanding of cultural narratives or mythologies about things "gigantic" (i.e., archetypal giants in familiar stories). In an interview with Odile Quirot, Courcoult describes why he is drawn to gigantic puppets: "For years, I wondered how one could tell a story to an entire town. On a plane to Rio, the idea of using out-sized marionettes came to me.... People have believed in giants [forever]. Every culture on earth has stories about them. I find the giant more powerful than God or religion—because it is more make-believe yet more human" (quoted in Harris 2007a, 3).

In an interview with Jean-Christophe Planche, Courcoult (2005) adds:

> Over three or four days I try to tell a whole town something intense which will be talked about everywhere, be it in the bakery or the bar, on the pavement or in the office. I try to move people and this ambition will not be restricted by financial means or the audience's culture. Therefore, I make attempts at popular theatre in the sense that I seek to gather together these people to tell them something poetic. I have seen adults crying as the giant leaves. They have obviously lived other things, sometimes difficult, and yet this makes them cry. I don't believe they are crying because [the Giant] is leaving but because of the loss of their imagination. Over several days, they have dreamt as adults and now it's finished. Most adults have difficulty dreaming. (2)

Giant puppets, like giants, can be said, then, to be "universal" in two respects—they are able, because of their size, to "tell a story to an entire town," and stories about giants resonate with audiences due to references to familiar archetypes, often archetypes from children's stories (Courcoult, quoted in Harris 2007a, 3).

The link between the quantitative and the qualitative aspects of scale are worth interrogating here. As I have argued, the relative size of the puppets to the size of members of the audience is not merely a quantitative difference but contributes also to a qualitatively different experience. Psychologists who study the perception of space, such as Daniel R. Montello

(1993), note that scale "has an important influence on how humans treat spatial information" (312). When it comes to our spatial perception, Montello and others have observed that not all spaces are alike; rather, we understand different scales of objects in the outside world using "multiple spatial psychologies" that differ not in "merely quantitative ways" but in "a qualitative way" (313). The human body plays an important role here: the distinctions between the multiple conceptions of space are based—importantly—on "the size of a space relative to a person" (ibid.).

Montello (1993) distinguishes four major classes of psychological spaces: *figural* space is a "pictorial or object space" that is "projectively smaller than the body" and thus may be perceived "from one place without appreciable locomotion" (315). *Vista* space is "projectively as large or larger than the body" but can still be "visually apprehended from a single place without appreciable locomotion" (ibid.). *Environmental* space is "projectively larger than the body and surrounds it" and is "too large and otherwise obscured to be apprehended directly without considerable locomotion," and thus usually requires "integration of information over significant periods of time" (ibid.). Finally, *geographical* space is "projectively much larger than the body and cannot be apprehended directly through locomotion" but must, rather, be "learned via symbolic representations such as maps or models that essentially reduce the geographical space to figural space" (ibid.).

For the present purposes, I define as "miniature" the figural pictorial or object space (any perceived image or object) that is "smaller than the body," and define as gigantic images or objects that occupy vista space, environmental space, or geographical space that is "larger than the body." The key difference between the quantitatively miniature and gigantic on the qualitative experience of scale is the sense that the miniature can be "apprehended" (seen or held) from a single place and all at once, whereas we can apprehend the gigantic only in parts.[7] Both the miniature and the gigantic reconstruct our sense of our own being, but the quantitative difference in the size of a space or object relative to ourselves gives rise to a qualitatively different experience: we can hold the miniature in our hands, but the gigantic envelops us.

Miniature puppet figures allow us to create a microcosm of our world within the bounds of the puppet play proscenium, but gigantic puppets inhabit our space and "look" upon our world as though we were miniature. Susan Stewart, in her extended cultural analysis of the miniature and gigantic, *On Longing: Narratives of the Miniature, the Gigantic, the Souvenir, the Collection* (1984), describes the miniature as "a metaphor for the interior space and time of the bourgeois subject" (xii).[8] Stewart argues that "the toy"—which she defines as a smaller-than-human object that can be apprehended—"opens an interior world, lending itself to fantasy and privacy in a way that the abstract space, the playground, of social play does not" (56).

If the miniature is an expression of private desire,[9] the gigantic, conversely, is emblematic for Stewart of the desire for collective experience, or the desires of a collectivity. As Stewart (1984) observes, "While fantasy in the miniature moves toward an individualized interiority, fantasy in the gigantic exteriorizes and communalizes what might otherwise be considered 'the subjective'" (82). She underscores the connection between the quantitative and qualitative aspects of scale when she adds:

> We cannot speak of the small, or miniature work independent of the social values expressed toward private space—particularly of the ways the domestic and the interior imply the social formation of an interior subject. And we cannot speak of the grand and the gigantic independent of social values expressed toward nature and the public and exterior life of the city. Aesthetic size cannot be divorced from social function and social values. (95)

In the foreword to the *Puppetry International* issue devoted to "mega-puppets," Andrew Periale (2007) points out that gigantic puppets can also have a different effect—they can elicit another affective response. He begins by pointing out that believers in God or a Creator of the Universe usually imagine this entity as "big, huge, even humongous" (2). He adds that for adults like himself, "being in the presence of giant- or mega-puppets" has "the powerful effect that [his] parents (by sheer dint of size) have long since failed to exercise over [him]" (unless, as he notes humorously, he happens to be "visiting them over the holidays") (ibid.). He explains that giant puppets, by making us feel small, reinforce "bonds of community," remind us that there are both "things and ideas in the universe bigger than we," and give us hope that "the humongous forces that rule our lives" are "benevolent and loving" (ibid.). John Bell (2007) reinforces the idea that being in the midst of giants produces in us a sense of modesty about our own power and agency in this world:

> I think it has to do with the obvious discomfort of scale that giant puppets bring with them. If the manipulation of hand puppets, marionettes, rod puppets, shadow figures, and other smaller-than-life forms brings with it a pleasing sense of security about the powers and abilities of human agency, giant puppets (even though they are also set in motion by human hands) perform a relationship in which humans are not the biggest things around. While the human-to-small-puppet ratio establishes a kind of confidence, the human-to-giant-puppet ratio inevitably brings with it a sense of unease and doubt. (26)

Bell observes that what is notable about giant puppets is how their "larger-than-human stature" makes us reflect upon "the relative limits of human agency in a world which appears to be governed by larger-than-life forces" (28–29).

The feeling of being in the presence of something larger than us can make us feel uneasy and, at the same time, give us a sense of wonder and awe (see Figure 11.4). Indeed, audiences watching Royal de Luxe perform-ances—especially children—experience both kinds of reactions, and often both at once (not unlike the child pictured in the film *Royal de Luxe et Le*

Figure 11.4 A child swinging on the arm of the Little Girl Giant. (Photo credit: Esther Simpson)

Mythe du Géant who clings to his father and yet despite his fear cannot help but watch the Giant through the cracks between his fingers). In her reflections on "the power of large-scale puppetry in public spaces," Prior (2006) describes how the impact of Royal de Luxe performances lies in the "universal human emotions" that are "evoked by the extraordinary skills of the animators in operating the mechanical people and creatures" and "the interactions that take place between passers-by and puppets" (2). Royal de Luxe includes viewers in their performances not only because the giant puppets have the effect of enveloping us, but also because there are no "lead" characters per se—the performances feature the puppets, but bringing the puppets to life is a participatory affair. The red-liveried technicians manipulating the puppets are "actors" and, as Harris (2007a) notes, "[t]he audience, too, is an actor" (7). Indeed, even the process involved in the animation of a Royal de Luxe performance (namely, the manipulation of puppets that in more traditional performances would be hidden behind the proscenium) is shared with the audience. Harris (2007a) points out that "[i]t is one of those paradoxes of the Giants that, seeing an unbelievable thing, and seeing plainly the levers and ropes and pulleys and humans required to make it work—for none of this is ever concealed in a Royal de Luxe performance—you believe in it utterly" (2).[10] In Prior's (2006) longer description of the Little Girl Giant, we hear a similar articulation of this magical-mechanical paradox:

> From the pod La Petite Géante rises up, a girl puppet in a green dress and white ankle socks that, although she towers above the crowd, has an air of gentle childhood innocence that keeps her firmly placed as a "little" girl. She has black hair that moves gently in the breeze, and enormous eyes that slowly close and open, her beautiful eyelashes sweeping down and up. She takes a while to find herself in this strange new territory, looking over the gathered crowd with a slow turn of the head, her eyes seeming to come into clear focus as she takes in her surroundings. The machinery—cranes, wires, ropes, pulleys—is fully visible. The large number of manipulators is clearly in sight above, behind and around her. There is no attempt to hide the business of animating this giant marionette, yet she is alive. We believe with total conviction, and our hearts reach out to her. All eyes in the large crowd are drawn to hers, and it seems that everyone feels, as I do, that they have made personal contact with an extraordinary being. (1)

Harris (2007a) posits that seeing the mechanisms of the giant marionette exposed, yet feeling as though one is watching something magical, is an experience common to art: "Indeed, all art is participatory owing to a quality that art historians call 'the viewer's share'—the finding of meaning in what is seen" (11–12). That is, although audience members can see how the puppet is manoeuvred, they can at the same time believe that the giant puppet has come to life—in fact, for some, seeing the mechanism required to move the giants may even augment the sense of awe at what marvellous creatures can be brought into being through a creative combination of human artistry, technology, material, and movement. Audiences marvel at Royal de Luxe's ability to bring such "beings" into being as well as the affective responses that these "inanimate" objects are capable of evoking.

Indeed, the focus of a Royal de Luxe performance from the perspective of both its creators and its audience seems to be less on the content of the story (which is intentionally "simple" and "archetypal," as Courcoult explains) and more on the creation of a shared affective experience.[11] As Courcoult says of the performances he creates, the public reaction is "as important as the form of the show" (quoted in Harris 2007a, 4). Also important to Courcoult is that Royal de Luxe's performances are financed by taxes and performed on the city streets so that they can reach a broad public. He states:

> I am proud that the shows we produce are financed by taxes … it seems fitting and beautiful that some tax money is dedicated to popular culture. By putting on the show in the public arena and free of charge I can reach people as they are, whereas in traditional theatre you only meet those who have dared cross the threshold. (quoted in Prior 2006, 2)

Prior (2006) points out that creating theatre in the open spaces of the city, accessible to a wide audience, is an ethos shared by numerous artists and companies who create gigantic puppet street theatre (2). She also observes that unlike the work of other street theatre puppet troupes whose performances are "overtly political," Royal de Luxe's work is "intrinsically political" because of "its very existence in public spaces" (ibid.). Prior argues that "puppets on the street have a unique role to play in the creation of a theatre that is genuinely egalitarian, that is political in its very existence, regardless of whether artists take a consciously political stance, and which does indeed, in so many varied and beautiful ways, display life in its clearest terms" (3). For Prior, then, gigantic street puppet theatre has the effect of transforming a place into a public space. In other words, street puppet theatre calls into existence— it performs and thus provokes—a public sphere by virtue of the gathering of people in public space. Her discussion of the political nature of such a space is interesting because in effect she suggests that public space is created by what takes place there—that the event, the people, and the performance, rather than the ownership designation of the physical place—is what creates "public" space as such. In the next section I expand on Prior's observations by suggesting that although large puppets have been used historically as media to convey political messages, the performances of Royal de Luxe are "intrinsically political" in that they create public spaces—and, as I argue, alternative affective encounters—in the open spaces of the city streets.

Imagining Hope

Courcoult (2005) explains that "imagining a show like an encounter with a machine" is "a legacy of Jules Verne" (1).[12] He goes on to explain that Verne was "a dreamer who was determined to make people dream" (ibid.). Helen Marriage, director of Artichoke, the producers who brought Royal de Luxe to London, remarks that "the drama of the encounter—the towering machine brought into the fold to become a personage—is theatre that steps just outside the possible" (quoted in Harris 2007a, 8). She remarks that "[a]udiences in general can only imagine what they already know" (quoted in Harris 2007a, 9). Royal de Luxe is interested in delivering not only what most people have never seen, but also what they might not ever have imagined possible. The dreamlike encounters with Royal de Luxe's performing machines turn mundane city spaces into places of possibility—spaces in which there is a distinctly hopeful atmosphere.

Ben Anderson and Adam Holden's work on "affective urbanism" is useful in thinking about the kind of shared experience that Royal de Luxe's gigantic puppets create in city spaces. Anderson and Holden (2008) understand cities as composed of "multiple, differentiated affects, feelings, and emotions" and seek to foster an "everyday urbanism" that is "attentive to the *taking place*" of these affective responses (145).[13] In his extensive work on hope as an affect, Anderson (2006) is interested in "how hope takes place"—in other words, he focuses on the "geographies of the affectual and emotional life" (733). He argues that "[h]ope, and hoping, are taken-for-granted parts of the affective fabric of contemporary Western everyday life. The circulation, and distribution, of hope animates and dampens social-cultural life across numerous scales: from the minutiae of hopes that pleat together everyday life to the larger scales of flows of hope that enact various collectivities" (ibid.). Audiences describe Royal de Luxe performances as having a powerful affective impact. People are often deeply moved personally, and feel a sense of sharing an affective experience with others. The "taking place" of these affects, feelings, and emotions transforms everyday spaces into spaces of alternative possibilities; the coming-into-being of another way of being in the cities inhabited by the puppets imbues these spaces with a sense of hopefulness by demonstrating some of their latent potential. As Anderson (2006) notes, "through affect we are able to open onto the diverse presences *within* 'everyday life'" (738).

Hope, or becoming hopeful, is of course a somewhat paradoxical experience since hoping for something to come into being is necessarily premised on the fact that it does not yet exist. Further, hope, which in Ernst Bloch's assessment "dwells in the region of the not-yet, a place where entrance and, above all, final content are marked by an enduring indeterminacy," also contains within its very structure the possibility that what is hoped for may never become actual (quoted in Anderson and Holden 2008, 155). The positive kernel (or presence) that is hope is bracketed by, on the one hand, an absent reality, and on the other, the possibility of an absence. Anderson and Holden (2008) agree that

> [t]here is, therefore, a point of danger, or hazard, folded into becoming hopeful that indicates that a good way of being has "still not become": in the sense that the present is haunted by the fact that the something good that exceeds it has yet to take place and that "the conditions that make it possible to hope are strictly the same as those that make it possible to despair." (quoting Marcel, 743)

Although I agree with Anderson and Holden's (2008) statement that it is "always from the context of specific diminishments that becoming hopeful emerges" (743), I would like to distinguish between two different temporalities of the emergence of hope or of becoming hopeful. It seems to me that in certain cases "specific diminishments" are evident at the outset and give rise to hope for something else, and in other cases, it is rather an event that evokes a sense of hopefulness that makes "specific diminishments" evident. In the case of Royal de Luxe performances, in particular, it seems that it isn't necessarily that people's hopes are answered, but that hopes people may not have even recognized or acknowledged existed are *created*. Thus, hope does not arise only from known "absences," such as the absence of safety and comfort; hope also arises when an "absence" is revealed or exposed as a result of a potential presence is introduced into quotidian life. Indeed, when first encountering performances by Royal de Luxe one may not expect to *become* hopeful. Nonetheless, Royal de Luxe's performances have the effect of introducing an alternative space that exposes the everyday as a place that *could* be different (i.e., more open to creative possibility, more playful, more egalitarian). Once the giant puppets leave town and that space of possibility disappears, audiences routinely remark how much they hope that the giants will return so that their city might again reveal its potential to become other than it is. In other words, Royal de Luxe can be said to perform and thus create or provoke spaces of hope.[14] Indeed, I suggest that in this way, Royal de Luxe creates theatrical spaces that, following the work of Michael Gardiner, can be said to function as "critical utopias" (1993, 179).

Critical Utopias as a Getaway from the Everyday

The imaginative utopian spaces that Royal de Luxe creates—spaces wherein we see ourselves as miniatures in the presence of giants—might be dismissed as escapist dreamscapes. Indeed, critics of "festival" (Bataille 1991), "spectacle" (Debord 1995), and the "carnivalesque" (Bakhtin 1984) argue that while temporally limited events that alter our experience of space can function as "a curious inversion of a state of continual war," they should not "be confused with more complicated and efficacious acts of resistance" (Read 2006, 523). I would like to complicate the simple dismissal of street performances under the category of "festival" or "spectacle" by suggesting that the alternative worlds that they create have a utopian function that is implicitly—even when not explicitly—also critical. Actualizing such dream-spaces, even if only for a fixed period of time, through, for example, the construction of another dimension created through a difference in scale, alters our perspective on the existing world and offers an alternative to what the existing world *could be*. As Gardiner emphasizes in his essay "Bakhtin's Carnival: Utopia as Critique," the term "critical utopia" identifies "self-critical utopian discourse itself as a process that can tear apart the ideological web"— that is, rather than suggesting that a particular utopian imaginary ought to replace the current state of affairs, critical utopianism is a "permanently open process of envisioning what is not yet" (Moylan quoted in Gardiner 1993, 179).

Thus, the *critical* aspect of a critical utopia is less a matter of content, or *what* the utopian vision looks like (i.e., we may not necessarily want giant puppets to permanently live among us), and more *that* a process of envisioning a different way of being is being performed. The very sight of Royal de Luxe's performances in one's everyday environs presents a juxtaposition that gives rise to a number of readings of those streets. Not all of these interpretations consider the performance and the transformation of these streets in a positive light or as presenting a vision of how we want to live, but the alternative reality that is created does dislodge the apparent fixity of "the way things are." The difference in scale created by the performance puts the city into relief in a way that may be critical *or* celebratory—what is crucial is that the possibility of an alternative possibility is enacted and experienced. As Gardiner (1993) underscores, the key to a critical utopian perspective is that it emphasizes "becoming" and objectifies "emancipatory ways of being as well as the very possibility of utopian longing itself" (179). Regardless of whether we'd like to live as miniatures in a giant puppet show every day, "Utopia represents a peculiarly well-suited vantage point from which to view our own social arrangements, because these are suddenly illuminated in a new and very different light. They now appear strange or even alien through a comparison with the utopian world, present-day society is estranged, rendered unfamiliar" (180). This momentary aesthetic and affective break creates a "dialectical tension" between the performance and reality that, even after the giant puppets leave, "results in a permanent oscillation between fantasy and praxis, escape and return" (186). Importantly, this break is one that is not only "in thought" but also "in experience, or enactment, or living possibility" (ibid.).

Critic Robert Eaglestone's review of *The Sultan's Elephant* emphasizes that the performance did more than focus his attention on the fantasy of the giant mechanical elephant puppet moving through the street—it cast a new light on the streets of London. He (2006) writes:

> The media made a great deal about the ways in which lampposts and street furniture had to be moved to let the Elephant pass. But for me, the change to the city was much more than that. In his essay, "The Origin of the Work of Art," Heidegger writes that an art work doesn't just foreground itself as an art work but also draws attention to the world in which it exists.... And so it was, for me, with the elephant. As people stood on what was usually the busy street, or sat on the curbs or steps of shops and offices, or looked out from windows, I was drawn to look not at the Elephant, but at the city streets again, and in different ways: their wideness, for example (as opposed to seeing them simply as lanes of moving traffic to cross); the differences in colour (the darkness of the tarmac, the roughness of the curb stones, and the red and yellows of the advertising). The hugeness of the elephant— its "out-of-scaleness"—made me look at the second, third and fourth stories of buildings around it, the details around their windows and the decorations on the roofs. (524)

Eaglestone (2006) affirms that this outsized spectacle made him "see" the city streets that, presumably, he typically simply takes for granted as he passes by. What he sees—and what he critiques in his review of the performance—

is not a troubling juxtaposition, but rather, a troubling complementarity between what he called an "orientalist spectacle" and the "great streets" of London. He reflects on the movement of the giant elephant through streets that feature grand, white, Victorian architecture "originally funded in no small part by empire" and passing monuments and statues of generals that led the colonial wars (525). He found that the huge elephant did not challenge these structures but served rather as part of "the spectacle of empire" and, indeed, "a celebration of Empire" (ibid.). Critic Alan Read (2006) praised the performance in part because he welcomed the change in affect in the streets—namely, the fear that had come to preside over London following the bombings on July 7, 2005;[15] however, he too viewed the Royal de Luxe performance as having missed an opportunity to offer a critique of the London locale:

> [A]s someone who works within the very streets the elephant occupied for a weekend, it should not go without saying that the opportunity for exposing the locality—one of the most entrenched power-bases in the western world, dripping with gentleman's clubs and business quangos, and confirmed in its utter hegemony by the continued presence of the alternative to orthodoxy, the orthodox ICA—to a more sustained, poetic critique, would not be beyond Royal de Luxe or those brave promoters, such as Helen Marriage, who stake their livelihoods and lives on such occasions. (523)

While I agree with these critiques of the content of *The Sultan's Elephant*, I maintain that although the performance was not explicitly critical of its environs (and thus, may well have participated, even reinforced, the same colonialist history it neglected to critique), it succeeded in casting light on a given state of affairs and inspiring critique that called into question whether what we take for granted is how things ought to remain. The presence of Royal de Luxe's puppets in the streets provoked a critical view of the London cityscape by providing one particular creative response to what is possible in a city. Moreover, as I have argued, the critical power of Royal de Luxe performances rests not only in the content of the story, but also in the affective dimension that is experienced as a "living possibility" (Gardiner 1993, 186).

In this chapter, I have focused on the importance of the critical power of affect especially in terms of an understanding of "critical utopia." The outsized performances of Royal de Luxe are not only critical of the everyday by comparing it with what could be, but also critical of the everyday by revealing what could be felt. The hope experienced by audiences contributes to the critical and creative power of Royal de Luxe's performances. As Anderson and Fenton (2008) note, "bearing witness to spaces of hope involves thinking of ordinary, quotidian, life as not-yet-become" (76). Creating spaces in which hope is experienced "heralds the possibility that the spatial/temporal here and now may become otherwise (whether hope is for a change from, or continuation of, that here and now)" (ibid.).

The creation of a space that feels full of hope opens the possibility for more lasting change to take place. The gigantic performances of Royal de Luxe do more than simply shed light on current situations and surroundings, or create a festive, spectacular, carnivalesque aesthetic space. Through the enormity of their art—by creating something people have not seen before (or perhaps not even thought possible)—Royal de Luxe invites people to imagine other impossibilities that might become possible, other dreams that might become realities, and other hopes that could come to be actualized. (Or, at the very least, hopes that could be hoped.) Hope, as Anderson and Fenton (2008) state so eloquently, "unsettles the spacing of the present" and invites people to conceive space as "animated by (im)possibilities, potentialities and virtualities" (79). Hope—like critical utopian visioning—is critical not only because of the creation of a vision of some alternative possibility, or something that is hoped for, but also for the very impetus, the drive, the ongoing desire for positive change that it invites and incites. And although we may not necessarily want to permanently live at the feet of giant puppets, Royal de Luxe's performance may also serve as a humbling reminder that we as humans, despite many of our actions, are neither the biggest nor necessarily the most important entities on the planet. And further, these gigantic puppets might provoke us to ponder that perhaps, when inhabiting a shared space with others, we, when playing giants, ought to be benevolent and kind.

Notes

I would like to thank Michael Gardiner at the University of Western Ontario for his thoughtful guidance on earlier versions of this project and his generous support of my M.A. research on puppetry, aesthetics, and politics. I would also like to gratefully acknowledge the support I have received from the SSHRC Joseph-Armand Bombardier Canada Graduate Scholarship, the Izaak Walton Killam Memorial Scholarship, and the Ralph Steinhauer Award of Distinction during my doctoral studies at the University of Alberta, where I developed many of the ideas in this chapter with the guidance and support of Rob Shields and the valuable feedback of fellow contributors to this project.

1 It should be noted that issues of scale have received attention in the field of human geography; however, "scale" in human geography routinely refers to levels of social/economic "scales" of networks (local/national/global) (Marston, Jones III, and Woodward 2005). For the purposes of this paper, "scale" will be related, as in architecture or urban planning, to relative physical size—the relationship between the human body and material objects (puppets) and the space of the built environment.

2 Royal de Luxe performances have included *Le Géant Tombé du Ciel* (*The Giant Who Fell from the Sky*) in Le Havre, France (1993); *Le Géant Tombé du Ciel: Dernier Voyage* (*The Giant Who Fell from the Sky: Last Voyage*) in Le Havre, France (1994); *Retour d'Afrique* (*Return from Africa*) in Cameroon (1997–1998); *Les Chasseurs des Girafes* (*Giraffe Hunters*) in Nantes, France (2000), and China (2001); *The Sultan's Elephant* in London, UK (2006); and *The Hidden Rhinoceros* in Santiago, Chile (2007) (Jahnke 2007: 1).

3 I say "certain" liberties because the rambunctious behaviour that gave puppets their "street appeal" has throughout history been kept under close surveillance by the authorities ready to censor shows featuring "politically suspect material" (Bell 2000, 18).

4 Royal de Luxe creates events that are highly participatory and extremely "popular" in both senses of the word.

5 A "site-specific" work articulates and defines "itself through properties, qualities, or meanings produced in specific relationships between an 'object' or 'event' and a position it occupies" (Kaye 2000, 1).

6 Architects at the University of Tennessee School of Architecture observe, curiously, that there may be "an actual phenomenological correlation between the experience of scale and the experience of duration." In an experiment with various scales of environmental models, they found that "the experience of temporal duration is compressed relative to the clock in the same proportion as scale-model environments being observed are compressed relative to the full-sized environment" (quoted in Stewart 1984, 66).

7 I would like to distinguish between the gigantic and what theorists such as Longinus, Burke, Kant, and Lyotard, among others, have termed the "sublime." Although their descriptions of the sublime (or descriptions of the experience of the sublime) differ, the sublime, in general, connotes an object or idea so vast that it is by definition beyond measure. Although the sublime may well be gigantic, I would not describe Royal de Luxe puppets as "sublime." The puppets may be large and inspire awe or even fear (and so be likened, perhaps, to the experience of the sublime in some of the above writers' descriptions); however, it is precisely that the puppets can be measured against the people in their midst, the buildings, and the streetscape that they have an effect that is not "beyond" this world, but very much grounded in it—the puppets do not help us "transcend" space but rather "transform" it. The puppets exist at a scale that relates to their surroundings, not at a level so lofty that it lies beyond thought or imagination.

8 Charles C. Gordon (2006) signalled a lack of discussion of scale in a different context—in what he called the "new technological revolution" in his "Considerations on Miniaturization." Describing the influence of miniaturization on

"artifacts of everyday culture and on the design of those artifacts," he too observes, "One effect of the processes of making things smaller is to contract the actor network involved in social processes and, in certain instances, to make individual something previously done in specific social networks" (211).

9   In *The Poetics of Space* (1964), Gaston Bachelard also argues that "imagination in miniature" not only takes us back to childhood, but also appears "at all ages in the daydreams of born dreamers" (149). He underscores that the miniature "stimulates profound values" (151); that, contrary to what one presume, "[m]inia-ture is one of the refuges of greatness" (ibid.) or, in sum, that "[v]alues become engulfed in miniature and miniature causes men to dream" (152). But the dreams and values that the miniature holds are for Bachelard (as for Stewart) those of "solitary dreamers" (181). Although the values and dreams may be "profound" or "great," they are intimate and private. The cocooning experience of the miniature (as opposed to the collective experience of the gigantic), Bachelard states, "detaches [one] from the surrounding world" (161).

10 As Prior (2006) observes, "there is no off-stage in this show" as "everything that happens ... can be viewed by the public" (1).

11 This perceived lack of attention paid to the story has invited criticism of Royal de Luxe performances. Kara Reilly (2007) writes that "it seems that, apart from the company's elaborate spectacles of mechanical wonder, there is little desire to tell a meaningful story" (5). Moreover, she adds that the stories are "fraught with problems linked to tourism, globalism, and neo-colonialism" (ibid.). As I further discuss below, a similar critique of the performances of *The Sultan's Elephant* in London has been levelled by Eaglestone (2006), who points out that the reliance on simple stories and familiar archetypes is problematic—it involves a failure to look critically at the traditions and scrutinize the history, context, and meanings of the stories upon which the performances are based. He described *The Sultan's Elephant* as "almost a set piece of orientalism"— "like a checklist of basic features from 'Orientalism 101'" in which "Here" was con-trasted with "a foreign amalgamated 'over there'" (525).

12 When Royal de Luxe puppets are not performing, some can be viewed in a new venue in Nantes imagined by François Delarozière and Pierre Orefice called Les Machines de L'Île. This venue currently features the giant elephant and will eventually include additional "monumental mechanical structures open to the public" (Malavida 2007, 4). This artistic project is described as "a blend of the invented worlds of Jules Verne, the mechanical universe of Leonardo da Vinci, and the industrial history of Nantes, on the exceptional site of the former shipyards" (7).

13 Anderson and Holden (2008) understand affects as "impersonal movements that constitute what a body can do," feelings as "interpersonal expressions of affects," and emotions as "personal qualifications of feelings" (145). (See Shields and Tiessen in this volume for more on affect.)

14 The presence of the puppets in the street has the effect of disrupting the "nor-mal" routines in the time/space in which their performances take place. In Anderson's (2006) terms, their presence and performance create hope through the creation of a "point of divergence" or, more specifically, a "moment of *discontinuity* in which a threshold is crossed through the creation of an

intensified connection with life (the 'glimmer' or 'spark' of hope)" (745). The puppets "surprise thought" and cause a rupture in everyday experience—not only in terms of location and duration, but also in terms of an affective experience of a place/time—that points to the potential, or possibility, of what could be or what could happen there (ibid.). (See Jackson and della Dora in this volume for more on hope as that which "surprises thought.")

15   Read (2006) noted that because the original performance of *The Sultan's Elephant* was postponed due to the London bombings on July 7, 2005, Royal de Luxe's performance was welcomed by many as a "celebratory festival" that brought back the "bright side of streets which know more troubled times" (523).

References

Anderson, B. 2006. Becoming and being hopeful: Towards a theory of affect. *Environment and Planning D* 24: 733–52.

Anderson, B., and J. Fenton. 2008. Editorial introduction. *Space and Culture* 11 (2): 76–80.

Anderson, B., and A. Holden. 2008. Affective urbanism and the event of hope. *Space and Culture* 11 (2): 142–59.

Bachelard, G. 1964. *The poetics of space*, trans. M. Jolas. New York: Orion Press.

Baird, B. 1965. *The art of the puppet*. New York: Macmillan.

Bakhtin, M. 1984. *Rabelais and his world*, trans. H. Iswolsky. Bloomington: Indiana University Press.

Bataille, G. 1991. *The accursed share: Vol. II, The history of eroticism*, trans. R. Hurley. New York: Zone Books.

Bell, J. 2000. *Strings, hands, shadows: A modern puppet history*. Detroit, MI: The Detroit Institute of Arts.

———. 2007. Mega-puppets and global culture. *Puppetry International: The Puppet in Contemporary Theatre, Film & Media* 22: 26–29.

Blumenthal, E. 2005. *Puppetry: A world history*. New York: Harry N. Abrams.

Courcoult, J. 2005. Extracts from an interview with Jean-Luc Courcoult by Jean-Christophe Planche. *Les Cahiers du Channel* 19: 1–4.

Debord, G. 1995. *The society of the spectacle*. New York: Zone Books.

Deleuze, G., and F. Guattari. 1986. *Kafka: Toward a minor literature*, trans. D. Polan. Minneapolis: University of Minnesota Press.

Eaglestone, R. 2006. The Sultan's Elephant. Review of *The Sultan's Elephant*, by Royal de Luxe, London. *Contemporary Theatre Review* 16 (4): 523–25.

Gardiner, M. 1993. Bakhtin's carnival: Utopia as critique. *Critical Studies* 3 (2): 20–47.

Gordon, C. 2006. Considerations on miniaturization. *Space and Culture* 9 (2): 210–14.

Harris, E. 2007a. Royal de Luxe: The Saga of the Giants, March 26. *3 Quarks Daily*. http://3quarksdaily.blogs.com/3quarksdaily/2007/03/royal_de_luxe_t.html (accessed January 5, 2009).

————. 2007b. Royal de Luxe II: Face-off in Reykjavik, May 21. *3 Quarks Daily.* http://3quarksdaily.blogs.com/3quarksdaily/2007/05/royal_de_luxe_i.html (accessed January 5, 2009).

Jahnke, M. 2007. Royal de Luxe: The theater group with pull, April 11. *Interesting Thing of the Day.* http://itotd.com/articles/635/royal-de-luxe/ (accessed February 5, 2009).

Kaye, N. 2000. *Site-specific art: Performance, place and documentation.* London: Routledge.

Latshaw, G. 1978. *Puppetry: The ultimate disguise.* New York: Richard Rosen Press.

Lefebvre, H. 2002. *Critique of everyday life.* Volume II. Trans. J. Moore. London; New York: Verso.

Malavida, D. D., dir. 2007. *Les Machines de L'Île Nantes.* Nantes: SEM Nantes culture&patrimoine.

Marston, S. A., J. P. Jones III, and K. Woodward. 2005. Human geography without scale. *Transactions of the Institute of British Geographers* 30: 416–32.

Montello, D. 1993. Scale and multiple psychologies of space. *Spatial information theory: A theoretical basis for GIS.* Heidelberg: Springer Berlin.

Periale, A. 2007. Big. *Puppetry International: The Puppet in Contemporary Theatre, Film & Media* 22: 2.

Prior, D. M. 2006. Puppets on the street. *Animations Online Edition* 17 (Summer). http://www.puppetcentre.org.uk/animationsonline/aoseventeen/feat_watchout.html (accessed February 5, 2009).

Read, A. 2006. The elephant in the street. Review of *The Sultan's Elephant,* by Royal de Luxe, London. *Contemporary Theatre Review* 16: 522–23.

Reilly, K. 2007. Puppetry of the spectacle: Royal de Luxe's giants. *Puppetry International: The Puppet in Contemporary Theatre, Film & Media* 22: 24–27.

Stewart, S. 1984. *On Longing: Narratives of the miniature, the gigantic, the souvenir, the collection.* Baltimore; London: Johns Hopkins University Press.

Urry, J. 2000. Mobile sociology. *British Journal of Sociology* 51 (1): 185–203.
————. 2002. Mobility and proximity. *Sociology* 36 (2): 255–74.

12

The Spatial Distribution of Hope
In and Beyond Fort McMurray

SARA DOROW
GOZE DOGU

[O]nce one has hope within one's field of vision, one discovers the astounding degree to which the constellations of feelings, discourses and practices articulated to hope permeate social life. (Hage 2003, 9)

Introduction

Fort McMurray, Alberta, has been hailed as a "land of hope" for workers and their families, for the Canadian national economy, and even for a car-bon-based global energy system. This town-cum-city serves as staging area for the development of the Athabasca oil sands, a deposit of bitumen covering an area of northeast Alberta larger than the province of New Brunswick (or Florida) and composing the second-largest known oil reserve on the planet. It is unconventional oil, in that it must be mined from the surface or underground pockets and then separated from a viscous combination of sand, oil, and water; the process requires much higher levels of financial and human resources than does the production of conventional oil. In the early years of the twenty-first century, as the right alchemy of financing, technology, government policy, and higher oil prices allowed the extraction of bitumen to take off, the population of Fort McMurray doubled to more than 70,000 in just eight years. The professionals, service sector workers, and especially trades people who migrated (and were often encouraged to migrate) from all over Canada and other parts of the globe inhabit spaces with and beside people who have called Fort McMurray home for decades or even generations. But "land of hope" means different things to these people, and as we argue in this chapter, these differences are revealed at the juncture of identity and place—in the social relations of co-presence (Massey 1994) among professionals and industrial workers, long-term and short-term residents.

Hage (2003) argues that in an era of flexible capital accumulation and reduced state welfare provision, hope is not only unevenly distributed across the social spectrum, but also increasingly scarce. Our exploration of Fort McMurray utilizes Hage's framework but shifts toward conceptualizing the distribution of hope as a matter of social relations to, in, and across space. Hage has said that the kinds of attachments people have to place (mostly synonymous with the nation in the case of his work) are contingent on a society's ability to distribute hope evenly, and this ability is increasingly compromised. While in basic agreement with Hage's argument, we fear his conceptualization of hope may inadvertently fix place and/or conceive of space as a series of "levels" from local to global. Doreen Massey's impressive body of work has asserted first, that both places and identities vary, and thus vary in relation to each other; and second, that any "place" (such as Fort McMurray) is "constructed out of a particular constellation of [globalized] social relations, meeting and weaving together at a particular locus" (Massey 1994, 7). In other words, the "big picture" of social and market relations (such as that of the oil sands industry) is in fact local, even as "local" is itself many things, constructed out of "the intersections and interactions of concrete social relations and social processes in a situation of co-presence" (138).

In this chapter we explore several co-present forms of "local consciousness" (perceptions of identities and belonging in and through place) among different groups of people in Fort McMurray, with the aim of reconceptualizing hope in terms of spatialized social relations. In that sense, through Massey's insights, we are expanding on Hage's framework. Analyzing the complex and uneven "relations of co-presence" in the particular context of Fort McMurray provides a unique lens on the social distribution of hope as a spatialized process; it alerts us to the differential availability and experience of hope as a matter of relations in and across places.

This framework informs our analysis of more than fifty interviews we conducted with a broad cross-section of people living and/or working in the Fort McMurray area; each interviewee was also asked to draw a sketch map of "your Fort McMurray." Participants included welders and truck drivers from out of province living in work camps, immigrants with engineering degrees recruited to work for the oil companies for several years, thirty-year residents teaching nursing or education in the local college, Aboriginal people born and raised in the area. The results, richly varied and sometimes wildly compelling, presented an opportunity to trace the uneven topography of where and how people "place" their hope. For many of the long-time residents, hope is embedded in and for the community of Fort McMurray itself; for many in the mobile worker population, Fort McMurray is where hopes for other places, times, or people are enabled or frustrated; and for yet another set of people, namely, recently arrived professionals in the oil business, hope is flexibly able to put down roots in this place (or a number of places) for as long as is possible or prudent. Across this range of narratives, relationships to and understandings of place speak to the spatialized distribution of hope, which in turn displays the uneven social imprint of the oil sands resource economy.

Fort McMurray and the Oil Sands

The municipal government encompassing Fort McMurray[1] touts it as Canada's energy capital, asserting in one of its flyers that with "a deposit that contains enough oil reserves to maintain production for more than 300 years[,] the [municipality], its partner investors and its people are building on that future—one with opportunity for all. Come join us. Come share in the energy!" This promise of opportunity, a hope built on the future longevity of the oil sands, is matched on the other side of the flyer by the size of the region's "big spirit": "Our land mass is unequaled, our oil industry is massive and our untapped potential is infinite in scale. But nothing in the region can compare to the enormity of our indomitable spirit."

Expressed in this way, Fort McMurray is a blurry concoction of sociopolitical space and the resource economy that surrounds and sustains it. The actual vast mining operations (sometimes compared to a moonscape, or even to Mordor),[2] where three-storey trucks load and haul two million tons of bitumen-soaked sand each day for processing and upgrading, sit mostly north of and thus almost entirely out of sight of the actual town site. Yet Fort McMurray and the oil sands are bound together in complex material and discursive ways. When a construction worker from Newfoundland or an environmental consultant from Nigeria says they work in Fort McMurray, the default assumption is that they work in the oil industry—whether they live in the town of 70,000, or commute by bus or plane in and out of the many work camps estimated to house at least another 20,000 people. Long-time residents of Fort McMurray, those who have lived there since long before the current boom or even before the first boom of the late 1970s, are more likely to mean the town itself when they refer to Fort McMurray. Even so, the oil industry figures into the place(s) of their Fort McMurray in myriad ways—after all, the two original companies, Syncrude and Suncor, have a three-decade history that reaches deep into the social and physical infrastructure of the town.[3]

The socio-spatial imbrication of industry and town is also evident in the discourses of Fort McMurray that circulate nationally and globally. As suggested by the "energy capital" flyer, some of these discourses are official, created by municipal and provincial government offices for the sake of attracting both investment and labour.[4] But more than this, the "big spirit" campaign was a direct response to some of the detrimental imagery of Fort McMurray that had hit the national and international media by 2006. The fast and vast growth of new mining construction projects between 2002 and 2006—investments of fourteen billion dollars and the influx of thousands of new residents—had quickly put very high pressure and high prices on social and physical infrastructure in Fort McMurray. Media coverage linked the oil boom to a gold rush mentality and a crude, masculinized, drug-ridden, family-unfriendly environment, an image captured in the nickname "Fort McMoney." A second wave of media focused on "dirty oil" prompted industry, government, and community leaders to warn and worry that environmental criticism would hurt industry, and thus the town. In short, Fort McMurray—the place that is both community and industry—found itself waging a battle over its ability to serve as a social backstop to the promises and vagaries of economic hope.

Hope, Space, and Neo-liberal Capitalism

In this section, we briefly consider the concept of hope in all its expansiveness and fragility, and aim to extend the more common temporal treatment to the important question of spatial distribution. In almost any theoretical treatise on hope, the future figures prominently. As Flaherty (1983) put it, "hope is conceivable only because we apprehend a malleable future" (335). But just as prominent is the idea that hope ties the future to the present. Hage (2003) quotes Erich Fromm on hope as a "vision of the present in a state of pregnancy" (10), and Steinbock (2007) asserts that the experience of hope is not only "directed toward the future" but is also actively engaged with the present, interested in "a possible transformation of the current situation" (285). Hage's framework of hope captures this temporal dimension well. He sees hope as an affect, as an enduring state of being where one holds the capacity to confront uncertainties, experiences a sense of agency and mastery over life, and has life pursuits and a belief in the future (25).

While hope is often defined as temporally enduring or sustainable, it is also understood as simultaneously fragile (Anderson and Fenton 2008). Steinbock (2007) argues that hope is really only hope because it is sustained in the face of contingency, over against that which threatens the possible. It is in fact this mix of longevity and fragility, argues Hage, that makes the affect of hope so compatible with capitalism. Identifying societies as mechanisms to distribute the experience of hope, Hage (2003) asserts that much of the "success" of capital accumulation has been due to the state's active role in distributing hope differentially, depending on the material and symbolic conditions in a society. The state socially distributes hope in part through the mechanism of national citizenship and belonging, but also through the "ability to maintain an experience of the possibility of upward social mobility" (13). In this way, hope underwrites political and economic aims, promising a dignified and meaningful life vis-à-vis the contingencies of the market.

A number of critics argue that these contingencies grow under neo-liberal capitalism to the detriment of the survival, let alone the even distribution, of "hope for life."[5] Indeed, the increasingly uneven and uncertain distribution of hope is Hage's entrée to a critique of neo-liberal capitalist relations. In *Against Paranoid Nationalism* (2003), Hage analyzes this unevenness as a complex of affect (resentment, guilt, envy, etc.) that becomes established in a nation in the formation of identities and across ethnic, social, and class lines. His aim is to explore what it means to belong to a community (i.e., nation) and what it is like to feel at home for migrants and "natives," and to offer a framework for identifying tensions (i.e., contingencies) around inclusion and exclusion. Hage posits that with neo-liberal capitalism, or what he calls "transcendental capitalism," sustained social (national) identification and secure, protected economic conditions are shattered for more and more people. These growing contingencies turn hope on its head. Hope is still generated by governing institutions, but it is traded on a contradictory and transparently shaky promise of economic abundance for all, and in the increasingly narrow terms of better jobs, more consumer power, and thus better lifestyles. Browne (2005) dubs this a fragile and illusory hope because the actual delivery of abundance (the fulfillment of hope) is indefinitely postponed. Hage (2003), following Bourdieu, emphasizes neo-liberalism's waning commitment to any kind of equitable distribution of hope, found most brutally in the dispossession of symbolic capital (16–18).[6]

Fort McMurray seems an extreme or perhaps exceptional example of Hage's conceptualization of the neo-liberal dissemination of hope. On the one hand, the numbers (at least until the fall 2008 economic "slowdown" during which we first drafted this chapter)[7] painted Fort McMurray as a relatively hopeful place to fulfill the promises of the market: it boasted an annual economic growth rate of 8.5 percent and the lowest unemployment in the country. For the time being, its contingencies appeared minimized, its opportunities to individuals widely accessible. On the other hand, oil (and especially unconventional oil) is a limited resource and a volatile commodity, subject to impermanence and uncertainty for people who hope to gain from working in its orbit; these are contingencies that certainly have been felt in Alberta, especially as the government has decreasingly committed to mitigating their effects (Harrison 2005; Macnab, Daniels, and Laxer 1999).

The rich and highly contingent "hopefulness" attached to Fort McMurray challenges us to adjust and extend Hage's theory of hope. Our research findings especially nudge us not only to consider how hope (as a temporally contingent affect) is unevenly distributed within Fort McMurray, but also to consider Fort McMurray as a node within the uneven distribution of hope (as a spatially contingent affect), nationally as well as transnationally. In other words, Fort McMurray stands in relation to other places—those many places to and from which financial resources and mobile workers flow. The work of Doreen Massey (1994, 2002) emphasizes two important and interrelated facets of these relations. First, a place, a locality, gains its particularity from the specific interactions and articulations of "social relations, social processes, experiences, and understandings" that come together in the varying and co-present identities of individuals, "but where a large portion of those relations ... are constructed on a far larger scale than what we happen to define for that moment as the place itself" (1994, 66).[8] These insights give us the theoretical tools to see Fort McMurray as a place that is articulated by a particular kind of political economy, a specific "instance" of neo-liberal capitalist relations, and especially one with a high labour mobility focused on one resource. But second, and following from this first point, people have vastly different kinds of relationships to even one geographically defined place, depending on their social relations to each other. This then means that Fort McMurray is not one but many places, possessing multiple and contested identities (i.e., multiple layers) formed through conflict, social negotiation, and difference among differently situated social actors.

Massey offers us ways to build on Hage via a spatial analysis that places hope without fixing place. That is, her understanding helps us see Fort McMurray as a node of neo-liberal capitalist relations (and more specifically of a globalized oil economy), but at the same time, as composed of multiple places. Massey brings our attention to the importance and relevance of studying the particular social relations of co-presence in a place like Fort McMurray, because it is here that spatially dispersed social action is filtered and informed. Massey is thus a pivotal addition to our exploration of the distribution of hope in Fort McMurray, not only because Hage's analysis is pitched fairly exclusively at the level of the nation, but also because this national space is taken for granted as the backdrop for his analysis of the social distribution of hope. Where Hage theorizes belonging and unbelonging as at least in part a matter of social and political attachment to place, Massey has insisted that such a perspective too readily fixes place. She points instead to how the great variation in people's sense of place might equally be a source of conflict or richness (1994, 6).

Adjusting our spatial view affects how we understand the varying kinds and qualities of hope distributed across the spectrum of people in Fort McMurray. First, we must see the temporalities of this place differently. As Anderson and Fenton (2008) put it,

> Hope unsettles the spacing of the present. The topos of the "not-yet" is not only a question of the temporal extension of the present into the future. It also involves thinking of space as animated by (im)possibilities, potentialities and virtualities—some of which we find in the past life of spaces, some of which can be predicted to occur in the future, and some of which are impossibilities "to come." (78–79)

But second, and even more importantly for our purposes here, hope itself can no longer be mostly a matter of temporal relations. When we add to the "not yet" of hope its "not here," the pregnancy and contingency of hope are not just about multiple temporalities, but also about multiple places in relation to each other, within the life of any one individual, or within any particular social relation; hope is stretched out spatially.[9] Hope is constituted by and through those spatialized social relations of co-presence.[10] How and where people see and experience hope thus maps the social relations of co-presence. Taken together, Hage and Massey form a conceptual legend for our reading of the visual and verbal maps produced by research participants in Fort McMurray.

Mapping the Distribution of Hope

Our social mapping of the spatial distribution of hope began with an analysis of people's "local consciousness" (Massey 1994) of Fort McMurray. In our study, this was based on a combination of narrative texts (interview transcripts) and visual images (the sketch maps we asked people to draw of "your Fort McMurray" using pens of several colours and one or two pieces of 11" × 17" paper). The maps were solicited in the latter part of in-depth interviews that asked participants about their history with Fort McMurray, experiences with everyday life and community, perspectives on the oil industry, and thoughts about the future.[11] This combination of visual and verbal social mapping was crucial to our theorizing of hope (even though we did not often ask about hope directly), since superimposing each pairing of map + interview one onto the other created a polyphony of stories about place and identity—the "co-presence" of which Massey writes. Drawing on the methodological strategies of Ommen and Painter (2005), we started with some simple quantitative analyses of what elements appeared on the maps, how often, and with what kind of detail or emphasis.[12] The patterns that emerged were surprisingly helpful as a starting place for roughly organizing the maps, and more importantly, asking qualitative questions about the spatialized distribution of hope that could further be applied to the interview transcripts.

Our initial crude division of the maps echoed a division in Fort McMurray that came up time and again during the research project between long-time residents and the so-called shadow population of mobile workers. Florence, a long-time resident and instructor at the local college, summed it up: "I think you have two factions of people here. I think you have the long-term people like myself, who tend to see the city with rose-coloured glasses…. Then you see the workers, like the people here not necessarily for the long term." But then when we literally laid out the maps along a spectrum from long-term to short-term residents and began to study their features alongside the interview narratives, we found that this temporal variation in people's relationship to place was complicated by their work and socioeconomic status, which in turn was implicated with family and home, as well as race and citizenship. And so we deal here with three rather than two social groupings; these richly but only partially reflect the population in Fort McMurray, and serve as a starting place for exploring the spatial distribution of hope.

We begin by considering the written and visual narratives of professional-class long-time residents, whose hope we find to be embedded—in other words, it is hope for this place called Fort McMurray. Their hopes entail middle-class nostalgia for stable place-based identity in a fast-changing, compressed global economy; the fragility of their hopes suggests a foreclosure on the possibility of place-based hope (especially in a town so dependent on a single globalized resource). We then move to the shadow population of oil industry workers whose hope is beyond this place, attached to other locales, and yet contingent on their ability to make money while here. This spatial disconnect between places of viable work and locations of social hope might be interpreted as a form of fragility or deferral, but we want to also consider the "not here" of hope as potentially transformative. And finally, a third group of people provides an important conceptual wedge, in that they are neither tied to place nor seemingly stuck between places. These are the short-term industry professionals, whose hope seems to travel with them; they selectively put down roots to make the most of their time in Fort McMurray while imagining their next (cosmopolitan) move.

Across all three groups, themes of home, family, and material well-being play into the constitution of hope, and hope is contingent in complicated ways on the viability of the oil industry. However, our analysis of individuals' relationships to the place Fort McMurray reveals that the contradictions and possibilities of hope are unevenly distributed. In this way, we cannot think of the three groups as discrete but as together constituting "social relations of co-presence." In the sections that follow, we consider each group in turn, providing illustrations from a few representative people from each grouping.

The Stalwart of the Community: The Long-Timers

By no design of our own, the first responders to our research posters and fly-ers and Internet postings had a certain profile: long-time residents of fifteen years or more, more often than not white women, usually working in professional capacities (this group included oil company administrators, teachers, city employees, and business people), and "community involved."[13] It became clear that no matter what people's work relationship to the oil industry, there was a complex symbiosis between the health and image of the industry and that of the town; many expressed a desire to counter the negative media depictions of Fort McMurray. Within this context, it was hope for Fort McMurray as their home and community that characterized their narratives. The problem for this place-embedded hope was when and how Fort McMurray would "settle into itself" (once again), overcoming the contingencies wedged between the sped-up, hyper-mobile, infrastructure-poor present and an imagined calmer, grown-up city of the future. (See Figure 12.1 for a sample long-timer map.)

Compared to the full spectrum of fifty maps, those drawn by the twenty long-timers were replete with place-oriented details of the physical landscape, the built environment, and social connections and activities. Inscribed on these details of place were nostalgia about the past, a desire to defend the

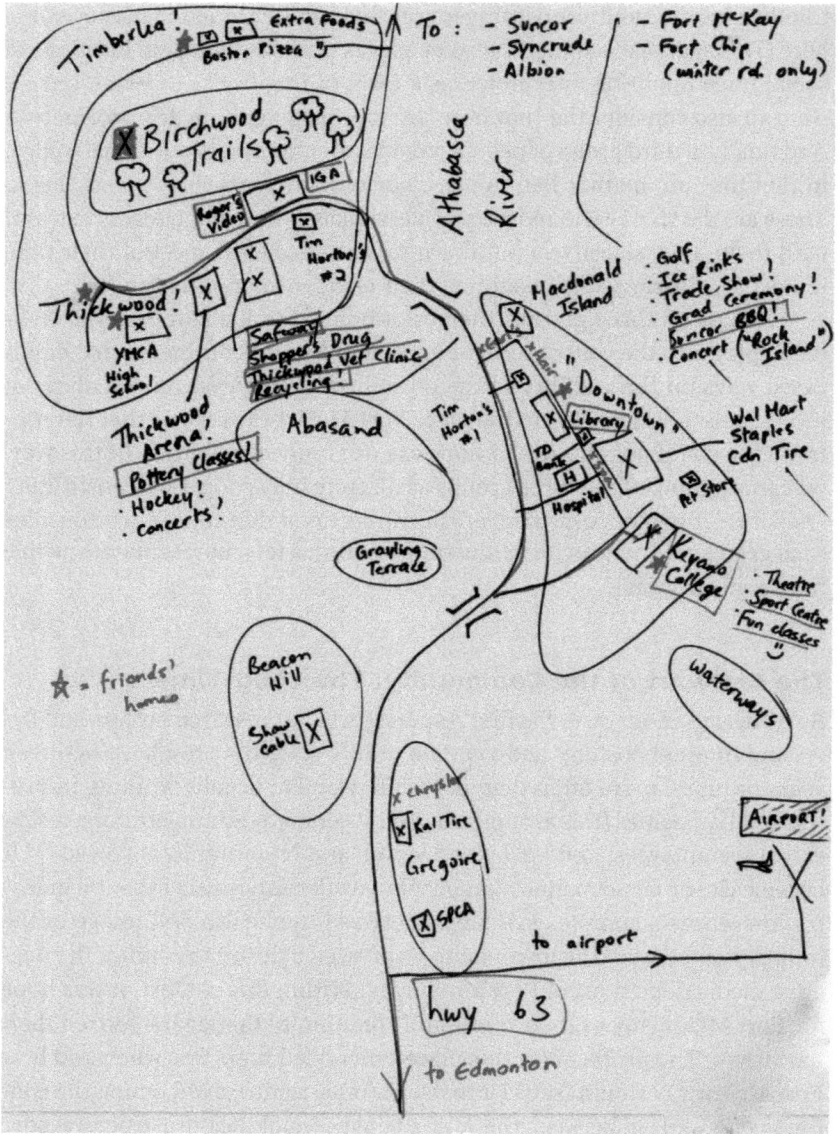

Figure 12.1 A long-timer's map

community of the present, and concern about what the current upheaval would mean for the future of the community. Unlike other respondents, long-timers wove historical narratives into their maps (the Abasand neighbourhood as older and built during the first boom, or what used to be where Walmart is now), including signs of the current growth (the twinning of the highway, or new housing developments appearing where there used to be forest) and reminders of the town's roots in oil (the Oil Sands Discovery Centre, or the ruins on the riverbank of one of the original mining sites). Many also bound themselves to place through the enduring family-like friendships they had made over the years. Others referred to a time when they didn't lock their doors, or when it took two hours to go to the grocery store because you kept running into people you knew—not because the lines were so long, as was now the case.

This nostalgia for the past fed a continuing sense of community-in-place: long-timers eagerly mapped recreation and entertainment spots, from volunteer activities to bingo and sports and church. Against the tides of change, these places and signs of community found endurance in a white, middle-class vision of access to nature, suburban living, family, and home ownership. The wooded trails around the suburbs most often appeared as a sign of "the good life," a place to go for walks, or for your children to play. This family-oriented suburban living was epitomized by Thickwood and Timberlea, newer subdivisions that, as Hilary put it, were becoming their own amenity-complete areas—it was getting to where "you didn't have to leave." Hilary noted that of all the mining towns where she and her husband could bring their skills, they had chosen this one because it had the best amenities for their children. This was a two-way street: it turned out that children's activities and family events had often helped to pave the way for many long-timers' own social networks and community involvement.

Nonetheless, long-timers felt their "family community" threatened by the exigencies of the recent boom—with uncertain implications for their hope in and for this place. The trails that Lynn lovingly drew on her map were made increasingly unsafe, she thought, by the single men living three or four at a time in the basement suites of her Thickwood neighbours' homes. The ethnic and racial diversity of schools and workplaces might be creating too many tensions. And for Brian, the increased cost of living and stretched public budget threatened the hockey facilities he had worked into his map. For some, downtown was a "no-go" zone of single men and drugs and bars that epitomized these problems. Indeed, the brunt of the blame for the current fragility of long-timers' place-based hope was reserved for the thousands of short-term and "fly in, fly out" (and mostly male) workers who called somewhere else home (a home where they paid taxes). These people are "just working here and have no investment," said Sharon.

The solution long-timers proposed was a reinforcement of hope in and for place. They wanted the mobile workers to settle down and give back to the community in the form of taxes and time. This solution married productive, reproductive, and consumptive lives—work, family, and home ownership—to each other and, most importantly, to place. Brian tied this to nostalgia for the first boom, when, sure, people came for the big dollar, but they often came with their families and made the transition "from boomtown to hometown." But there were contingencies on this solution that long-timers grudgingly knew were written into the uneven distribution of hope across the very spaces they mapped. These included the extremely high cost of living, and the inability of the physical and social infrastructure to keep apace with the growth of the oil industry and thus the town. In other words, mobile workers turned out to be not so much a cause as a symptom, a facet, of the strong "winds of change" brought by the oil economy. For this reason, admitted Sharon, she thought people outside of Fort McMurray should know "that the streets aren't paved with gold here, in that's it's not just a piece of cake to live here." These co-existing but contradictory messages—"just call this place home!" and "it's difficult to call this place home anymore" —speak to the uncertainty, or impossibility, of the kind of place-based hope espoused by the long-time, community-minded middle class. Such hope is amenable neither to adapting to change-in-place nor to being transferred elsewhere.

The Flexibilized Labourers: Oil Industry Workers

Long-time professionals' hopes for place sit in tension with the spatial and temporal metrics of the Athabasca oil sands in the early part of the twenty-first century. As existing projects expand and dozens of new ones are started, tens of thousands of skilled and unskilled labourers are needed to construct the roads, build the processing plants and pipelines, transport people and goods, and staff the work camps. These are the people we include in the category of "industry workers."[14] We interviewed thirteen such people, most of whom were males with some kind of trade certification working shifts and living in work camps or sharing rented apartments. While most were white and Canadian-born, two were Aboriginal, and three had come to Canada as refugees from Africa. (See Figure 12.2 for a sample industry worker map.)

Industry workers' maps and narratives often suggested a suspension of time and place. One respondent said that when he is in Fort McMurray

Figure 12.2 An industry worker's map

(living in camp), "time does not move," while another said he and his partner were just "biding our time here." Similarly, their sketch maps were
either quite abstract or quite minimal in their depictions, with few of the
conventional signs of place-based identity: only one of the thirteen maps
included any trees or rivers, recreational spots were rarely depicted, none
included schools or churches, and details of neighbourhoods were almost
absent. For some, the actual town did not make the map at all or made it
there in negative terms (Mark labelled it a "shit hole" and Ben as "not fun").
Gadeshi at first stared at the blank sheet of paper we gave him, declaring,
"I don't have a life here, how could I draw it?" The oil sands were often
depicted in very generalized pictures and words, and often connected with
pollution and/or cash.

As much as long-timers laboured to demonstrate and uphold their
vested hope in place, industrial workers' detached and negative depictions
of Fort McMurray seemed intent on the opposite: their hopes were quite
spatially dispersed from Fort McMurray, tied to other people and places—
places like Edmonton, Toronto, Nova Scotia, India, Somalia. Fort McMurray figured into the hopes of the industry workers predominantly as a place
to make some money. In fact, half of their sketch maps made reference to
money, signalling that the whole point of being here was to leave with cash
in your pockets to fulfill hopes and plans elsewhere. Ben, who had been a

"mobile worker" for fifteen years, put a check mark next to "work" and "money" on his map, and added, "I am yet to leave.... When you leave you have a good life, it is all about the quality of life. This is what you have worked towards. You don't want to live here for the rest of your life." Lucas, who was making over a hundred grand a year as a heavy hauler truck driver, created a balloon called "make money" on his map with the attached wish list: buy house, [open a] night club, see stuff, travel. This is not to suggest that these spatially dispersed hopes were always temporally deferred. Some participants were regularly sending money to their far-away families, and one was even using the money he made in the oil sands (from the "capitalists taking our stuff," as he wrote on his map) to support a broad activist network.

This particular trans-local construction of hope both demeaned the quality of life in Fort McMurray (seen as variously chaotic, dirty, unsophisticated, or conservative) and imagined fulfillment in other (sometimes nonspecific) places and times. In between were stopgap practices that helped to tide people over: most of the workers' maps included escape hatches to places that temporarily mitigated the stark reality of spatially deferred hope. Some of these escape routes led away from Fort McMurray. Mark went regularly to Edmonton on his days off to spend time with activist friends; next to "E-town" he wrote "this place keeps you sane." Ben said that he and his partner got away on vacation when they could to "get out of this mindset ... go and get your sanity back." Other sanity-keeping places were isolated local spots attached more to the individual than to the rest of Fort McMurray. Lucas labelled the SPCA where he had done some volunteering "my Zen." And Gadeshi's limited places of escape were attempts to survive mentally and financially: the Tim Hortons where he would meet up with other East African drivers during their off hours, and the YMCA Immigrant Settlement Services office where he regularly sought help to find a job that would pay enough to allow his family to move from Toronto.

Hope is kept alive, Hage (2003) tells us, through the "experience of the possibility of upward social mobility" (13), the promise of living a dignified and meaningful life. For many of the labourers we encountered, this promise depended on transforming the opportunities of "Fort McMoney" into hopes for other places and (often) other times, which in turn was contingent on getting a good-paying job in the first place, then saving the money needed in a fathomable amount of time (especially given the high cost of housing for individuals not receiving a living-out allowance from their employer). Ben had not yet checked "leave" off his list of plans for Fort McMurray because he didn't think he had enough money yet. Lucas admitted that he wasn't very good at saving his money, which caused him to worry he would be "trapped" or "end up like them," as he wrote on his map. As part of the now regularized global phenomenon of "flexibilized" labour, industry workers had to be concerned with the economic contingencies that might affect their window of opportunity in Fort McMurray. Orienting ourselves to their spatial relations helps us to see that they hoped for more meaningful lives for themselves and in some cases, their families. These hoped-for lives just weren't associated with the place where money could be made. Fort McMurray went from "a place to find work!" to "just a place to work."

The Flexible Cosmopolitans:[15] Short-Term Oil Industry Professionals

We have seen that for both the long-timers and industry workers with whom we spoke, hopes were usually deferred into an uncertain future, suspended either until Fort McMurray settled down or they could leave. By contrast, short-term professionals (people who had been working in the oil sands for several years or less and did not intend to stay past four or five years) seemed to carry with them many of the tools for fulfilling their hopes; their symbolic, human, and social capital provided opportunities for them to actively engage their hopes in a number of places. Fort McMurray was an especially good place to temporarily cultivate hope, depending in part on family and work situations. More than half of the ten participants in this category had families with young children, although two of them were regularly making trips to Calgary or Edmonton, where their families resided. All but one had some kind of professional degree (engineering or business related), and while most were relatively early in their careers, half were immigrants to Canada with oil industry experience in other countries. (See Figure 12.3 for a sample cosmopolitan map.)

The cosmopolitans' sketch maps were an intriguing hybrid of the long-timers' and the industrial workers'. They tended to be more abstract and less detailed than those of the long-timers, but included more place details than the industrial workers' maps. When these details did appear, they were often individualized, such as the location of their own child's dance class or a gym where the participant worked out occasionally. If neighbourhoods appeared, their character was often defined by one particular spot within them of direct significance, such as a colleague's home, a badminton club, the downtown office of their company, or the participant's own house. But like the industrial workers, they also often included arrows leading out of Fort McMurray

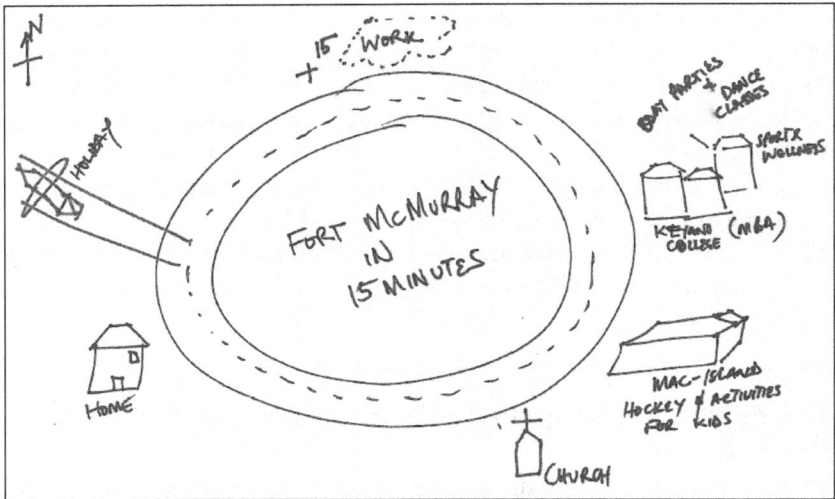

Figure 12.3 A cosmopolitan's map

with words like "go home" or "holiday." Facets of the natural landscape were scarce, and the oil sands usually appeared in fairly general terms.

The mapped spaces of the cosmopolitans' lives gave identity not so much to Fort McMurray as to themselves.[16] Many of the roots they had selectively put down in Fort McMurray were offshoots of their portfolios of degrees, networking skills, globalized identities, and personal values. Fort McMurray seemed to offer enough of the right things right now for creating a life. These included classed expressions of personal fulfillment: wine events, gym memberships, dinners out, and learning to play a musical instrument one had always wanted to learn. Even their complaints about Fort McMurray's lamentable shopping or "frontier" way of doing business were often narrated as limiting the exercise of their personal and professional identities. What they sought was fertile ground to enhance their skills and reproduce their quality of life—what Bourdieu (1994) has called the potential to "accumulate being." Their hope was to do just that while they were in Fort McMurray, even as they imagined where they might go next and do the same. Efosa, for example, saw time in Fort McMurray as a way for him and his wife, Charlotte, to advance their career options. Efosa, Charlotte, and Pete, all immigrants, noted that because of a tight labour market, the oil sands industry was one of the most likely spots in which to gain the "Canadian experience" needed to open up their professional choices in other places in Canada. In other words, it could make them more flexible cosmopolitans.

This "transferable" hope (which of course came with some limits) was underwritten by the consistent feeling that one could go elsewhere, either permanently or temporarily. Like the industrial workers, some of the short-term professionals built holidays into their maps; these escapes to relatively exclusive destinations in the Rockies or to international locales were narrated not only as a way to endure Fort McMurray, but also as an expected part of a cosmopolitan life. The bigger point for many of the respondents was that they could potentially exercise their self-fulfillment in any number of cities or countries. Charlotte and Efosa were considering Australia for their next career move.

This ongoing ability to "experience the possibility of upward social mobility," to make one's self at home where you are, is enhanced by family. We were struck by the dominance of participants' homes/houses on their sketch maps, but also by how often their social connections in Fort McMurray were catalyzed by their children and families, which in and of themselves constitute a kind of cultural or symbolic capital. Pete's narrative is perhaps an exception that proves the rule: an immigrant from Korea, he had a wife and daughter 700 kilometres away in Calgary. On his map he drew a dotted line leading from his house in Fort McMurray (labelled "boring time") to Calgary (marked "call → caring"), representing the spatially dispersed hopes of his personal life. What Pete and other participants with families shared, however, was an expressed interest in providing experiences for their children to "accumulate being," including going to university, or growing up in multicultural environments. Cosmopolitans' narratives of family were linked to home ownership, but unlike the long-timers this was not perceived as a long-term investment in the place. Rather, the suburbs of Fort McMurray were a good place to capitalize both symbolically and materially on investments in a fairly short period of time.

So for short-term industry professionals, skills and identities and even "home" could be re-placed; in this way they were somewhat buffered from the neo-liberal state's withdrawal from ensuring an equitable distribution of hope, and they could in fact self-actualize because of flexibilized accumulation. When Hage (2003) tells us, "capitalism goes transcendental, so to speak. It simply hovers over the Earth looking for a suitable place to land and invest" (19), it is the cosmopolitans who best match the spatial distribution of hope this implies.

Concluding Remarks

For all the people in Fort McMurray, hope is contingent to some degree on the market. This in itself, as Hage has argued, is a sign of the times. But the market also appears in a particular way in this locality, that is to say, in a natural resource economy characterized by the demand for a large mobile workforce, the high cost of housing, a history of close company–town relations, frontier "family values," and, of course, the unpredictable price of a barrel of oil. The particularities of the Fort McMurray context are manifested in multiple forms of people–people and people–place relations—in the different positioning of workers within the political economy of one industry (e.g., professionals and labour)—and this is reflected in the uneven distribution of hope.

Hope is placed in a variety of ways. In Fort McMurray, family is a catalyst for the long-term and short-term professionals to attach to place, although for long-timers, family is further constructed as the key to settling and making it "home." For those who had families elsewhere, especially industry workers but also some of the cosmopolitans, their kin networks were often fundamental to the spatial dispersion of their hopes.

But perhaps most intriguing is how hope was wedged between place and mobility: the ability to experience the possibility of a meaningful life, and to actively engage with hope in the present, lay at the juncture of this place (which was different things to different people), and the un/desirability or im/possibility of being in, or going to, other places. Hage (2003) asserts that the enemy of societal hope is "a sense of entrapment, of having nowhere to go" (20). While he does not necessarily mean this literally, our spatial analysis suggests how hope might be contingent on real or imagined, short-term or long-term forms of staying or going. In other words, our participants' social maps suggest a spatialized dialectic of hope and entrapment.

Long-time residents did not necessarily want to leave, but Fort McMurray was changing before their eyes in ways that squeezed their place-embedded hopes.[17] Ironically, the oil industry both sustained and threatened their hopes for this place, revealing a spatialized form of the emaciation of hope. It would seem that flexible accumulation is only partially compatible with attachment to place, which in turn creates a squeeze on the possibility of nurturing place-embedded hopes.

Industrial workers in many cases wanted to leave this place, but could or would not do so until they had made enough money to fulfill hopes elsewhere. On the flip side, a few were interested in settling with their families but found the cost and pace prohibitive. Their hope was stuck between here and elsewhere, immobilized in part by their dependence on the flexibilized labour requirements of this booming resource economy, and at the same time deferred to other places (and usually times). But individual circumstances can also trick the spatial and temporal confines of hope: for a couple of these workers, coming to Fort McMurray had enabled an active engagement with hope. One such example was a sixty-year-old woman who told us that coming to live in a work camp and drive a bus for an oil company (the centrepiece of her map was a bus with a white horse on top) had freed her from a life of family obligations at home in eastern Canada.

But this kind of flexible spatialized hope applies most readily to the cosmopolitans, who while certainly not free to go wherever they wanted when they wanted, carried with them multiple forms of capital that allowed them to actively engage with their hope in any number of places—to be less "stuck" than the other two groups of people between this (changing) place and the uncertainties of moving elsewhere. Perhaps most telling is the difference between the "escape hatches" they and the industry workers built into their maps. While almost purely sanity-keeping mechanisms for the latter, these exit strategies were also meaningful enactments of hope (and of self) for the former. If hope is unevenly distributed and increasingly scarce under "transcendental capitalism," as Hage (2003) has argued, then the "cosmopolitans" seem best situated to actively engage in it, to connect the dots between present and future, and to experience the possibility of its fulfillment.

By approaching Fort McMurray as multiple places—as many things to different people—and also as a node of spatially diffuse capitalist relations (following Massey's conceptualization), we can see how hope, which is usually conceived of temporally, is spatially distributed. This distribution of hope maps the uneven social relations of co-presence as a matter of class and family and temporality, as we have seen, but also, as we have only been able to touch on, gender and race and citizenship. But then most importantly, hope itself becomes a matter of place, a spatialized affect.

Notes

1   Fort McMurray is formally part of a larger municipality, the Regional Municipality of Wood Buffalo. The RMWB covers some 68,000 square kilometres of the northeast corner of Alberta, with a population of 90,000, making Fort McMurray its largest (and only) centre, along with a number of much smaller rural and historically Aboriginal communities; the RMWB area also encompasses almost all of the Athabasca oil sands. So just as "Fort McMurray" often stands in for industry, in popular discourse it stands in politically for the whole of the RMWB.

2   After her visit to the oil sands in fall 2008, Council of Canadians chair Maude Barlow famously compared the look and feel of its environmental impact to the wasted landscape of Mordor in *The Lord of the Rings*.

3   The literature on resource communities, mining towns, and ghost towns is abundant (for a review, see Gill 1990 and Robertson 2006), and Fort McMurray can indeed be considered a mining town. However, what makes Fort McMurray an interesting case is the scale and extent of the operation. It is a bigger and seemingly longer-lasting version of "the mining town," and this makes the fragility of neo-liberal capitalism all the more apparent, as Young and Matthews (2008) argue.

4   This can be understood as a feature of contemporary global capitalism. Paulsen (2004) writes, "In an era of increasingly mobile capital, places vie to distinguish themselves from one another so as to attract positive attention from investors [and] what it takes to attract attention from preferred investors is shifting from generic qualities of any place to the more specific characteristics of a unique place" (246–47).

5   Hage (2003) points to Nietzsche's differentiation between "hope for life" and "hope against life," the latter type breeding passivity rather than engagement.

6   In a related cynicism toward the ideological power of hope, Sparke (2007) analyzes a discursive "double movement" in the neo-liberal capitalist (U.S.) state's promotion of the war on terrorism: generating fears of geopolitical instability while at the same time distributing hope in geo-economic liberalization as the answer to that instability. Alberta oil is in fact regularly pitched to investors as stable (located in a peaceful, democratic, rationally regulated economy) relative to many other petroleum deposits.

7   As we wrote this, the economic crisis that began in fall 2008 (including surprisingly low oil prices) generated stories warning of a dangerous curtailing of new oil sands projects, but also stories marvelling at the relative economic health of the industry. By March 2009 this optimism had dimmed in the face of what were reported to be 20,000 layoffs and the cancelling of many planned projects.

8   This relational aspect of place has also been under the radar of theorists with different understanding/conceptualizations of place than ours. Hui in this volume discusses Hetherington's conceptualization of place as a relational process between identities and materialities.

9   Perhaps, then, Nietzsche's "hope against life" might also be considered as a "hope against here," where withdrawal from active engagement is in fact animated by and in other places.

10 These social relations are stretched out over space. Spatial social relations, according to Massey, involve not only class relations, but also gender and other forms of exclusion/inclusion (such as race). In *Space, Place and Gender*, Massey sums up the overall aim of the book as "to formulate concepts of space and place in terms of social relations. Throughout, there is an assumption that one aspect of those [spatial social] relations which is likely to be important is that of class" (1994, 2), but then she adds other aspects to it, by asserting that class itself "is insufficient. Among the many other things that clearly influence that experience, there are, for instance, 'race' and gender" (147). It is also worth nothing here that she and Hage share this rich and complex understanding of social inclusion and exclusion, in terms of what Massey would call the power geometry of social differentiation (149).

11 Interviews ranged from one to three hours, and were conducted over an eighteen-month period, during four separate field trips to Fort McMurray.

12 Ommen and Painter (2005) conducted a discourse analysis of students' sketch maps of a South African city, treating drawers as "embedded agents who, through their sketches, reveal the ideological tensions of their specific geographic, historical and socio-economic position" (508). The contingencies on what ends up included, excluded, emphasized, delimited, etc., on paper say something about "the world of the drawer, its values, issues, ideologies, and current state," and also about "a particular place within a particular period" (508) (and we would add, within a particular global configuration, in relation to other places). Similar techniques are used in cognitive mapping; see Huynh et al. (2008) and Kitchin (1994, 1).

13 The gendered and racialized aspects of these participants' narratives deserve a full treatment, but there is not space in this essay to give them justice. A post-colonial reading of Aboriginal "long-timers" is also in order, but again, we must regrettably save this for future work.

14 There are also hundreds of mobile workers in the retail and service industry in Fort McMurray, but for this chapter we have focused on those working in the oil industry, directly or by contract.

15 The historical generation of the term *cosmopolitanism* (and *cosmopolitans*) is diverse. The majority of the debates around cosmopolitanism revolve around four different discourses: national/anti-national, a form of citizenship, a form of consumption, and a form of subjectivity (Binnie and Skeggs 2006, 222). We are interested in the last two discourses, and this forms our basis for conceptualizing the interviews that constitute the third group as cosmopolitans. Here, cosmopolitans are seen as elite professionals in high-status occupations, members of what Leslie Sklair (2001) calls the transnational capitalist class. In a way, the cosmopolitans are a conceptual mix of embodied cultural dispositions (Bourdieu 1984) and the privileged, empowered subjectivity of the power geometry of space-time compression (Massey 1994).

16 Thielbar (2005) has asserted that cosmopolitans are attached to a larger social world, and their attachment to a particular locality, although not necessarily tangential, is different from that of people who have more "placed" existence (243–54).

17 We must note that in some cases their identities no longer matched the place in another way: they were considering leaving because their children were grown and gone.

References

Anderson, B., and J. Fenton. 2008. Editorial introduction. Spaces of hope. *Space and Culture* 11 (2): 76–80.

Binnie, J., and B. Skeggs. 2006. Cosmopolitan knowledge and the production and consumption of sexualised space: Manchester's Gay Village. In *Cosmopolitan urbanism*, ed. J. Binnie, J. Holloway, S. Millington, and C. Young, 220–45. New York: Routledge.

Bourdieu, P. 1984. *Distinction: A social critique of the judgement of taste.* London: Routledge.

————. 1994. *Practical reason: On the theory of action.* Stanford, CA: Stanford University Press.

Browne, C. 2005. Hope, critique, and utopia. *Critical Horizons* 6: 63–86.

Flaherty, M. O. 1983. The sociology of hope. *Contemporary Sociology* 12 (3): 334–35.

Gill, A. 1990. Women in isolated resource towns—an examination of gender differences in cognitive structures. *Geoforum* 21 (3): 347–58.

Hage, G. 2003. *Against paranoid nationalism: Searching for hope in a shrinking society.* Annandale: Pluto Press.

Harrison, T. 2005. Introduction. In *The return of the Trojan horse: Alberta and the new world (dis)order*, ed. T. Harrion, 1–22. Montreal: Black Rose Books.

Huynh, N. T., B. Hall, S. Doherty, and W. W. Smith. 2008. Interpreting urban space through cognitive map sketching and sequence analysis. *The Canadian Geographer* 2 (2): 222–40.

Kitchin, R. M. 1994. Cognitive maps: What are they and why study them? *Journal of Environmental Psychology* 14: 1–19.

Macnab, B., J. Daniels, and G. Laxer. 1999. *Giving away the Alberta Advantage: Are Albertans receiving maximum revenue from their oil and gas?* Edmonton: Parkland Institute.

Massey, D. 1994. *Space, place, and gender.* Minneapolis: University of Minnesota Press.

————. 2002. Don't let's counterpose place and space. *Development* 45 (1): 24–25.

Ommen, C. v O., and D. Painter. 2005. Mapping East London: Sketching identity through place. *South African Journal of Psychology* 35 (3): 505–31.

Paulsen, K. E. 2004. Making character concrete: Empirical strategies for studying place distinction. *City & Community* 3 (3): 243–62.

Robertson, D. 2006. *Hard as rock itself: Place and identity in the American mining town.* Boulder: University of Colorado.

Sklair, L. 2001. *The transnational capitalist class.* Oxford: Blackwell.

Sparke, M. 2007. Geopolitical fear, geoeconomic hope and the responsibilities of geography. *Annals of the Association of American Geographers* 97 (2): 338–49.

Steinbock, A. J. 2007. The phenomenology of despair. *International Journal of Philosophical Studies* 15 (3): 435–51.

Thielbar, G. 2005. Localism-cosmopolitanism: Prolegomenon to a theory of social participation. *Sociological Quarterly* 11 (2): 243–54.

Young, N., and R. Matthews. 2008. Resource economies and neoliberal experimentation: The reform of industry and community in rural British Columbia. *Area* 39 (2): 176–85.

Spectacular Enclosures of Hope
Artificial Islands in the Gulf and the Present

MARK S. JACKSON
VERONICA DELLA DORA

There are no more unknown islands.
Saramago (1999, 11–12)

Timeless in appeal. A destination that captures the imagination and doesn't let go. Like nothing else. Found nowhere else. The World. Epic.[1]

Introduction

In José Saramago's allegorical short story "The Tale of the Unknown Island" (1999), the unnamed protagonist of the fable demands of his king a boat. Once royally gifted, the man proposes to set sail on a voyage of discovery in search of "the unknown island." The king, on hearing the request and proposition, scoffs, "There are no more unknown islands ... only the known islands are on maps ... what is this unknown island you go in search of?" The man replies that if he knew that, then the island wouldn't be unknown now, would it? Irritated at the man's insolence, but curious as to his conviction, the king presses further: how do you know there is an unknown island? "Simply because," comes the reply, "there can't possibly not be an unknown island" (11–12).

Saramago's play on the logical possibility of unknowns reveals itself, within his simple and beguiling tale, as a disarmingly clever meditation on desire and hope. The story is written both as an allegorical lament and as a poetic corrective to a bureaucratic, modern world convinced of its known, and thus enclosed, horizons. Dreams and love, reminds Saramago, are the means to redress our present, bereft as it is of imagination, optimism, and openness to the transformative possibilities of the unknown. Saramago uses the archetype of the island as an iconic metonym to summon forth deeply embedded, age-old cultural longings for exploration, imagination, and self-discovery. In his hands, the figure of the island, and its promise, exposes a culture defeated by its own circumscription.

Their physical boundaries clearly demarcated, islands, by definition, delimit the ostensibly known. At the same time, however, the *imaginative* geographies of islands remain fraught with paradox. Seemingly recognizable boundaries beckon both as harbingers of safety and as omens of insularity. Islands at once configure, through their iconicity, ancient narratives of desire and fear, hope and desolation, nostalgia and the unknown. As such, they continue to be both objects of quixotic fascination and loci of determinate action. In the island stories that enervate largely Western cultural narratives, more often than not the fascination for islands lies in their active capacity to represent control and ownership. But, at the same time, they also signify the beyond to, and escape from, the present's all-too-encompassing turmoil. So, despite the fact that modernity celebrates its progressive rendering of the world in numerous and manifest ways—including the detailed mapping of all islands and, thus, possible knowable spaces—the prospect of there *not* being an unknown island remains deeply disturbing for a geographical and sociological ethos steeped in presumptions of progress and expansion.

It is as though the icon of the island acts as both driver to and supplementary excess of the modern ethos of discovery, mapping, and control. Hence, for Saramago's king and would-be sailor, wary skepticism and yearning for the unknown in the context of a world confident in its geographical omniscience play against each other in an allegory on the perils of a world without refuge from ourselves. Pertinent questions emerge from the story. What happens when the world becomes full, mapped in its entirety, and taken as known? Where then will we set sail in search of ourselves and, hence, others? What will beckon us? Will we erect our own imaginary beacons? Or will doing so simply revert an already myopic gaze through mythic or illusory nostalgias?

Saramago's fantasy is an allegory on the present to come. While we do not, in this chapter, presume to assert that our global present is one named and completely closed to the promises of difference—like that of the world over which the unnamed king presides—it is also the case that there are influential spatial and social events that do represent, in some subtle and not so subtle ways, enclosures against today's perceived uncertainties and threats.

These curious spaces manifest desires and nostalgias for place removed from eternal turmoil and vagary by encasing their promises in precise, known, and delimited terms. We are familiar with these promissory spaces. They have long inflected many of our everyday expectations. Cruise ships, resorts, gated communities, amusement parks, and other similar self-enclosed "lifestyle" spaces affectually allure with twin promises of "relax and enjoy." As promissory spaces, they enclose their retreat from a supposedly joyless and strained world by delimiting emergent possibilities, and thereby control the impacts of indeterminacy and uncertainty on "a world" insulated from the "rest of the world."

Emblematically, the past few years have seen the emergence of a number of iconic artificial island projects in the Persian Gulf and in other parts of the world. Mainly intended for a wealthy elite of foreign investors, these self-contained spaces can perhaps be considered as the ultimate "promissory spaces" of late modernity. In this chapter, we shall interrogate these new spaces as symptomatic of an attempt to fortress hope by articulating place, for the few, through nostalgic desire and enclosure. It is in the island and, as we shall suggest, no more so than in the varying contemporary forms of the *artificial island*, that nostalgia, desire, and hope come together to articulate place and sociality in specifically curious, if also sometimes troubling, ways.

Places as diverse as Qatar, Russia, Thailand, Spain, Portugal, Slovenia, the Netherlands, the Bahamas, South Korea, and Pakistan are all proposing artificial island projects as part of their socio-economic development strategies. These numerous island developments manifest different forms and functions specific to their regional conception and location (see Jackson and della Dora 2009). In this chapter we focus on the new artificial island developments in the Persian Gulf. These, we argue, are particularly significant as they act as reconfiguring loci for globalizing spatial forms. As a somewhat sympathetic commentary has recently remarked, "The Gulf ... is not just reconfiguring itself; it's reconfiguring the world" (Koolhaas 2007, n.p.). Furthermore, the Gulf island developments articulate specific geographical and sociological discourses, both in their material form and in the rhetoric that surrounds them. Gulf islands embody the next logical stage in an urbanized habitus predicated on fortressing, privatization, and technologically mediated distantiation. In what follows, we shall address the visual materialities and the spatial politics of Gulf island developments to ask questions about the role these contemporary sites have in placing nostalgia, hope, and desire within the spatial imaginaries of our global present.

The chapter is structured in five parts. In the first two sections, we relate the peculiarity of island imaginaries and the speculative character of the new artificial islands. The third part analyzes the visualization of the present artificial island developments and projects in the Gulf—their construction as promissory places of hope in online marketing videos and other interactive media spaces. The last two sections address the politics of island emergence and representation. Have these emergent spaces become material symptoms of a late capitalist modernity resigned to securing itself against a planet rendered known, completed, and now waste? Are they the spaces we imagine when we have convinced ourselves that there are no more unknown islands? We conclude with a reflection on the implications these places have for an affective politics for thinking the anticipatory interconnections of wish and longing.

Artificial Islands as Meta-geographies

The worldwide phenomenon of the artificial island has become a significant defining imaginary and material form of twenty-first-century development visions. Countries clamouring to reinvent their urbanizing coastlines in order to attract tourist dollars, to energize real estate markets, and to revitalize moribund, or previously absent, cityscapes have turned to new construction technologies (GPS, large-scale sea dredging, vibratory soil settlement, etc.) to "islandize" their geographies. Perhaps the most familiar and popular developments are the well-known islands shaped as palm trees, "World maps," and stylized "universes" off Dubai's coast in the United Arab Emirates. Less well known is the fact that, since the beginning of the Gulf's island constructions, and within a few years, an island-mania seems to have exploded across the globe. Countries within and beyond the Gulf are currently at work reinventing the earth by engaging projects to build their own artificial islands. The Gulf island developments, not solely limited to Dubai (Oman, Bahrain, Qatar, and Saudi Arabia—although the latter in the Red Sea—all have artificial island developments as part of their real estate–driven development strategies), have assumed an iconic capacity as affectual and socio-economic spaces, and circulate as such. Constructed by developers and speculators largely as tickets to participating in a "globalized community," and received by wealthy buyers and media as such, the iconic power of artificial islands lies largely in their very ontological status—in their "islandness."

The appeal of the Gulf island developments as archetypes of urban expectation (and thus as "spaces of hope") similarly lies in their very insularity.

Chiefly, the sociological affects of "building islandness" are to enhance unthought prescriptive capacities for insularity, remove, control, imaginative freedom, and security, and, moreover, to align those affectual resonances with economic, developmental, and technologically responsive ends.

Artificial islands are neither a new phenomenon nor single of purpose. Tenochtitlán, reed habitations in the Tigris-Euphrates, Portuguese colonial trading ports in Japan, ancient crannogs in Scottish lochs, and perhaps more familiar things like international airports, parking lots, and waste removal sites all employ artificial islanding techniques.[2] Two characteristics, however, make the new Gulf and "post-Dubai" artificial island projects different from "traditional" artificial islands. The first is the scale of their self-proclaimed spectacular appeal. The islands off Dubai's coast (still under construction; two have been inhabited since 2006, and a third, Deira, the largest, will be completed in 2015) are shaped in the form of three gigantic palm trees surrounded by circular breakwaters. At its completion, Palm Deira will extend for 12.5 by 7.5 kilometres, whereas Palm Jebel Ali is expected to accommodate a population of 1.7 million people by 2020. The World, a fourth island project initiated in 2004 and close to completion, is an archipelago of private artificial islands arranged in the shape of a world map, each island available for cash and customizable to reflect its wealthy owner's desires (Florian 2008). Once the Palms Trilogy, the World, and other forthcoming projects, such as the the Universe archipelago, are complete, over 950 kilometres of beachfront property will have been added to Dubai.

The second characteristic of the new artificial islands is that whatever their purpose, they delineate on a global scale and in globally networked ways new assemblages and geographies of desire and fear, inclusion and exclusion, escapism and alienation from natural and social Others. Reinforcing social distinction through symbolic and spatial creation, the islands naturalize exclusion, while at the same time disciplining desire in those excluded from the physical space. Our argument, then, hinges on examining the sociological and geographical significance of the interaction between these two processes.

We argue that contemporary artificial islands are new "meta-geographical terra-forms" (cf. Beaverstock, Smith, and Taylor 1999; Lewis and Wigen 1997; Taylor 2001). We shall define these terms in turn. By "meta-geographical" we mean that these new island forms are spatial structures that normalize and naturalize people's expectations, knowledge, and interactions with the world. They exploit and mobilize often unconscious social frameworks to shape historical, cultural, economic, political, and, perhaps, even natural appreciations of contemporary possibilities and expectations for being in

the world. In-vogue tourist destinations, new spaces for urban regeneration, and, more significantly, models of ideal gated communities, artificial
islands can be characterized as new dream-spaces emergent within global
capitalism's "hyper-commercialized, neo-liberal and individualizing escapism"
at the same time as they articulate key definitional characteristics of national
and communal identity (Giroux and Kellner 2003, 119). Their newness and
imaginary, often speculative complexities reveal multiple, and frequently
competing, discourses significant for thinking about contemporary socio-spatial reorganization. Indeed, what is significant about them as technological
spaces is the fact that they attempt to assert techniques and rhetorics of
place that order social interactions through constructions of *naturalized
place*.

   Terraforming, the second of our invoked terms, literally means "earth-
shaping." A neologism that comes from science fiction, *terraform* was first
coined in 1942 by American writer Jack Williamson (1989; see also
Williamson 2003). Given its science fiction provenance, terra-forming first
referred to the technological altering of an alien planet, a hypothetical process
of deliberately modifying the planet's atmosphere, temperature, surface
topography, or ecology to be similar to those of Earth in order to make it habitable by humans. In 1961 astronomer Carl Sagan proposed the terraforming of Venus; he imagined seeding the atmosphere of the planet with algae,
which would remove carbon dioxide and reduce the greenhouse effect until
surface temperatures dropped to comfortable levels. In 1976 NASA officially
addressed the issue of terraforming (or planetary modelling) and concluded
that it was possible for Mars to be made into a habitable planet. Thirty years
later, Venus and Mars have not been terraformed, but the Arabian Sea has.
Indeed, *terraforming* is the term used by the developers of the artificial
islands that are being fabricated in the Persian Gulf. Its use exposes the presumption that whole worlds can be shaped to meet human hopes, desires,
and expectations.

   Terraforming in Dubai implies the epic creation of your own private
island-world *from scratch*, from a sea surface marketed as an empty space
waiting to be inscribed by human imagination and action. And what's more,
not unlike the original science fiction invocation of the term, terraforming
represents itself as a viable option precisely when the earth, as we have come
to know it, is perceived as known and full and needing to be escaped. When
we have no choice *but* to invent and colonize space, even our own terrestrial
space, we must write the earth anew. Interestingly, terraforming as earth-
writing (a "geo-graphing") is literalized in the emergent islands of the Persian Gulf. An epigram composed by Dubai's emir, Sheikh Mohammed bin

Rashid Al Maktoum, features as an "earth poem" on the Palm Jebel Ali's crescent. Spelled out in sand and stone, the island poem will read, "It takes a man of vision *to write on water*" (emphasis added). The meta-geographical significance of islands as new terraformed spaces extends as much, then, to the very character and presumption of their earthly construction—sometimes even their literal shape—as it does to the kinds of everyday life shaped consequently therein.

Speculative Meta-geographies

Adding beach frontage to potential housing and property is the key reason for the Gulf's island developments; in real estate terms, beachfront property is more valuable than non-beachfront property. In Dubai, a city that only twenty years ago was a relatively small, desert-bound trading port, the real estate market depends almost entirely on its willingness and capacity to add value. The city-region's property development market thus legitimizes its often exorbitant exchange values precisely through the construction of ever more spectacular and enticing additive and exchange values: island beachfront, golf courses, marinas, leisure amenities, skyscrapers, malls, etc. If this exchange value can appeal to imaginative cultural geographies that speak to long-held social and private desires for exclusivity, remove, isolation, and control, while at the same time offering access, amenity, and cosmopolitan luxury through a nearby city, then so much the better.

The constructed promise of these spaces is also significant for a second key feature of these developments. They are or have been built entirely "on spec"—that is, they are speculative developments, meaning that a developer anticipates that a demand exists or will form for a product when it is put on the market. Most of the properties and islands are largely sold before they have even been built and, as such, depend upon a desire being created through the spatial promise of their iconic islandness. Again, the promise of the imaginary spaces to deliver, as consumables, the ontological allure inherent in an idealized island geography is key to recognizing the unique significance of these residential and resort developments.

As we mentioned, Dubai is not the only region investing in the work of "islanding" in the Arabian Peninsula. Oman, Qatar, Bahrain, Kuwait, and Saudi Arabia are also at work building artificial residential and commercial islands in an effort to bring foreign capital to the region. For example, the Pearl-Qatar promises an exclusive paradise in the making, according to the developer's website: "An Island Rediscovered ... where Pearlesque names, crafted from an intriguing mix of Italian, French, Spanish and

Arabic, summon up the charm of the old world, and the spirit of the new."³ Bahrain's addition to the islanding and urbanizing Gulf is called Durratt Al Bahrain.⁴ The project's promotional and marketing literature tellingly emphasizes much upon which these speculative spaces depend: "island living and city style. It's the desert and the sea, it's a holiday and a home, it's a place to be together, it's adventure. It's one world that offers you endless possibilities."⁵

What these and other similar dwelling forms explicitly aim to create, or as the Pearl-Qatar rhetoric boldly claims, "rediscover," is an environment steeped in the nostalgias and fantasies of island life. Bucolic repose, quiet remove, unhurried pleasure, and easy abundance are all advertised and sold, not as found or chance consequences of difficult passage and discovery, but as purchasable forms of life shaped by technology and economic opportunity. But, more than this nostalgic rediscovery, the Gulf's residential and touristic island spaces also work to bring together, and thus absolve, in a kind of progressive synthesis—in a technological rendering of place—the very antithetic paradoxes that have long characterized traditional island spaces. Adventure *and* security, escape *and* familiarity, isolation *and* cosmopolitan diversity, tranquility *and* excitement are promised, brought together, and ostensibly sustained through the geographical terraform of the artificial island. What emerges, then, from the traditional island narrative is the claim of the spaces to offer the possibilities of control and determination. But, at the same time, as technological spaces, their domestic promise also revels in their capacity to construct adventurous diversity and distinctly exotic and unfamiliar geographical spaces. Not unlike the historical promise of the early suburb to bring together city and country life,⁶ the residential and resort island promises the best of both worlds with none of the downsides typically associated with island life: isolation, insularity, elemental danger, and abandonment. Antitheses and tensions are experienced as paradoxes of adventure and threat, and dissolve one into the other through promissory technics of place (Berman 1988, 15).

The catalytic agent, the *artificial* island, is explicitly invoked as textual *and* economic referent. Regeneration depends upon added economic value, and repeating patterns of iconicity translate themselves outward from Dubai as the epicentre of wealth and lifestyle creation. The idea of the island becomes a crucial part of a "re-export model, ... [an] empirically perfected development package of financial inspiration and exportation ... [to] the largest swath of the globe barely touched by globalism"; they are indeed working to reconfigure the world (Bouman, Khoubrou, and Koolhaas 2007, 283).

Developing city-regions abutting the Gulf, in addition to those culturally connected by way of religious, linguistic, or proximate sympathy (regions as disparate as Gujarat, Rabat, Damascus, and East Timor), have followed suit by invoking the Gulf model of added-value development to attract foreign capital and global attention. For example, Gujarat's International Finance Tech-City—GIFT for short—promises to become one of the world's largest finance centres, built, as its website boasts, "on a perfection of purpose."[7] Its centrepiece, the 400-metre-tall Diamond Tower, will sit on the manufactured waterfront of Fortune Island, an artificially constructed island and water attraction at the centre of the 200-hectare business district and surrounding integrated townships. But GIFT is being built on the outskirts of Ahmedabad, a city of approximately 8 million people located 120 kilometres inland from the Arabian Sea. The built island space, sitting at the centre of the project and housing the planned city's proposed centrepiece, has travelled inland; an iconic capacity to communicate promise, spectacle, and technologically ensured futurity inheres in this movement. Once again, it is the dynamic relationship within this spatial, island ontology that defines the iconic exclusivity of the project.

Of course, one of the significant features of the nature and attraction of these travelling island terraforms is the fact that they are spectacularly unnatural; their "technicity" adds value, economically and iconically. Their iconic shapes account for much of their speculative lure as socially significant spaces. Once we have exhausted the natural world as possible, and thus potential, once it becomes perceived as full and known, and thus without allure and excitement, we turn to creating it as speculative fantasy.

Virtual islands

Like the past, islands seem apart from the everyday present; in continental eyes they are exotic, out of this quotidian world.... To Enlightenment savants, islands seemed especially evocative of the past, both in their physical nature and in the habits and culture of their human inhabitants. By the late eighteenth century, islands had become iconic sites of bygone ways of life elsewhere extinct or fast succumbing to modern progress. (Lowenthal 2007, 208–9)

Whether spaces of reverie or nightmare, islands are largely nostalgic spaces. That is, they are often narrated as places concerned with loss. But they are also deemed to be places for recovery and self-regeneration; island images of paradise symbolize the "no longer," island images of utopia the "not yet"

(Baudet in Gillis 2004, 65). They are the favourite sites for visions of the past *and* of the future. Great Renaissance geographical discoveries were often anticipated by invisible islands in the Atlantic: Sebastian Muenster's imaginary places—Die Nuew Welt, Fortunate Isles, and the Hesperides— mapped in 1544, are apposite examples, as are the fabled Island of California, Antilia, and Saint Brendan's Isle (see Gillis 2004, chap. 4). Sixteenth-century cosmographers, such as André Thevet, provided seemingly accurate cartographic representations of imaginary islands accompanied by written accounts. The rhetorical power of the map contributed to the resilience of Thevet's imaginary islands: some of them survived as actual islands on British Admiralty charts well into the twentieth century.[8]

If the map of the Atlantic has become emptier than five centuries ago, today the Persian Gulf seems to be following the inverse trend. Visions of fantastic islands are starting to crowd its waters and, once again, to colonize a geographical imagination through economic imperatives of capitalist accumulation, feeding from the medieval belief that "anything marvelous was always an island" (Royle 2001, 11). Nowhere are islands, speculation, and representation connected so intrinsically as in the Gulf. As we have mentioned, only a small percentage of the island real estate in the Gulf has been completed, but a much larger percentage is already sold out, even before the surfacing of these terraforms from the sea—all the housing on Palm Jumeirah was gone in a mere fifteen days (Bouman, Khoubrou, and Koolhaas 2007, 44). What the island property owners in Dubai purchase is a vision whose appeal lies in the promise of its materialization.

Nakheel, Dubai's premier developer, which is constructing the Palms and the World, advertises itself as "a company that turns extraordinary visions *into tangible reality.*"[9] The focus of the company, Nakheel's official webpage states, "is on building icons that embody innovation and progress, creating a legacy of value for generations to come."[10] The very existence (or rather, the possibility for coming into existence) of the new artificial islands is entirely dependent on visual representations. The Gulf islands are visions in that they require imagination both by producers and consumers. Like the imaginary islands in the Atlantic of Renaissance explorers (or the unknown island in Saramago's tale), the islands of the Gulf imply futurity. Whether *in fieri* or (as it is often the case) not yet commenced, the Gulf islands require more faith in images and promotional videos than in tangible reality. Yet, as we shall see, the two are not disconnected.

What the investor ends up buying is first of all an image, a virtual space (see the introduction and conclusion in this volume on virtuality). As Marcus Doel and David Clarke (1999) note, however, "real virtuality has nothing to do with resemblance. Still less does it concern a false approximation or a final resolution. (Virtual) reality is nothing but immanent creation and experimentation" (280). In the case of the artificial islands in the Gulf, digital technologies do more than "anticipate" the future: they blend it with the present and set the viewer in a hybrid oneiric dimension in which the two become inseparable.

It is thus not fortuitous that all the promotional island videos follow a standardized pattern. These videos generally open with an orthographic view of the islands rapidly emerging from the water—with the cartographic vision being sketched on the blank sea surface. The Palm Jumeirah and the World, for example, are presented in their latest stage of construction, as viewed from an airplane. But in the twinkling of an eye the visual angle shifts from perpendicular to high oblique, and it then suddenly decreases, setting the viewer a few feet above sea level. The viewer is rapidly taken on a bird's-eye tour of the islands, as if on board a small helicopter. But here is the wonder: as the visual angle shifts, aerial views of the islands-in-becoming's barren sand and asphalt turn into Edenic greenery and luxurious villas facing an impossibly turquoise sea. Without realizing it, the viewer is transported into a dreamlike virtual world of 3-D digital simulations subtly marketed as reality. Scenes of dredgers pumping out the sand and charismatic engineers at work (but never of Pakistani immigrant workers!) and interviews with satisfied buyers are injected here and there, further confusing "what is there already" with "what has yet to come." Sand, asphalt, and impossible paradisaical visions blend in an indistinguishable continuum. As the videos approach their end the visual angle increases again: the viewer is returned to the cartographic godlike view from the airplane, and the Edenic island-worlds are transmuted into stylized symbols—into commodified icons of themselves.

As Briavel Holcomb observes in the case of cities marketed for tourism, "because the product is usually sold before the consumer sees it, ... representation of place, the images created for marketing, the vivid videos and persuasive prose of advertising texts can be as selective and as creative as the marketer can make them—a reality check comes only after arrival" (quoted in Bouman, Khoubrou, and Koolhaas 2007, 40). The artificial islands in the Gulf, however, are virtual spaces in multiple and less traditional ways than other tourist destinations. They are not simply marketed through impossible digital "visions from above": they are literally constructed "from above" and *through* visions—from the sheikh's initial approving gaze on three-dimensional models, to the whole process of dredging, which is itself based on GPS technologies (i.e., on visualization through satellites, rather than from the ground).

The Dubai and post-Dubai artificial islands find their fulfillment also "from above." Their elaborate iconic shapes are virtually invisible from sea level. They can be seen only from an elevated spot: from the top floor of the Burj al-Arab (the world's only seven-star hotel), from the millionaire's private helicopter, from the airplane approaching DXB (Dubai's international airport). Perhaps more significantly, these islands are also visible to the booming global population of virtual explorers who scour the expanse of the Gulf through Google Earth in search of new islands and curios. Hybrid creations of sand and technology, the Gulf's artificial islands can be visually grasped (and thus appreciated) only through technological mediation.

Their virtual ontology makes the islands geographical objects best suited to being viewed from above. As Holcomb has observed, "the island is the lowest form of spatial organization. Pure accumulation, it has an iconic form and a certain perimeter and location. It can be reached by dramatic arriving.... The surface of the island reveals everything there is, all its contents" (quoted in Bouman, Khoubrou, and Koolhaas 2007, 40). Whether from the air or through Google Earth, the Gulf's artificial islands arouse curiosity; they invite exploration and closer scrutiny, like the insular worlds in miniature depicted in Thevet's book of islands.[11] Therefore, even those islands that are still under construction (such as Doha's Pearl) are accompanied by interactive links offering utopian renderings of how they will look upon completion, in a future that returns to the present as promise, beckoning and gesturing to the continuing paucities of the present.

Aspiring to flatness, the new icons circulate their iconicity through spectacular, if virtual, visibilities, thus inverting the modernist promises embodied in verticality. Unlike Corbusier's unbuilt vertical visions, or even those visions realized as today's skyscrapers (see Pak in this volume), the island projects remove the populist promise by seeking to hide and disperse their physicality except through mediated and hyper-real spaces of simulation. This distancing reifies the relationship between island habitant and onlooker, and creates "a powerful, exclusionary cognitive barrier transcending the need for obtrusive physical barriers" (Rofe 2006, 316).[12]

Perhaps even more intriguingly, artificial islands, and their associated urban features, whose construction has not yet been started—for example, Madinat al-Hareer in Kuwait, Waterfront City in Dubai, or even the more distant Federation Island in the Black Sea—are mapped onto Google Earth as were Antillia and other Atlantic imaginary islands of the past onto geographic technologies of the time. As Baudrillard (1983) writes, "It is the map that precedes the territory" (166). The map and, in this contemporary case, its imaginative, interactive geographies work to disperse and elide, on the one hand, but also to promote and exemplify, on the other, the boundaries of islandness. The very confines between the real and the virtual that the island has always already thrown up thus circulate telegenically as spectacles of aspirant consumption through dispersed assemblages of capital (Bouman, Khoubrou, and Koolhaas 2007, 44).

The horizontal invisibility of new islands in the Gulf works not only from outside, i.e., from the perspective of the viewer looking at them; it also works from inside. Panoramic views might appeal to the tourist spending a night at the Burj, but no longer to the millionaire seeking an exclusive insular retreat. The most expensive of the islands in the World archipelago do not face Dubai's skyline; rather, they face the open ocean. The marine horizon implies futurity. It is the elemental line through which we construct the world; it is where finitude and the infinite meet; it is the element in which thing and process blend into each other, a line of encounter between what is there and what has yet to come (Farinelli 2007, 31–32). As such, the horizon is not only a metaphor of the Gulf's islands-in-becoming, but also one of their most desired features. Exclusivity requires as complete a visible separation as possible. The ultimate backdrop of this separatist lifestyle is one constructed with reference not to an extant world, but to a dispersed world of imaginary futurity. A picture from Dubai without iconic backdrop is the most sought after experience in Dubai: Dubai without Dubai (Bouman, Khoubrou, and Koolhaas 2007, 276).

In the following section we shall address how the visual grammars of the island places and their circulations discipline desire and hope through the spatial imaginaries of neo-liberal enclosure.

Disciplining Desire

Nowhere but in a place like this can the world be so richly re-imagined.[13]

The Gulf islands and their promises signal a spectacular re-centring of development and consumption geographies; they participate in a shift toward a "new global capital of the world in the making [whose] imagery is transmitted long before its reality" (Bouman, Khoubrou, and Koolhaas 2007, 276). Strategically positioned in an oil-rich region, and midway between Europe and the developing economies of China and India, Gulf cities bare no bones about efforts to locate themselves at the centre of complex consumption- and trade-animated nexuses of globalizing flows (financial capital, real estate investment, tourism, mobile labour, air travel, etc.). Indeed, the branding slogan for Dubai's largest holding company, Dubai World, is "The sun never sets on Dubai World."[14] Dubai World manages the Dubai government's development projects and, with over ninety subsidiaries, includes under its purview all of the Emirates' island developments, the world's largest mall, numerous resorts and hotels, the Dubai ports and authority, dry docks, shipping lines, and much else. The tagline of the company, of course, is a conscious subversion of the British colonial saying, "The sun never sets on the British Empire," and actively works to re-centre the imperial imaginary away from its former colonial master through corporate and city branding whose global reach is not at all dissimilar to that of the seventeenth-century East India companies. History returns in new and interesting ways.

Today, however, sun, sand, and spectacle converge on dispersed telegenic—rather than traditionally mapped—imaginary horizons. These horizons are mediated through the participatory visualizations of the many who travel to and from the islands without ever leaving their homes. The creation of the island spaces has the effect of seeming to be neutral with respect to negotiated histories. Emptied of intrinsic value and reinscribed—literally— through imperatives of added economic value, the ocean spaces have not had to, at least on the surface (and the surface is what matters) evidence themselves as aggressive or exclusionary; they have not had to displace anyone.[15] Visible to most only through a tele-mediated godlike viewership, or barely evident on the horizon, the islands mask their physical mechanisms of exclusion. This has the effect of rendering their spectacular spaces unassailable and unattainable (Rofe 2006, 315). Instead, the twinned logics of affluent seclusion and hyper-visible remove reify each other—and discipline desire in interesting ways.

Characteristically fungible, the desires of the late modern, consumptive viewer are targeted and heightened through a distanced but tantalizingly close interaction—"look but can't touch."[16] The empathies of the excluded viewer are directed through the imaginary geographies of the island as iconic site of aspiration, consumptive possibility, and futurity, but within the expectation that they will always be out of reach and largely unknown, and, crucially, if for those very reasons, deeply desirable spaces. It is important to emphasize that the capillary dispersion and reification of desire for the imaginary possibility of these places happens through conduits or assemblages of capital and consumption. The process is no different from the more local and intimate consumption of commodities in arcades, exhibitions, malls, etc. Nor, as we mentioned, is it much different from the way that suburbs, condominium developments, and gated communities have long sold themselves. Rather, it is a scalar amplification of these well-worn processes.

The physical layout of Gulf island developments reflects a gating, but the layouts also replicate, in some instances, panoptic conformations. Take, for example, Palm Jumeirah. The original of the Palm Trilogy, Jumeirah is an island complex made up of sixteen stylized palm fronds extending from a central trunk. The complex roughly encompasses a diameter of five kilometres and is made up of 92.2 million cubic metres of carefully placed sand. Each of the fronds accommodates homes and apartment complexes. The fronds themselves are surrounded by three crescent islands that act as breakwaters. The central trunk is planned to house numerous hotels, accommodations, and leisure facilities. At the centre of the trunk, however, a 62-storey mixed-use luxury hotel and residential building destined to become a landmark icon in Dubai's skyline[17] rises above the palm complex. The tower, built and operated by the Trump Organization, will, when complete, dominate the surrounding archipelago. The tower will offer its guests and permanent residents 360-degree views of Jumeirah from the comfort of a luxury environment—and "without being seen." Clad in reflective gold glass, the tower will in turn be visible from all locations on the island, as well as the mainland itself.

The panoptic "physio-political technique" (Foucault 1995, 223) of the Palm extends its governance through a morality tied firmly to constructing and disciplining consumptive desire as an unthought affect within and beyond the island development. Although Jumeirah (like the other island developments) invites viewing from above, at the same time, as we have suggested, those who live there are invited to look out toward the horizon, into the ocean, while remaining conscious of its centrepiece's regulatory economy of exclusivity and the material enclosures rendering that economy and landscape possible. As a couple featured in a promotional video for Palm Jumeirah exclaim as they are filmed purchasing a house on one of the artificial islands, "We couldn't have believed this was possible, to have a gated community with your own private beach, in the centre of the Hong Kong or Singapore of the Middle East, you know, which is Dubai, and here we are."[18] Dubai becomes the world. Significant, however, to island places like Palm Jumeirah is the fact that they, as the Trump Dubai evidences, work explicitly as beacons, as surveilling spectacles whose reach extends into the networked apparatuses of fabricating and consuming spatial imaginaries.

Unlike utopias of the past, in many of these places, the projected politics of inclusion materialized through ideal socio-spatial arrangements are elided in favour of a legitimating participatory discourse that derives its validity from economic rationales, wherein discourses of security (protection from terror, crime, inequality, difference, etc.) work to legitimate a spatial evacuation of nonmarket moralities. Thus, two things make these spaces noteworthy: first, this elision raises the status of profit and expediency as the criteria both for planning (to make plans and have policy-relevant plans, one must assume a *polis*) and for dwelling; and second, crucially, these island places circulate as spectacular icons of the affectually possible, but as possibilities constrained by the material, and myopic, horizons from which they emerge.

Artificial islands are different from traditional gated communities in that they reinforce spatial difference through the symbolic registers of insular exclusivity as they circulate as "visions from above." In other words, the spatial construction of social difference and exclusion operates not simply through traditional disciplinary and panoptic technologies such as walls, moats, or surveillance cameras, but also through the highly mediated disciplinary production of an iconically and geographically normalized *desire*, a desire that increasingly feels, as given, hierarchies and imaginaries of place circumscribed through resolutely corporate and privatized productions. The prescriptive locus of disciplinary force and production is thus not interested in shaping a modern, public subject (as, arguably, in Foucault's characterization of disciplinary power),[19] but rather in shaping a desirous consumer for whom the governmental ideal of a polity or public is irrelevant, or even discarded. Interestingly, these gated island spaces are also articulated within, or as part of, built assemblages that work specifically to rearticulate the discursive resonance of "city-ness," spaces that have traditionally be wrapped within concerns of the public sphere. For example, Dubai's larger planning imperatives articulate segmented and highly privatized visions of specialist zones, each branded by the appellation "city": Media City, Health City, Education City, etc. The effect, like the more literal artificial islands, is to isolate and marketize space, but more importantly, to marketize the imaginary possibilities of cities and citiness.

Those who employ islands as technologies of place are not interested in collective embrace, punishment, or correction; they are interested in producing consumptive desire in a world that needs to be reimagined as "The World" (compare this to Shields on desire and Las Vegas in this volume). Or, as Rem Koolhaas, one of the designers of the island-based Waterfront City in Dubai remarks, "the world is running out of places where it can start over ... THE GULF will be the terrain where the current crisis of the metropolis has to be confronted" (Koolhaas 2007, n.p.). Reshaping expectant desire and aspiration is key to this reimagination. In an echo of Foucault's emphasis on the governmental discipline of the soul, the World's third guiding principle, entitled "RARE," articulates a steeling of desire and its affectual force *within* the soul: "Imitators are everywhere, but innovators can still be found, if you know where to look. Innovators that create singular destinations, in singular cities, places so uncommon they pull at the heart, captivate the mind and take up residence in the soul."[20]

As terraforms dependent entirely on technologically sophisticated construction techniques directed "from above," these island places are enabled almost exclusively for, and by, "an electronic capitalism [which] enables the most successful to secede from the rest of society" (Reich quoted in Spivak 2008, 161). Indeed, there is no pretence to polity in their productions of imagined place. For example, the Pearl-Qatar website boasts of the project's ability "to redefine an entire nation ... as an exclusive destination of aspirations ... a lifestyle of incredible qualities ... a world of opportunities available for both individual and corporate investors."[21] Those able to afford the exclusivity and the luxuriously privatized spaces are deliberately secluded and physically removed from a mainland that holds the potential to threaten their supposed privilege and aspirant stability. Artificial island spaces thus erase the conditions for public space, becoming a resistant outside to marketized space (Brown 2003, n.p.). As concentrations of spectacular wealth, these spaces materialize, through display, the "exclusion of a margin that is rejected into misery" (Raffoul and Pettigrew 2007, 3) and bypassed as unredeemable. "[T]he world is running out of places where it can start over."

Excluding the margin to the beyond of hope, Gulf "islanding" developments work to enclose place in undifferentiated spheres of consistent, deferred promise. They seek the beyond to the political frontiers that the modern city throws up in a symbolic, reactionary "revanchism" of the world (Smith 1996, 211). They attempt to reinscribe place—a deeply nostalgic practice—wherein possibilities of a good or value standing outside of a totalized spatial calculus are unknown because the imaginary space of the present, one that actively removes itself from continental history, has been conceived as an economic and material totality; "there are no more unknown islands."

Enclosing Hope

Hope ... dwells in the region of the not-yet, a place where entrance and, above all, final content are marked by an enduring indeterminacy. (Bloch 1998, 341)

The Gulf's artificial islands are not hopeful places. They are not hopeful places because they do not foster the continual surprise of thought (Anderson 2006,

745). Recent work by geographer Ben Anderson (2006) on the politics of affect and how "hope takes place" suggests that hope is dependent on the intrusion of the outside. It is porous and permeable. It is characterized by a transitional openness to the multiplicities of the harmonious and the disharmonious. Hope is a process, rather than a finality, that reminds us of the present's emergent pluralities and partialities (Anderson 2006, 734, 749). The Gulf's artificial islands, as enclosed and secluded places, work to preclude the multiplicities and social permeabilities of difference. Their techniques of place sequester and homogenize through economic rubrics of sociality. This, of course, is neither new nor surprising. Just as gated communities have long been noted as enclaves of fear and as places that actively promote a defensive, reactionary insularity (cf. Blakely and Snyder 1995; Dupuis and Thorns 1998, 2008), so today, in new and exaggerated forms, Gulf island developments unapologetically literalize this insularity, and do so in a way that rearticulates desire and the geographically imaginable.

What is important to recognize about the islandness of these spaces is less that they are physically gated communities than that their very spectacularity and mobility, as icons of a terrestrial geography of possibility, enclose imaginative horizons of life. They imagine precisely by enclosing the horizons of the always already plural *socius*. Ecologies of community, difference, and indeterminacy—the very connective openings through which we attune ourselves in multiple ways to affecting and being affected—are deliberately limited in the physically manifest places and fundamentally limited in the specular *imaginaries* of the Gulf's artificial islands. This is not hope as Bloch and his interlocutors have imagined it. For them, it is in the attitudes and ethics of indeterminacy that hope emerges *qua* hope, not, as it is represented in the islands, as some determinacy of desire (Massumi 2002). The economic and social enclosures of these island residences do, to some degree, experiment—as islands spaces have long done[22]—with the redefinition of home or vacation. But they do so only in so far as the experiment returns a certain determinate security. Less the *socius* open to possibility, they are nostalgias for the securities of monetary return, social determinacy, risk avoidance, luxury and pleasure, and freedom from the worries of inequity. These enclosures enervate the imaginaries of the island fantasy places and, crucially, travel as imaginary visions of futurity.

Conclusion: Floating Islands

You have to leave the island in order to see the island. (Saramago 1999, 27)

In this chapter we have engaged the artificial island projects in the Gulf as new types of iconic and technologically mediated spaces that nevertheless rest on (and indeed magnify) pre-existing narratives and spatialities, such as those of the traditional gated community. Born of technological "visions from above" and graspable *only* from above, these island forms naturalize and materialize extreme visions of neo-liberal privatized seclusion. In so doing, they lure potential investors with the promise of possible "new worlds" or escape from the corrupted world of modernity, and thus with the hope for a "better life (style)." At the same time, however, as we have tried to show, these spaces also "enclose hope" within their very panoptic conformation— metaphorically *and* physically. In their different incarnations, these fantasy islands might thus be envisaged as both floating utopian visions and ultimate social experiments.

The "virtual" islands of the Gulf, however, are not the first artificial island experiments floating in the Western geographical imagination. Eager buyers in the Gulf, David Lowenthal (2007) reminds, "ignore the fate of the first proposed (post-Noah, pre-*Titanic*) island cum cruise ship, Jules Verne's 27-square-kilometre *Floating Island*, housing ten thousand American millionaires in untold luxury (1895). Cruising at eight knots an hour, this 'ninth wonder of the world' was wrecked in a South Pacific storm running aground on New Zealand" (206). Today, real, hyper-mobile floating islands such as that described by Verne are a reality. In a way, they represent the apotheosis of the utopianism and cynicism described above. While the well-known failed case of *The Freedom Ship* has garnered recent attention, another circulatory expression of luxurious isolation quietly sails ceaselessly but largely unnoticed around the world. It too is called *The World*. This cruise ship is advertised as "the only private community at sea offering residential options." The company promises on its website, "*The World* allows us to participate in the ever changing and always exciting diorama that is our globe—all in a luxuriously secure environment"[23] Like its more fixed island relatives, the cruise ship is now home to over sixty permanent residents and promises the familiar predicates of neo-liberal dwelling: private community, luxury, exclusivity, and security.

If the Trump tower promises its visitors a 360-degree panoramic view of Palm Jumeirah and the surrounding region, like nineteenth-century panoramic rotundas,[24] *The World* cruise ship sets its residents within a mobile panopticon from which they can enjoy a filmlike sequence of views of the world—a dioramic sequence of ephemeral surfaces of which the passenger becomes a detached spectator. The experience of being alive, of "Living," as *The World*'s promotional literature puts it, becomes a commodified, capitalized, and hypermediated performance of seclusion and excluded separation from the potentials of vulnerability and exposure. The ship's *Weltbilt*, or "world-picture" (Heidegger 1977)—that is, the way it renders and practises the world through its representation of it—like those of its fixed island cousins, is a profane, material mythologizing of the modern technical wish image. The dream-world then is of *The World* rematerializing itself through a reified vision of a technical capacity to except oneself from the consequences by which one's escape is made possible.

This dream is very different from the redemptive one with which Saramago ends his short story, to which we return by way of conclusion. It is a dream that preserves the possibilities and paradoxes of the island imaginary, but that also preserves the possibilities for hope. After the king grants the unnamed sailor a boat—also unnamed—the man begins to explore his vessel and its seaworthiness with an unnamed female companion, who also bequeaths herself to the island adventure. In the evening, under a rising moon, they share a simple meal of bread, cheese, and olives on the ship's quarterdeck. As they eat, they reveal their anxieties for the next morning's setting sail; they will be sailing into the unknown. Tired, they go below to sleep. The man dreams. He dreams of his ship setting sail; of it fully provisioned with sailors and animals and seeds and earth and rain; and of the ship blessed with the bounty of the earth turning slowly into an island. He dreams of trees and flowers growing from the ship's provisions, up around the mast and sails, of roots penetrating the hull, and the sails becoming a canopy of emergent life. He dreams of birds emerging unbidden from the trees, and of them singing in the flourishing, windswept treetops. The man-made technicity of ship becomes a place full of life, diversity, and potential as it sails through the dreamt unknowns of the oceans. When the man wakes, he is in the arms of the woman. Together they christen their ship *The Unknown Island*, and they set sail to the possibilities and freedoms the unknown provides in the form of hope.

Notes

1 Narration to a promotional video, "Video 1," for Dubai's "The World," http://www.theworld.ae (accessed January 10, 2009).

2 Examples might include the New Kitakyushu and Kobe airports in Japan, Peberholm in Denmark, additions to the Hong Kong airports, and, on a perhaps less spectacular scale, Tronchetto, Venice's public car parking island.

3 The Pearl-Qatar, http://www.thepearlqatar.com/main.aspx (accessed February 18, 2009).

4 *Durratt Al Bahrain* translates as "Bahrain's collection of precious gems or pearls" and continues the luxurious and exclusive motif represented by the treasured and rare.

5 Durratt Al Bahrain, http://www.durratbahrain.com (accessed February 20, 2009).

6 This union of the best of the country and the best of the city is, of course, still promised in depictions of suburbs today. See Park in this volume.

7 Gujarat International Finance Tec-City, http://www.giftgujarat.in (accessed February 20, 2009).

8 See also Thevet, A. 1586. *Le grand insulaire et pilotage d'André Thevet, angoumoisin, cosmographe du Roi: Dans lequel sont contenus plusiers plants d'isles habitées, et deshabitées, et description d'icelles* as quoted in Lowenthal 2007, 203.

9 Emphasis added, http://www.thepalm.ae (accessed January 22, 2009).

10 "About Nakheel," http://www.thepalm.ae/about-nakheel.html (accessed February 20, 2009).

11 *Isolarii*, or island books, were "visual catalogues," or atlases, that featured maps of different islands on each page. The maps were usually accompanied by notes about the island's history, geography, climate, economy, customs, antiquities, legends, and "curiosities." Cristoforo Buondelmonti's *Liber Insularum Archipelagi* (1422), the first island book, included only Aegean islands. *Isolarii* produced during the following century encompassed islands from all over the world. The last *isolario* was published in 1699 by the Venetian cosmographer Padre Vincenzo Maria Coronelli.

12 As we have argued elsewhere (Jackson and della Dora 2009), island fantasy spaces share two significant and on the surface contradictory characteristics. The first is that they are built to be immediately recognizable (as iconic forms); that is, they are built to be recognized in their artificiality. Yet the ways by which they are to be noticed and appreciated has shifted within the changing contexts of people's interactions with the geographical world. They are also built to be invisible—at least from ground (or sea) level. If the icons of modernity had to be vertical landmarks (the Eiffel tower, the Empire State Building, skyscrapers in general, etc.), and the fancy icons of postmodernity have to be equally visible, it seems that the new cultural icons aspire to flatness. A French tele-journalist recounts visiting the World with Hamza Mustafa, the project's general manager: "We boarded two boats and headed toward The World.... Nothing but water and sky lay before us. If I hadn't known we were heading toward new land not yet visible on the horizon, I would have said we were

heading to Iran.... I asked the marketing director if the project would ever be visible from shore. 'No, [he said] except maybe on a clear day from the top-floor restaurant of the Burj Al Arab, the world's only seven-star hotel.' Having once redefined luxury, Dubai has now released it from the confines of icon. Invisible is the new look" (Bouman, Khoubrou, and Koolhaas 2007, 266).

13   "The World's Principle VII: Legacy," http://www.theworld.ae/world-principles .html (accessed January 18, 2009).

14   Dubai World, http://www.dubaiworld.ae (accessed January 12, 2009).

15   This is not excepting the now notorious exploitation of the labourers who toil on the islands and in the Gulf cities' many developments. For more on the work camps, wages, and inequities of the workers living in the Emirates, see Davis 2007.

16   This is a play on Walter Benjamin's (1999) contention that "world exhibitions were training schools in which the masses, barred from consuming, learned empathy with exchange value. 'Look at everything; touch nothing'" (201, G 16, 6).

17   This condensed description is based on sound in http://www.trumpdubai.com/ (accessed Nov. 1, 2010).

18   http://www.thepalm.ae/jumeirah/news-media/video-gallery-1/the-palm/ (accessed January 21, 2009).

19   "The expiation that once rained down upon the body ... must be replaced by a punishment that acts in depth on the heart, the thoughts, the will, the inclinations" (Foucault 1995, 16).

20   "The World's Principle III: Rare," http://www.theworld.ae/world-principles.html (accessed January 18, 2009).

21   The Pearl-Qatar, http://www.thepearlqatar.com (accessed February 7, 2009).

22   "For geographers, anthropologists, ecologists and biologists, islands hold a particular attraction functioning as small-scale spatial laboratories where theories can be tested and processes observed in the setting of a semi-closed system" (Royle 2001, 20).

23   *The World,* http://www.aboardtheworld.com (accessed February 10, 2009).

24   Panoramas were large canvases (up to 165 by 400 feet) set in special circular, windowless buildings (rotundas) illuminated through a large light dome. Visitors would view the landscape painted on the canvas from a covered platform set in the middle of the building. Canvases would feature very realistic renderings of distant exotic landscapes, European cityscapes, war landscapes, etc. Panoramas were advertised to the public as "surrogates of reality," allowing visits to distant places without leaving one's hometown. On the difference between panoramas and dioramas, see della Dora 2007.

References

Anderson, B. 2006. Becoming and being hopeful: Towards a theory of affect. *Environment and Planning D* 24: 733–52.

Baudrillard, J. 1983. *Simulations,* trans. P. Foss, P. Patton, and P. Beitchman. New York: Semiotext(e).

Beaverstock, J. V., R. G. Smith, and P. J. Taylor. 1999. World-city network: A new metageography? *Annals of the Association of American Geographers* 90: 123–34.

Benjamin, W. 1999. *The arcades project*, trans. H. Eiland and K. McLaughlin. Cambridge, MA: Belknap Press.

Berman, M. 1988. *All that is solid melts into air*. New York: Penguin.

Blakely, E. J., and M. G. Snyder. 1995. *Fortress America: Gated and walled communities in the United States*. Working Paper for Lincoln Institute of Land Policy, USA.

Bloch, E. 1998. Can hope be disappointed? trans. A. Joron. In *Literary Essays*, 339–44. Stanford: Stanford University Press.

Bouman, O., A. Khoubrou, and R. Koolhaas, eds. 2007. *Volume / Al Manakh*. Amsterdam: Stichting Archis.

Brown, W. 2003. Neo-liberalism and the end of liberal democracy. *Theory and Event* 7 (1): n.p.

Davis, M. 2007. Sand, fear and money in Dubai. In *Evil paradises: Dreamworlds of neoliberalism*, ed. M. Davis and D. Bertrand Monk, 48–68. New York: The New Press.

della Dora, V. 2007. Putting the world into a box: A geography of nineteenth-century travelling landscapes. *Geografiska Annaler: Series B, Human Geography* 89 (4): 287–306.

Doel, M., and D. Clarke. 1999. Virtual worlds: Simulation, suppletion, s(ed)uction and simulacra. In *Virtual Geographies*, eds. M. Crang, P. Crang, and J. May, 261–83. London; New York: Routledge.

Dupuis, A., and D. Thorns. 1998. Home, home ownership and the search for ontological security. *Sociological Review* 46 (1): 24–47.

———. 2008. Gated communities as exemplars of "forting up" practices in a risk society. *Urban Policy & Research* 26 (2): 145–57.

Farinelli, F. 2007. *L'invenzione della Terra*. Palermo: Sellerio.

Florian, J. 2008. Dubai's Palm and World islands—progress update. AMEinfo.com. http://www.ameinfo.com/133896.html (accessed February 18, 2009).

Foucault, M. 1995. *Discipline and punish*, trans. A. Sheridan. New York: Vintage.

Gillis, J. 2004. *Islands of the mind*. New York; London: Palgrave.

Giroux, H., and D. Kellner. 2003. *Public spaces/private lives: Beyond the culture of cynicism*. New York: Roman Littlefield.

Heidegger, M. 1977. The age of the world picture. In *The question concerning technology and other essays*, ed. W. Lovitt, 115–54. New York: Harper.

Jackson, M. S., and V. della Dora. 2009. "Dreams so big only the sea can hold them": Man-made islands as cultural icons, travelling visions, and anxious spaces. *Environment and Planning A* 41 (9): 2086–104.

Koolhaas, R. 2007. *The Gulf*. Baden: Lars Müller.

Lewis, M. W., and K. E. Wigen. 1997. *The myth of continents: A critique of metageography*. Berkeley: University of California Press.

Lowenthal, D. 2007. Islands, lovers, and others. *The Geographical Review* 97 (2): 202–29.

Massumi, B. 2002. Navigating movements. In *Hope: New philosophies for change*, ed. M. Zournazi, 210–44. London: Pluto Press.

Miéville, C. 2007. The Freedom Ship. In *Evil paradises: Dreamworlds of neoliberalism*, ed. M. Davis and D. Bertrand Monk, 251–61. New York: The New Press.

Moles, A. 1982. Nissologie ou science des îles. *L'Espace Géographique* 4: 281–89.

Raffoul, F., and D. Pettigrew. 2007. Introduction. In *The creation of the world or globalization*, J.-L. Nancy, 1–17. New York: SUNY Press.

Rofe, M. W. 2006. New landscapes of gated communities: Australia's Sovereign Islands. *Landscape Research* 31 (3): 309–17.

Royle, S. A. 2001. *A geography of islands*. London; New York: Routledge.

Saramago, J. 1999. *The tale of the unknown island*, trans. M. J. Costa. London: Harvill.

Smith, N. 1996. *The new urban frontier: Gentrification and the revanchist city*. New York: Routledge.

Spivak, G. C. 2008. *Other Asias*. Oxford: Blackwell.

Taylor, P. J. 2001. Visualizing a new metageography: Explorations in world-city space. In *The territorial factor: Political geography in a globalising world*, ed. H. Knippenberg and G. Dijkink, 113–28. UvA, Amsterdam: Vossiuspers.

Williamson, J. 1989. *Seetee Ship*. Ojai, CA: Bart Books.

———. 2003. *Terraforming Earth*. New York: Tor Science Fiction, Macmillan.

Conclusion
A Roundtable on the Affective Turn

ROB SHIELDS
ONDINE PARK
TONYA K. DAVIDSON
the CONTRIBUTORS

Ecologies of Affect started with the ambition of demonstrating the importance of affect in everyday urban experience. As themes emerged, we realized that they themselves overlapped. We therefore wanted to make a place for these intersections between and across the chapters and to address the ways in which the sum of the book was more than its individual parts. This book is its own ecology, an expression of place and of the diversity of a non-institutionalized interdisciplinarity.

In order to prepare this concluding chapter, we gathered the contributors for a fruitful roundtable discussion of emergent themes that had arisen during the writing and revision process, after the original commissioning of the chapters. The editors undertook to write up the discussion, which we present as a collectively authored chapter. We therefore synthesize and reconsider the key themes across the book, the tensions that developed, and emergent directions for further research.

We see this book as a series of relationships between the cases. A common theme is the intersection of the intangible with the material world in the form of qualities and relationships that shift bodies and things from one category or status to another or that relate the present to its past (as in the memory of a historical moment) or future (as in the promise of latent capacity). The chapters converge on questions of space as place, scale, imagery and of time as historicity and affective temporality. This is a matter not only of a shared concern with the place and time-space of the cases, but also of complex spatiality and temporal qualities, which are revealed in the chapters as they theorize hope, nostalgia, and desire. These yield an ethical and political engagement with affect which integrates it into the play of power across the uneven resources and unequal terrain of struggles for emancipation from oppression and of desires for a better world. We see affect as relevant to individual expression and identity, as well as an essential element of social life. It is thus part of the political stakes of formal public spheres and of micro-political interactions. Pushing this further, affect is both an outcome and a medium that resonates with discrimination and revulsion as much as appreciation, respect, and interest in the Other.

Virtual and Material

Nostalgia, desire, and hope are three modalities of affect. Collectively, the contributors suggest that the intangibility of affect is more than a convenient fiction, a psychological concept, or a merely subjective perception or idea. Instead, we identify affect as virtual, a real but intangible thing or capacity. Through case studies, we discover the inter-relation of the virtual and the material. This comes out across discussions of the capacities of things and people, the affordances of objects, and the performativity of social processes and imaginaries by which these capacities are actualized. In this manner, objects and environments are materially rearranged. Subjects do not simply realize scripts like reading the lines of a play, but fully actualize their capacities to enact social roles creatively, acting out within the constraints of a time and place their capacity to be human. This means not simply acting as a stereotypical consumer, citizen, or tourist, but doing so with character. The virtual implies emergent behaviour and creativity of both bodies and things rather than the predictable patterns of robots. This can be a continual and spatially distributed process, whereby people's material interactions form virtual places that then re-form relationships to the material. Many of the chapters are focused on the moment of enactment of the virtual when it has material effects (see chapters by Shields, Vallee, Tiessen, and many others).

We argue that ephemeral, ghostly, unsettling, immaterial, and dreamlike experiences shape our relationships to place. These experiences leave traces in, and are produced through, the material world. Such traces include not only utilitarian physical worlds, but also the props and material supports that concretize nostalgia, hope, and desire. These include such objects as the souvenir mug of East Germany in Winkler's discussion of *Ostalgie*, representations such as the posters in Buffam's chapter on the Edmonton youth centre or Cambre's proliferating images of Che, Davidson's inherited photographs of a family homeland, the suburbias of Park's picture books, and even the artificial islands toured by Jackson and della Dora. Our cases add something new to the literature on affect by emphasizing its fleeting character. We find affect to involve a process of moving from virtual to actual and back again (see Shields's chapter). The term "syncresis" is advanced to capture this element of performativity or enactment—the flickering back and forth of affect and behaviour. This is similar to a figure–ground image: our perception continually reverses itself from between two different forms that can be discerned but not at the same time, one in the internal and the other in the external spaces of an outline. Affect, like the object of desire, is always liminal, escaping—fleeing.

In some cases, this gives rise to hybrids. Buffam's chapter on the space of the youth centre shows an in-between space (for example, between excluded and included, dominant and oppressed), while souvenir objects, cityscapes, storybook suburbs, and artificial islands all function as affective objects about which it is difficult to dissociate the virtual, abstract, and material. Objects afford an emotional engagement with the past that isn't otherwise possible. It exists in the experience of them. Might one also speculate that the allure of a desired technology or fetishized object lies in its *promise* of experiences and relations to the world and others that are to come, in the future, even if one dare not hope to actually experience them? Whether a photograph sits idle in an album or a mountain bike is at rest, innovations are often fetishized and desired for both their qualitative promise and their material capacities or affordances. Along with memoirs and diaries, aren't all materialities animating a hybrid experience of affect? They are the "scaffolding" of affect, as Davidson argues.

If affect is not ephemeral, it is also not epiphenomenal. The contributors to this book demonstrate that virtualities such as affect *matter*. That is, affect is not a question of secondary symptoms, nor merely a derivative effect caused by something else, such as a primary cause or phenomenon. Furthermore, affects are of interest as causes in themselves and as an undertheorized aspect of causal mechanisms and chains. The vision one has of these is changed by attention to affect and other virtual aspects of the world of bodies and things such as capacities and affordances. The difference that attention to affect makes is that it forces a recognition of the importance of qualities and intangible objects, and leads to causal mechanisms being understood less as situations of instantaneous impact and more as processes in which an interval or liminal zone is opened up between cause and effect, where impacts are seen to gather their force, to be shaped and even in some cases deflected or amplified.

Relation

Relations are an interesting a priori phase space from which to open the discussion of affect. Relations imply and induce spaces that are characterized by affectivity between phenomena such as bodies and things. For example, nostalgia is relative to some thing: it is a relation. Hope is toward a thing or toward a particular disposition of things. Emphasizing not so much the gaps as relations between the virtual and material—as well as between states and objects or bodies in any process—Tiessen draws on Barad's notion of intra-action to remind us of tight processual relationships that have a formative effect on outcomes. If the term "interact" means gross activity that presumes the prior existence of independent objects, to "intra-act" designates "ontologically primitive relations," which, out of a field of interacting phenomena, produce states that we cast as meaningful, if reified, objects (Barad 2007, 815). "Things" that come to be named and known are always relations and processes. A car is always rusting, for example, biodegrading into a state that will one day be little more than lumps of plastic or metal. The virtual character of that collection of materials allows us to continue to recognize it as "a car" or "my car" even as it rusts or when it has lost its wheels or been crushed. The close, syncretic relation of the virtual to the material could also be described as an example of intra-action.

Approaching desire via affect—in other words, taking a Spinozan approach to desiring—locates it within a relational process: desires are stages along a process from the virtual to the actual and back again. Desire is also seen to be a productive, syncretic moment. It is situated in a continuum between creative imagination and material labour and social action. Like the return of a pendulum, or longing for elsewhere (see Dorow and Dogu's chapter), an iterative process brings one's capacities and the affordances of one's environment to bear on desires and expectations, which are relative to one's circumstances. This is more widely understood today as a Nietzschean and Deleuzian approach to affect, understanding desire as productive. But this needs to be extended to affect in general, for it is clear from the foregoing chapters that nostalgia creates a world and hope creates a world, each of which has a flickering and fleeting quality but nevertheless produces effects.

As Cambre, Hroch, and Park show, images appear as more than representations or false substitutes for actual objects or scenes. In their capacity to evoke and provoke, they are directly engaged with the affective, as well as with a mimetic or documentary plane of meaning. This is significant also for cases of memory and the capacity of remembrance of the past to move agents in the present. While memories have to be "worked up" as a performative effect of the brain, they do not remain within the sphere of mental representations but are enacted as bodily action.

Time and Space

Within this book, questions of space and time are foregrounded. The affective dimensions, tones, or modalities that are nostalgia, hope, and desire can be said to operate like temporalities, "as if." However, reflecting synthetically, we are past pinning them to specific temporalities, namely nostalgia to the past, hope to the future, and desire to the present. There is, instead, a flickering process of moving between these affects, folding time and space into complex conjunctures and relationalities. This folding of affect is noted by theorists of hope (see Tiessen's and Dorow and Dogu's chapters for summaries), but the folding of temporalities is a further implication, where past, present, and future lose their distinctness, where time is reversible. One may hope nostalgically to return to the past. One may despair that a desired future will never arrive, that the present will not change. Affects work in time and unfold in time. You can have mixed feelings, literally. Hope, desire, and nostalgia can be had all at once. If anything flickers it is affect. One's "in-the-moment" sensation of experience is flickering: a trans-temporal inter-relation. The affectual modalities of nostalgia, desire, and hope are both playful, like gigantic puppets, and heavily burdened and also politically divisive, like the discourses of childhood hope enacted in the inner-city Edmonton youth centre, the images of Che Guevara on the wall in Palestine, or a skyscraper added to St. Petersburg's skyline.

A spatial theme that we converge upon is place and place-making. Across the contributions, place works like a hologram, flickering between various temporalities and affectual registers: nostalgia, desire, and hope are produced simultaneously. Place as hologram emphasizes the quick and ephemeral, the mobilities of both affectual relationships with place and the properties of the places themselves, and the mobilities among places.

In memories and representations, places are abstracted or fictionalized, becoming almost like fairy tales, but they also become mythic in the sense of containing a reserve charge of affect (as opposed to the literary sense of mythical and myth). "Virtualized," place becomes not just personal (or subjective), but portable and mobile.

Affect "takes place" as an event (*occursus*) in a context (*situo*) to modulate the understanding and relationship to place and environment, as Shields argues. Whether it is the nostalgic eighteenth-century Swiss soldier suffering homesickness, the mountain biker shortcutting along a desire line, or the hopeful billionaire fantasizing about living on future artificial islands, affect intervenes to change the co-constitutive intra-relations between bodies and with objects. As Vallee's and Davidson's chapters show, objects of nostalgia, such as the phonograph's songs or heirloom baby clothes, demand return and repetition. If Winkler doesn't contemplate the return visit, Hui shows that return tourism is in many cases able to realize the potential held as affect in migrants' memories of place.

Mobilities and Scale

In a globalized context, movement and travel are possible not only for bodies, but also for images, as Cambre demonstrates, and imaginaries, as Jackson and della Dora show. Affects may arise out of movement or tangible, material mobilities. In considering how escape destinations such as Las Vegas relate to industrial and resource communities such as Fort McMurray (at the heart of the Athabasca tar sands in Alberta), or the relation between Pak's future-imagined cityscape, present-day St. Petersburg, and memories of storied pasts, one can see that there is a circulation of specific affectual modalities (hope, nostalgia, desire), a kind of circuit or exchange set up between different places and times.

One virtue of a focus on affect is that it gets us out of a static approach where we deal only with reified objects in slices of time. Instead, it answers the trans-disciplinary demand for recognition of mobilities of all kinds (Urry 2002; Appadurai 1996; Lee and Lipuma 2002; Gandhi 2006) and Whitehead's process ontology (see, for example, the 2008 special issue of *Theory Culture and Society*). This can also be read in terms of the ecological thread that runs through the chapters, from the mountain biker's relation to the environment to puppets' performative creation of an environment, from idealizations of suburban nature to the creation of artificial islands.

Issues of scale cut across the papers in the shape of personal engagements with desire, hope, and collective formulations that circulate in different ways. Scale is spatial, social, and political, encompassing scales of interactions, scales of meaning, and scales of engagement. One might ask: at what scale should life be lived? The relationship between larger phenomena such as *Ostalgie*, which is a much more broadly shared sense of nostalgia, versus the personal return trip to a mother country demonstrates two different scales of engagement with nostalgia. Hroch shows how scale, in the form of giant puppets, produces a new space of representation by transforming the relative sizes of street objects in relation to the bodies that inhabit. Jackson and della Dora consider the attempt to enlarge the world itself, which has become too scaled down, by literally creating new territorial spaces. In our research, scales are often counterposed, in collision, or intersecting: global/local, miniature/gigantic, urban/region, historic/ephemeral.

A political theme emerges at two scales: at the micro level of specific interactions and relations and at a macro level where capacities may be systematically frustrated or resources reduced. Reflecting on our discussions, we can observe that prioritizing relations as an ontological premise is a methodological shift away from static structural positions to emergence, to "how things go." It entails directly asking, "What's happening?" in an engaged manner as opposed to stopping at a neutral description of an assemblage or of the balance of powers. This has an ethical and political import. For example, affect throws new light on issues of race and demands for cultural recognition and respect, evincing micro-political attractions, fissures, and displacements that are engendered by its relational vacillations. It also changes how we approach material culture and the physical aspects of phenomena, from exclusion to migration, graffiti and T-shirts, and even to building artificial islands and global networks of escape. Affect thus cuts across the concerns of the social sciences, producing a set of meta-reflections while at the same time suggesting a methodological shift that takes affect as animating micro-politics. At this scale, a play of affects can be seen in which bodies are mobilized by their mutual capacities, limits, and potential. Indeed, this is the ethical "stuff" of politics—loves, hates, affections, loss, and alienation.

For example, spaces of desire or nostalgia often have restrictions on access, which depends not only on economics, but also on agents' bodies marked by race, class, gender, ability, and ethnicity; on subjects' differential place attachments; and on their different capacities to "be attached" to places and held to them. These differential attachments and capacities anchor or attach us elsewhere and to other times, whether as tourists, visitors, cosmopolitan residents or integrated migrants who "pass" as locals, as Dorow and Dogu show. But Hui considers those with attachments to place who are excluded as exiles or desirous outsiders.

The politics of hope, too, play out both temporally and spatially. Hope is not simply related to an open future, something that is only temporal, but it can be "placed" spatially and politically. A youth centre can become a place of hope that acts upon and reinscribes as well as transforms the racially uneven distribution of hope. The cognitive sketch maps of Fort McMurray drawn for Dorow and Dogu often locate hope in escape destinations off the page. But their interest in community and their critical position on the uneven distribution of hope is validated because, in an affective analysis, intangibles matter as they are so entwined with the concrete world of health, access to material resources, and life chances.

A Research Agenda

Ecologies of Affect gestures toward a future research agenda, temporal and spatial, material and virtual. From these studies, we draw a mandate for broadening the objects of social analysis to include affect. In the context of this book, linkages are created with histories; with sociologies and critical traditions that have run through British and other currents of cultural studies; and with contemporary writing on embodiments, geographies, transnational cultures, nonrepresentational theories, and the political economy of globalization. This breadth is exceptional in North American social science scholarship, which has stressed specialization and micro-analyses.

Taking Spinoza's notion of affect seriously also returns social science to some of its forgotten foundations such as the work of Tarde, forsaken for Durkheim's more stable focus on institutions and social facts, an engagement that is also advocated by Latour (2005) in his recent work on the "sociology of associations." It also suggests a re-reading of classics with an eye to process and perhaps against the grain of how they have been categorized or institutionalized in disciplines such as sociology, for example, Robert Merton's neglected essays on Whitehead or on creativity.

Many of our contributions deal with questions of embodiment. We reach out to a politics of gesture and attention. Spinoza's interest in the flow of affect within situations and its applicability to the interpersonal as well as its original intention as an approach to resolving Descartes' subject–object dichotomy has further implications for spatial analysis. Post-humanisms, such as those associated with references to Deleuze, haven't reached out to an ecological vision. Affect, central to Deleuze's philosophy, offers them this (see Introduction). It displaces the fixed, reified subject in favour of a radically in-process mind-body, which is unified with the body and clearly placed in a context and in a flow of intra-relations by which its capacities are realized or frustrated, but by which it becomes always something new; paradoxically, this is what we generally understand when we speak of "being oneself."

All the contributors discuss the relation between the spatialization of sites and objects and their capacities as places able to "host" nostalgia, hope, or other affects. One can imagine specific places where one indulges in dreams—fantasies of happiness or aspirations to wealth, success, or status. These places might include a casino, a shopping mall, a suburb, or the personal auditory space—possibly as small as the cranial space separating a pair of earphones—of the listener who consumes a nostalgic song. The relational identity of places is built on differences that are affective. There is a habitual association of affect with specific places. One may feel one's capacity to be extended or amplified by, for example, the opportunity to travel or to consume leisure time in a tourist destination away from the pressures of everyday responsibilities and one's status. But this regime of placing affect also amounts to a geographical governance of human affect, of relations to oneself, and of the exercise of capacities that may be restrained in everyday life and allowed to blossom only during "time off" or in leisure spaces. This sense of restraint and loss is a further thread. It is particularly evident in chapters on hopelessness, such as Jackson and della Dora's on the loss of frontiers as the world comes to be understood as closed, mapped, finite, and with dwindling nonrenewable resources.

We see this book as offering a set of critical studies, not as a paean to good or happy feelings. Affect is commodified and sold commercially as any of the examples of *Ostalgic* mugs, Che T-shirts, cookie-cutter suburbs, Las Vegas, or Tin Pan Alley illustrate. Affect is also mobilized politically, as Benjamin warned in his critique of what he called the "aestheticization of politics," often to obfuscate and intensify historical matrices of subjugation. If politics works through affect to structure the distribution of resources and access to life chances, there is both need and considerable urgency to a critical approach. We close with this sense of the necessity of acknowledging affect in social and cultural research. This book engages in a wider project, an "affective turn" in research agendas. There is much to do.

References

Appadurai, A. 1996. *Modernity at large: Cultural dimensions of globalization.* Minneapolis: University of Minnesota Press.

Barad, K. 2000. Reconceiving scientific literacy as agential literacy. In *Doing science + culture*, ed. S. T. Reid, 221–58. New York: Routledge.

Gandhi, L. 2006. *Affective communities: Anti-colonial thought, fin-de-siècle radicalism and the politics of friendship.* Durham, NC: Duke University Press.

Latour, B. 2005. *Reassembling the social: An introduction to actor-network theory.* Oxford: Oxford University Press.

Lee, B., and E. Lipuma. 2002. Cultures of circulation: The imaginations of modernity. *Public Culture* 14 (1): 191–213.

Theory, Culture & Society. 2008. Special section on A. N. Whitehead. 25 (4): 1–117.

Urry, J. 2002. *The tourist gaze.* London: Sage.

List of Contributors

Bonar Buffam is a Ph.D. candidate in the Department of Sociology at the University of British Columbia. His research explores the racial intersections of law, civility, and the public life of urban spaces. His current research project documents the racial publics and geographies that emerge through the circulation of texts about illicit urban economies in Vancouver and Chicago. His work also appears in *Law, Text, Culture* (2009) and *Social Identities* (forthcoming). He can be reached at hbuffam@interchange.ubc.ca.

Maria-Carolina Cambre is a doctoral student in Educational Policy Studies at the University of Alberta. Her dissertation research is titled "The Politics of the Face: Manifestations of Che Guevara's Image and Its Renderings, Progeny, and Agency." Conceptually, this thesis has transported her to other places such as the disciplinary interstices between art, sociology, and anthropology and methodologically to the Shangri-La between phenomenology, semiotics, and arts-based research. Virtually, she can be found here: http://www.ualberta.ca/~mcambre/.

Tonya K. Davidson is a Ph.D. candidate in Sociology at the University of Alberta. Her research interests include cultural memory, material culture, and the built environment. Her dissertation research is on the dynamic social lives of a series of monuments in Ottawa, Ontario. Tonya is currently teaching in the Sociology department at King's University College, the University of Western Ontario. She can be found at http://www.tonya-davidson.ca.

Veronica della Dora is Lecturer in Geographies of Knowledge at the School of Geographical Sciences, University of Bristol. She is the author of *Imagining Mount Athos: Visions of a Holy Place from Homer to World War II* (University of Virginia Press, 2011) and co-editor with Denis Cosgrove of *High Places: Cultural Geographies of Mountains, Ice, and Science* (IB Tauris, 2008). Her research interests and publications span cultural and historical geography, history of cartography, Byzantine and post-Byzantine studies, and science studies.

Goze Dogu is a Ph.D. candidate in Sociology at the University of Alberta. Her research interests are diverse and include petro-capitalism and "oil culture," political economy of immigration and racialization, politics/policies of food, and critical analysis of public policy. Her dissertation research is on the problematization of natural resources in Alberta's oil and gas royalty and tax framework, and attempts to theorize the discursive knowledges and technologies around nature and valuation of natural resources. She can be reached at gdogu@ualberta.ca.

Sara Dorow is Associate Professor of Sociology at the University of Alberta. She heads a SSHRC-funded research project on the challenges and possibilities for "community" in Fort McMurray, Alberta, at the heart of the largest oil industrial development in the world. She is also the author of *Transnational Adoption: A Cultural Economy of Race, Gender, and Kinship* (New York University Press, 2006). Dr. Dorow may be reached at sdorow@ualberta.ca.

Petra Hroch is a Ph.D. student in Sociology (Theory and Culture) at the University of Alberta. Her doctoral work is supported by a SSHRC Joseph-Armand Bombardier Canada Graduate Scholarship, Izaak Walton Killam Memorial Scholarship, and Ralph Steinhauer Award of Distinction. Petra's research interests include art, design and aesthetic theory, environmental ethics, and social and political theory. Her work has been featured in *Walter Benjamin and the Aesthetics of Change* (Palgrave Macmillan, 2010).

Allison Hui is a Ph.D. student and Commonwealth Scholar in the Department of Sociology at Lancaster University, UK. Her work examines how what people do and where they do it are intertwined, bringing together theories of mobilities and of practices in an empirical study of leisure pursuits. She is also involved in the ESRC-sponsored Social Change, Climate Change working parties, and is a convenor for the British Sociological Association's Postgraduate Forum. She can be reached at a.hui@lancaster.ac.uk.

Mark Jackson is a Lecturer in Postcolonial Geographies at the University of Bristol. His research interests and publications lie at the intersections between philosophy and social theory, post-colonialism, urban studies, social history, political ecology, and visual studies.

Olga Pak is a Ph.D. candidate in the Department of Sociology at the University of Alberta. Her research interests pertain to social imaginary, nostalgia, urban ethics and aesthetics, social history and cultural studies of Soviet and post-Soviet Russia. Olga's dissertation project explores post-Soviet urban transformations in Russia. She can be contacted at pak.olga@gmail.com.

Ondine Park is a Ph.D. candidate in Sociology at the University of Alberta and a researcher at the City-Region Studies Centre. She is interested in contemporary exemplars of the "normal": social, cultural, and spatial practices and forms that are ubiquitous, taken for granted, and normative. Her research interrogates the ways these are represented and reproduced, and how they are imagined or wished to be normal. Her current work focuses on desire, the idea, and promise of the suburban good life. http://www.ualberta.ca/~opark.

Rob Shields is Henry Marshall Tory Chair and Professor in the Departments of Sociology and Art and Design, University of Alberta. He is founder and co-editor of the journal *Space and Culture*, and founder of *Curb* magazine. His most recent works include *What Is a City? Rethinking the Urban after Katrina* (ed., with Phil Steinberg, University of Georgia Press, 2008) and *Building Tomorrow: Innovation in Construction* (ed. with André Manseau, Ashgate, 2005). He directs the City-Region Studies Centre.

Matthew Tiessen completed his doctorate in Critical Theory and Visual Culture at the University of Alberta with the support of a SSHRC Doctoral Fellowship and Killam Memorial Scholarship. Matthew's research engages theories of digital and visual culture, mobility, virtuality, and ethics. His writing has been featured in *CTheory*; *Rhizomes: Cultural Studies in Emerging Knowledge*; *Space and Culture*; *Pli: The Warwick Journal of Philosophy*; and *What Is a City? Rethinking the Urban after Hurricane Katrina* (University of Georgia Press, 2008). Matthew teaches in the Communication Studies department at Wilfrid Laurier University.

Mickey Vallee received his Ph.D. from the University of Alberta, where he now teaches courses in sociology and music. He is currently co-editing a hypertext glossary of terms by Deleuze and Guattari with Rob Shields (http://www.deleuzeguattari.com) while writing a book on Lacan and the virtual structures of recorded music. He is delighted to see this anthology released just after the birth of his second daughter, Anouk.

Anne Winkler is a Ph.D. candidate in Sociology at the University of Alberta. She is interested in commemorative practices in the post-socialist context. In her dissertation project, Anne examines the representation of East Germany in museums. She may be reached at awinkler@ualberta.ca.

Index

culture, 20, 25, 33, 34, 87, 100, 105, 254, 266n8, 294, 301, 323, 324; popular culture, 27, 106, 225, 227, 231, 259
currency, 23, 88

D

Davidson, Tonya K., 9, 213n2, 318–19
Davis, F., 86–87
death, 55, 78, 85, 90–92, 99, 163n13, 222, 233, 234, 235, 238
Debord, Guy. *See* spectacle
DeLanda, Manuel, 131, 135–36
Delarozière, François, 249, 267n12. *See also* Royal de Luxe
Deleuze, Gilles, 4, 10–11, 12–13, 82n2, 116, 118, 129, 132–34; 138; 139n1, 139n2, 230, 246, 320, 324. *See also* affect; assemblage; deterritorialization; Guattari; haecceity; minor art; Spinoza
della Dora, Veronica, 4, 12, 13, 200, 203, 268n14, 313n12, 314n24, 319, 322, 323, 325
democracy, 33, 37–38, 147, 149–50, 151, 154, 156, 161, 290n6
de-modernization. *See* re-feudalization
departure, 66, 72, 73–74, 80–81, 93–94, 162
Derrida, Jacques, 240
desert, 10, 92, 105, 106, 109, 299, 300
designer rebellion, 229–30, 235–36, 241n6
desire, 1–12, 51, 57, 66, 73, 75, 85, 90, 108, 113–15, 127–40 (*passim*), 143–65 (*passim*), 169–90 (*passim*), 197, 198, 201, 202, 205, 209, 305–8, 317–25 (*passim*). *See also* dream; good life; utopia
desire line, 11, 127–31, 322
destinations, 2, 11, 72, 107, 109–16, 122n4, 162, 229, 287, 293, 298, 303, 309, 322, 325
deterritorialization, 145, 152, 161, 231–32
development: neo-liberal, 274–77, 287, 290n3, 290n6, 295–316

(*passim*); speculative, 106–7, 108–9, 110, 122n4, 297, 299–301, 302. *See also* real estate
diagnosis, 85, 90
diaspora. *See also* displacement; exile; migrants, 57, 61n7
Didi-Huberman, Georges, 235–36
disavowal, 134, 188, 198–99, 201, 204, 206
discipline, 33, 95, 155, 163n10, 198, 204, 206, 207, 208, 210, 297, 305–9
displacement, 32, 85, 90, 92, 121, 154, 197–99, 323
Dogu, Goze, 12, 13, 111, 113, 203, 320, 323–24
domestic sphere, 2, 10, 52, 99, 177, 179, 186, 212, 256. *See also* home; suburbs
Dorfman, Ariel, 227
Dorow, Sara, 12, 13, 111, 113, 203, 320, 323–24
dream, 12, 30, 44, 106, 150–51, 156, 218, 232, 252, 253–54, 260, 265, 267n9, 293–94, 312, 324–25; American dream, 174; dreamer; dreamlike, 13, 260, 303, 318; dreamscape, 262; spaces of, 106, 298, 312, 324–25
drugs, 109, 202, 204, 206, 208, 211, 274, 281
Dubai, 122n4, 293–316
dunamis, 203
duration, 88, 119–20, 132, 252, 266n6, 268n14
Durkheim, Émile, 324

E

East Germany. *See* Germany
ecologies, 1, 4–7, 13–14, 121, 138, 185, 197, 198, 212, 298, 310, 317, 322, 324; definition, 6
economy. *See* affect: affective economy; capitalism; market; oil
Edmonton (Alberta), 1–3, 12, 13, 14n1, 14n2, 197–213 (*passim*), 283, 284, 285, 318, 321

elsewhere, 111, 112, 227, 282, 283, 287–89, 320, 323

empire, 263–64, 306

enclosure, 294–95, 309–13; neo-liberal, 305

encounter, 67, 73, 77, 86, 89, 114, 116, 118–21 (*passim*), 137, 144, 169, 170, 172, 176, 198, 204, 220, 232, 238, 239, 249–50, 254, 260, 261, 305; ethics of, 118–19. *See also occursus*

entertainment economy, 23, 92, 106, 110, 114, 129, 246, 281

environment, 2, 6, 7, 91, 105, 111–23, 129, 131–39, 158, 159, 181–85, 203, 238, 255, 273–74, 287, 307, 312, 318, 321, 322, 327

escape, 10, 11, 23, 47, 56, 78, 105–23 (*passim*), 177, 211, 248, 263, 284, 287, 289, 298, 300, 113, 322–23; "escape attempts," 109–13. *See also* line of flight

Esterhazy, Prince Nicholas, 92–94, 96

Ethics. See Spinoza

ethnography, 6, 9, 12, 13, 44, 45, 47; ethnographic studies, 43–61, 197–213, 271–91. *See also* autoethnography

event, 6, 25, 38, 51, 73, 86, 88, 205, 245, 251, 253, 254, 260, 262, 282, 321. *See also* co-presence

everyday, the, 3, 5, 6, 29, 30, 33, 35, 106, 110, 111, 116, 127, 134, 144, 155, 173–75, 245–62, 278, 295, 302, 317, 325; critique of, 175, 185, 325

everyday life, 3, 5, 6, 13, 20, 23, 27, 29–30, 33, 170, 176, 177. *See also* Lefebvre

everyday things, 4, 6, 27

exception, 12, 119, 134, 147, 173, 181, 185, 188, 198, 212, 240, 252, 275, 276, 287, 306

exile, 43–45, 47, 50, 51–52, 227, 323. *See also* diaspora; displacement

experience, 4, 5, 8, 23, 25, 47, 52, 66, 68, 72, 73, 77, 79, 86, 89, 91, 98, 100, 106, 109, 116, 119, 121, 144, 146, 153, 155, 159, 173, 177, 180, 204, 218, 220, 223, 231, 234, 238, 245, 249, 254, 256, 260–65, 275, 284, 286, 288

expression, 23, 27, 28, 113, 132, 137–38, 151, 158, 171, 175, 186, 230, 237, 240, 256, 287, 312, 317, 318

eyes, 91, 97, 208, 234, 237, 287, 301

F

face, 27, 43, 54, 157, 217–41 (*passim*), 252, 305. *See also* Levinas

family, 11–12, 19, 23, 43–61 (*passim*), 67, 68, 76–78, 81, 93, 96–97, 98–99, 112, 118, 169–90 (*passim*), 209, 212, 236, 271–91 (*passim*), 319; Las Vegas as escape from, 109, 111; Romantic family unit, 177; vacationers, 112. *See also* grandparents; photographs

Fanon, Franz, 206

fantasy, 13, 86, 90, 108, 109, 113, 114, 118, 135, 177, 256, 263, 295, 302, 310, 311, 314

fear, 5, 6, 8, 10, 106, 114, 203, 234, 258, 265, 295, 298, 311

feeling, 4, 5, 43, 46, 51, 52, 76, 77, 96, 100, 113, 119, 146, 152, 227, 238, 271

festival, 2, 14n2, 246, 262, 265, 268n15. *See also* liminal; ritual; spectacle

flickering, 7, 8–9, 11, 12, 13–14, 106, 119–21, 221–22, 319, 320–21. *See also* affect; ambivalence; contradictory; flow; flux; syncresis

Florensky, Pavel, 217, 219

flow, 6, 87, 96, 107, 109, 114, 119–20, 129, 260, 276, 305, 324; overflow, 239–40

flux, 5–6, 114, 115, 119, 133. *See also* affect; ecologies; flickering; flow; syncresis

force, 4, 6, 98, 132

Fort McMurray (Alberta), 271, 276, 279, 284; boomtown, 274, 282; "energy capital," 274, 283; negative portrayal of, 274, 279, 284. *See also* oil: economy

314n15, 2, 5, 25, 26, 33, 112, 118,
204, 206, 212, 253, 260, 264,
271–91 (*passim*)
worlding, 12, 294–96, 308–9

Y
youths, 12, 28, 50, 55, 90, 95–96,
98–99, 118, 158, 197–213 (*passim*),
218, 225–26. *See also* children

Z
Žižek, Slavoj, 97

Environmental Humanities Series

Environmental thought pursues with renewed urgency the grand concerns of the humanities: who we think we are, how we relate to others, and how we live in the world. Scholarship in the environmental humanities explores these questions by crossing the lines that separate human from animal, social from material, and objects and bodies from techno-ecological networks. Humanistic accounts of political representation and ethical recognition are re-examined in consideration of other species. Social identities are studied in relation to conceptions of the natural, the animal, the bodily, place, space, landscape, risk, and technology, and in relation to the material distribution and contestation of environmental hazards and pleasures.

The Environmental Humanities Series features research that adopts and adapts the methods of the humanities to clarify the cultural meanings associated with environmental debate. The scope of the series is broad. Film, literature, television, Web-based media, visual art, and physical landscape—all are crucial sites for exploring how ecological relationships and identities are lived and imagined. The Environmental Humanities Series publishes scholarly monographs and essay collections in environmental cultural studies, including popular culture, film, media, and visual cultures; environmental literary criticism; cultural geography; environmental philosophy, ethics, and religious studies; and other cross-disciplinary research that probes what it means to be human, animal, and technological in an ecological world.

Gathering research and writing in environmental philosophy, ethics, cultural studies, and literature under a single umbrella, the series aims to make visible the contributions of humanities research to environmental studies, and to foster discussion that challenges and reconceptualizes the humanities.

Series editor
Cheryl Lousley, English and Film Studies, Wilfrid Laurier University

Editorial committee
Adrian J. Ivakhiv, Environmental Studies, University of Vermont
Catriona Mortimer-Sandilands, Tier 1 CRC in Sustainability and
Culture, Environmental Studies, York University
Susie O'Brien, English and Cultural Studies, McMaster University
Laurie Ricou, English, University of British Columbia
Rob Shields, Henry Marshall Tory Chair and Professor, Department of Sociology,
University of Alberta

For more information, contact
Lisa Quinn
Acquisitions Editor
Wilfrid Laurier University Press
75 University Avenue West
Waterloo, ON N2L 3C5
(519) 884-0710 ext. 2843
Email: quinn@press.wlu.ca

**Titles in the Environmental Humanities Series
from Wilfrid Laurier University Press**

Animal Subjects: An Ethical Reader in a Posthuman World, Jodey
Castricano, editor / 2008 / 324 pp. / ISBN 978-0-88920-512-3

Open Wide a Wilderness: Canadian Nature Poems, Nancy Holmes,
editor / 2009 / 534 pp. / ISBN 978-1-55458-033-0

*Technonatures: Environments, Technologies, Spaces, and Places in the
Twenty-first Century*, Damian F. White and Chris Wilbert, editors /
2009 / 282 pp. / ISBN 978-1-55458-150-4

Writing in Dust: Reading the Prairie Environmentally, Jenny Kerber /
2010 / 276 pp. / ISBN 978-1-55458-218-1 (hardcover),
ISBN 978-1-55458-306-5 (paper)

Ecologies of Affect: Placing Nostalgia, Desire, and Hope, Tonya K.
Davidson, Ondine Park, and Rob Shields, editors / 2011 / 360 pp. /
illus. / ISBN 978-1-55458-258-7